DATE DUE

D0041195

An Island Called California

UNIVERSITY OF CALIFORNIA PRESS

BERKELEY/LOS ANGELES/LONDON

ELNA S. BAKKER
FIGURES BY GERHARD BAKKER

An Island Called CALIFORNIA

AN ECOLOGICAL INTRODUCTION TO ITS NATURAL COMMUNITIES

Second Edition, Revised and Expanded

University of California Press
Berkeley and Los Angeles, California
University of California Press, Ltd.
London, England

© 1971, by The Regents of the University of California

First Paperback Edition, 1972
Second Edition © 1984

Printed in the United States of America

5   6   7   8   9

Library of Congress Cataloging in Publication Data

Bakker, Elna S.
   An island called California.

   Bibliography: p.
   Includes index.
   1. Ecology—California. 2. Natural history—California. I. Title.
QH105.C2B3 1983   574.5'09794   82-17453
ISBN 0-520-04948-9

to NANCY THOMAS NEELY
who started it all

Contents

Illustrations

Maps

Figures

Preface

Around the year 1510, some eighteen years after Columbus' discovery of the New World, Garci Rodríguez Ordóñez de Montalvo of Spain wrote a highly popular though decidedly fanciful account of a queen who ruled over a rugged country of Amazon-mannered black women. Among other quaint customs was the feeding of surplus males to trained griffins, keeping only enough men, either born to them or captured by raiding vessels, to serve as studs to these enterprising women. Gold was the only metal known, incidentally.

Montalvo is not hesitant about locating his mythical queendom. He instructs: "Know ye that on the right hand of the Indies there is an island called California, very near the Terrestrial Paradise. . . ." Fact and fiction were not altogether inseparable in those days when tales of the New World spread through the homelands of the returned adventurers. Inn and courtyard rang with truth and fantasy mixed, at best, in equal proportion. No wonder then that the early explorers making their arduous ways up the west coast of Mexico drew what seemed to them the obvious conclusion that the land across the Sea of Cortez would continue to be separated from the mainland. If so, this surely was the famous island of griffins and bold rocks, California.

In time, of course, the misconception was corrected. Baja California is a peninsula, and lands to the north are fixed more or less firmly to the North American continent. I say "more or less" since the San Andreas Earthquake Fault is supposedly shifting the portion of California west of this great rift to the north. Be that as it may, there is ecological validity in thinking of California in insular terms. Not only is it isolated by a combination of topographic and climatic features, it differs from the rest of the continent in a number of significant ways which, involving as they do both species and the natural communities where they live, form some of the basic themes of this book.

During the years of writing the first edition the author was working as a consultant naturalist for The Oakland Museum, part of a team developing an exhibits program that features an ecological orientation of California's biotic communities. The visitor to the Natural Sciences Division of this museum complex is invited to think of the visit as a "walk across California," beginning with the Golden Gate, turning south at Mono Lake, and ending in the deserts of southern California.

It seemed logical to pattern this book in the same fashion— to take a slice of central California from west to east, a transect some 65 miles (105 km.) wide whose southern border is latitude 37° 20″ (San Jose) and whose northern edge lies along the 38° 14″ parallel (Petaluma). (See Map 4.) The boundaries are admittedly arbitrary, but they enclose representative examples of the biological communities typical of the state's heartland.

Within the decade following publication of the first edition, it became apparent that a second edition was imperative. Both popular and scientific literature abounded with summaries of research recently conducted in California, much of it gathered into such splendidly useful books as the *Terrestrial Vegetation of California* by M. G. Barbour and J. Major (John Wiley, 1977). At the same time, it was decided to include three new chapters on southern California, making the book more appropriate for use throughout the state.

Among the many patient people whose expertise, and generosity with time and helpful suggestions provided invaluable aid are: Gerhard Bakker whose knowledge, encouragement, and artwork have greatly contributed to the completion of both manuscripts; Edith Kinucan, research assistant; Dr. Richard Vogl, Botany Department, California State College at Los Angeles; Dr. Hans Jenny, Soils and Plant Science, University of California, Berkeley; Dr. C. Don MacNeill, Natural Sciences Division, The Oakland Museum; Don Greame Kelley, formerly Acting Curator, Natural Sciences Division, The Oakland Museum; Dr. Robert Stebbins, Museum of Vertebrate Zoology, University of California, Berkeley; Dr. A. Starker Leopold, School of Forestry and Conservation, University of California, Berkeley; Dr. H. Thomas Harvey, Department of Biology, California State College at San Jose; and Dr. Jack Major, Botany, University of California, Davis. All of the above reviewed the portions of the manuscript appropriate to their special fields. Those whose thoughtful guidance proved invaluable in producing the second edition include Dr. Ted Hanes, professor of Biology and Director of the Fullerton Arboretum at California State University, Fullerton; Gayle M. Groenendaal, research geographer, Bioworld Associates; Dr. Carey Stanton, president, Santa Cruz Island Company; Janine Derby, forest botanist, U.S. Forest Service, San Bernardino National Forest; and Dr. Dean Wm. Taylor, research biologist, Mono Basin Research Group.

All photographs were taken by Bruce Barnbaum with the exception of those illustrating Chapters 3, 11, and 22, which were taken by Gerhard Bakker.

Elna S. Bakker
Los Angeles, California, 1984

Map 1. California

An Island Called California

Sunset, Santa Monica Beach

1. The Seashore

Where the far edge of California gives way to the ocean, landscape shifts to seascape, a meeting ground with its own kinds of confrontation of the two great worlds supported by our planet. Beaches fringe a restless surf; headlands thrust obstinately into churning swells; and islets persist in spite of the sea's aggression. These are outposts of California, stubborn and steadfast.

Stony point, sand or pebble beach, lagoon, and cliff are common features of shorelines everywhere, created by the struggle of the two adversaries, land and sea. Each supports typical aggregations of living things that vary from one habitat to another. Rock outcrops often usurp the beach line. Where they do, pools and shallows shelter distinctive forms of life found only in such environments. Here, at low tide, one can rummage for their treasure, peering into little bowls encrusted with all manner of living things—slippery and smooth or roughened and calloused—or crouching beside channels through which the wavelets pulse in gentle rhythm. Then thoughts can move like curious fingers over this small portion of the world of the sea, now open for a while to inspection.

Even the smallest tide pools are worth investigation for their rich assortment of organisms. In no other kind of place can one see more animals in a single visit. Though terrestrial soils may harbor enormous quantities of living things, it is usually difficult to observe them and their behavior without special equipment. Tide pools, on the other hand, are readily viewable, and their inhabitants for the most part are large enough to be easily seen.

Changes in tide level hinder or aid their exploration. The best times are during the very low tides occurring regularly along the California coast. Then one can venture out to usually inaccessible rocky heaps and reefs, and discover miniature groves of sea palms, perhaps catching a glimpse of an octopus slipping like a spurt of dark fluid behind a sheltering projection. To the curious but untutored observer, a tide pool visit can be a frustrating experience. A first reaction often is, "I want to know what they are!" If so, he is in good company as this quest for understanding has been the starting point for a number of avocational and professional experiences in natural science. But simply identifying the organisms found here does not tell the whole story of tide pool life, and we are now beginning to discover just how complex and interwoven are the threads of the drama.

For many years natural scientists were largely concerned with discovering and naming plants and animals or with learning how their various systems and organs functioned. In the early decades of the twentieth century they became interested in the communities in which these plants and animals live together. Before, it was enough to know that a fairly small greenish-purplish crab was *Pachygrapsus crassipes*, the lined shore crab, which lives on rocky shores of western North America, scavenging on bits and pieces of organic debris, scuttling into crevices or under rocks for cover. But the shore crab does not live alone. It occurs with other crabs, and a number of plant and animal species share the same tidal environment. They all have evolved ways to cope with their watery home, making use of it in terms of food and shelter. They are living things on which the struggle for survival has not only imposed adaptations for life in tide pools, but has established patterns of interrelationships. A shore crab is aware of some of these interactions and connections in the web of his existence. This bit of debris is good to eat; that one is not. This approaching thing may be dangerous; that one is harmless. This place is too dry to live in; over there is better. With these perceptions, it places itself in a community and sees its world as one in which it lives with other creatures in a place best suited to its inherited habits.

Shorelines provide some of the most fascinating natural communities in California. Their inhabitants reflect the great wealth of living organisms present in the ocean ecosystem, a term used to describe a more or less self-contained unit of nature that includes both physical environment and the plants and animals found there. Tide pools and beaches are on the edges of this world-within-a-world and depend on its food resources in a variety of ways.

The coast of California has several types of littoral communities, depending upon their substrate, or base, and their position with regard to tide levels. There are two low and two high tides each day, but of unequal height. They are described as a higher high water, a lower high water, a higher low water, and a lower low water; and they rotate through a twenty-five-hour period as each tide is approximately one hour later than that of the preceding day. Twice a month the shore experiences extreme tides. When the sun, earth, and moon are in a straight line, their combined tug causes spring, or extra high and low tides. When the sun and moon are in right-angle position with regard to the earth, their influence is less, as the respective pulls tend to cancel each other out. The ensuing neap tides, as they are called, have a small rise and fall. Excessive spring tides occur in May and June and in November and December, prior to and around the summer and winter solstices.

One of the often observed features of rocky shores is the zonation of their plants and animals. The organisms of the littoral are stratified, for the most part, according to the amount of aerial exposure to which they are subjected during tidal rise and fall, though other factors are also at work. Five zones have been described for the coast of California. The top or splash zone is the highest. Here live animals which can protect themselves from desiccation by withdrawing into shells, or may require only an occasional wetting, or are more adapted to life in the air rather than in water. Generally, the upper part of this zone receives moisture only from spray and unusually high waves. The lower part is visited by the higher of the two daily high tides. Next down are the midlittoral or intertidal zones; the higher one (zone 2) is reached by both high tides, that is, it is covered and exposed twice a day, and the lower (zone 3) extends down to mean lower low water and is exposed once a day. Zone 4 is usually under water. Only the so-called minus tides, or extreme lows, will uncover it. Below this is the subtidal zone (zone 5).

The water on which most animals of rocky shores depend for oxygen, moisture, and food is present or absent according to zone and time; they must adjust to the tidal rhythm, meeting its demands in some way, or perish. Ironically, surf can be their worst enemy, necessary though it is for the life of the community. Not many living things can take the unleashed power of wave surge and splash. This is not the only danger. They, like other creatures, must have some defense against hungry neighbors. A few individuals of each species must remain alive long enough to mature and reproduce if the species is to survive.

How does life go about minding its affairs in this warring ground of land and sea? One only has to do a little rocky shore exploring to begin to understand. It is not necessary to wait for an extra low tide; midlittoral zones will serve nicely. Central California has many beaches along semiprotected open coasts where easily accessible rock outcrops with pools abound: around the Monterey Peninsula, near Santa Cruz, Año Nuevo Island, Moss Beach, and, north of the Golden Gate, Dillon Beach, Tomales Point, and Shell Beach. From Point Sur south to Morro Bay access to tide pools may be more difficult, but by the same token a visit more rewarding as they are likely to be less disturbed. The rocky shore of Rancho Montaña de Oro State Park west of San Luis Obispo has excellent tidal life. At present, military installations and private ranches restrict much tide pool exploration between Point Sal and the Gaviota area in Santa Barbara County. Along the remainder of the southern California coast, tide pools are scattered on rocky headlands, some of the most well-known being around the Palos Verdes Peninsula, Laguna Beach, and Dana Point and Little Corona, south of Newport Beach. In places the sedimentary rocks have been upended, and weaker strata have been worn away leaving crevices, some large as a bathtub and some as small as a tea cup. These are the jewels of the shoreline, their still surfaces broken only by the occasional surge of the wavelets characteristic of low tide in quiet waters.

The higher ledges of the splash zone are populated by animals more oriented to life on land than in the sea. Rock lice, relatives of the common sow bug, slip into cracks well above the tide line. Surf avoiding, they are independent of actual contact with water. Slightly farther down are the first of the real marine organisms, at this level highly specialized to resist desiccation. Acorn barnacles scatter themselves on rock that is occasionally quite dry. They are able to exclude sun and air by retreating behind tightly closed doors. When the welcome floods of high tide wash over them, they quickly open and fling out legs to grab what crumbs they can from the rich larder of the sea. Unlike the scurrying rock lice or stationary barnacles, species of littorines, also called periwinkles, wander about on rocky faces at the lower level of the splash zone. These little snails seem to need only an occasional wetting. Like many other marine animals, they have an operculum, a door with which they can block their shell openings, protecting themselves from air. Limpets, other slow-moving molluscs, clamp their oval-shaped shells firmly to rocks; the tight seal keeps the soft-bodied animal inside from dehydrating. Many of them tend to be night active, when the danger of desiccation is less.

The rocky midlittoral has many hazards for its residents. Even the dwellers of pools whose water levels do not fluctuate much regardless of tide height must contend with possible changes in temperature, oxygen level, and salinity. Breaker impact is of great importance, particularly along the eastern Pacific shore. Large waves generated by wind and storm patterns travel great distances to slam against cliff and headland. The mid- and lower-zone creatures on the outer rocks of the open coast withstand an incredible amount of buffeting and have evolved many adaptations to the now weak, now strong cadence of surf. Limpets and barnacles are admirably designed to withstand wave action. Water hits and runs harmlessly off their sloping shells. Branched animals such as stony corals absorb wave shock easily. Purple sea urchins are sometimes found in very wave-swept positions. With tough spines they scrape round cavities in the rock. By settling into these, after wandering out for food, they escape some of the surge stress. Many tiny animals such as certain isopods, cousins of the rock louse group, seek shelter in their spines. Living in the same turbulent waters are California mussels, common starfish, and leaf or gooseneck barnacles, often in such abundance as to exclude other forms. The sturdy starfish, attached to the substrate by the suction of its tubed feet, can regenerate an arm if one is lost in combat or by wave action. Mussels cling to these sea-battered outer rocks by means of byssal threads, extruded by a gland in the foot. Barnacles use a natural cement for secure fastening. Snails such as the turbans found at midtide and low tide levels are protected by shells and cling to the rocky surface with muscular feet. Sea palms, erect seaweeds with frondlike clusters on flexible "stems," meet the full force of the breakers. Their holdfasts grip the rocky foundation, and the stem is strong and pliant enough to bend but not break with each new wave. Many intertidal organisms use rock fissures, overhangs, and other possible refuges to escape wave impact.

Seaweeds are the most numerous in the midlittoral and subtidal zones. They cannot endure the prolonged dehydration of the undependable splash zone, nor can they descend too far from sunlight. Rockweeds and nail brush appear rather high in tidal stratification. Any pool with permanent water from tidal residue usually has a colorful display of seaweeds. It is these more than anything else that give texture and variation in hue to most pools, notwithstanding the more spectacular animals such as red and blue sea stars, purple and burgundy sea urchins, and brilliant orange-red solitary corals. Another richly colored stony coral is seen occasionally off southern and Baja California, and clusters of these fire-hued polyps reward skin divers and other more adventurous explorers of the subtidal zone. By far the most spectacular corals in southern California are three or four species of horny corals known as the gorgonians. Largely confined to warmer latitudes, they include sea

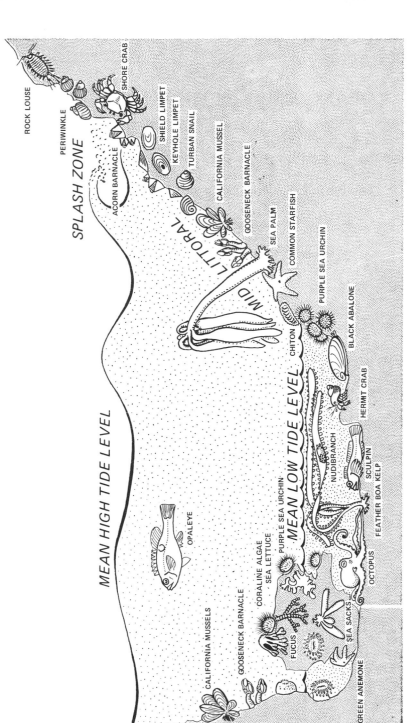

Figure 1. Typical homesites of intertidal and subtidal species

fans and sea whips. Those offshore southern California are usually found in deeper water and look like small trees whose branches appear to be blossoming with richly red, purple, or salmon pink polyps fringed with tiny tentacles. Another organism that resembles and is somewhat related to the foregoing marine invertebrates is a beautiful red to purple hydrocoral, close cousin to the hydroids referred to later in this chapter. It forms encrusting sheets or branching structures. Offshore the southern California coast, it occurs intertidally in the northern part of the state. Limy seaweeds known as coralline algae grow like stiff pink lace on walls, in crannies, and even on mussels and other shells. The cabbagelike "leaves" of red laver and red fan, the waving ribbons of red sea feather, red point, and lissom red sea fire enrich the brocade of tide pool sides with hues ranging from orange through russet to purple-red. The double rows of bladelets on the fronds of agarweed have deeper tones of red. The larger species in this group are commercially harvested for use in food and pharmaceutical products.

True browns are contributed by the oar weeds—prevalent plants of lower tidal zones in central and northern California—feather boa, a number of rockweeds, ruffled sword, and seersucker. Beds of sea lettuce, one of the loveliest of seaweeds, are salad green. Ocean pincushion and green rope live lower on the littoral and are richly emerald. Many seaweeds are olive in hue, and yellow, black, and lavender are not uncommon colors. *Gigartina* is one of the more common genera of seaweeds along the California coast and is as remarkable for color variation, ranging from light rose to nearly black, as it is for the bumps or outgrowths on the blades of some of its species. A number of them are so coarse in texture that they are given the common name of Turkish towel. Two of the more interestingly shaped seaweeds are sea grapes, looking very much like their name, and sea sacks, pouches that resemble about-to-be blown up balloons. Some species of red algae are found at depths down to 600 feet (180 m.). Because of their pigmentation they can absorb and thus use blue and green light, the most deeply penetrating wavelengths of solar radiation in water.

A number of the larger seaweeds such as the feather boa kelp (the common name is inspired by blades and air sacs projecting from the stipe like the plumes of Edwardian era finery) and oar weed require footholds in lower intertidal zones or just below. Both of the giant kelps, bull and bladder, are firmly fixed to rocks in even deeper water, below the realm of the littoral. Inflated bladders at the base of the "leaves" float the long, ropelike stipes of the latter up through the intertidal regions to the surface. The equally long stipe of bull kelp enlarges near the water surface to become an enormous tapered air chamber from which a cluster of blades, sometimes 12 feet (3.6 m.) long, spreads out. The brown bulbous tops of the air chambers gently rising and falling with the ocean swell are common sights to those familiar with the central and northern California coast. In southern California bladder and feather boa kelp are joined by beds of elk kelp whose blades branch antlerlike from a large float at the end of a stipe often 90 feet (27 m.) long.

By and large, however, the algal group that includes the oar weeds, large kelps, and sea palms are the most conspicuous brown seaweeds north of Point Conception, and certain rockweeds, much smaller plants, are often the most prominent brown algae south of this coastal landmark. The change in dominance of species is largely because of warmer water. The California Current, a south-flowing offshore stream of cold water, parallels the coastline until it turns east at Point Conception. The current, on the other hand, continues south and west, allowing the southern coastal waters to become warmer. Since cool water tends to favor the growth of marine plants, it is no surprise that beds of seaweed north of Santa Barbara County are luxuriant, some almost junglelike with rich vegetation. Though the marine algae of southern California are less lush, they make up for it in diversity as they have a larger number of species.

As we discuss plants and animals in the various parts of the state's shoreline in these first three chapters, it will become apparent that because of changes in the temperature of coastal waters, climatic patterns, topography, and other influential factors, the southern coast differs in varying degrees from the rest of maritime California. Nevertheless, the state shares with the west coast of North America the distinction of having one of the world's richest seaweed floras (that is, all of the kinds of plants in a certain place and time), comparable with those of Japan and Australia in both diversity and luxuriance.

Much of the plant and animal life of zone 4 is restricted to this tidal level. Many organisms of the midlittoral tend to remain above the rocks and crannies that usually are submerged. Those that live below have certain advantages. Surf impact tends to keep the larger kinds of seaweed from higher and thus more exposed sites. A number of animal species are replacements for kinds living in higher zones. Rock crabs, close relatives of the commercially harvested market crab, take the place of shore crabs. The solitary green sea anemone commonly is found below the masses of the midtidal aggregated sea anemones. This elegant creature looks as though it was painstakingly carved from jade because of the one-celled alga living in its tissues. At this depth one will rarely find the higher-dwelling limpets but instead will see giant keyhole limpets, a related gastropod. The abalones, another group of close cousins, are more at home in low and subtidal waters as are many brittle stars, sea cucumbers, and chitons, or sea cradles. Though the familiar sea stars of higher zones are present, the most characteristic representative of this group at this depth is the huge, many-armed sunflower star. Its mottled skin is soft to the touch rather than having the leatheriness typical of the more common species. The giant red sea urchin is another animal that supplants its relative, the purple sea urchin, at lower tidal levels.

While examining the wonderfully rich life of the intertidal rocks, look for channels that run from pool to pool. Here, wave pulse drifts the shredded sea lettuce back and forth as though a tired woman were waving tatters of green chiffon. Rockweeds stiffen and relax as the current ebbs and flows. Unraveling and ragged kelp blades drift coiled in great tangles. On uneven surfaces between the basins, clumps of partly exposed seaweed curl with the flexible crispness so peculiar to these plants. When the upwelling water, back flow or insurge, quickens the pool edge, opalescent bubbles gather and burst in their own tiny rhythms. Hermit crabs skitter and fuss on toothpick-size feet, retreating into or peering out of their portable homes. Blennies, young opaleyes, and sculpins slip in and out of fronds of rockweed. Nudibranchs, small, often colorful shell-less molluscs, glide over the rough surface, their naked gills rippling delicately; sea stars and sea urchins creep about on tube feet. Smells hover from decaying seaweed and that briny something which belongs only to the beaches of cool and temperate lands. From overhead, or just where the breakers begin to curl, comes the shrill yet muted keening of a gull or a sea lion's hollow honk. Bird and seaweed, hydroid and crab—practically every major division of living forms is represented in the crowded communities of rocky shores. To gain just a little understanding of how their residents live together is to begin a new adventure.

Beachcombing, unlike tide rock exploring, is a gentle sport, and a very pleasant thing to do—alone, with congenial people, or with a dog. Your four-footed companion should be tractable, however, content to walk quietly by your side if you so command. Of course, there is hardly a better place to run a dog, with waves to chase, shorebirds to harry, and a host of glorious smells. So, if taking home a wet and dirty canine is no problem, its company may enrich these pleasurable intervals of sand and wind and surf, as many people have discovered.

There are ways and ways to beachcomb. If your feet can take it, barefoot is best. There is nothing like shoes full of sand, particularly wet, large-grained sand, to make the experience disagreeable. Even sandals are a nuisance as the damp grains encroach between foot and sole. Very high tides compound the problem. You never know when an aggressive wave will chase you back to softer sand, which should be avoided if possible. It is hard to walk through, and it is rather spare of interesting flotsam. Try to keep to the narrow strip of firm wet sand between lower swash zone and high tide mark. Then, barefooted and in swimsuit or dungarees, you will not have to worry about an occasional footwetting.

Beaches vary in place as well as time. Steeper shores have coarser sand. The converse is equally true, and gentler slopes have finer sands. These patterns are closely related to beach position, and a natural sorting out results from the combination of several factors—prevailing swell direction and coastline configuration among them. Many headlands on the central California coast curve to the south, thus protecting inlets and bays to the east. The beaches behind these jutting cliffs reflect this sheltering influence. The most protected are flat, and the sand is fine grained. As the shore opens out to the full force of the northwest swell, the most common wave direction here, the strand slopes sharpen and their grains are larger.

Where bay indentations bite into the coastwise cliffs, they are often sealed off, or almost so, by sandspits across their mouths. The headlands flanking them are subjected to constant battering. Particles torn from the parent rock are picked up by currents that travel parallel to the bay mouth, generated by waves hitting the shores at an angle due to wind and land patterns typical of the coast. Swept by these longshore sea streams, the fragments drop as they encounter the quieter waters of the bay, enlarging shoreline beaches and building sandbanks across its mouth. Gradually the headlands erode back to where the bars have formed, and a comparatively straight coastline is the result.

The long spit beaches with their enclosed lagoons are the beachcomber's boulevards. The flats to leeward are the communal residence of myriad plants and animals preferring muddy bottoms and quiet water. Eel-grass, a true flowering plant, is frequently found in dense patches in these shallower areas and, when uprooted, lies in windrows in place of the piles of seaweed so characteristic of the outer edge.

Where the coves are narrow or the parent rock of larger beaches is a certain nature, the sandy fringe may be reduced to practically nothing, and cobble—collections of surf-rounded pebbles—paves the shoreline. Then the lap and swish of the sea has a sound heard on no sand-bottomed beach. This is the clatter of thousands of pebbles settling into place with each receding wave. Such sibilant soughing is quite different from the roar and crash of breakers pounding reefs or headlands.

Aside from the great slow rhythms of coastal uplift and downdrop, erosion and buildup, beach appearances can change from day to day, from season to season. Tides rearrange the shore-edge debris. Storms toss up new tangles of deep water kelp that are often host to creatures, or their remains, less adventurous folk rarely see. The casual visitor down for a picnic or for the day has a whole new world of discovery. One can enter it with but a handful of the bits and pieces from these undulating ribbons of flotsam following the wave line of high tide. Here are the empty cones of acorn barnacles strewn about or still adhering to fragments of rock or to shells secreted by other animals such as mussels and red abalones. Many intertidal forms stay quite clean of encrusting growth, and one can pick up clamshells, starfish, and black abalone looking scrubbed and polished in comparison to molluscs and crustaceans more hospitable to free riders. You can make the acquaintance of some of the more attractive snails by carefully checking over these little mounds of debris. Purple olivellas which live in the fine sands of bay mouths are a collector's joy when perfect and tinted a soft violet. Delicate pectens are the seashells of tradition with fluted fan and squared-off side projections. Several clams have sun-ray markings in pink, violet, and tan. Occasionally there are the dainty slipper shells or the craterlike hillocks of their ribbed cousins, the limpets, as well as polished tusk shells, one of a group of elongated, pointed shells so beloved by the American Indians for ornamentation. Horn snails and the banded black-(or gray-) and-white barrel snail occur in lagoons or bay flats and should be looked for there, not on seaward shores. Rock snails and top shells, on the other hand, live in more open waters and their convoluted spirals are often part of the wave-line litter.

Crab remains are common. The cast-off exoskeletal parts, which are periodically discarded as the animal grows, are paper thin or hard as a china plate, depending on the species. Sand dollars are the delight of children who carefully collect them for their perfection of shape and the embroidery of their markings. The "dollar" is the husk covering the soft and vulnerable animal inside, now dead and washed away. Alive it was bristly, much like its cousin the sea urchin whose globe-like casing is also part of beach debris. *Donax,* the little shore-dwelling bean clam whose shell often has small round holes drilled by predaceous boring molluscs, occurs as far north as the San Luis Obispo area. Among beach debris more commonly found in southern California are wavy top shells, distinguished by their large size (up to 5 inches—13 cm.—in height) and scalloped ridges, and chunky pieces of intertwined white tubes broken off from the midtidal colonial home of tube snails. The gem of the southern beaches, according to many collectors, is the chestnut brown cowry, the only true cowry in California's waters. It is richly dark on top, shading to white where little serrations mark the opening to the shell's interior. Extremely fortunate finds are the exquisitely fashioned little murex shells that are related to the tropical beauties of any extensive collection.

All along the coast keep an eye out for evidence of boring clams. Scattered in among pebbles you might find rock fragments pitted with round holes quite frequently still cradling the bivalve responsible for the hole. These are dug by chemical means or abrasion. The half-shells, opening and closing in a rotary motion, scrape away the rock particles with the help of sharp ridges on the two valves.

Most of the small rounded pebbles scattered on a sandy beach testify to the grinding action of waves. Rockhounds have learned to tumble handsome rock specimens by observing the power of water, sand, and motion. Jadeite and moonstone, jasper and agate—skin-smooth and grape-round—are the gems of the beach, free for the finding. Crystal clear and looking more mineral than animal, jellyfish and a host of relatives litter the beach from time to time with gelatinous lumps. *Velella*, often called "by-the-wind-sailor," is a small animal whose aggregations drift with the winds and sea currents, hoisting sails of clear plasticlike material. From time to time they are cast up on shore by the thousand, to die and end as flotsam. Much different in color and shape are the egg cases of skates, related to rays and sharks. They look like rectangles of black leather with four hooked projections at each corner. These catch on to kelp fronds, anchoring the case until the embryo within matures enough to emerge from the open end. Wave-ground bits of broken bottles can also be found, as well as knotted twists of driftwood and the snarls and clumps of seaweed—small worlds even now, though ripped from their rocky substrates.

Turn over a pile of kelp and hundreds of beach hoppers and the smaller sand fleas burst like sparks from a beach party bonfire. These little amphipods seek any shelter available on the shore, including driftwood, abandoned picnic litter, and the sand itself into which they burrow. Some are nocturnal, others day active, but all must protect themselves from desiccation though, oddly enough, they will drown in water. They are flattened like their relatives the isopods, or sow bugs. However, amphipods have a humped look as though pinched by two fingers pressing in on each side of the thorax or chest. A sowbug appears to have been flattened by someone pressing a finger down on the top of its back as it scurries along.

But the real treasure of a pile of decaying seaweed is revealed to the casual beachcomber in forms of life seldom seen except by skin divers and tide-pool explorers. One may find baby octopi, kelp crabs, and nudibranchs still alive in the masses of wet seaweed abandoned on the shore by the giant waves of winter storms. Crustaceans seeking the shelter of sea-weed and kelp beds such as broken-back and skeleton shrimp stir and wiggle, still alive though their storm-loosened home was heaved up on shore. Sea spiders, small worms, sponges, and tunicates together with stray sea stars, sea lice, and many other intertidal forms spend all their lives in the "roots" and "stems" of the great plants of the kelp forest. Storm wrack is an excellent place to look for these animals as it provides mois-ture, shelter, and even food.

Here and there in a pile of the larger algae are the torn shreds of smaller and more delicate species: braided hair, mer-maid's hair, and delicate sycophant, for example. But a day or two of sun and dry air soon reduce these fascinating heaps of sea hay to unattractive snarls, their stems dried to leathery thongs. Any still-attached leaves are now toughened and shriveled. The little sea creatures so abruptly torn from their home in the littoral must die unless some high wave gives them reprieve and carries them back for a second chance at life. Odds are they are doomed. Their remains will feed the sand fleas, beach hoppers, and flies that are the last to use the friendly shelter of the castaway kelp heaps. Little groups of yellow-rumped warblers, small yellow and black land birds, hunt among these drying piles for the abundant insects now thriving in place of marine animals.

Though many shorebirds closely resemble each other, their differences become readily apparent with careful observation. Gulls are easy to identify, particularly while standing as they often do on one leg facing into the wind, their satiny gray and white plumage sleek against firm, fat bodies. While in flight, they can be confused with terns, elegantly slim close relatives. Gulls have a dignity about them and are rarely guilty of any-thing more frivolous than a proprietary interest in the garbage and refuse of dock and harbor. Sanderlings, on the other hand, collect in fussy little flocks as the small white birds scamper up and down the beach with the precision and unity of a corps de ballet. They spray out and converge in wonderful rhythm, moved this way and that by the attack and retreat of breaking waves, feeding just along the fringe of the surf.

A variety of probers enriches the bird life of the shore. Marbled godwits, whimbrels, willets, red knots and other large sandpipers work their way over the wet sand hunting for small crustaceans, bivalves, and worms. A number of smaller sandpipers or "peeps" busily search for tiny organisms exposed by wave surge or buried just under the sand surface. Snowy plovers and other short-billed birds pick over the sea wrack with its fly-infested seaweed and organic debris. Birds preferring rocky shores and reefs are surfbirds, black turnstones, wandering tattlers, and black oystercatchers. One of the few birds to nest on the sandy shore has now been declared an endangered species by the California Fish and Game Commission. The colonial-nesting least tern is so disturbed by human intrusion that breeding is impossible where people are in close proximity. Fortunately there are a few isolated areas in the southern half of the state (it does not breed north of Monterey Bay) where nesting can continue without interruption.

Though large numbers of birds are supported by the shoreline's bill of fare, aside from organic flotsam, beaches seem quite devoid of the rich marine life of intertidal rocky habitats. The substrate itself accounts for this paucity. Sand is not only abrasive, but it shifts constantly with wind and wave, and sessile animals such as sea anemones rarely get a foothold on this unstable flooring. Many burrowing marine organisms, however, find the wet sand of the intertidal beach zone a most acceptable home. It is easy to penetrate and provides an excellent cover for protection against predation, wave shock, and dehydration. What appears to be quite sterile harbors a variety of animals which in turn are food for the shorebirds so closely linked with the beach. Another type of natural community lives here though it may not be as spectacular and obvious as in the case of tide pools.

One of the most observable species is the sand or mole crab. Every habitual swimmer along the coast has had the experience of feeling prickles under his feet as he walked down into the surf, particularly at low tide. These are the antennae and heads of small egg-shaped crabs waiting for food to be washed to them by the incoming waves. Their dependence on the tide for food has resulted in a kind of migratory behavior. They travel up and down the beach slope always within reach of the wave edge.

Clamming is a common and popular beach sport. In digging for clams, one's spade may turn up many sand beach residents. The Pismo clam of southern California and the razor clam of northern shores are excellent eating. They feed by means of siphon tubes that extend to the surface, enabling these bivalves to burrow deep in the sand. The razor clam can dig itself in very rapidly, using the strong muscles of its foot as a tool. Small crustaceans live here, too. Ghost shrimp are dwellers of sandy flats, and apparently get their food from the tiny organisms living in the mud they ingest while digging their burrows. Gray shrimp and the shrimplike opossum mysids are often found in swash pools along the more open coast. Sea cucumbers may surprise the clam digger who associates these living lumps with the crevices of the lower tidal rocks. Bristle worms or polychetes are much at home here. Their large family includes the sedentary tube-building worms. Some secrete lime, forming tube masses underneath rocks along the shore. Others are dwellers of sand or mud flats and line the tubes with mucus; a few species, apparently, even construct a mucus net with which to catch food particles. One bristle worm, so named because of the spines along its body, is bright red. From 1 to 2 inches (2.5–5 cm.) long, it is found about 18 inches (46 cm.) below the sand surface. This is too far down for the probing bills of shorebirds, but other marine worms are numerous enough to be important items in avian diets.

Out on the flats or on the lagoon side of bars and spits where the sand is clean and relatively free from mud, several species of brittle stars, the channeled basket snail, large white moon snails, and sand dollars make their homes. Sand stars, burrowing anemones, sand clams, and several types of crabs join them, appreciating the calm water behind the barriers closing off the open ocean.

Any discussion of how plants and animals live together leads quickly to the consideration of food sources available for the community and the various ways in which these are obtained. Food is present on the littoral in greater abundance than meets the eye. A vast network of eaters and eaten is woven from the strands of interaction among the organisms of the shore. This food web, as it is termed, is an extremely important aspect of any natural community. Its designs are determined by what species are present, meeting conditions imposed by both physical and biological environment. It is a complex of endlessly repeated feeding patterns, or food chains, consistently characteristic of the community.

The organisms of the shore are but part of the larger marine world, its fringe actually, adding to and taking away from its great supply of nourishment but having little impact on the total oceanic ecosystem. Here as everywhere, green plants initiate the strands of the food web as they are the only organisms capable of making food. From another point of view, they form the base of a numbers pyramid (see Figure 2). An explanatory word about these two terms is in order. Food webs stress the feeding relationships among species—who eats what or whom. Numbers pyramids show the comparative number of organisms involved in specific food energy transfers.

Phytoplankton (plant plankton) is a major basic component of both food webs and numbers pyramids. For the most part it consists of bacteria, microscopic algae such as diatoms and dinoflagellates, and other tiny free-floating organisms. Dinoflagellates give rise to the red tides that poison oysters, mussels, and fish in epidemic proportions. Whole shorelines are strewn with dead animals during major outbreaks. The summer peaks of these organisms, called "blooms," are responsible for the prohibitions against eating shellfish in this season. California mussels are often under quarantine for much of the year.

Like most plants, diatoms and dinoflagellates make their own food through photosynthesis, the process of combining water and carbon dioxide to make simple sugar through the use of the sun's energy. They are the food factories of the open sea and are the most important source of plant-derived nutriments. Seaweeds, the other great crop of the sea, are decidedly less significant, though some animals of the littoral do feed directly on them or their dead remains. Snails such as the midzone black turbans, various limpets, abalones, and chitons (or sea cradles) move out herdlike onto the village commons and upland meadows, as it were, feeding on the lush and prodigious growth of algae, both microscopic and larger forms. Sea urchins scavenge but also harvest seaweed. In contrast, huge numbers of animals depend in whole or in part on plankton. All the plant-eating forms feeding on the vegetative, or producer, base are first order consumers. They constitute the sec-

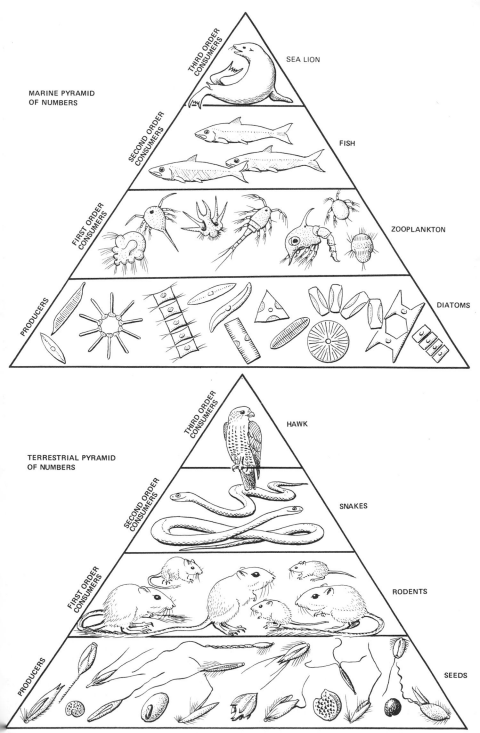

MARINE PYRAMID
OF NUMBERS

THIRD ORDER CONSUMERS — SEA LION

SECOND ORDER CONSUMERS — FISH

FIRST ORDER CONSUMERS — ZOOPLANKTON

PRODUCERS — DIATOMS

TERRESTRIAL PYRAMID
OF NUMBERS

THIRD ORDER CONSUMERS — HAWK

SECOND ORDER CONSUMERS — SNAKES

FIRST ORDER CONSUMERS — RODENTS

PRODUCERS — SEEDS

Figure 2. Marine and terrestrial pyramids of numbers

ond level in the numbers pyramid which, with them, begins to taper upward from the base, since there are fewer herbivorous feeders than plants. Food webs, on the other hand, become larger as more food chains are involved, their species feeding on plants or preying upon each other. Zooplankton, the smallest of these first order feeders, includes the larval forms of sea animals, and organisms such as copepods, other tiny crustaceans, worms, and one-celled animals known as radiolarians and foraminifers. Most feed on phytoplankton and some on each other. Both types of plankton are consumed by larger organisms ranging in size and species from tiny invertebrates to fair-sized fish. It is often impossible to differentiate among those which eat plant plankton only, those dependent on animal material, and species which eat both. It is simplest to assign all to first order consumer rank.

The next step is reserved for the second order consumers. They eat the animals that feed on plants. Starfish eat plankton-feeding mussels; gulls hunt for small fish, some of whom are dependent on the plankton "sea broth," sieved out by gill rakers. Many shoreline numbers pyramids end right here. Gulls and their fish-eating neighbors, brown pelicans, have very few predators. But other pyramids mount higher and higher, as small fish are prey for larger fish which in turn are victims of still larger fish. The carnivorous fish share the larder with other second, third, and fourth order consumers, such as the fish-eating birds to which we have referred, sea lions and others. The upper levels of the pyramid can only support a few individuals; attrition of food sources and strong competition among like-size carnivores limit their numbers.

Occupants of the top level have few or no predators, and death is the result of disease or old age. Not many kinds compete with them; their only enemy is man. In the open ocean killer whales and sharks, barracuda and other large meat-eating fish occupy top positions. In coastal waters few creatures dare tackle elephant seals, sea lions, and true seals. Only when these imperial animals die and scavengers and decomposers work over their remains does the nutrition cycle begin again. Then the nutrients captured in their flesh are released for the use of other marine forms. During life, however, their nitrogenous wastes contribute to the ocean's vast storehouse of nutritious compounds.

An incredible number of living things are involved in the journey from plankton to shark: millions of tiny plankton organisms, thousands of little fish, hundreds of larger fish, and one shark. Its body is but the small remnant of a vast amount of biological intake and output on the part of all the creatures in the pyramid: the production of offspring, food hunting, growing, digesting, warding off disease and enemies, eliminating wastes, and so on.

Though we have alluded in passing to various types of food-getting behavior on the part of shore-dwelling animals, we have not covered the matter by any means. Minute forms of plant and animal plankton occur by the trillion in offshore waters. Many animals of the littoral feed entirely on plankton served to them by the surge and drift of tidal flow. Bivalved molluscs—oysters, clams, mussels, and scallops—open their shells and trap the tiny particles on mucus-covered gills. Sponges, tunicates, and barnacles also utilize the same food source. The seawater-flooded internal chambers of sponges have cilia, or hairs, which help move minute organisms toward ingestion. Hydroids are small, sometimes delicately plumed animals living in colonies like coral. Each individual animal, called a polyp and usually indiscernible to the naked eye, weaves a set of stinging tentacles in a tiny dance for bits of food brought within reach. Such meals may include organic fragments resulting from predation or decay. Flower-resembling sea anemones make use of stinging cells at the tip of their petallike tentacles. These capture and transfer bits of food, including tiny animals, to the digestive cavity with a quick infolding action unexpected of such placid-looking creatures. Anemone congregations are often disguised by a blanketing of shell bits, sand, and gravel.

Many animals feed on the remains of other organisms. Rock crabs are notorious for being scavengers—that is, they will eat anything edible, alive or dead, including picnic refuse. This is almost as true for the little hermit and shore crabs so active in the higher midzones of rocky shores and the larger commercially valuable crabs of lower levels. They hunt about for any bit of plant and animal debris within their range. Beach hoppers and fleas forage in the wrack piles, eating the decaying seaweed or the detritus caught in it.

Starfish are outright carnivores. They clutch such shell-protected animals as snails, barnacles, and mussels in their many-armed embrace. Able to exert enough pressure to pry loose or open the shells of their victims, they need but the smallest crack in order to begin a remarkable process of feeding behavior. Everting its stomach, located in the middle of its body, the starfish slips this organ inside the opened shell to begin digestion. Nudibranchs, also aptly called sea slugs, often feed on hydroids, avoided by many marine predators because of their stinging cells. Sea slugs collect the "unpopped" cells in special tissue on their backs. A number of snails are predaceous and use a grinding organ called a radula to cut holes in the shells of clams, oysters, and other molluscs.

Though not of the shore communities, sea otters, one of California's most prized sea mammals, live in beds of giant kelp just along the outer edge of the surf. Frequently accused of depleting the abalones of the central California coast, research indicates a preference for purple sea urchins. They crack them open against rocks and eat the juicy insides. One of the more striking wildlife experiences of our coast is to see a group of these attractive mammals swimming or floating on their backs midst a tangle of bobbing kelp bladders.

It is perhaps apparent by now that seashores have several unique features. One is the presence of sessile, or stationary, animals that depend only on the bounty of the tidal currents to bring them nourishment. This particular way of being an animal is almost unknown on land. Any similar habit is largely confined to freshwater environments. Even there, very few species remain stationary for their entire lives. Terrestrial creatures must forage for their food; no kind current shoves the banquet table within their reach.

The vast numbers of animal species and individuals are impressive. Except for insect swarms or bird flocks, nowhere else do we see so many organisms in such concentration. The great beds of barnacles, mussels, and sea anemones, so characteristic of tidal life, have no land-dwelling counterparts. For the most part it is plankton, wave-served and free for the taking, that is mainly responsible for such great abundance. The richness of this soup and its universality in seawater, though there is some variation in density from place to place, account for much of the profusion of sea life, serving as the almost inexhaustible support for broad and crowded consumer levels resting on it.

In any situation where dining goes on so lavishly, other creatures suffer. The young, nature's deposit in the evolutionary bank, have a particularly hard time of it. To compensate for the inevitable destruction of much of their progeny, most sea creatures reproduce in astronomical numbers. Their presence in the communities of today testifies to the survival of enough individuals to insure the continuation of the species.

The famed grunion, a small, smeltlike, inshore fish of southern California, has a truly remarkable tactic for breeding. A member of the silversides family, it is the only marine fish on our coast to strand itself for spawning. When about a year old and 5 inches (12.7 cm.) in length, they undertake their first "run," on one of three or four nights following each full or new moon from late February to early September, in other words, during spring tides. The timing is even more precise than that. Females, each accompanied by several males, swim ashore and deposit their eggs in the sand in a one- to three-hour period immediately after high tide. The eggs are fertilized by sperm deposited on the sand near the female. The exquisitely tuned timing prevents the eggs from being washed out by high water as, chances are, no higher tides will occur until the next spring tides when the baby grunions hatch and are carried out to sea.

Many marine invertebrates have several stages of development, some of which are incredibly different from the parent animals. E. F. Ricketts and J. Calvin, in *Between Pacific Tides* (Stanford University Press, 1968), a classic for anyone interested in intertidal forms, sum it up neatly: "It is a grotesque business, as bewildering to the average man as if he were asked to believe that rosebushes give birth to hummingbirds, and that the hummingbird's progeny become rosebushes again." One common jellyfish, *Aurelia*, produces as offspring a larva which looks like a small flattened oval blob with tiny hairs or cilia. It swims to rocks or seaweed where it eventually settles. After losing its cilia it develops tentacles and behaves like a sea anemone except that it builds layers of itself which break off and drift away to become jellyfish. In larval form it is merely part of the freely drifting bits and pieces, or plankton, and is available to any open mouth. The mortality rate is understandably high. Only a few individuals become large or developed enough to hunt for a toehold in the already densely populated tidal zone. Creatures die, making place for newcomers to the community, but competition is keen for the vacancies. Crowding intensifies in lower tidal zones as the longer hours of inundation decrease the risk of dehydration and increase the time available for feeding. Predators requiring water for mobility also have longer periods of time in which to pursue prey, so, as mentioned above, competition for space is extreme.

Consequently, many species are indiscriminate about the substrate upon which they come to rest or to anchor. Barnacles make their permanent homes on mussels as well as rocks. Many snails—red abalone, for example—carry tiny communities on their backs. Hydroids, bryozoans, other small forms, and seaweed live contentedly, not alarmed in the least when their homes occasionally move about. Indeed, some animals not only tolerate but welcome a disguising thatch on their backs. Masking crabs are famous for carrying about bits of seaweed or sponge as camouflage.

Among the marine plants well adapted to crowded conditions are epiphytic seaweeds, species with established footholds on larger forms. Common though this type of relationship is among plants, particularly in the tropics, one usually doesn't think of seaweed as being very much given to this habit. But in an environment where rhythms of moisture, temperature, and sunlight are fairly reliable, sea plants adjusted to such fluctuations thrive, and the inevitable crowding is the result of favorable conditions in general. Plants have taken to living on each other in an attempt to circumvent the limitations of specified space. Such seaweeds as delicate sycophant and tassel wing sprout in rosy fronds from the host algae. Some types actually do penetrate the tissues of the substrate plant in a kind of semiparasitism, but these are few. Wrinkled, moderately branching algal "stems" support more epiphytes than those which are multibranched or smooth stiped. Bryozoans and other tiny sedentary animals often attach themselves to kelps and smaller seaweeds. Some form crusty or mossy patches, others a jellylike scum.

Defense from each other is, necessarily, a strong thread in the pattern of tidal life. Many of the safeguards against wave crash and desiccation serve to protect tidal creatures from predation. Strong muscles hold a limpet firmly to the rock or keep bivalves shut tight against danger. Snails merely retreat behind an unappetizing mound of lime. Food-getting devices such as stinging cells, claws, and spines are useful defensive mechanisms. A few tidal species are suspected of having unpleasant-tasting flesh. Sea spiders and kelp crabs, brittle stars and shrimp weave and scramble through the lush kelp patches, safe from the attention of larger predators, which rarely penetrate such jungles. In the labyrinthian world of sea cliffs and rocks, there are crevices, crannies, and caves, some never uncovered even by the lowest tides. These provide excellent hiding places for shy animals, like octopi. They avoid their enemies by swiftly slipping into sheltering cracks or beneath overhangs. Rock projections protect many animals preferring the sandy or cobbled floors beneath them. Beds of sea anemones and mussels accommodate thousands of tiny organisms seeking to hide themselves. Sponges and other colonial animals take refuge in communal living. A large number, including tube worms, dig burrows in which they reside. Lime tube builders are quite secure, for a mouthful of rock is not pleasant eating. The colonial sand-castle worm, as its name implies, uses mucus in cementing sand to form large masses of tubes that adhere to rock faces at low tide zones.

With all of the perils and risks involved in living in the littoral, there is, as in all natural communities, a marvelous balance of success and failure. Take success to mean the ability of the individual to reproduce itself and the species to continue. California shares, with other shore-fronting lands, the oldest natural communities on earth. Life which we assume to have begun in ancient seas has changed less in this environment than in any other. We look back a hundred million years when we investigate tidal rocks and shores. That is not to say the individual aggregations of organisms of the littoral have undergone no change. California's coast is a rising one. Old wave-worn terraces occur high on the sea-facing bluffs. Erosion is constant along cliffs facing the open ocean. Softer strata are worn away. The undermined remains crumble into the froth-fretted surface below, destroying old habitats and presenting new homegrounds for tidal pioneers. Aside from these drastic shifts, many of the risks and hazards of life on land are missing. There are no threats from fire and periodic prolonged drought. But man, that most tireless, efficient, and voracious predator of all, has become an invader. Abalones, spiny lobsters, and edible crabs, once common in the coastal waters, have decreased alarmingly; strict conservation measures are imperative to insure their survival.

Nowhere else in the natural world are two such richly different environments so close together. To seaward are fish and brown pelicans in measured flight just above the outer breakers; to land, cliffs or sand dunes with wildflowers and white-footed mice. Surf and bluff are natural fences bordering these strips of beach often no more than fifty feet wide, if that. The highest tide wave-line marks the last stronghold of the sea. From here on, cold and heat, wind, rainfall, and soil determine what will live here.

The coastal dunes and cliffs are in themselves communities and have their own kinds of specialness. Shore dunes are found where the land slopes gently to the sea. Almost as soon as one goes inland from the high tide mark, the sea strand (beach) plants appear. Most are perennial, nonwoody, succulent (thick or fleshy stems and leaves), and there are surprisingly few, about thirty in all. They usually form hillocks and help create the undulating landscape so characteristic of dune topography. There is a distinct shift in distribution from north to south. From Point Reyes northward, the strand vegetation is dominated by beach grass (purposely introduced in the 1800s and since naturalized), American dune-grass, silver beachweed (beach bur), and the little pink heads of sea rocket (another nonnative), accompanied by two other important species, beach morning glory and a yellow-flowered sand verbena. South of Marin County the grasses gradually lose their dominant position, and most of the other plants mentioned above, with the exception of beach morning glory, become more significant along with sea fig, with its rosy sunbursts, the densely foliaged spikes of seascale, and beach pea, whose flowers are clusters of little pink and white bonnets. These last three species occur farther north, but they are more characteristic of central California beaches. This colorful assemblage continues into southern California, but with some change. Beach pea is absent south of Monterey County; the yellow-flowered sand verbena is replaced by a pink-flowering species, and salt grass and the silky yellow whorls of Hottentot fig increasingly are in evidence. A number of other plants are supporting performers with this all-star cast, such as maritime blue grass, beach strawberry (Santa Barbara County and north), and the sunny little circles of beach evening primrose, and they play more or less important roles depending on their range as well as on local factors such as degree of dune stabilization and competition from introduced species.

Distribution varies with distance from the high tide mark. Only a few stalwart plants such as beach grass, the sand verbenas, and sea rocket can cope with the severe conditions of the lower beach. Sand is a poor substrate for a number of reasons. It is low in nutrients, rainwater rapidly drains through it, and it is easily picked up by the wind. The more barren sand dunes not only shift and wander, but wind-driven sand is very abrasive. Salt-laden sand is even more of a problem (see Chapter 3). Succulent tissue helps store what water the plant can absorb. The brisk winds encourage plants to grow in small, dome-shaped mounds, mitigating the consequences of exposure, and the minute white hairs that give a characteristic grayish tint to the foliage serve to reflect potentially damaging heat.

Though soil salinity decreases behind the foredune, airborne salt from fog or spray as well as the intense heat and light bounced up from the sandy surface continue to make the dune area inhospitable but by no means uninhabited. Indeed, as we shall see, many coastal dunes, particularly in the northern part of the state, support a large number of plants. The rhizomes, or underground root-producing stems, of beach grass and American dune-grass stabilize large foredunes, arresting them from advance. The woody roots of other strand plants form smaller hillocks. Behind these sheltering mounds are often more open dunes, being pioneered by typical strand and other plants, and stabilized ridges that are host to dune scrub and even forest communities.

In the northern coastal counties, the beach plants that persist behind the foredune are joined by many wildflowers such as California poppy, wallflower, thrift, goldenrod, and seaside daisy. Common shrubs of the dune scrub are bush and tree lupines, coyotebrush, beach sagewort with its handsome silver-green feathery foliage, and wild buckwheat. Hollows between the sandy mounds are often more moist than the surrounding dunes. Water-tolerant rushes and sedges first encroach on such sites followed by prickly tangles of blackberry and thickets of willow and wax myrtle. Red alder is one of several dune broadleaf trees though a number of cone-bearing trees are at home here. Sitka spruce joins beach pine on dunes in Mendocino County northward; other components include Douglas-fir and grand fir. While salal, huckleberry, and red-flowering currant are common throughout much of the coast in central and northern California, two plants of the dune forest—bearberry and a type of reindeer lichen—are more restricted in their distribution, the latter particularly so as it is confined to the northernmost coastal counties. Both occur in boreal latitudes and may have survived this far south from colder times.

Sea-facing dune slopes often have fewer shrubs than the lee or less exposed sides, and nonwoody strand plants are more extensive on the windward sides, demonstrating the capability of these species in meeting the harsh dune environment. South of the Bay Area, dune scrub, or shrubby growth, loses many of the species that so enriched the vegetation described above. Bush lupines and coyotebrush continue to be prominent along with the pioneering beach plants. Mock heather is very important, joining bird's-foot trefoil, croton, and golden yarrow. California sagebrush, however, begins to replace beach sagewort, and the northern wild buckwheat gives way to a southern species. From Ventura County south, almost all of the northern shrub elements of dune scrub disappear, but their places are taken by shrubs more characteristic of chaparral, coastal sage scrub, and even desert scrubs, communities of plants we shall be meeting farther along. Lemonadeberry and bladderpod are typical examples.

The open spaces of sand between clumps of vegetation are guide books of information about the animals that live here. The tracks of beetles and lizards, wild mice and other small mammals criss-cross over the fine dune sands. Even the lightest pressures by the smallest of feet tell stories of what went where, and sometimes why, as trail intersects trail in a revealing pattern.

Very few dedicated beachcombers of the California coast will top the last dune without pausing and looking westward once more—out to the restless horizon of breaker crest and trough, to sanderlings and kelp piles, to a beach perhaps already wiped clean of his footprints by that erratic housekeeper, the tide.

Sea Cliff, Montaña de Oro State Park

2. Sea Cliff

Sea cliffs form some of the great sceneries of the world—
Côte d'Azur, Norwegian fiords, White Cliffs of Dover, and California's cliffs of Mendocino and Sonoma, Point Reyes, the
Golden Gate, Point Lobos, and along the spectacular coastline
north of San Simeon. Relatively unspoiled cliffs continue
south around Point Conception, but with the exception of a
few places on the Palos Verdes Peninsula and Torrey Pines
State Reserve, near La Jolla, coastal bluffs below Gaviota suffer
from highway construction, urbanization, and uncontrolled
recreational use.

Where headlands drop into the sea, there is a glorious pageantry of color and motion as wave follows wave, confronting the terrestrial outposts in endless procession. First comes the subtle shift in blue or green as the breaker is born. Then the infant swell slides toward land increasing in height until it crests and spills down upon itself in a white cascade. Now, when it is almost spent, tracelets of foam break away and eddy gracefully around the rocks and reefs at the foot of the cliff face, slipping seaward in the pull of the back surge.

The greatest joy of a shore watcher is a curling wave breaking directly against cliff foot or tide rock. Then, in a sweep of aquamarine and indigo its fluid ice shatters in a shower of blue-white crystals. There are the marvelous sounds of impact, as well, in this crash and splintering.

California shorescapes would be far less interesting if they were all beach flats and dunes. Coastal mountains are responsible in part for such dramatic views as those along the Scenic Highway south of the Monterey Peninsula. The Santa Lucia Range drops sharply to the sea in an incomparable meeting of land and ocean. The actual sea cliff itself, the portion being eroded by wave action, is but part of a great downsweep of mountain. The highway, the only interruption of these plummeting curves, seems tacked on like makeshift decoration. This is not to quarrel with its being there. This country suffers little from being seen and admired. But conservationists cannot be less than grateful to the far-sighted citizens who fought inappropriate commercial development. Today California can claim one of the great unspoiled coastline drives in the world.

Whether natural seawalls are backed by steep mountain, coastal plain, or broad shelves and benches—common along much of the coast—they are under constant attack by the sea. Wavelet and comber bite and lick at their bases, nibbling out rock fragments which, surf-tossed, grind away still more rock. Compressed by the upslope of the shore, breakers hitting cliffs increase in volume and strike these faces, broadside as they often are, with tremendous power. The softer shales and sandstones of the coastwise sedimentary series erode quickly. Whole chunks drop away undermined by the constant gnawing. The harder rocks persist in headlands such as Point Reyes and Bodega Head. The Farallon Islands, 30 miles (48 km.) west of the Golden Gate, are made of the same ancient granites as those two famed promontories and have resisted untold centuries of battering.

The sea-facing cliffs of southern California are notoriously unstable, falling to block major highways for days and collapsing in slumps that have tumbled dozens of homes downhill. They are comprised mainly of Tertiary (geologic time from the Dinosaur Age to the Ice Age) shales, sandstones, and other sedimentary rocks, usually marine in origin. Not only are such rocks highly subject to wave undercutting, two other conditions contribute to their instability. Most of the rock layers in slippage areas slant sharply seaward, and underlying shale beds, interacting with underground moisture, behave like lubricants. They become slippery, and overlying rock and soil layers may start a downward slide as inevitable as the descent of an escalator.

Straight-sided islets known as stacks enrich the shorescape. They, too, have been successful in withstanding the attack. Either tougher rock or protection from exposure to full wave strength has enabled them to remain. Uncountable rocks and reefs are scattered around them and along the cliff base. In Sonoma and Mendocino counties, coves circle around to break into stacks and rocky clusters connected by arches that hover over breakers tumbling back and forth through the spanway. Such an inlet on a golden summer day is enchantingly lovely with a gentle wind nudging the needles of the firs and pines along the cliff tops, the silver of splash and slide-off, the turquoise of surge and swell.

Many coves are usually friendly places, and no better sites for picnics exist if they are accessible and open to the public. The larger inlets have beaches built by currents traveling along the curve of the cove head and endlessly working over the sand and pebbles of the little strand. In narrower coves the waves, confined as they are, crash into each other coming and going. These little pockets, or surge channels, are extremely dangerous for human exploration and are best left to be viewed from above.

Beaches also occur on the more open cliff-faced shorelines lacking cove indentations. South of San Francisco, in San Mateo County, wave attack against the foot of coastal hills has resulted in some remarkably straight cliffs with long beaches between the few and scattered headlands. North of Point Reyes, the west side of the peninsula is bordered by broad straight strands and inshore dunes around Abbotts Lagoon. The rocky slopes of the ridge have been partially smothered in sand dredged up from the sea bottom. Prevailing currents are parallel to the shore, and cross-current action which would aid in creating indentations is negligible.

The cliffline is broken at points along the coast, particularly where river valleys enter the sea. Frequently their mouths are semisealed across by bars, stretches of beach, or dunes that separate the open sea front from the lagoons and tide flats to the rear. California has a predominantly rising coast. One can deduce this from such topographical features as wave-cut terraces on the hills above the present shoreline and ancient stacks now standing as isolated remnants on the coastal plains that were once strands and beaches. Very recent subsidence, however, has drowned the mouth of the major river system of California and created San Francisco Bay. This estuary contains vast acres of mud flats rich in bird and invertebrate life. Tomales and Bolinas bays and Drakes Estero are also prime examples of tide marsh shorescapes in striking contrast to neighboring palisades. The first two are drowned mouths of rift valleys formed by the famous, or infamous, San Andreas Fault. Drakes Estero is a typical valley system flooded most probably by the same subsidence that made San Francisco Bay.

Some cliffs are mere bluffs with easy access to the beach. Others like Duxbury Point, at the outer end of Bolinas Bay, are practically unscalable, and their beaches and reefs are lonely places where only seabirds congregate. But all along the coast, people have managed to wear footpaths, often overgrown by vegetation and hardly discernible, that wind down these steep faces to disappear in the talus and boulder heaps of the cliff base. Sea-edge precipices are by no means always sheer or perpendicular. They may have ledges, gullies, knobs, and slopes where plants establish themselves and seabirds create a world of their own.

A cliff is not an easy dwelling place. Water even in a climate of relatively high rainfall is scarce for several reasons. Shallow soils cannot hold much moisture, and runoff is particularly rapid on steep gradients. The cool winds constantly blowing inland from the ocean are in themselves drying; they carry away moisture from the leaf surface and leave salt deposits instead. Salt-burdened soils and atmosphere are additional hazards likely to be encountered by plants attempting life on a sea cliff habitat. Such conditions amplify any tendencies to dryness on the part of the environment.

Many plants simply cannot manage such a site at all. They need more water or deeper soils, less salinity or less wind. One or several of these limiting factors prevent many of the plants usually found near the coast from even a reconnaissance on sea bluffs. Some, however, do very well. They germinate in cracks where soil has begun to accumulate, rain water lingers longer, and there is shelter from the wind. In time the shrubs force a network of roots through rock joints and breaks, maintaining a tenacious hold on life. Or they find toe space on a barren ledge and proceed to build a soil base, often with the debris from their own discarded parts such as leaves and flowers. An existing clump of plants is an invitation for seedlings to try to establish themselves in the same place, if there is enough soil to go around. Gullies with their catchment hollows are host to many plants whose careers may end with the next great storm as they are torn out and tossed into the sea below.

Among the specific forms frequently found growing on sea cliffs are the carpetlike sea fig and Hottentot fig, which conserve water in their thick triangular leaves, and hang in untidy masses from the cliff edge or spread over the bluffs in coarse friezes. A close relative, the naturalized ice plant, is also succulent. Tiny blisters cover the surfaces of leaves and stems to give them a jeweled look. Live-forevers have reddish rosettes of fleshy water-storing leaves. Their near relative, stonecrop, retains moisture in much the same way.

From San Luis Obispo County north, the shrub ocean spray feathers out in plumes of creamy white along gully sides and occasionally on the more open bluffs. Coyotebrush, prostrate blue blossom and other coastal forms of ceanothus, and bush monkeyflower are typical cliff shrubs and have many of the drought-resistant features discussed in more detail in Chapter 4. Up to 6 or 7 feet (1.8–2.1 m.) tall, the spectacular tree lupine has corn-kernel yellow or, more rarely, lavender blossoms. Though characteristic of sandy places, like their dune bush cousins, they often cluster in the lee of low ridges and the gravel of road cuts. Where the bluffs fold back along canyons and river valleys, the more protected locations may encourage masses of stunted sword fern, berry vines, paintbrush, cow parsnip and other umbels, and blue blossom ceanothus.

Small flowering plants are not uncommon: rock cress, seaside daisies, evening primrose, thrift, golden yarrow, and wallflower are small flares of pink or yellow among the quieter grays, whites, and rusts of wild buckwheats. These last look like awkward handfuls of dried twigs even when they are in full bloom. Dock is the same rusty color, though much more leafy, and is another dweller of rocky outcrops overlooking the sea. Some of the most frequently encountered plants are grasses, forming little ledge-top hummocks that are colonies of coastal prairie, a community we shall meet later on. Indeed, adventurous pioneers are commonplace on these bracing heights. Readers familiar with the first chapter will have noticed by now that many of the plants of the dunes are cliff dwellers as well. Though the habitats differ in a number of ways, both experience almost constant wind and air-borne salt. These two physical features of the maritime environment continue to harass vegetation inland from the immediate coast, and several important plants of both dune and cliff dominate the adjacent coastal scrub, another community discussed further along. On the other hand, enterprising scouts from these inland communities attempt to establish themselves on these often precarious slopes.

Though many of its succulents extend the length of the state, sea cliff vegetation of southern California differs quite widely from that to the north. There is a superficial resemblance. Coyotebrush continues to be a prominent shrub, especially in draw bottoms and along the base of the cliffs. Buckwheats are some of the most common residents of the habitat, but they are not the same species as those in the northern half of the state. The striking large yellow lupine is rare south of Ventura County, but its visual impact in the landscape is replaced by giant coreopsis (San Luis Obispo County to Los Angeles County). Ragged brown sticks out of season, in spring they burst out with plumes of bright green feathery leaves and large clusters of sunshine-yellow flowers. A smaller species of maritime coreopsis occurs in San Diego County and south.

Analogous to the relationship between cliff inhabitants northward and their adjacent plant communities, most of the southern sea bluff shrubs are hardy members of the coastal sage scrub, the neighboring community inland in most places. They include bush-sunflower, lemonadeberry, laurel sumac, goldenbush, bladderpod, black and white sages, and California sagebrush, which extends north to Marin County where it contributes to the sea cliff vegetation. Cacti comprise a prominent group of plants. The velvet cactus is rare now, but clumps of prickly-pear stand out like collections of old-fashioned hair brushes among the shrubby growth.

Full-grown bushes away from the coast, many shrubs are stunted, sometimes to prostration, on sea bluffs. Sea breezes and salt spray are responsible for the natural pruning and keep exposed thickets in hedgelike form. The drying power of salty wind kills any pioneering twig daring to venture beyond the protective mass of compacted foliage. It is interesting that many of the adaptations typical of alpine and desert plants prove useful to vegetation on this relatively moist and comfortable coast.

A prime reason for some cliffs, smaller offshore islands, and rocks being devoid of plants, or almost so, is the continuous congregation of seabirds, to a spectacular degree in some places. One of the best known such rookeries is the Farallon Islands, those last pieces of California where the immense loneliness of the open sea begins. Exposed and storm-scarred, their aged granite is broken and cracked. There is hardly any covering vegetation except for a few low-growing plants such as the succulent Farallon weed and some introduced grasses and other nonnatives. The result is a ceaseless weathering of rugged terrain. Though now they serve as a navigational facility with a Coast Guard station, beacon light, radio signal transmitter, and radar equipment, at one time they were major contributors to the markets of San Francisco. It seems that there were not enough laying hens around this thriving city in the 1850s. So the Farallon Egg Company was formed, and at one time 120,000 seabird eggs were gathered in two days and sold for a dollar a dozen. The practice finally came to an end when the islands were declared a bird reserve in 1909, but by that time the bird population had decreased considerably. Fur seal and sea otter skins were another source of income for early-day exploiters of this tiny outpost.

Many of the birds that nest on these and other coastal islands north and south of the Golden Gate, such as the Channel Islands off the southern California coast and those of British Columbia and Alaska, are truly seabirds. That is, they spend most of their lives on the open ocean, coming to shore only during the summer breeding season. If they could have evolved ways to incubate eggs out at sea, they might conceivably have done so. Birds such as Cassin's auklet, ashy storm-petrel, and Xantus' murrelet, which breeds on the southern California coast, behave as though land is to be avoided whenever possible except for the period of reproduction. This, however, may extend for several months. On the other hand, cormorants, western gulls, and oystercatchers are true shorebirds in that their activities are never far from shore the year around.

Though the Farallones are the most famed of these California seabird rookeries and have a large number of species and a great number of individuals, some coastal cliffs—on Point Reyes and Año Nuevo Point, for instance—have well-developed nesting colonies. Offshore islets, like Seal Rocks close to San Francisco's Cliff House, are frequently used. These natural communities differ from most others in being almost exclusively the homes of birds, either nesting, or nesting and roosting; there are few mammals, except for sea lions and seals on skerry or beach. Plants are extremely scattered or nonexistent in the crowded rookeries. Seedlings would soon be trampled or buried by nesting activity. Guano accumulations, up to a foot thick, preclude the successful establishment of vegetation except perhaps for lichens, those hardiest of plants. Birds such as cormorants and western gulls use plant materials for their nests and depend on dried seaweed, twigs, or grass brought in or washed ashore. Bare ground nesters, if they make any preparation at all, line the nest depression with rock fragments or pebbles, harsh substrate for something as fragile as an egg.

Few nesting sites are as crowded as those of seabirds. The great gannet concentrations of Newfoundland and islands of the North Sea are so congested during breeding season that it is difficult to walk through them, if the birds remain stationary, without stepping on some offspring or parent. California murre colonies on the ledges of coastal promontories and islands are often equally crowded. To the enterprising bird watcher they appear as a solid mass of gurgling, restless gray. On the Farallones, in their avian heyday, they most probably outnumbered the neighboring species also nesting here. Though the islands never quite regained the bird populations of pre-egg-company days, they still support large colonies. One would suppose that much competitive struggle takes place as the birds arrive from the open sea in March and April looking for nest sites. It is hard to believe that there is little or no fighting for nesting space which is so limited.

Natural communities have their own laws of supply and demand. Desert regions are short on water, and desert dwellers must compete successfully for their share or die. Most communities have limits on the supply of food available to their animal residents. Each species has its own requirements and preferences, and competition for food is primarily between individuals of a species in any given environment. Any severe limiting of the supply intensifies competition, and ultimately the individuals competing for the diminishing food source die of hunger, change their diet, or move to better feeding grounds.

For the seabirds along the California coast, however, food is relatively abundant. Upwelling cold offshore currents carry nutrients which support a rich plankton population, attracting fish in heavy concentrations. Both for their own use and that of their offspring, the birds prefer nesting close to this abundance.

Ample though the source may be, many seabirds have developed additional ways to increase efficiency of food finding. Such birds as auklets, guillemots, loons, puffins, murres, and cormorants are divers and need not depend on surface feeding. Brandt's and double-crested cormorants have carried this a step further. The latter have been observed feeding cooperatively in San Francisco Bay. Flocks form closely packed lines and advance with some of the birds diving all the time. The fish are steadily driven forward, and escape is unlikely as up to a fourth of the flock is underwater on the attack. Pelagic cormorants, another local form, dive deeper than the other two resident relatives and will go to considerable depths in search of food, so A. C. Bent reports in *Life History of Petrels, Pelicans, and Their Allies* (Dover, 1964). Such interspecific division of the habitat allows a more efficient use of its resources.

Thus food is rarely a problem, nor is water, for these birds are adapted to drink seawater. What is scarce, however, is nesting space on the smaller islands and where suitable sites are limited. Over the thousands of years that these places have been host to seabirds, patterns of behavior have developed tending to lessen the burden of competition for breeding room. A basic ecological tenet states that species occurring in the same community cannot have identical sets of life habits, that is, they cannot live in precisely the same way. One type of mouse might be night active, its cousin diurnal. One sparrow species looks for seeds on the ground, another forages in shrubs. Each form operates in certain ways that may be slightly or largely different from every other possible competitor in the community. It has adjusted to fit one of the many variations in the shared habitat. This functional status or role of a species is called its ecological niche.

A physically limited community such as a rocky, barren seabird colony or collection of colonies would appear to offer little in the way of nest site diversification or, in other words, not many niches for various breeding site requirements. There is a range of accommodation, however, more than one would suppose.

Three closely related cormorants live on the California coast: pelagic, Brandt's, and the Farallon or double-crested. Each species has a slightly different pattern of nesting behavior, with enough diversity so that the three forms avoid getting in each other's way. The first cormorant prefers very narrow ledges on sheer seawalls. It appears to nest later than the Farallon and earlier than the Brandt's, both of which choose less steep slopes and broader shoulders.

The demure Cassin's auklet and the harlequin-billed tufted puffin, or sea parrot, dig burrows often three to four feet long in grassy banks and slopes. These tunnels occur by the hundred; and rather incredibly, no tunnel ever seems to intersect another, though they may be in close association. Many birds breed in these tunnels, most of them being used year after year, and there is evidence that some individuals wait until later in the season when burrows are being vacated by earlier nesting couples. Western gulls use either cliff ledges or, more commonly, the gentler sea bluff slopes, while California (common) murres prefer narrow rock ledges. Ashy storm-petrels seek rocky crevices, and brown pelicans build simple nests of sticks or debris on rocky or brushy slopes on offshore islands. Some birds occasionally use old puffin burrows. Guillemots— stubby little black-and-white birds—seek great sea caves, features of shoreline cliffs which have been carved by wave action in weaker rocks at surf level. Here they huddle by the hundreds on ledges and in crannies under arched ceilings, which are sometimes sparkling mosaics of rich color. These crystallized mineral deposits, incidentally, result from seepage percolating down through cracks in the rock above.

Thus, even tiny islands and severe cliffs provide more types of nesting niches than one would suppose, and competition for breeding sites is considerably lessened by differences in

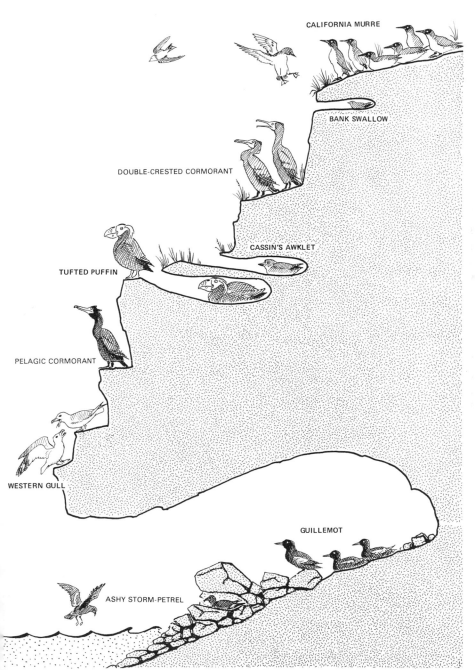

Figure 3. Typical nest-site preferences of some California seabirds

breeding habits. Other factors are also at work. When conditions are at saturation point, there is evidence for some colonies that the nest site area is used in shifts, one species succeeding another as the season progresses.

Each bird when finally settled has defenses against overaggressive and impatient neighbors. Territoriality is a strong pattern of bird behavior. Crowded though these colonies might be, each owner defends its nest vigorously against theft of material or usurpation of space. Swift stabs or bites with sharp bills warn intruders against invasion of territory which, in such congested conditions, is the area within reach of the nest owner's bill. The same action is used in defense against predation from western gulls, ravens, crows, and other potential enemies.

There are other protective devices against predators. Some species seek shelter in more inaccessible nest sites—hard-to-reach-into cracks, burrows, and similarly restricted places. The massing of colonially nesting birds is in itself a deterrent to harassment. But threatening situations, approaching human beings, and the like will drive many seabirds from their nests, leaving them and their contents open to various hazards. Cassin's auklets and ashy storm-petrels are nocturnal and confine their feeding and brooding exchanges to the night hours when danger is less.

Close association may have additional positive features. It is suggested that colonial birds are stimulated to breed simultaneously, thus hatching their chicks at about the same time. This supposedly confines predation to a short interval and does not allow prey-predator relationships to strengthen into what would be leisurely exploitation if the food supply were continuous. In many ways cooperation for defense is simplified by colonial behavior.

Birds breeding close to the surf level must be wary of another predator; young sea lions can develop a taste for eggs, though older ones seemingly are not interested. Sea lions, elephant seals, and true seals are the most important mammal members of sea cliff communities. Because of their awkwardness on land and bulky size, they inhabit the lower cliff ledges and reefs. From time to time, smaller mammals make their home here. Rodents, rabbits, and predators such as skunks and foxes, which often patrol sea bluffs, are found on some of the nearer islands, including the Channel group off southern California. Regardless of the presence of some predatory species, the fact remains that isolated bluffs and islands are the safest places for colonial seabirds. Difficulty of access helps protect the vulnerable throng, where little or no concealment is attempted by ground-nesting birds and whose equipment for defense is somewhat limited.

The larger sea mammals have their own breeding rhythms. Among the sea lions and elephant seals, competition is less for space than for mates, the females of the harems. The battles between mature males are famed in natural science literature as adventurous souls have looked in awe through the fog of desolate coasts on these violent struggles. The male northern fur seal, a migrant species along the California coast, exhibits an intense territoriality during breeding. He truly fights for space when he defends what he considers his ground, that is, where his pups will be born and he will mate with his harem. Any newcomers will be challenged and driven off, unless he is past his prime and gives way to stronger youngsters who must win their territories through the defeat of older bulls.

Like bits of foam on wing, flocks of gulls curve and circle past the cliff face. Long-throated and slim, cormorants pause on a perching point before taking off for their feeding grounds. Oystercatchers investigate likely looking limpets and mussels as they patter over the reefs and rocky shoals on salmon pink feet. And the black swifts that also share the crannies of these battlements flash by in fleet arcs hunting for flying insects of little interest to their fellow cliff dwellers. They are busy places, these rough, inhospitable-looking precipices, particularly when rookeries are present and it is breeding season, and noisy, too, when a shrill cacaphony breaks through the colony as something disturbs the compacted throng. Life is zestful here, out on land's edge, with winging, calling birds and spindrift blowing off a swelling sea.

Snowy Egret, Upper Newport Bay

3. Salt Marsh

To many people, tidal flats and marshes are unattractive, particularly where man has used them as dumping grounds. Californians have been guilty of this practice, allowing unsightly fills around the southern edges of San Francisco Bay and on the shores of Richmond and Berkeley, where discarded tires and other such repulsive flotsam are strewn about in abundance. A kind of "we-just-drive-by-them, we-don't-notice-they-are-there" attitude enables the more insensitive to be ignorant of these awkward landscapes. However, this wasn't so easy some years back when the famed "East Bay Perfume," an overpowering mixture of sewer smells, crouched in wait for those commuting on the shoreline highway. Fortunately, much of this essence has now succumbed to modern technology. Only the faint memory of those heady days lingers in the air.

Ecologically, these too-often despised acres are of deep interest. They are among the world's most productive. One plant species alone, cordgrass, produces five to ten times as much nutrient material and oxygen per acre as one of our most prized crops, wheat. It is doubtful if cordgrass will ever become a widely used commercial food crop, but in the economy of the salt marshes it is of tremendous importance. A few herbivorous forms, such as insects, eat it fresh, but when decayed by bacteria into tiny particles, it is the main dish on the banquet table for the invertebrate feeders, as well as a few fish, of the baylands. It also contributes nutrients for the beds of algae that help link these backwaters with the sea.

By all standards, San Francisco Bay is the state's largest and best known estuary. Most every young geography student, if asked what is California's most striking and scenic feature, will answer either the Golden Gate or Yosemite Valley. Historically it is unequalled, as much of California's story begins here, ends here, or passes by. Geologically it is the state's prime example of a drowned river mouth, whose topography prior to flooding was such that a north-south trending valley was already in existence. It is this basin which gives it a butterfly shape. The northern wing, or embayment, is technically San Pablo Bay and the southern is San Francisco Bay proper. The combined Sacramento and San Joaquin rivers flow into this huge backwater at Carquinez Strait, and Suisun Bay behind it is where the two great streams converge as they flow toward the bay. An enormous amount of sediment has been deposited on the bay floor and is exposed by low tides draining off the shallows and gently sloping shores around Palo Alto, San Leandro, San Pablo, and the flatlands north of Vallejo. There are several places, however, where rocky hillsides drop abruptly into the waters of the bay—for instance, around the bridge terminus at Richmond, the Golden Gate itself, and the Tiburon Peninsula. It is this fringing of hills that gives beauty to this inland sea; and patterns of island, cove, and headland, particularly on Marin's bay-facing shores, are charming daughters of this meeting of Coast Range and ocean. In less dramatic places, great expanses of mud flat and marsh gently ease out to permanent water. On a foggy day when the tide is in, one can become totally confused over what is land and what is water. Then gray floats over gray, and only ship whistles and the muted thunder of traffic on a nearby bridge enforce a reality of their own.

Four other central California coastal wetland areas are well known: Bolinas Lagoon and Tomales Bay of Marin, with

Drakes Estero between the two, and Elkhorn Slough of Monterey Bay. Farther north salt marsh is more or less extensive in Bodega Bay and in estuarine bays and neighboring lagoons at the mouths of the Smith, Klamath, and Eel rivers. South of Monterey, Morro Bay State Park has a number of acres of tidal flats as do Goleta Slough and Carpenteria Marsh in Santa Barbara County. North of Malibu, Mugu Lagoon is well worth a visit though access is limited because of the nearby naval installations. Anaheim Bay and Bolsa Chica Slough still have some relatively unchanged wetlands, but the gem is Upper Newport Bay, which, after considerable struggle in the courts of Orange County, finally was declared a wildlife sanctuary. About a dozen streams drain the coastal slopes between San Clemente and the Mexican border and terminate in wetland-fringed lagoons, some of which are biologically productive. Mission Bay, once host to a large tidal marsh, is now almost completely developed into resort and recreational facilities. Only remnants of marsh remain in San Diego Bay, but Tijuana River, just north of the border, enters into some marsh and mud-flat habitat as it exits to the sea.

The two major types of coastal wetland environment are mud flats and salt marshes. There are differences between them, though we often loosely interchange the terms. Marshes usually begin at the mean lower high tide level, that is, they are covered by the highest tide of the day. Their plants, though adapted to prolonged feet wetting, are limited in the length of continuous inundation or exposure they can endure. Tidal flats are intermediate between the open water of bay or lagoon and the surrounding marshes. They extend down from mean lower high water to extreme low water and are submerged and exposed twice a day. Few plants can tolerate the many adversities of such an environment. What vegetation is present is mostly composed of unicellular and larger forms of algae with the major exception of eel-grass, which is common in saltwater shallows, including the tidal drainage creeks that seldom become completely dry. The cordgrass and pickleweed of the marsh are also intertidal, but the former is able to withstand up to twenty-one continuous hours of submergence. Pickleweed begins its best growth around the average higher tide line. Conditions vary, but one can generalize by saying that cordgrass growth is the deciding feature. Below its coarse and tangled masses are the tidal flats. Where it begins and above, the landscape takes on the characteristics of a marsh. Both marsh and mud flat are drained by a network of meandering creeklets that accommodates the flood and runoff of both the tide and freshwater streams flowing in from surrounding uplands.

Flat or marsh, these bay shallows are home or favored resting place for many living things, harsh and problematic though they appear. Certainly they are inhospitable to most of the native plants of California. If one should drop seeds of bush monkeyflower in among the pickleweed, though they might germinate, it is doubtful they would ever mature. They simply are not adapted to life in a salt marsh.

Adaptation, or the successful meeting of environmental conditions, is the main business of life. It is one of the central themes in the story of evolution, that great and grand unfolding of the potential in the living organism. Adaptation does not happen, species-wide, overnight. It takes place within the framework of species survival, within the slow spiraling of evolutionary history through what is known as natural selection. Those best fitted to meet certain conditions survive; those less so do not, or have a harder time of it. These conditions are both physical and biological or, in other words, involve terrain and neighbor. Such features as temperature range, exposure to sun and wind, soil variation, and amount of available moisture are primarily physical in character. Residence in biotic communities also means interaction with other living things. Competition and predation are two of these interrelationships upon which we have already touched. Both types of environmental impact are of equal importance to a living organism. A limpet,

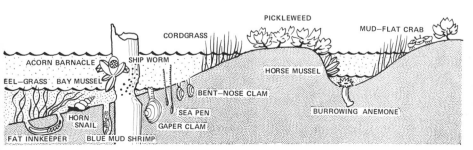

Figure 4. Tidal mud-flat zonation

to remain alive, must avoid being eaten as well as avoid death from dehydration.

The earth's history is one of inconstancy. Seas have invaded and withdrawn; ice masses have pushed forward and retreated; volcanoes have erupted and subsided; temperature ranges have widened and narrowed. Biological change is a key process in the ability to survive these fundamental habitat variations, and its major mechanism operates within the germ cell itself. Abrupt changes, or mutations, cause organisms to differ from their parents. Most mutations have no survival value; indeed, they are often detrimental. But some of them increase the organism's ability to cope successfully with threatening environmental factors. And what is most important, since the change occurred in genetic material, the new characteristic will be transferred to offspring for their benefit as well. For example, a forebear of a certain strain of rabbit developed hind legs that were longer than usual and, being able to better elude its predators, survived, while its shorter-legged cousins succumbed, moved away, or developed some other means of escape. Its descendants benefited by their lengthened hind legs, and today the jack rabbit is legion in the wild areas of the West. Natural selection favors the transmission of beneficial mutations, but weeds out those that are harmful. Animals can adapt in several ways: changes in behavior, in anatomical structure, and in physiological processes and functions. The same is true of plants, if we use the term "behavior" in a broad sense. Most broadleaf trees living in climates with severe winters lose their leaves during the cold part of the year, and their metabolism slows down to wait the season through in a kind of hibernation.

To return to the coastal wetland habitats, what are the conditions this environment imposes on the members of its communities? Certainly, they must accept daily tidal ebb and flow with occasional springs and neaps. Some of the mud flats will always be under water in sloughs and channels, and the upper edges of the marsh will be above the high water mark, though occasionally dampened by the highest tides and at times thoroughly wetted by wind-driven waves, freshwater floods, rain, and changes in water level. Variations in salinity are to be expected. The percentage of salt content in tidewater near stream and river outlets drops considerably in the winter and spring months when storm runoff increases. Out in the salt pans and shallow ponds, temperature ranges are broad. Organisms living in these pools not only must survive abrupt changes in salinity—during rain storms, for example—but must also withstand a possible rise or fall of 50° F. (28° C.) in water temperature. By either flooding or increased turbidity, tidal action can reduce the amount of light received by submerged plants, thus affecting their ability to photosynthesize.

Muddy substrates give rise to other difficulties. Waterlogged, salt-impregnated, and deficient in oxygen, marshes and mud flats appear unable to offer much in the way of plant habitat. Nor is this all. They are unstable and rearrange their drainage sloughs, filling in here, slumping there, particularly during the wintertime when high waves, tides, and runoff slosh and splash over these lonely-looking flatlands. Where banks have been built up along the channel sides because of root accumulation, undercutting can occur. Plants act as silt traps, and the masses of vegetative tissue in themselves are responsible for sediment deposition, especially during floods. Denser, more cohesive mud tends to remain in place, particularly when stabilized by plant concentrations. Then the drainage ways shift more slowly. Sand flats rarely develop well-defined, more or less permanent channel systems. This accounts for their absence from much of both Bolinas Lagoon and Bodega Bay.

It is indeed testimony to the tenacity and resourcefulness of life that not only do organisms live here, but they thrive to the point of being among the world's most productive species. How and in what manner have they adapted themselves to these pans and sloughs?

Zostera, or eel-grass, is probably one of the most interesting species of coastal lagoon vegetation. A seed plant, it lives a life of submergence, neighbor to sea lettuce and other algae such as various primitive unicellular species. Blue-green or golden brown, the latter vividly stain the dark gray tidal muds. Sea lettuce and eel-grass are both a brilliant green; so color is by no means missing in what is often thought of as a very drab environment. *Zostera* is a hydrophyte, or water plant. It is found only in bays and saltwater sloughs. The surf grasses of the rocks of the outer shore are different, though they too are real seed plants and are adapted to life in wave surge. In the calm shallows of lagoons there is little need for structural rigidity, since the water itself provides a supporting medium. Instead of stiffening tissue, eel-grass has air spaces in its blades and stems to take advantage of the buoyancy of water and to store oxygen needed for metabolism. Anchored in the sands and muds of bay floors, it supplies a relatively stable habitat for many invertebrates, some of which could never be at home in bay waters otherwise. Eel-grass, particularly when dead and decomposing, is a source of food. In addition, many species of small algae are epiphytic on its blades, sometimes covering them until the original leaf surface can no longer be seen. These in turn are homes for microscopic algae such as the diatoms so abundant in plankton. Its thickets shelter many other organisms. The tiny white "flowers" of certain hydroids blossom on the blade tips. Nudibranchs and little snails such as the fragile bubble snail slowly maneuver through the interlacing stems. Transparent, skeleton, and pistol shrimp share the micropolis with marine worms, some of them tube-building.

Once above the weaving ribbons of this little community, plants and animals must make their peace with a world that is rained on, tide flooded, sun warmed, drained off, and mud stuck. There are noticeable vegetation patterns as well as drainage systems. As indicated elsewhere in this chapter, salt marsh vegetation has two more or less distinct zones—a lower one dominated by cordgrass and a higher one where pickleweed and other succulent plants become important. There is accumulating evidence that the maximum length of continuous exposure or, conversely, submersion is a major factor in the distribution of salt marsh plants. The tidal flood of the lower marsh may last more than six hours, but exposure is limited to the fifteen-day period between spring tides. Submergence is often less than six hours in the higher marsh, and exposure may be weeks or months in duration, awaiting extreme high tides. This dual marsh system is typical of central and northern California; as we shall see, southern California has a third zone between the two just described. Cordgrass, incidentally, does not occur north of Humboldt Bay.

Cordgrass advance is largely responsible for marsh expansion as it stabilizes new mud deposits. San Francisco Bay is filling in naturally as well as artificially. Though parts of its shoreline have subsided due to the pumping out of underground water, thousands of tons of silt are constantly being dumped by the rivers and streams entering the bay. As the floor builds up, the land is elevated above the critical submergence level for cordgrass (about 4.5 feet [1.3 m.] above mean lower low tide), which then moves in. Even without human interference it is estimated that it will not take long, geologically speaking, for much of the bay to become first a marsh and then a meadow.

Cordgrass has several adaptive devices that allow it to survive prolonged submergence. It is equipped with hollow passages in its leaves and roots so that air can move readily throughout the plant even while underwater. In general, oxygen levels are low in the dense sediments of a salt marsh, though by no means is this vital gas completely absent. All tidal lagoon plants able to make food take carbon dioxide from the air and give off oxygen during the process of photosynthesis which then returns to the water, soil, and air to be available for the other great life process, respiration—the oxidation of food to produce energy.

Only a small number of plants can tolerate soils of high salt content. Called halophytes, these species have modified in various ways to cope with the substrate. Cordgrass and its distant cousin, salt grass, which lives at a higher level within the marsh, excrete excess salt by means of special glands. Films of salt crystals often cover their leaves in little white patches. That cordgrass thrives is indicated by the 3- to 4-foot (1–1.2 m.) tall stems and rank growth. In places it gives the flats much the appearance of an upland meadow. A perennial, it spreads by runners, producing in springtime very hardy youngsters that account for the plant's success as a colonizer.

Pickleweed, indicative of the higher marsh and the most widespread group of coastal wetland plants, is another story. It, too, is a halophyte; and its fleshy, segmented, leafless stems exemplify an additional modification to saline soils. Storing water within its tissue, it uses a device employed by cactus and other succulent desert plants. At first glance, it seems somewhat absurd to imply any similarity between the two habitats, for certainly if a place is a marsh, it is not a desert. To understand this peculiar state of affairs, it is useful to know something about osmosis, the movement of water through the membranes that enclose living cells. Water moves from a less concentrated solution to a more concentrated one. Cell sap is usually more concentrated than soil water. Therefore, water flow is into the plant until equalization is approached. But, when the outside water is loaded with dissolved salt, as in a salt marsh, it is more concentrated than the cell liquid, and osmosis is reversed. Ordinary plants will wilt and die under these circumstances, losing water to the soil rather than taking it in. In effect, a salt marsh is a chemical desert with conditions as severe, if not more so, as those of a climatic desert.

Halophytes have the ability to concentrate organic compounds or soil salts in their cell fluids and so maintain the internal concentrations necessary for osmosis. The plant's metabolic processes, however, impose additional burdens. Transpirational moisture is lost as vapor through the leaf pores or stomates (see Chapter 4), leaving behind potentially toxic accumulations of salt. Halophytes have developed a number of mechanisms to control the amount of salt in leaf tissue. Succulent plants such as pickleweed store water to dilute excessively saline cell sap. Nevertheless, at the end of the growing season so much salt has been retained that perennial pickleweeds wither to dry stems, losing both cell liquid and its load of salt. The grasses referred to above, as well as sea lavender, rely on glands, special salt-excreting cells, to solve their problem. Saltbushes, described more fully in Chapter 18, have tiny glands on their foliage that store salt until full enough to burst and deposit their contents on the leaf surface to be blown or rinsed away.

Sodium and chloride ions—the electrically charged particles that make up sea salt—are excessively available in coastal wetlands. Only a few plants require sodium to any degree, and toxicity from high soil concentrations of this element is a constant threat. On the other hand, potassium, an essential element for growth, is not only in short supply, but it is chemically similar to sodium. Through a process known as active transport, many halophytes assist the passage of potassium ions into the cell. Carrier subunits of the root membranes selectively bind themselves to the ions and convey them across the membrane, releasing them as free ions. There are two mechanisms involved in active transport, and one—of great advantage to halophytes— is far more resistant to competing ions of the chemically similar sodium. Most of these procedures to regulate both the intake and excretion of salt require expenditures of energy, and it is not surprising that only a few plant species have adapted to life in a salty habitat.

Soil salinity is by no means uniform throughout the marsh. The amount of salt present is modified by tidal flooding, intrusions of freshwater, and evaporation. As a result, the most saline soils occur around mean high water, in other words, where cordgrass gives way to pickleweed. Salinity tends to decrease both landward and shoreward from this meeting ground of the two marsh zones, but it also varies with the season, increasing in depth in the wet months and rising during the dry period.

It should not be inferred that salt marsh plants require high soil salinities for best growth. Indeed, it appears that most would do as well or even better in freshwater habitats. Though some halophytes germinate when salt concentrations are rather high, the majority sprout when rainwater or some other source of freshwater has temporarily diluted the salt content. In sum, halophytes put up with their salt-ridden world, but they don't need it.

It is no accident that pickleweed replaces cordgrass right where soil salt concentrations are highest. Though unable to cope with the prolonged and frequent submersions endured by cordgrass, pickleweed is more tolerant of high soil salinity, but only to a point. It avoids the salt-impregnated pans that develop along the inland edges of coastal marshes in warm climates. Regardless of these environmental limitations, pickleweeds are a remarkably tolerant group of plants. Cordgrass is missing in many tidal wetlands throughout its range in California. Where this species is absent, and even where it is present, pickleweed is a vigorous mud-flat invader. The two plants are not mutually exclusive. Their territories have some overlap, the degree depending upon local circumstances, and there are large colonies of an annual species of pickleweed in among cordgrass in southern California.

Though the little swollen segments of its branching stems often look like tiny pickles strung together, pickleweed gets its name from its use as a pickle. It has other culinary uses as well. Worldwide in distribution, four species occur in California. Two are bushy perennials, and their fleshy little joints grow out green and juicy in the spring and remain so during the summer. They turn an attractive scarlet in the fall and then, as noted above, dry into woody-looking twiglets. Their root masses are of great importance to the tortuous channelways as they give stability to slough banks and sides. The smaller annual species are not as widespread in California, and one, referred to earlier, is confined to the southern part of the state. Salt grass and *Frankenia*, with its inconspicuous pinkish flowers, are two other halophytes in close association with pickleweed.

At higher elevations, such as the dikes that build up along the drainage channels, are plants that must live through a long, dry summer as well as cope with more or less salty soils. Saltbushes and their succulent relative, sea blite, grow with gum plant, *Jaumea, Lasthenia,* and the introduced brass buttons, members of that large and cheerful family, the sunflower group. Bird's beak, arrow-grass, and sea lavender contribute hues of green or purple while dodder, that ubiquitous parasite, drapes tangles of orange-colored string over pickleweed and other bushes. Tules and other bulrushes and cattails are indicative of brackish water, usually where freshwater streams enter the salt marsh. Finally, a more hospitable environment for most plants is encountered on the bluffs and uplands above the marsh. The usual weeds and some of the more common wildflowers—mustard, wild radish, scarlet pimpernel, filaree, fiddleneck, goldfields, and wild oats among others—green up in spring and dry to straw in summer. Representatives of adjacent plant communities appear at suitable levels above the wetlands—the herbs, shrubs, and trees of the coastal hills. The increasing diversity of vegetation as one goes inland reflects the change from the severe stresses of the lower marsh to the essentially freshwater and thus less demanding world of the surrounding hills. Pickleweed and cordgrass are lonely monarchs in their wet and salty realm because few plants are equipped to compete with them. Farther inland, competitive stress becomes increasingly influential, replacing the rigorous requirements of the marshland's physical environment. The easiest places in which to live are the most popular.

In the larger tidal wetlands of southern California cordgrass and pickleweed retain their command of the lower marsh. The higher marsh is characterized by pickleweed, sea blite, salt grass and other salt-tolerant grasses, and many of the halophytes previously discussed such as sea lavender and *Jaumea*. In between is a transitional low cover of stunted members of the low marsh along with saltwort and the annual Bigelow's pickleweed, a species not found north of Los Angeles County. Smaller, shallow lagoons are more subject to environmental variation, particularly when tidal access is blocked by closed inlets. Consequently, marsh vegetation is much poorer here, and a number of such tidal areas in southern California lack cordgrass, saltwort, and other typical low marsh plants. Instead, they have more weeds, encouraged where freshwater provides much of the soil moisture.

We have already become acquainted with many of the animals for whom the lagoons and their intertidal flats are home. In the deeper waters of San Francisco Bay live fish, jellyfish, and other swimming forms. Some of the most readily observable organisms have small communities of their own on wharf pilings, concrete docks, and boat slips. In and among the seaweed clumps one can see creatures often thought more typical of the tide pools out on the reefs and rocks of the surf-splashed littoral. Sea stars and sea cucumbers are by no means uncommon and may even prefer these quieter waters. Several anemones join them; one introduced species is an unusual and striking combination of orange and green. Tiny hydroid colonies fan delicate feathers through the food-carrying currents. Various bristle worms compete with barnacles for tasty particles. Sea spiders and small crabs hunt for edible debris that may have settled on the sessile forms. Concentrations of moss animals spread brown fuzz over piling and barnacle alike. Pouch-like animals known as sea squirts wait along with the hydroids for dinner. Among the host of gastropods—by and large the snail group—traveling up and down the stained dock sides are file and shield limpets and unicorns. Several bivalves are very much at home here, often to the detriment of their man-made substrate. Bay mussels, originally from Europe, form brittle, dark purple masses. The arch enemies of all who have to do with the maintenance of shoreside installations are shipworms, in reality boring clams. Their long thin bodies appear more wormlike than clamlike; but the boring tool, a small shell at the front end, establishes their relationship. Not only are there native borers, such as the San Diego shipworm, but one of the most destructive, a foreign *Teredo*, appeared on the West

Coast some years back and added its efforts to the thousands of dollars of damage these pests cause every year. Gribbles, wood-boring isopods, also attack untreated wood.

Recent research on tidal marshes and mud flats has turned up some surprising data. These desolate-appearing stretches are very fertile in that nutrient flow through them is greater than in adjacent and apparently more prosperous natural communities. Several factors account for this. Tidal currents not only deliver food and oxygen to residents of the flats, but remove wastes. Many kinds of nourishment are produced in the lagoons themselves, plankton, large and small algae, various grasses, and other plants. All of these forms not only contribute fresh vegetation to the menu, but they add to the organic enrichment of the muds and sands when their dead remains are broken down by the anaerobic bacteria living in the oxygen-poor substrate.

A third reason for the fertility of this environment can be found in the presence of what are known as nutrient traps in many estuaries. Salinity differences between incoming freshwater on one hand, and seawater on the other, are responsible. Ocean water, being heavier, sinks to the bottom, and freshwater floats above. Vertical and horizontal turbulence is created by the meeting of these two water masses with resultant eddies that mix the nutrients, diffusing them and making them more available. Other factors contribute to the high fertility of baylands, and one specific to San Francisco Bay should be mentioned. Mussels occur here by the thousands. They excrete phosphate-rich fecal pellets which are excellent fertilizer for marsh plants.

Because of the various types of food offered here, many invertebrate animals of the coastal wetlands are either filter feeders or deposit feeders. The filterers depend upon tidal currents to bring them sustenance in the form of tiny particles of plankton, decayed vegetation, and so on. When surrounded by water, such molluscs as mussels, clams, cockles, or pectens open their shells and strain out tidbits with cilia on mucus-covered gills. Deposit feeders actually ingest the rich oozy mud, and nutrient material is extracted from what would be an unsavory mess to human consumers. The unwanted sediments pass out as waste. According to a book, which the author highly recommends, *Coastal Ecology: Bodega Head*, by M. G. Barbour, R. B.

Craig, F. R. Drysdale, and M. T. Ghiselin (University of California Press, 1973), the deposit-feeding animals tend to remain in zones above mean higher low water whereas the filter feeders dominate the zone below this tidal demarcation. The authors are of the opinion that the length of submergence time is the deciding factor. Organisms feeding on matter suspended in water find it advantageous to remain where the tide is in much of the time. The deposit or "slurp" feeder, as Joel Hedgpeth calls it in his very useful little book, *Seashore Life* (University of California Press, 1964), on the contrary, can ingest mud at any time, regardless of tidal movement, as long as it is damp enough. One "slurper" is the California horn snail, the most abundant snail in the high tide zone of mud flats.

Scavengers such as the hairy hermit crabs and the little mud-flat crabs (*Hemigrapsus*) hunt about as their tide pool cousins do, looking for edible flotsam. The latter are the common larger crustacean of tidal shallows. They scuttle along the channel beds like swiftly moving shadows, popping into their burrows which often honeycomb the slough banks. Mussels form great congregations on channel banks. These shell-studded masses are bound together by the same sticky strings that fasten the tide pool mussels to their substrate. They are crawled over and lived upon by many smaller lagoon-dwelling species. But tidal mud, that surprising source of food, is the best home of all to the burrowers which make the most of this easily penetrated material. Burrowing anemones, sea pens, boring clams and piddocks, sand clams and gapers, bent-nosed clams and bristle worms are safe under the inches of sticky overburden they put between themselves and their would-be predators. One of the most famous burrowing tube worms is the fat innkeeper. This odd creature can be up to a foot (.30 m.) in length and its permanent U-shaped burrow several feet (1 m.) long. A filter feeder, it has a funnel of mucus and strains its food through that device by pumping water through its burrow. So efficient is this sausage-shaped animal that there is plenty for other organisms as well. A pea crab, a worm, and a small fish live in the tube, dependent on the bounty. Such a relationship is called commensalism, where one organism feeds from the efforts of another or derives some other benefit, without harm to the host. It is adaptation carried to a remarkable degree.

Crawling around on top of the sediment floor and ready to return into their shells are horn snails and the predaceous moon snails in company with barrel snails. Basket snails share a device with other species of their group, a natural siphon through which these animals can take in clean water while rummaging about in bay mud. Like the fat innkeeper, ghost and mud shrimp are also burrow dwellers. Where oysters are bedded, both native and introduced, oyster borers and oyster drills are never far away. Some of these predatory species came along with their transplanted hosts and set up shop close to oyster colonies now supporting an active shoreline industry. Commercial oyster harvesting is much more characteristic of the northern half of the state than the southern, and it extends north to the famous oyster beds of Puget Sound.

A number of tide-flat organisms are restricted to the warmer waters of southern California and south. In the same group of invertebrates as sea stars and sea urchins is an animal with the seemingly inappropriate name of sweet potato cucumber. Actually it is a sea cucumber that looks very much like its vegetable counterpart, and it burrows into mud or fine sand with equal impartiality. The lancelet or amphioxus, a primitive vertebrate, apparently prefers sandy beaches at the mouth of bays, and the porcelain sand crab remains in the sandy floors of quiet waters. A low or subtidal resident of either mud or sand flats, the sea pansy—close relative of sea anemones—is a gaudy purple, heart-shaped mass studded with food-capturing polyps. It is also found in deep water sandy bottoms. In contrast, the little fiddler crab is characteristic of the high tide zone of sand and mud flats, digging burrows above the high water line. The large cloudy bubble shell is another common resident of southern mud flats.

When the tide is in, the creatures of the salt flats are busy opening shells, waving antennae, sucking up mud or waiting hopefully in their burrows for the food drifting by. Watching for low water just behind the dikes and pans are the "second table" feeders, the waterbirds. As the hours pass and the tide makes its inexorable way out the Golden Gate or past the mouth of Newport Bay, the waiting birds flock on the newly exposed flats, for now it is their turn. Pintails and mallards, joined in winter by American widgeons and shovelers, along with coots and herring and other gulls, work their way over the squishy surface hunting for worms, shrimp, and little molluscs. Clapper and black rails are shy residents of pickleweed and cordgrass jungles and forage along the slough sides ready to disappear into the marsh if startled or disturbed. Avocets with orange flushed heads and precise markings of their cousins, the black-necked stilts, reflect neatly patterned images in the mirror of the marshlands. Stepping along, they swish back and forth with slender bills wonderfully adapted for feeding in shallow water. Many birds are less concerned about waiting for low tide levels. Egrets and great blue herons stand sentinel in the shallow water of the marsh edge at all times of the day with eyes watchful for fish, shrimp, and other swimmers. In winter a legion of diving and fish-eating ducks gathers here during high water—canvasback, goldeneye, greater and lesser scaup, redbreasted mergansers, and ruddy ducks. Kingfishers, looking like little figures out of some Bonapartian campaign with their jaunty cockades and rust, blue, and white uniforms, perch on bayside wires. Terns flash and hover, competing with the herons for the fish of high tide.

Many avian winter visitors settle here for a prolonged period of rest and feeding in preparation for the strenuous summer breeding activities inland and north. Divers such as grebes and loons, those birds of folklore with their ringing, haunting calls, winter here. Glaucous-winged gulls, dunlins, western sandpipers, long-billed curlews, and black-bellied plovers share these teeming flats with willets, short-billed dowitchers, greater yellowlegs, and whimbrels. Some are migrants and do not intend to stay long. They use these marshlands of the Pacific flyway system as a major wayside stop. Others settle in, much like the northerners who flock to Florida to escape the cold of winter.

As these mud-flat feeders investigate the now uncovered bill of fare, the algal colonies stretched over pool and bank sides are also in action. Using the unimpeded sunlight, they photosynthesize, producing the nourishment needed for more plant tissue. As on sandy beaches and in tide pools, food chains, single-strand associations of food webs, are building. Examples of typical linkages taking place at times governed by tidal rhythms are: in tide, fish and swimming crustaceans/diving birds; out tide, molluscs and worms/mud-probing birds.

Another rhythm superimposes itself on that of the tide, day and night periodicity. Coons pad down to the shores and hunt for tasty shrimp during the darker hours. Meadow mice and salt-marsh harvest mice patter through runways, confining their more adventurous feeding to nighttime. Shrews though furred and small are not rodents, but are insectivores. They join the many nocturnal predators such as owls and skunks.

Someone has suggested that an answer to the "tide flats are ugly and uninteresting, let's fill them in" way-of-thought would be a handsome book illustrated by inspired photographers. In color they could present the exciting vignettes, the telling details of life in this rich and varied community. Perhaps a November twilight with a pink-washed sky reflected on a pool in which a stilt is feeding in all his elegant charm; or a closeup of the scarlet tips of pickleweed just before winter turns them into dried wisps. Then there are the feathering "plumes" of hydroids on eel-grass, and the exquisite shells of the bubble snails; cordgrass, harvest-gold and frost-spangled on a December morning. Even the reticulation of a dried mud pan has its own austere but striking design.

And there are the groups of ash-gray and white gulls, facing the wind on piling tops, or one-legged on the wet and shimmering flats of low tide, waiting for the slow and subtle inundation, the gradual, almost undetectable water lift along grass stem and slough side.

Summer Fog, Malibu Creek State Park

4. Patterns on the Hills

Anyone driving the 118 miles (190 km.) between Dubuque and Cedar Rapids, Iowa, on a summer day will see the following: some towns, several rivers, livestock, crop fields, other cars, people, billboards, buildings, and woodlots. They add up to a pleasing, prosperous-looking landscape or a deadly bore, depending on one's viewpoint. Central Iowa has its seasonal changes, but it does not have scenic variety. Considering its enviable position in the farming world, it probably doesn't care. Corn is King, and healthy stands of this crop are the best views possible to their owners.

In contrast, anyone driving the 15 miles (24 km.) from Mill Valley to Bolinas Lagoon (via Panoramic Highway) in Marin

County, just north of the Golden Gate, will pass through or alongside seven of the major natural communities found in California: chaparral, coastal scrub, grassland, coniferous forest, mixed evergreen forest, beach strand, and salt marsh. This mosaic of plant associations is quite bewildering to the casual observer. Why is grassland adjacent to a dense redwood forest? Why is there a patch of scrub here and a magnificent stand of Douglas-fir there? Common sense would suggest a reasonable uniformity of natural vegetation in the five crow miles between these two points. Marin County, however, is only a segment of many square miles of similar coastal landscape.

Two of the seven have already been discussed, salt marsh and coastal strand. Their most important determining features are obvious: the salt floods of the tide and the nature of their substrates. The other five are not as clearly self-explanatory. This chapter will deal with coastal scrub, grassland (or coastal prairie), chaparral, and mixed evergreen forest. The major coniferous forest types of this part of the transect deserve their own chapters as do other outstanding communities—foothill woodland, freshwater marsh, and streamside vegetation.

This crazy-quilt arrangement is characteristic of many California hillsides, not only sea-facing flanks. The inner Coast Ranges, those east of San Francisco Bay, for example, may have slightly different floras, but they share many species and communities with the fog-hooded mountains to the west. In many places man has seriously disrupted this natural patterning, and it is difficult to guess what the native vegetation was like. Eucalyptus and Monterey pine—the first from Australia and the latter, though a California native, once confined to isolated groves immediate to the sea—replace natural tree and shrub growth. Orchards and crops, to say nothing of urban sprawl, have all but obliterated any hints of the original plant cover. But enough wild country remains throughout much of central California, making it possible to surmise what was once there and bring it into ecological focus.

This part of the state, hill-and-valley California, engenders its own special kind of love and loyalty. To most people acquainted with the region the phrase "rural California" means tree-sprinkled hills and ranches snug in valleys reached by wandering dirt roads. Unless they are really familiar with the geography of the West, few people will think of the flat farm acres of delta rice or Fresno orchard. Popularly, countryside California is pastoral California, the gentle topography of coastal range and foothill slope. Before we begin to discover some of the answers to the puzzle of their occurrence, it is appropriate to describe each of the four communities that lie in such curious patterns on the hills.

Coastal Scrub. To someone without botanical training this low-growing shrubby cover looks much like true chaparral, which often occurs above it on coastal bluffs. Many species are common to both communities, yerba santa, coyotebrush, and poison oak, for example; but coastal scrub is characterized by the predominance of subshrubs, 1 to 5 feet (.30–1.5 m.) in height with semiwoody stems growing from a woody base.

Two main types of coastal scrub have been described. The northern assemblage—called northern coastal scrub—spreads northward from Monterey County to southern Oregon in patches that are often interrupted by other communities described in this chapter and elsewhere. Its southern counterpart—coastal sage scrub—extends south to Baja California. A broad transition zone begins in northern San Luis Obispo County and continues northward to Marin County. Several southern species, with their characteristic summer drought leaf-dropping habit, contend with coyotebrush, the dominant plant of the northern community, creating a relatively open, one-storied cover on the coastal hills. California sagebrush is much in evidence as far as its northern limit in Marin County, but black sage loses ground in Monterey County though it persists inland to Contra Costa County. Such visitors from the south are gradually replaced by species more typical of northern coastal scrub until the community emerges as distinct, mesophytic (more moisture-requiring) vegetation near Point Reyes Peninsula. It has a low-growing cover of shiny-leaved salal, fronds of bracken and sword fern, snarls of poison oak and blackberries and other related berries, and a number of herbs, frequently rank in growth, including yerba buena, cow parsnip, golden yarrow, pearly everlasting, and a few grasses. Coyotebrush, the "beach bum" of the lot, blue blossom and other ceanothus, wax myrtle, and snowberry are often members of the shrub layer, though the whole collection may be understory to bishop pine and Douglas-fir.

As so often in California the community is a mixed bag of plants—contributions from grassland, chaparral, and forest whose input depends upon latitude and slope aspect as well as propinquity. In certain places along the northern coast several species of lupine are supreme, delighting us with their seasonal color that is in such contrast to the less showy coyotebrush. It appears that the prostrate varied lupine is successful near the lip of the sea bluff, coping with salt spray, strong winds, and perhaps higher summer temperatures, whereas tree lupine prefers a less extreme environment several hundred yards (meters) away from the bluff face.

California sagebrush and black sage are two prominent plants mentioned above and should not be confused. The sagebrush species belong to the daisy family and include the Great Basin sagebrush spreading over many miles of the arid West. The sages are in the mint family. Both groups usually have pungent, spicy odors. Everyone has personal tastes about smells, but to some the sagebrushes are more biting, almost acrid. The true sages have more a perfumelike essence just as their distant cousin lavender does. One of the delights of wandering through coastal scrub is its fragrance, as a number of plants of this community have leaves containing aromatic oils and resins. Whatever its local variations, coastal scrub is one of the typical vegetations of road cuts lining the hairpins of Highway One, in Marin County and south of San Francisco Bay, climbing over the bluffs above the beach, crowding in brushy fields between stands of evergreen trees.

Coastal Prairie. These bits and pieces of grassland on the outer ranges from Santa Cruz County northward contrast greatly with the shadowed groves of cone-bearing and broadleaf trees that are also a part of the coastal mosaic. In summer they look like scarves of gold velvet artfully draped over ridgetops and between the dark folds of redwood or Douglas-fir. Spring-green grasses, either native or introduced, blow in the onshore wind with grace and delicacy, but unless cropped by livestock, they are tawny tangles by summer. Wild bulbs such as Douglas iris, blue dicks, blue-eyed grass, and mariposa lilies, and other wildflowers embroider these open slopes, accompanied by sedges, rushes, and ferns.

Patches of prairie alternate with coastal scrub and forest on maritime bluffs, extending inland some miles (kilometers) on warm slopes and ridgetop balds. Because of the relatively cool, humid climate along the north coast, the basic assortment is enriched by nodding trisetum, Pacific reedgrass, and tufted hairgrass, species common at higher elevations or in northern latitudes or both. A number of bentgrasses and a variety of melicgrass are found nowhere else than in these stretches of coastal prairie, accenting the uniqueness of these grassy "islands." The species more representative of northern habitats gradually lose ground southward along the coast, but many are common the length of the state. Most of the original prairie grasses are perennials; nevertheless, nonnative annuals such as wild oats and soft chess have encroached since livestock introduction, shouldering aside the old-timers and thoroughly altering the composition of the prairie. There is evidence, however, that the perennials are encouraged to return when grazing is restricted.

Like most meadowlands, these fields are tunneled by rodents. Meadow mice, sometimes called voles or field mice, are at home in the turf. They tunnel elaborate runway systems through the grass roots. Harvest and deer mice are plentiful in prairies. Harvest mice weave sheltering balls of dry grass; deer mice nests, lined with dry vegetation, are usually tucked in burrows or buried under logs and rocks. All of these small rodents eat seeds, berries, and other nutritious plant parts. Meadow mice are fond of green stems and leaves, and where the animals occur in large numbers they can be very destructive to crops and native vegetation alike. Mice are juicy feasts for keen-eyed and sharp-eared predators. Night-active habits protect harvest and deer mice somewhat, though owls and bobcats are constantly alert to their presence. Voles are busy at all hours. They are safe in runways, as long as their activities are undetected; but snakes, hawks, weasels, and the larger carnivores such as coyotes and gray foxes watch or listen for telltale movement and noises.

Chaparral. This is the typical brushy growth of the hillsides that means wild California to many people. It is the dangerous community in that so many destructive wildfires originate in its highly flammable vegetation. It is also one of the most effective plant barriers against ground travel by the larger animals. Man and deer alike find mature chaparral with its profusion of stiff twigs almost impossible to enter. One can crawl through it, but this means of getting somewhere is fatiguing and painful. Imitate the deer and follow their trails if you go exploring.

The word *chaparral* has an interesting history. It comes from the Spanish, *el chaparro,* meaning the evergreen scrub oak. This in turn has a Basque root, *chabarra,* which also refers to scrub oak. The *-al* suffix is common to many of the Spanish place names throughout the West, being added to the root word to indicate the phrase "the place of." We get the cowboy's chaps from the leather pants or *chaparajos* he used when riding through this dense prickly cover. It must have been very gratifying to the Spanish settlers in California when they discovered a land so much resembling their own, even to the same type (though not the same species) of shrublike oak.

Though chaparral is one of our most distinctive natural communities, covering about 8 percent of the state, it is not confined to California. It occurs in southern Oregon, extends into Baja California, and even emerges as an upland island of brushy growth in central Arizona at about 4,000 to 5,000 feet (1,200–1,500 m.) in altitude. In southern California it spreads from nearly sea level to 5,000 to 6,000 feet (1,500–1,800 m.), wrapping around the Transverse and Peninsular ranges to mingle with the plants of the desert to the east and north. It continues up into the northern coastal mountains where it tends to remain in the inner ranges, and it is part of the foothill mosaic in some areas of the Sierra Nevada.

Chaparral consists for the most part of shrubs that are admirably adapted to a summer drought/winter rain climatic pattern. Its most active growth season is late winter and spring when soil moisture and air temperature curves meet for optimum growing conditions. Summer through early fall is the time for rest, unlike plants of regions having summer precipitation and cold winters where the frost season is the time of inactivity. Summer dormancy is shared by most chaparral plants, but some photosynthesis and other fundamental life processes continue throughout the dry months on a limited basis. This reduces both the need for water, an essential ingredient in foodmaking, and the gas exchange that though necessary in such processes unfortunately allows the escape of precious water vapor. In addition, the thick leathery nature of the leaves typical of these plants helps retard moisture loss. Evergreenness is also of survival value. It allows the plant to take advantage of rain whenever it arrives without having to produce a new set of photosynthetic equipment, that is, leaves. The fact that long-lived foliage uses nutrients more efficiently is important in less fertile environments as is the ability to store these necessary substances in leafy tissue for later growth.

All of these features are of great advantage when dry years hit, and the rainfall is less than normal. Brushy hillsides may suffer but are not put out of business; most mature, healthy shrubs manage to stay alive until the next rainy season. Many of these plants experience some leaf drop each summer, decreasing the amount of water-wasteful foliage, but during prolonged droughts the shrubs have recourse to another strategy. This is die-back—the loss of branches until only one or two life-sustaining limbs may remain.

In a subcommunity of its own, chamise, the most common chaparral shrub, often covers warmer, drier knolls and ridges with the uniform texture of broadloom carpetry, interrupted here and there by isolated clumps of other shrubs. Chamise has very small, needle-thin, water-conserving leaves, well adapted to its xeric (dry) sites. There is a rough correlation between leaf size and the aridity of the habitat—more mesic (moist) areas should support shrubs with larger leaves. Ceanothus, another genus of plants typical of brushy hillsides, tends to replace chamise on moister sites in northern California. A number of these species have leaves from 1 to 2 inches (2.5–5 cm.) long and half again as wide. Various manzanitas and scrub oak, other frequently encountered associates, also form chaparral communities of their own where local conditions permit. Mingling with these common brushy species are redberry, coffeeberry, silk tassel, hollyleaf cherry, chaparral pea, a number of currants and gooseberries, elderberry, and toyon, a handsome shrub that often becomes a small tree. A number of shrubs preferring more mesic places are winter deciduous—squaw bush and hazelnut among them—and drop their foliage during the cool season, but most of the species typical of xeric sites are faithful to the evergreen habit.

In addition to the water-conserving features discussed

above, other adaptations are characteristic of xerophytic (drought-adapted) plants. The steep, easily eroded slopes, so often home to chaparral, in general have soils that are thin, coarse, and incapable of holding much moisture during the drier part of the year. Most chaparral shrubs have two sets of roots, one long enough to tap moisture sources deep in fractured bedrock. The other is a system of lateral roots that takes advantage of moisture near the soil surface. Leaves of many species are cutinized, that is, have a varnishlike or waxy coating which serves to waterproof the leaf. Such leaves are often shiny, reflecting and thus reducing solar heating. The culprits responsible for most of the water lost from leaves are stomates, tiny openings in the leaf surface. The carbon dioxide for photosynthesis enters the leaf through these little pores, but transpiration, the escape of water in vapor form, takes place here as well. In idling away the long, dry summer, chaparral plants make less food, and the stomates need not remain open to permit the entry of carbon dioxide. Their closing obviously retards transpiration at the same time, an enormous benefit to these harassed plants. In many xerophytic species the openings are tucked down in pits, protected from drying air flow, or they are located on the under surface only. A few chaparral shrubs have leaves so oriented that just the edges of the blades receive sunlight rather than the broad leaf surface.

By no means is chaparral always the brown-green of the dry period. Urged along by the bounty of springtime, ceanothus sprouts little bursts of tender new foliage and blossoms in puffs of blue or white. Tree poppies display vivid yellow flowers that closely resemble those of herbaceous cousins. Vines like wild rose and wild peas, such as pride-of-California in San Diego County, spread pink blossoms over fence and shrub. Wild currants have sprays of rose and white. Pale lavender bells hang from yerba santa stems. The justly dreaded poison oak is one of the few coastal plants to turn a lovely crimson in late summer and fall before it loses its leaves completely. Toyon is aptly called Christmas berry. The clusters of its small beadlike fruit ripen to a brilliant scarlet in winter.

Herbaceous plants are not absent. These have juicy, in contrast to woody, stems and are usually what is meant by the term "wildflower." On the tops of road banks and in the more open slopes, light and space encourage yellow mariposas and tidytips, star lilies, blue dicks, shooting stars, globe lilies, and the little pink and purple pagodas known as Chinese houses. In the rich wet soils of seepages and marshy places, look for yellow monkeyflower, miner's lettuce, buttercups, and cow clover. Lupine, fiddleneck, purple nightshade, bird's-foot trefoil, and tar-weed grow in roadside shoulders, while locoweed, clarkia, chia, paintbrush, several penstemons, and farewell-to-spring—that poetically named harbinger of summer—are at home in cracks and soil pockets of steep canyonsides and road cuts.

Though these brushy areas appear forbidding and formidable, they shelter a surprising number of animals within their concealing thickets, many with night-active habits. One well-known but seldom-seen mammal is the dusky-footed wood rat. Its stick-and-twig home may be several feet high and just as broad, containing a complex of runways and living quarters which it leaves at night to scout for house material and food such as leaves, bark, and fruit. Then it becomes interesting to nocturnal predators—owls, skunks, and ringtails. The wood rat's nest at times is more of an apartment house than a private residence. Lizards, insects, amphibians, and the commensal California mouse—one of the white-footed or deer mouse types—find the wood rat's construction efforts very convenient, and the mouse often robs its stored food. Gray foxes dig into wood rat lodges, tearing them apart with their front paws. Running skillfully through the stiff-twigged maze, these attractive members of the canine family are on the lookout for other small dwellers of the coastal shrublands. Heermann's kangaroo rat, California ground squirrels, brush and pocket mice, the Sonoma and Merriam chipmunks, and brush rabbits are among their victims. Gophers, rodents of more open country, rarely expose themselves to such attentions and are careful to plug the holes of their feeding tunnels. But gopher snakes and weasels are only too successful, from the gopher's point of view, in entering.

Reptiles are extremely common in the brushlands, partly because of the large number of rodents. Pacific rattlesnakes, racers, and gopher snakes slip through leaf litter and other debris. Alligator lizards, skinks, and fence lizards are frequently encountered by hikers in brushy country. One can readily startle them out of their hiding places or from sunning spots while poking about rocky outcrops and under fallen limbs.

Several birds are so much a part of chaparral and scrub that they occur nowhere else. The wrentit, a shy bird with a long wrenlike tail, has a bouncing ball whistle that accelerates cheerily through the thickets. Scrub jays rasp raucously while diving in long bright blue glides from one vantage point to another. California thrashers sound like less talented students of their virtuoso cousin, the mockingbird, as they fuss about in the underbrush along with brown and rufous-sided towhees. A large number of birds typical of chaparral are neutral gray or brown in color. Thus they match the dull tones of the vegetative cover, which increases their chances of escaping predation. Goldfinches, rufous-crowned sparrows, kinglets, and bushtits work over the scrubby growth for tidbits on their way to other communities. California quail are common companions on a sunny morning hike through the chaparral. (A most interesting relationship between the breeding success of California quail and springtime annual plant abundance has come to light. It appears that during years of poor rainfall, the sparse and stunted herbaceous growth has certain compounds that when eaten by the quail inhibit brood production, a nice example of population controlled by the pressures of supply and demand.)

Mixed Evergreen Forest. Though lacking the imperial stance of an old-growth stand of redwood trees, these groves are delightful. Whereas most of their trees are not deciduous, they resemble in many ways the hardwood forests of the East. The streamside jungles of the interior California valleys share many of the same genera present in the eastern woods, but the mixed evergreen forest has the same sun and shadow interplay as groves of deciduous trees in Pennsylvania and Ohio. Most of the hardwoods of this community are broad sclerophylls, the technical term for plants having broad evergreen leaves (in contrast to the narrow-leaved conifers) with a stiff, leathery texture that, like foliage of chaparral plants, aids the tree in withstanding summer drought.

A digression here, for a moment. The word *genus* refers to the first of the two words of a Latin name of a plant or animal. It specifies to which branch of its family tree the organism belongs. The plural of genus is *genera*. A family of living things is made up of genera and their species, for example: family, Pinaceae (pine); genus, *Pinus;* species, *ponderosa*. This is the yellow pine so familiar in the mountainous West. No other plant in the world is named *Pinus ponderosa*. A specific name, such as *ponderosa* (heavy) or *albicaulis* (white-stemmed), may be repeated without limit; but the names of genera and higher groups are unique. The word *species* is both singular and plural. The word *specie* refers only to coin, not to an organism. One speaks of a species of ground squirrel as well as many species of ground squirrels.

To return to the forest trees, their leafy masses look as though they have been cut from a rich assortment of fabrics in every shade of green. The madroño has large, dark green leaves of heavy satin in pleasing contrast to its red and chartreuse bark. Tanoak, giant chinquapin, and the coast and canyon live oaks spread out swatches of coarse green homespun. The leaves of bay, or California laurel (Oregon's myrtlewood), are cut from deep green brocade. The most frequently encountered cone-bearing tree, Douglas-fir, drapes its branches with lacy strands whose green is tinted either yellow or blue depending upon location. Black oak foliage is fashioned from spring grass-hued taffeta. It and California buckeye are the deciduous members of this largely evergreen community, but they lose their leaves at slightly different times. Buckeye leaves begin to wilt, turn golden brown, and drop toward the end of summer. Black oak waits until fall. Where moisture concentrates in canyon bottoms and gully floors, other deciduous types—willow, big-leaf maple, and alder—contribute tawny brown, golden yellow, and even hints of crimson with the advent of the cold season.

Mixed evergreen forest extends the length of California's coastal hills and mountains, changing components to meet the various requirements of climate, soil, elevation, and topography. It needs less moisture than the redwoods or the mixed conifer forests of the Pacific Northwest but demands more mesic sites than foothill woodland, chaparral, coastal scrubs, and grassland, but all are interlocking pieces of a very complex Coast Range mosaic. From Marin County northward, the Douglas-firs stand parade-ground straight above the hardwoods, which undulate around them like exuberant hoop-skirted belles. Clustering under their taller associates, particularly in moister places, are salal, barberry, huckleberry, rose-bay, hazelnut, and ceanothus whereas poison oak, several manzanitas, and other shrubs tolerant of drier soils are typical of more xeric sites. Bracken and sword and other ferns enrich the shrub layer with both texture and color. In the most productive habitats trees and shrubs combine to form an often dense cover under which such herbs as oxalis, fairy bells, and heart's ease and other violets are sparse or rich as conditions permit.

This basic mixture of Douglas-fir, madroño, tanoak, bay, giant chinquapin, and black and live oaks is scattered in fragments on the outer coastal mountains but is more widespread on the inner slopes of the North Coast Ranges. In Siskiyou and neighboring counties a few members of the lush coastal forests of Oregon and Washington such as western yew and western hemlock venture onto moist, deep-soiled slopes and into draws. Sugar and yellow pines, more typical of California as they are found on all its major mountain ranges, accept somewhat drier sites. In its more xeric environment the forest is dominated by canyon live oak and other hardwoods. Though oaks are present throughout the entire range of mixed evergreen forest, each species has its own homegrounds. Canyon live oak probably has the broadest tolerance of site conditions. It is comfortable on moist stream banks as well as steep rocky slopes from southern Oregon down into Baja California. Coast live oak, the familiar *encina* (or *encino*) of coastal valleys and slopes, disappears just north of Sonoma County. Black oak is restricted to higher elevations south of the Bay Area. Interior live oak is locally present on Mount Diablo, Mount Tamalpais, the mountains of Santa Cruz County, and the Santa Lucia Mountains. As the northern dominants such as Douglas-fir and tanoak become less important and drop out, one by one, from the coastal hills southward from Santa Cruz County, coast and canyon live oaks continue to hold their own in the wooded landscapes of southern California. Scrubby forms of canyon and interior live oaks group in little hilltop thickets, miniforests, if you will, on Mount Diablo and other mountains in the Bay Area or mingle with other shrubs in both chaparral and woodland. Not only is the mixed evergreen forest an important as well as delightful piece of the coastal picture puzzle, it is often the transitional community, edging the coast redwoods on its wetter borders and sharing grassy patches with foothill woodland in its drier extensions.

The animal inhabitants of the wooded areas are much the same as those of the chaparral, with some differences. Mule deer readily move from one community to another, but tend to avoid the solid masses of thick chaparral. They prefer the more open brushy slopes. Favorite foods include the juicy tissues of herbaceous plants and spring-new sprouts of shrubs. They drift through the forest and along game trails, browsing as high as they can reach conveniently or nibbling at the grasses and forbs of the herb level.

Certain animals such as the gray squirrel are restricted to an arboreal life. One of the pleasures of exploring a patch of coastal forest is to see the down-feather tail of this tree squirrel flipping from side to side, or a bright eye peering over a limb. Since acorns are preferred food, oak trees are paramount in the life of this attractive animal, and its bulky nests are usually built in their limb crotches. A characteristic three-step food chain in oak groves is acorn/gray squirrel/hawk, but the tree-based life of the squirrel protects it from severe predation. If it eats the eggs of the black-headed grosbeak, common and typical bird of the broadleaf forest, a four-step chain ensues: seeds/grosbeak (in the form of eggs)/squirrel/hawk. The squirrel then moves to the rank of a second order consumer.

With this background of introduction to four of the many communities of the outer Coast Range, it is possible for us to pick up some of the pieces of our puzzle and attempt to fit them together, keeping in mind that five types of coniferous forest also flourish here: closed-cone pine, redwood, mixed conifer, yellow pine, and relict cypress. It should also be re-stated that no one really knows exactly why all these peculiar patterns exist where they do. There are many research problems still remaining for future ecologists.

Any understanding of the factors governing the distribution of biotic communities begins with climate, and California has several climates; the state's relief features and its position with regard to neighboring land and ocean have resulted in a series of climatic spectra almost as varied as its topography. Because of its latitudinal range, California experiences a gradual increase in rainfall from south to north, from the near desert conditions of San Diego to the temperate rainforest of the Pacific Northwest. Its mountain ranges have heavier rainfall on their seaward sides and lighter precipitation on their eastern flanks because of what geographers call rainshadow (see Figure 5). Winds are forced to rise when confronted by a mountain barrier in their path. Any moisture-laden air masses they may bear become cooler during the upward journey. Such chilling increases condensation, and higher slopes are often soaked by resulting downpours or snowfalls. On descent the clouds are warmed and, already relieved of much of their moisture, may dry to the point of complete evaporation. Some major storms, particularly in winter, do continue on across the mountain ranges of the Far West, but by no means is this true for all. Most of California's winter rainfall comes from storms generated over the Pacific Ocean and carried east by winds known as the westerlies. The Coast Ranges are the first physiographic or relief barriers they meet; and rainshadow accounts for the fact that Santa Cruz, on the shoreline, receives roughly 24 inches (60 cm.) of rain a year while, across the ridge, San Jose may have only 13 inches (33 cm.).

So placed, maritime central California has what amounts to a moderate rainfall with many local differences based primarily on topography. Of equal if not greater importance is seasonal distribution. California shares what is termed the Mediterranean-type climate with four other regions in the world

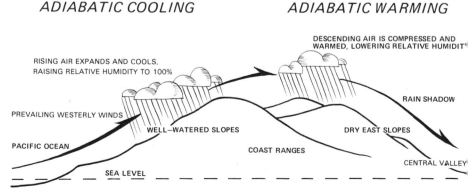

ADIABATIC COOLING   *ADIABATIC WARMING*

DESCENDING AIR IS COMPRESSED AND WARMED, LOWERING RELATIVE HUMIDITY

RISING AIR EXPANDS AND COOLS, RAISING RELATIVE HUMIDITY TO 100%

PREVAILING WESTERLY WINDS

WELL—WATERED SLOPES

RAIN SHADOW

DRY EAST SLOPES

PACIFIC OCEAN

COAST RANGES

CENTRAL VALLEY

SEA LEVEL

Figure 5. Precipitation pattern of central Coast Ranges

experiencing summer drought and winter rain. The extreme northwest corner receives occasional summer rain from storms that manage to slide down from Oregon, and higher ranges throughout the state have their share augmented by local thunderstorms. Masses of warm moist air, often associated with tropical storms, wander in from the south, bringing rain to the desert and even southern coastal areas in summer. In general, however, vegetation must be adapted to dry summers which are longer in the south and shorter in the north. Not only that, the Pacific High may deflect winter storms traveling east from the mid-North Pacific or down from the Gulf of Alaska. This pressure hump is a huge cell of air settling from aloft in what has been termed the Horse Latitudes, a subtropical belt of notorious calms in windjammer days. During the summer it bars from most of the state the rains that keep coastal Oregon and Washington green the year around. These two states, however, are on the edge of this great mass of high pressure, and rainfall decreases in summer here as well. The Pacific High usually weakens or moves south in the winter, following the sun, but sometimes it forsakes its customary course and continues to block off needed rain. At other times an extension of the Pacific High or a separate ridge develops, both circumstances having the same drought-producing effect. The causes of these changes are as yet not well understood, but there is some evidence that they are associated with anomalous patterns of sea surface temperatures. If such periods of lower than normal rainfall are set in train season after season, then California can have a series of dry years to worry farmers and forest rangers alike.

Another factor complicates matters. In summer, the northwesterly winds that prevail along the California coast—aided by the Coriolis force—push away surface water, resulting in the upwelling of cooler subsurface water. As moisture-heavy air flows landward from the ocean it passes over the cold water offshore. Enough condensation takes place to cause fog or drizzle, but not real rain. These summer mists, so disheartening to those who hope for a sunny day at the beach, are of extreme importance to coastal plant life—cropland and brush, Eucalyptus grove and redwood stand. This natural air conditioning forces many San Franciscans to wear coats in July while Bakersfieldians swelter in sports shirts. Anyone driving in one June day from Market Street to Bishop, east of the Sierra, could have this temperature and weather schedule:

```
 9:30 A.M. . . . San Francisco . . . 55° F. (13° C.) . . . fog
11:30 A.M. . . . Manteca . . . . . . . 95° F. (35° C.) . . . cloudless sky
 3:30 P.M. . . . . Tioga Pass . . . . . 40° F. ( 4° C.) . . . rain and sleet
 6:00 P.M. . . . . Bishop . . . . . . . . 90° F. (32° C.) . . . mostly clear skies
```

By now it will be obvious that there are many California climates. They account for much of the variety in its natural landscapes. Brushlands owe their scrubby growth and appearance to the summer drought experienced by most of the state. Such features as small leathery evergreen leaves and bushy habit are adaptations to regions of cool wet winters and warm dry summers. The same characteristics help the brush species live through periods of less than normal rainfall when the Pacific High is in stubborn command. The shrubs of the coastal scrub have many of these modifications. Some species, such as California sagebrush, have the ability to go dormant to the extent that their leaves desiccate and fall off during the dry season.

The evergreen trees of the coastal forests enjoy the same type of protection as chaparral in that they do not have to produce new foliage each year. One common species, buckeye, is deciduous, but to balance the energy needed for growing new leaves each year it loses them in late summer and remains inactive for the rest of the dry period. Its large thin leaves are ill-equipped for dry season dormancy, and their loss is another way to limit life processes during this critical time. Other trees of the broad-sclerophyll forest have many of the same evaporation-retarding leaf features as the brush species: waxy "waterproofed" leaf surfaces (cutinization), and stomata sunken to cut down on water loss.

Grasses have their own adjustments to the climate. Shallow rooted, they make use of surface soil water. When this disappears during drought, perennial grasses die back to underground runners, stem bases, and root masses, and the annuals live through the time of tension as seed. Most grasses are more xerophytic than brushland or forest plants and, in the coastal areas, often occur where conditions are dry. One such example is the Mattole River valley in Humboldt County where grassland persists though redwood forest might be expected. It is assumed that the prevalence of local dry winds, the result of downdrafts peculiar to the inner face of the King Range, is responsible for the anomaly. In like situations, forbs—herbs, or green plants, minus grasses—react in much the same way.

In general, extensive chaparral is confined to summer-drought regions with an annual rainfall range of from 10 to 25 inches (25–63 cm.). Desert occurs where the precipitation range is roughly from 8 inches (20 cm.) downward. Forests need more moisture than either brushland or desert, but there is a fair amount of variation. Areas supporting redwoods can receive as little as 25 inches (63 cm.) per year or as much as 100 inches (254 cm.). Thus, rainfall accounts for the overall pattern of California's vegetation: fir trees on the Sierran slopes, creosote bush on the flats of the Mojave Desert, and manzanita on Mount Tamalpais. But it does not explain why a fern-carpeted tract of Douglas-fir should abruptly open out to the scruffy confusion of chaparral, nor why ponderosa pine, one of the dry-climate conifers, appears in the middle of a redwood forest. These sharp community shifts occur over and over in a region remarkably uniform in climate. This section of California enjoys moderate rainfall and maritime influences that keep temperature ranges small. Logically these sea-edge slopes should have but one type of vegetation, perhaps brush adapted to the lack of summer rain and making use of the summer fogs. If one were to envision a hypothetical vegetation diagram based solely on central California maritime climate, its moderateness and uniformity might indicate something like that shown in Figure 6.

Figure 6. Hypothetical uniform chaparral-type vegetation

The famed redwood forest is a vegetation type commonly thought to be admirably suited to the coastal climate of California, but its distribution is by no means universal. In fact, in the San Francisco Bay region, these giants are held to pockets here and there. The extensive groves come into their own farther north. Man's inroads on the redwood stands in the transect aside, there are local restrictive climatic differences, more— and more influential—than one would realize. San Francisco is notorious for having its foggy streets and its sunny streets. The sea mists swirl in through natural draws and along channels formed by the valleys of this hilly city. In the warmer and more protected sections, housewives can garden in cotton dresses. In others, shoppers must button into wool coats against the chill and clammy winds. All along the coastal mountains, warm sheltered valleys huddle against exposed ridges, and a drizzly morning in Sausalito does not necessarily mean fog in Palo Alto.

Fog plays no unimportant role in central California's climate. According to Harold Gilliam's handbook, *Weather of the San Francisco Bay Region* (University of California Press, 1962), parts of the Berkeley Hills receive moisture equivalent to 10 inches (25 cm.) of rainfall each year from fog drip alone. Fog not only lowers air temperatures and raises humidity, it eases the effect of summer drought by forming drops that build up behind veins and other tiny dams on leaf surfaces. When heavy enough, they fall in sparse but noticeable showers. Since the redwoods are not as adjusted to summer drought as, for instance, the shrubs of the chaparral, they depend on both fog drip and its atmospheric humidity as a climatic "bridge" spanning the dry months between rainy seasons.

There are local differences in rainfall even in a relatively limited area. Mount Tamalpais creates its own small rainshadow. Its northeastern slopes receive less precipitation than its southwestern flanks which directly confront the storm-bearing winds. This is also true of many individual peaks and hills in the coastal ranges and accounts for some of the variation in plant cover.

The sea-facing bluffs and headlands of California seldom support thick tall forest. They are harassed by strong salt-laden winds that are essentially drying. Stunted scrub or prairie is typical of these exposed positions. What woody plants are present have the twisted and tortured habit of wind punishment. Clumped here and there on the seaward bluffs of Marin are hedgelike mounds of California bay and other broad-sclerophyll trees in more sheltered hollows or behind rocky outcrops. The appearance of these thickets is due directly to salty wind. It kills any exposed branchlet or twig venturing outside the protective masses of leaf and stem by dehydrating the vulnerable tissue.

But in the fog-visited and wind-sheltered canyons of the coastal hills, trees stand proud and straight. Just as mountain barriers cause rainshadow, passes and ridges channel and deflect wind which, when persistent in strength and consistent in direction, modifies the vegetation in its path. Where canyons open out to the sea, the benevolent bath of fog tempers the heat of summer. Such localized climatic units (microclimates) are due to the varied topography typical of many regions of California. Land and the great weather forces operate together in significant partnership.

In addition to affecting climatic patterns, features of the land exercise considerable control upon natural cover. The coastal hillscapes are rugged, broken by faulting and erosion. Ridge and gully succeed each other the length and width of the range system. Canyon bottoms are forested not only because of their sheltered positions; rainwater drains off the steep slopes above them and collects in permanent or seasonal streams on the ravine floors. Even where there is no visible flow, underground moisture concentrated here supports trees unable to live on drier substrates. We must now modify our hypothetical hillside to accommodate these additional situations (see Figure 7).

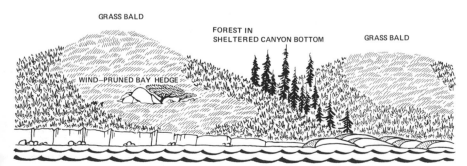

Figure 7. Exposed and sheltered sites in coastal hills

Another local variation of humidity and temperature must be taken into account. It, too, is due to rugged relief. In non-tropical regions, the direction of slope face or aspect, as it is sometimes called, is of great importance. As California is north of the equator, its southward-facing slopes get the benefit of the direct light of the sun, and those facing north are slighted. Solar radiation striking perpendicularly to a surface is more powerful in its effect than that which is oblique or glancing. Therefore northward-facing slopes are cooler than those facing south. Consequently, the soil retains moisture longer and can support more mesophytic vegetation. Southwest exposures are the most stressful for plants, warmed as they are by the lingering afternoon sun. Such xeric sites as these along the central California coast are predominantly chamise chaparral or elements of coastal sage scrub that are highly drought-resistant, for example, California sagebrush and black sage, whereas the north-facing slopes have a richer cover of less xerophytic shrubs or even trees. Coastal prairie is a typical occupant of both wind-blown ridgetop and dry south-facing slope while brushland and forest keep to either the cooler north-facing hillsides or deep-soiled valley bottoms. In moister places, chaparral takes the sunny slopes, and mixed evergreen forest keeps to the cooler shady hillsides. Such heavy growth in itself creates more mesic conditions. Wind is slowed and soil temperature and evaporation much decreased by the dense vegetation. Our diagram now undergoes another change; the shaded, humus-rich, north-facing slopes are cloaked with forest, and the warmer, drier south faces have brush or grass (see Figure 8).

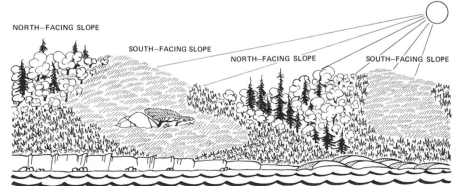

Figure 8. Differences in slope-face direction

These basic moisture patterns are further complicated by other influences. What ecologists call edaphic conditions are very much involved with the coastal mosaic. These have to do with the specifics of soil and are responsible for some of the abrupt changes in vegetation. Two such local substrate circumstances are noteworthy—outcrops of serpentine and exposed beds of ancient marine sands. The former occur in many places in California, particularly in the Franciscan rock series of the Coast Ranges where intrusions of molten material, at one time, forced their way into the earth's crust. Some of these, peridotite for one, were transformed into serpentine, a reddish or greenish rock, which usually weathers to very infertile soils. The outcrops are high in magnesium and heavy metals and poor in enriching substances such as phosphate, potassium, and calcium. They tend to be highly basic as well, that is, on the strongly alkaline side of the pH scale, another detrimental feature. Though some of these soils are waterlogged in winter, others are too thin to hold much moisture. Such conditions mean poverty for most plants and result in semibarren hillsides with widely spaced, starved-looking bushes or trees. Those that survive are short on branches and long on moisture-seeking roots. Many species found on serpentines seldom occur elsewhere. By enduring the unfavorable chemical ratio, they benefit from the absence of competing plants. There is evidence, moreover, that certain harmful soil organisms avoid serpentine sites; consequently, tolerant species such as leather oak and certain types of manzanita and ceanothus have several advantages in addition to their ability to live on a hostile substrate.

"Fossil" sand dune areas in the Santa Cruz Mountains are comparably infertile. Much eroded, these old loosely consolidated sand deposits have become badlands, and their coarse soils are poor water holders. Where they occur, the surrounding evergreen forest immediately changes to open woodlands of dry-climate pines such as knobcone and ponderosa. Manzanita and live oaks provide a sparse and casual understory.

The broken bedrock of the hillsides has encouraged another adaptation on the part of broad-sclerophyll shrubs and trees. Interstices or cracks allow roots to penetrate deep beneath thin soils typical of these communities for water that has percolated into the fracture system. With a crowbar and a little energy one can pry apart the exposed root-sundered rock slabs of a roadcut or gully side and get an idea of the extent of this living network. Where ridgetops and hillsides are steep and heavily eroded, they may be too thin-soiled for either the larger trees or lush grassland. Then the aggressive brush with its moisture-miser leaves and enterprising roots comes into its own.

Talus faces of fractured rock are uneasy substrates and along with outcrops of bare rock account for barren patches appearing here and there on the hillsides. Only very hardy species such as digger and knobcone pines or the most drought-resistant shrubs can struggle along on the poor terrain. At the other extreme, seepages, springs, and local surfacing of the underground water permit more mesophytic species to intrude among those more spartan.

Soils differ in their ability to hold water largely because of texture. Sand, gravel, or cobble soils take in moisture quickly, but it rapidly sinks through these natural sieves, leaving the upper horizons relatively dry. Fine-grained soils, on the other hand, tend to take up water more slowly but retain it for a longer period of time. Soils of broad valley floors commonly contain much fine-grained clay and silt. Though deep, when underlain by impervious layers through which water is unable to percolate, these poorly drained basin bottom soils are waterlogged in the wet season. Since the moisture confined to upper horizons readily evaporates in summer, leaving baked surfaces, crisscrossed with cracks where it has stood the longest, such soils are usually dry. Chaparral shrubs rarely venture out onto these fickle substrates. They do better on the rocky soils of the steeper slopes where, with long exploring root systems, they can make use of reliable water sources deep in fractured bedrock. Shallow-rooted and quick-growing species such as grasses and weedy forbs are well suited to heavier soils of gentle slopes or valley floors, as they can take rapid advantage of seasonally available water held close to the surface. A number of clay-heavy soil types are responsible for grassy balds in the northern Coast Range conifer forests. Some of them are vertisols which expand and shrink in response to changes in soil moisture. Such movement discourages the root development of tree and shrub seedlings attempting establishment on these unstable substrates. The soils of the Yorkville series tend to slump and creep, particularly in the wet season. Another soil series, weathered from certain schists—highly metamorphosed rocks—that are in contact with serpentine, is high in magnesium. Both keep tree growth at bay. Other patches of grassland occur on sandy soil, some surprisingly burdened with poor drainage. Some of the best soils in the area are thick, well-drained accumulations in the bottoms of ravines and canyons. When sufficiently moist a good part of the year they support forest or woodland incapable of growth on drier, thinner soils.

Soil organisms and chemical nature account for many specific plant associations. The rate of decomposition, or reduction of plant and animal debris to nutrients necessary for the growth of living things, depends on many factors—climate, the presence or absence of organisms responsible for such decay, vegetation, and the parent rock itself. If the process is slow because of the type of plant cover, drought, or long cold winters; if the bedrock resists disintegration; if certain soil elements are hostile to decay or if the substances so released are drained away through leaching or erosion, fertility suffers. Not only are pH values (acid-base ratios) of great significance in controlling decomposition rates, they determine the distribution of certain species. Some plants tolerate or do well on acid soils, whereas others grow best on those that are basic or neutral. Because of the evergreen nature of chaparral, duff accumulates slowly. Not only are the leaves small in size, but they drop infrequently. Decomposition proceeds quickly at the start of the rainy season when the soil receives reviving moisture and when the temperatures warm up toward the end of spring. Decay rates are slow the rest of the year. For these and other reasons, chaparral soils tend to be infertile. All of these features play their part in community placement, and our hillside should indicate an example or two (see Figure 9).

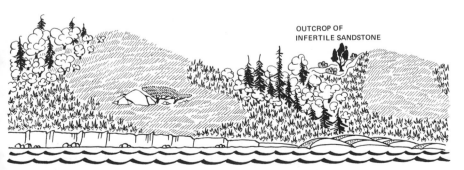

Figure 9. Edaphic influences

California's natural vegetation has another unusual aspect—its ability to survive the plant kingdom's most spectacular enemy, fire. Shocked and distressed as we are to hear of a disastrous fire, it is some comfort to know that the brushlands and forests of the state have built-in defenses against total destruction; it is poetic justice of a sort, because they are very fire-prone. Volatile oils, responsible for the pungency of scrub and chaparral, are highly flammable. Tinder-dry accumulations of discarded branches and other debris litter the thickets. Natural fires from lightning strikes have swept through the shrublands since their establishment far back in geological time (paleobotanical history, important to the understanding of the coastal mosaic, will be discussed in Chapter 5). When the American Indians entered what was to become California, they came as users of fire. With it they opened brushfields for hunting and seed gathering. It also escaped from campfires, as it still does today. Through millions of years a kind of equilibrium was reached between the native plants and fire. Fire is useful to chaparral because it clears out the dead wood and deposits ash, which is a rich source of nutrient material previously locked within living plant tissue as well as the slowly decaying debris. There is evidence that soil oxygen is increased by fire, and it removes toxins released by many chaparral plants that inhibit growth of possible competing species. Though the newly exposed soil dries out more rapidly, the plants in competition for its moisture are fewer in number and much reduced in size. Recently burned soil presents another problem in that it often becomes very water-repellant because of heat-concentrated substances from certain plants that tend to decrease moisture absorption. Under certain circumstances, however, fire leaves deposits of ash and charcoal that form protective crusts. In addition, the removal of litter and duff improves the seedbed considerably for plants whose seeds require bare, mineral-rich soil for germination. Many investigators report an increase in the soil organisms responsible for decomposition following fire.

A number of adaptations to the ravages of fire have evolved ensuring the survival of brushy species. Many of the most typical chaparral plants crown sprout after burning, that is, they start new stems from buds on the root crown which are activated when fire destroys growth-inhibiting hormones in the unburned stem. Such species as chamise are flourishing shrubs again several years after fire has reduced them to black and lifeless-looking snags. Though chaparral shrubs are prolific seed producers, some species of manzanita and ceanothus are so adapted to periodic burning that their seeds readily germinate only when heated enough to scarify the seed coat. Then water can easily penetrate and initiate growth. Though the new burn provides an environment greatly to the advantage of the seedlings, there are potential threats—prolonged summer drought or an exceptionally dry year, and the reverse, herbaceous competitors flourishing with abundant rainfall. Young shrubs whose roots have nodules of nitrogen-fixing bacteria evidently have a better chance for survival. The root crown sprouters have a much easier time of it. Because they are already established plants with access to stored food and water and are equipped with well-developed root systems, they can begin new growth immediately after the fire. They also have an advantage over herbaceous rivals as they eventually shade them out or release toxic substances into the soil.

Grasslands are little damaged by most burning. They recover about as readily as they go up in flames. Annual species, by their very nature, assure renewal after fire. If the seed crop has fallen to the ground by the time of the burn, chances are it will escape injury and be ready to begin new growth in the next rainy season. Perennial grasses are almost as immune to fire damage. Their root masses are safe underground, and they will resprout as soon as weather conditions are favorable.

According to scientists who have studied the coastal mosaic, much of its seemingly inexplicable character is due to fire. Species and even communities may be shifted about when a vegetative cover is so destroyed. Each type of vegetation has its own route and rate of recovery. Forests may take a hundred years to return to former magnificence; brushlands can regain their previous aspect in a decade.

Almost all of the regenerating scrub and chaparral regions of California have an herb interval when quick-growing grasses and forbs, uncommon in developed brushland, dominate the postburn landscape. In many instances, the pioneering herbs are strictly fire types. The seeds have lain dormant underground since the previous burn, sprouting only when heat treated so that water may enter and awaken the embryo. Many spectacular wildflowers, including the delicately beautiful fire poppies and pale yellow whispering bells, belong to this unusual group of plants. At any rate, newly opened brush areas with their ash-rich soils invite invasion by these quick-growing plants that require sunlight and space.

Postburn interaction between coastal sage scrub and chaparral is a prominent feature of many natural landscapes in southern California. Most of the scrub species such as California sagebrush and California buckwheat are somewhat weedy in nature. They propagate with ease because numerous seeds are readily dispersed by wind or other means. Once established on the burn, the semiwoody branches grow rapidly. There appears to be similar activity on the part of the elements of the scrub reaching central California. Yerba santa, black sage, and lotus (bird's-foot trefoil) are reported to be common invaders of recently burned chaparral on Mount Diablo. Seed-reproducing ceanothus and chaparral pea also pioneer following fire.

Throughout both herb and subshrub stages, chaparral recovers slowly by sprouting from seeds and root crowns, and eventually it reigns supreme. By denying light and producing toxic substances, it drives out the temporary species whose seeds lie dormant, waiting until the next great sweep of the fiery broom. Most trees of the mixed evergreen forest resprout, with the notable exception of Douglas-fir, but after a heavy fire the length of time necessary for a complete return from herb and shrub domination is much greater than that for brush.

The fire-induced herbaceous stage, under certain soil conditions, can be prolonged indefinitely by frequent burns. Many prairie balds exist for no other reason than recurrent fires staving off the return of shrubby growth. Any woody sprouts and seedlings attempting life in thick grass are subject to destruction in the next dry season. On the other hand, in the absence of burning, brush often invades grassland, extending its domain at the expense of the prairie.

The interested observer sees California's hillsides from but one point in time when he first asks about their puzzling vegetation patterns. A beginning student of plant ecology, given an introductory assignment of driving along Skyline Boulevard from San Francisco south to Santa Cruz and attempting to explain the hillside mosaic, is able to base his opinion only on what he sees during that drive. He does not have as yet the background to interpret the landscapes from the point of view of passing time. After study and research he will gain this ability and remember that what he sees today is not necessarily what will be there in ten years (if man leaves it alone), nor what was there before disaster removed the stable community adjusted to meet certain conditions. Some of the prairies and brushed slopes, looking so out of place in the midst of a Douglas-fir or redwood forest, may be initial stages in the recovery, after destruction, of wooded landscapes.

Such changes as these fit other pieces into the puzzle. We must now amend the diagram to include the effect of fire, adding grassland that has replaced chaparral and forest burned a year or so ago. Patches of coastal scrub on the sea-facing bluffs complete the picture (see Figure 10).

The animals of these burned communities are much affected by the holocaust that has flamed through or over their homes. Since this type of catastrophe occurs more often in the less humid interior of California, a discussion of what happens to them during and after a fire may be found in Chapter 11.

Man, himself, has many ways of controlling the natural landscapes over which he has assumed jurisdiction. He can alter their composition and change their appearance, using such methods as deliberate burning or the bulldozer. He can plow a grassy field and bring a piece of Iowa's uninspiring but money-making cornland to California valleys. By introducing livestock or encouraging herbivorous wildlife he can prevent the natural shift from temporary meadow to brush or forest. Mule deer relish acorns and nibble here and there on tender

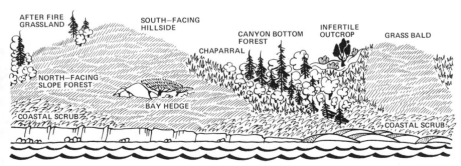

Figure 10. Typical vegetation mosaic

shoots of shrubs. By such feeding preference, large mule deer populations maintain grassland which would otherwise revert to woody vegetation.

Lumbering can be as disastrous an upheaval in the life of a forest community as fire or flood. If left alone, the normal transitional stages will return the cut-over land to the type of community for which it is best adapted. But man, the ever-active meddler, insists on manipulating nature, promoting those species most useful or worthwhile to him, eliminating those less profitable or desirable. By accident or on purpose, by carelessness or with considered reason, he has completely disrupted much of the orderly progression of cause and effect that for millions of years has played its drama upon forest and rangeland. Where the wilder areas are still tolerated, management has been substituted for the living world's own long-evolved controls—competition and the struggle for survival. To fire, climate, relief, and substrate we must add man as a determining factor in California landscapes which reflect a complex of interacting components, each exerting its influence, each contributing its answers to the puzzle of the patterns on the hills.

Bishop Pines, Marin County

5. The Fire Pines

A good introduction to California's coastal pine trees can be found in John Steinbeck's *Tortilla Flat:*

A high fog covered the sky and behind it the moon shone so that the forest was filled with a gauze-like light. There was none of the sharp outline we think of as reality. The tree trunks were not black columns of wood, but soft and unsubstantial shadows. The patches of brush were formless and shifting in the queer light. Ghosts could walk freely tonight, without fear of the disbelief of man; for this night was haunted, and it would be an insensitive man who did not know it. . . . The wind rose as they walked and drove the fog across the pale moon like a thin wash of gray water color. The moving fog gave shifting form to the forest so that every tree crept along and the bushes moved soundlessly like great dark cats. The tree-tops in the wind talked huskily, told fortunes and foretold death.

There is no place more suited to ghost-haunted nights and wandering shadows than a grove of California's coastal pine trees. Unlike their upright inland brothers, the yellow and sugar pines, many older individuals of these species lean and twist, throwing out tufts of foliage here, pulling in gnarled old branches there. The words "pine tree" often bring mental images of trees that are straight and tall and tapered. Many of the ninety-odd species of this genus, however, do not grow that way. They are crooked, almost arthritic in appearance, and deliquescent, that is, the trunks fork into limbs which in turn branch out to boughs and twigs. This is a habit commonly associated with such trees as oaks or elms but not conifers. However, the Aleppo, stone, and Japanese pines of gardens and parks are deliquescent, branching and rebranching into picturesque poses. Not all of the pines of the western interior, for that matter, have a central polelike trunk and tapered shape. The digger pines, pinyons, and timberline species such as bristlecone and limber pines have as spreading and irregular crowns as many broadleaf types. The coastal kinds often combine the two habits. A relatively straight trunk with the characteristic side snags of tapering conifers will suddenly umbrella into spokelike branches that angle off in all directions, supporting rounded rather than pointed tops. Young trees are usually of traditional conifer shape. Wind and salt spray may be responsible for picturesqueness of habit, as dense and more sheltered stands of Monterey pines are usually straight boled and isolated individuals in exposed sites are prone to irregular shapes.

The engaging interplay of line and texture and the subtle gradients of color from the rich green out at needle tip to the dark inner heart of old and matted foliage endear them to their admirers. Place these old fellows on headlands and bluffs, back them against the tapestry of the sea, enshroud them with fogwisp bits of lichen—and they grant you a striking landscape.

California has a rich representation of pine types. It has as natives almost one-fourth of all the species of the genus, *Pinus*. Many forms from the Orient, the Mediterranean, and central Europe have also been introduced as ornamentals. What is termed the California Floristic Province extends north to Coos Bay and southeast to Ashland in southern Oregon and into Baja California as far south as El Rosario. As it is the part of the state that lies west of the Cascade-Sierra Nevada-Transverse-Peninsular range axis, it excludes the deserts which are shared with other states. Eight endemic pines occur within the province; these are species restricted to a particular locale and occurring natively nowhere else. By no means is this the end of California's bid for forestry fame. It has a truly remarkable group of cone-bearing trees including three world records: the tallest, coast redwood; the largest in diameter, big tree; and the oldest, bristlecone pine. In addition, it has a large share of all the coniferous trees in the West.

The list below might prove helpful in stressing just how extraordinary is the story of California's conifers. One asterisk indicates which of these western coniferous species occur in the state; two show those endemic to the California Floristic Province. Species restricted in the West to Canada and Alaska are not included; only those growing in the continental forty-eight states, in other words, below the forty-eighth parallel, are listed. Also excluded is Texas, east of the Pecos River.

Pines

whitebark*
western white*
sugar*
limber*
southwestern white
Mexican pinyon
one-leaved pinyon*
two-leaved pinyon*
four-leaved pinyon**
foxtail**
bristlecone*
chihuahua
yellow*

Washoe*
Jeffrey*
Apache
digger**
Coulter**
Torrey**
beach*
lodgepole*
Monterey**
island** (species status unsure)
knobcone**
bishop**

Firs

Santa Lucia**
silver*
lowland (grand)*
subalpine*

white*
red**
noble*

Junipers

creeping
common*
California**
western (Sierra)*
alligator
red-berry

one-seed
Utah*
Ashe
drooping
Rocky Mountain

Spruces

Engelmann*
blue
white

weeping**
Sitka*

Cypresses

Macnab**
Modoc**
Arizona
Arizona smooth
Piute**
Cuyamaca**

Tecate**
Monterey**
Pygmy**
Gowen**
Abrams**
Sargent**

Odds and ends

mountain hemlock*
western hemlock*
Douglas-fir*
big-cone Douglas-fir
   (spruce)**
redwood**
big tree**
incense cedar*

western red (canoe) cedar*
Port Orford cedar*
Alaska cedar*
western yew*
California nutmeg**
western larch
alpine larch

(Note: it has been proposed that lodgepole pine should be divided into four subspecies—beach, or shore, pine; pygmy
pine, a very localized form in Mendocino County; the Sierra
Nevada-Cascade lodgepole pine; and the Rocky Mountain
lodgepole pine. The bristlecone pine has been divided into
Pinus longaeva, Great Basin; and *P. aristata*, Rocky Mountains.)

Of the seventy-four conifers in the West, fifty-seven occur in
California, and twenty-seven are endemic to the California
Floristic Province. The neighboring state of Arizona has thirty-
two coniferous species, but only one is endemic. It is no exag-

geration to conclude that the province is an outstanding world leader in its number of cone-bearing trees, both endemic and wide-range species.

Its twenty-seven endemics are dispersed sporadically throughout the state. Some are confined to very small areas, others have wider distributions. Not all will be covered in this chapter, which features three fire pines—Monterey, bishop, and knobcone—along with five of the native cypresses— Sargent, pygmy, Gowen, Monterey, and Abrams. Related species found only in southern California and southern extensions of more ubiquitous species will be discussed in a later chapter. The three pines have far more in common than membership in the yellow pine group, occasional deliquescence, and residence in coastal California. Often referred to as closed-cone pines, they, along with the brush and trees of the sunburnt hillsides, have adjusted to the inevitable presence of fire. The three species bear tightly closed, somewhat lopsided cones that cling to trunk and branch. Solitary cones or pairs are not unusual, but these pines are unique in that several are often whorled around the supporting stem. Clusters of a dozen or so have been collected that look for all the world like a colony of prickly gray barnacles that has renounced its tidal home and exchanged a wharf piling for a tree trunk. Here the cones remain year after year, unable to release their seeds unless fire melts the resinous coating that glues the scales together. The heat of the summer sun, foraging insects and rodents, and even the wear and tear of weather can open the cones as well. Of the three species, knobcone has the most persistent cones. Hanging onto trunk or bough, the clusters weather to driftwood gray, looking drier and less alive with each passing season. There are many examples of the growing trunk slowly incasing its attached cones, burying them deep in woody tissue. Only sawing open lengths of felled timber reveals these nurseries, some still stubbornly closed. Once released, the seeds readily germinate and produce hardy offspring. In no way do the seedlings indicate that the parent seeds may have waited for years, locked up by a habit that is fire insurance as good as any in the plant world. When burning has been the instrument of release, conditions for germination vastly improve. Two if not all three closed-cone pines, like so many California conifers, need bare mineral soil as a seedbed. Fire removes duff and other organic matter, releases nutrients from old dead as well as newly burned vegetation, reduces the competing shrub cover, and provides full sunlight.

Knobcone pines are the least maritime, but they have the widest distribution and reach the highest elevation, roughly 5,500 feet (1,650 m.), of the three. Occurring generally between chaparral at their lower border and forest at their upper edges, these assemblages of small coniferous trees and scrawny shrubs, with or without other arboreal associates, seem poorhouse-bound, and with reason, as we shall see. They grow as far south as two mountainous areas in southern California (San Bernardino and Santa Ana mountains), neglect the southern Sierra Nevada to reappear in the foothills of Mariposa and Calaveras counties, and struggle along on their typically dry, rocky, often steep ridges west of Lake Tahoe. From San Luis Obispo County north to the southern Cascades of Lane County, Oregon, they are scattered on the outer Coast Ranges, though rarely on sea-facing bluffs, but they are more common on the inner Coast Ranges and the Klamath Mountains of northern California and southern Oregon. With equally drought-tolerant associates, they form edaphically controlled "islands" surrounded by the more mesophytic mixed evergreen forest and other moisture-requiring communities.

They are serpentine specialists. This slippery-feeling rock contains possibly toxic amounts of nickel and chromium in addition to magnesium, an element that inhibits plants from taking up calcium. Though very infertile for most plants, serpentine-derived soils are host to hardy pines such as knobcone, which may be dwarfed, however, on unweathered serpentine where the soil is so thin it is practically nonexistent. Characteristic low-elevation serpentine sites in the Klamath Mountains produce open woodlands of incense cedar and the xerophytic Jeffrey and knobcone pines with an understory of scrubby forms of tanoak, bay, and canyon live oak. Dwarf types of ceanothus, coffeeberry, and silk tassel huddle beneath in a second layer of impoverished-looking shrubs; indeed, they all appear to be poor relations of their wealthier kin on more mesic or fertile slopes. Opening out on the still more xeric sites are parklike expanses of widely spaced trees and grass-covered floor. Knobcone pines are not confined to serpentine and related soils, but the habitat usually has some prohibiting feature—moisture-

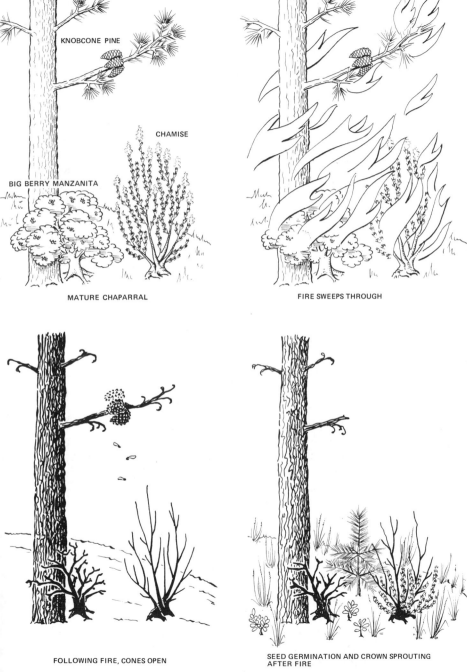

KNOBCONE PINE

CHAMISE

BIG BERRY MANZANITA

MATURE CHAPARRAL

FIRE SWEEPS THROUGH

FOLLOWING FIRE, CONES OPEN

SEED GERMINATION AND CROWN SPROUTING AFTER FIRE

Figure 11. Stages in return after chaparral and knobcone pine fire

leaking sandy soils, soils of high acidity, infertility for one reason or another, and droughtiness in general.

Bishop and Monterey pines have a more restricted range. Never far from the ocean, their striking bluff-top groves seem designed by Japanese printmakers. The two-needled bishop pines frequent swampy places as well as ridges and slopes and, in widely separated stands, are found usually within several miles (a dozen or so kilometers) of the ocean. With what is termed a discontinuous distribution, they occur here and there from Trinidad Head in Humboldt County, to Mendocino County where they form dune forests or mix with pygmy pine and pygmy cypress on the Mendocino white sands, and to Inverness Ridge in Marin County. South of San Francisco they neighbor their close relative, Monterey pine, on Huckleberry Hill near Monterey. Bishop pines also occur in the San Luis Range near Point Buchon, in the Santa Inez Mountains and Purisima Hills in Santa Barbara County, on the coast of Baja California south of Ensenada, and on offshore Cedros, Santa Cruz, and Santa Rosa islands. Apparently needing more moisture than knobcone pines, their maritime position guarantees humidity from sea spray and fog. Bishop pines often occupy north-facing exposures, making best use of precipitation that, particularly in the southern part of their range, is adequate but seldom plentiful. In more favorable habitats they mingle with the more mesophytic conifers—redwood, Douglas-fir, lowland fir, and the like. Where edaphic conditions are more rigorous, they may form relatively pure stands such as those on Huckleberry Hill, a site burdened with soils that are high in acid, low in nutrients, and poorly drained. Dense groves also occur on thin acid soils developed from diatomaceous shale in San Luis Obispo County.

Monterey pine, a three-needled form, is the most limited in homesite of the three. It is confined to hills and slopes around Monterey, to scattered groves near Año Nuevo Point, to tracts at Cambria Pines, and to Guadalupe and Cedros islands, off Baja California. Like bishop pine, it is often located on sandy substrates, in many instances derived from marine sediments, and is within reach of summer fog. Both coastal species have been planted extensively in parks and gardens, along roadsides, and in re- and afforestation projects, particularly overseas.

All three fire pine forests have typical shrub layers. For this reason Huckleberry Hill is well named. A brushy growth of manzanita and huckleberry is understory to Monterey pines on this low rise just to the north of Carmel. These and other members of the heather family—salal, rose bay, and Labrador tea—are frequently found in the shrub layer of bishop pine forest along with other woody and semiwoody plants of chaparral and scrub. The more drought-resistant shrubs such as various drysite manzanitas and chamise are commonly associated with knobcone pine. On serpentine soils it is accompanied by the stunted plants typical of this stressful substrate and the endemics that are confined to it. One often sees madroño, live oaks, bay, and other broad-sclerophyll trees mingling with bishop, Monterey, and even knobcone pines unless conditions are too severe.

It is difficult to discuss the Monterey pine without reference to a neighboring conifer, the Monterey cypress. This tree is even more limited in range, as its home is on the cliffs and headlands around and southeast of Point Cypress and Point Lobos, one of California's most beautiful state parks. Monterey cypresses are extremely photogenic. Exposed to the salt sting of the western winds, they have been harried and driven, forced to bolster their position with buttress roots that twist and curl into great woody snarls. Their branches are quite as grotesque and struggle to keep aloft parasols of scalelike leaflets.

Gowen cypress is the fourth native conifer found on the Monterey Peninsula, enriching this scenic elbow of California. All of them have settled into limited locations. Monterey cypress has taken possession of the granitic sea cliffs on two famous points; two small groves of Gowen cypress occur close by. One is 1.5 miles (2.4 km.) from Point Lobos; the other grows inland on the same Huckleberry Hill where the two coastal fire pines meet. Here they are mixed with bishop pine on thin, acid, poorly drained, sandy soils in an "island" surrounded by Monterey pine. This last species fills the gap between the two cypresses, growing upslope from Point Cypress to the summit of what must be one of the most botanically interesting hills in the entire state. It appears to mingle with bishop pine only around the edges of the island and does not penetrate into the latter's stronghold. At any rate, Huckleberry Hill is the only place in the state where bishop and Monterey pines associate with each other.

The other three native cypresses of coastal California have more or less limited ranges. The pygmy cypress is also, and more appropriately, called the Mendocino cypress as it is the tallest of all California cypresses, under the right conditions, and it is confined to Mendocino County. The stunted form lives on the white plains of podzolic soil derived from the sterile sandstone of ancient marine terraces along the Mendocino coast, notably near Fort Bragg. An impervious iron hardpan layer prevents roots from extending to any depth, and consequently they are incapable of obtaining subsoil moisture in spite of a relatively heavy rainfall. The shallow surface soils are dry in the summer but are waterlogged in winter. As they are among the most acid, nutrient- and oxygen-deficient soils found in California, these beds form an extremely poor substrate. These conditions have resulted in forests of stunted cypress, pygmy pine (a dwarf subspecies of lodgepole pine), and short-statured bishop pine accompanied by many of the same heather-family shrubs mentioned earlier in this chapter. There is speculation that such acid-tolerant plants metabolize compounds that bind iron from the surface soil. When released, the iron is leached down into the subsoil where it cements grains of quartz into the impervious layer. Where roots have been able to penetrate the hardpan or the soils are deeper and have more nutrients, the conifers so dwarfed on the white plains increase in size. Away from the barrens, flourishing Mendocino cypresses mingle with other coniferous species of the northern coast.

Abrams or Santa Cruz cypress grows above the summer fog belt in dry, often shallow sandy soil on four sites in the Santa Cruz Mountains. In one of these locations—ancient marine sand deposits near Bonny Doon—stunted forms of it and knobcone pine occur in open groves, joined by yellow pine on the deeper soils. Sargent cypress has the widest distribution of the five. Though it lives in the summer fog area in Sonoma County, its gray, waxy foliage allows it to occupy drier sites in the middle and inner Coast Ranges from Mendocino County south to Mount Hamilton, with scattered occurrence in Monterey, San Luis Obispo, and Santa Barbara counties. Whereas other coastal cypresses claim unfriendly sand deposits or salt wind-harassed headlands, Sargent cypress is almost entirely restricted to that other common producer of infertile soil, serpentine. It may be a stately tree on north-facing slopes or in canyon bottoms, consorting with trees of mixed evergreen and other forests, or it may crowd together in stunted thickets. It also joins chaparral and woodland in the inner Coast Ranges.

Leather oak, Jepson ceanothus, and a form of Mexican man-zanita are frequently encountered serpentine associates. Only the sea cliff wind fighters tie themselves in knots. When young or in more protected localities, the cypresses are the fa-miliar pyramids or spires of coniferous tradition though some species tend to become broad-crowned with age regardless of location. Individual pygmy cypresses have been found growing as tall as 100 feet (30 m.) where better soil conditions permit. In color they vary from the rich dark green of the humidity-requir-ing Monterey cypress to the soft gray-green of the interior, drier Sargent cypress groves. The tiny evergreen scales are water-conserving, admirably adapted to climatic as well as edaphic drought. As the small round cones tend to persist, remaining on the tree for some years, the California cypresses have been de-scribed as closed-cone trees. Only fire seems to guarantee seed dispersal and, by providing full sunlight and bare mineral soil, vigorous germination. The seedlings eventually develop into dense, even-aged stands. Too frequent burns, however, threat-en propagation, particularly if the trees are destroyed before they are old enough to produce cones.

Of these eight trees—three pines and five cypresses—seven are endemic, all are conifers, all are drought resistant, all are fire-adapted, and all occur in scattered sites on coastal hills. Again, it is appropriate to ask why. Why are some of these spe-cies confined to two or three tiny pockets and grow naturally nowhere else in the world? Why doesn't California have just one or two kinds of cypress, like Arizona, instead of this flock of cousins, most of them poor relations living on their little plots of serpentine or other dry infertile soils? Why are the fire conifers, with their marvelous adaptation, often confined to some of the worst real estate in California, from the point of view of plants?

Remnants of once widely distributed populations or floras are termed "relicts." They are the last remaining descendants of forebears that occupied larger territories. To fully under-stand our eight conifers we need to probe a bit into California's geological past. During the Dinosaur Age (from 225 to 65 mil-lion years ago) much of what is now the Coast Range and the Great Valley was covered by shallow tropical seas. Where the Sierra Nevada was to rise, a series of low mountains bordered the Pacific shoreline. During the first epochs following the end

of the age dominated by the great reptiles, the coastal mountains were emerging, produced by interaction among several
of the crustal plates that form the lithosphere of our planet.
The coastal region from Washington to central California supported a temperate rainforest, reflecting a gentle landscape
and a warm humid climate, that graded southward into an
evergreen subtropical woodland. Palms, tree ferns, and cycads
flourished in plentiful summer rainfall along with numerous
tropical and subtropical trees. At the same time a group of low
hills and intervening basins extended from British Columbia to
New Mexico. The northern section of this cordilleran region
(central Idaho and north) had forests of what is termed an Arcto-
Tertiary geoflora (Arcto refers to its northerly center of distribution, Tertiary to the geological time period in which the flora
grew). It was comprised of spruce, cedar (genus *Chamaecyparis*,
which includes Port Orford cedar and Alaska cedar), fir, Douglas-fir, redwood, and other conifers whose descendants are the
arboreal comrades of the forests of the West Coast. It also included such familiar hardwoods as alder and maple and many of
the heather-family shrubs we have just discussed. Surprisingly,
it also contained a large number of trees no longer native to
western America—dawn sequoia and gingko, which have returned to us as horticultural finds in Asia, and persimmon,
liquidambar, elm, and beech, among others, now confined to
the eastern part of our continent. This was a wonderfully rich
mixture of trees that must have been a botanical paradise.

South of central Idaho the ancient cordillera supported a
vegetation that reflected a drier, warmer climate. Though it included many of the conifers referred to above, a number of its
associates were sclerophyllous trees and shrubs that were ancestral to present members of chaparral and woodland along
with genera now typical of the mountains of central Mexico. In
what is now the sagebrush country of the western interior, a
mixed evergreen and deciduous hardwood forest covered
much of the landscape.

About 15 million years ago seas still covered much of the
Great Valley and isolated portions of the Coast Range. At the
same time the climate of the West was becoming cooler and
drier, particularly in summer. The mesophytic mixed forest of
the interior was forced to move toward the more humid, milder
coast. It in turn was followed by the conifers so long estab-

lished in the cordilleran region. They replaced the escaping deciduous species and finally reached the coast on their own march westward.

Just before and continuing through the Ice Age, the Cascade-Sierra Nevada-Peninsular range complex was rising to its present elevations, and massive structural uplift was in progress over much of the West. Most of the interior was now blocked off from storms arriving from the Pacific and moist air masses heading northwest from the Gulf of Mexico. Though the coming Ice Age with its intensified pluvial periods would ameliorate the condition, the West was becoming steadily drier. The approaching colder temperatures would eliminate many species or drive them to lower elevations, but because of decreasing summer rain the Asian and Eastern American species lost ground completely, leaving us with but one or two deciduous hardwoods (for example, boxelder) that are shared with the rest of the continent. Even before the Ice Age the western interior had become so drought-ridden that it could no longer be host to the redwoods and spruces pausing here on their advance to the coast. Instead, it could only support grassy steppes, scrub, and woodlands and forests of more xerophytic conifers.

While the more or less mesophytic Arcto-Tertiary conifers and hardwoods were moving west to their present locations along the coast and on the mountains of the Pacific states, another geoflora was also on the move. This was the Madro-Tertiary (Madro refers to the Sierra Madre of northern Mexico), established soon after the Dinosaur Age in the central and southern cordilleran regions. It featured the sclerophyll shrubs and trees that later became so familiar in California's natural landscapes. Their prototypes most probably evolved on locally dry areas of rainshadow and infertile rocky outcrops to become widespread sclerophyll woodlands and dry tropic forest over much of southern California, the Southwest, and northern Mexico. These community types intergraded with the Arcto-Tertiary geoflora where they came into contact in the central cordillera and the intermountain West. The result of this meeting ground enriches many of our natural communities, for example, the mixed evergreen forest with its Arcto-Tertiary Douglas-firs mingling with madroño and coast live oak, both left from Madro-Tertiary times. In addition to the live oaks and other sclerophyllous trees so characteristic of present-day woodland and forest, there were dry climate pines, junipers, cypresses, and many genera now absent from California but common in more southern latitudes—palms, wild figs, and relatives of the avocado. Such sclerophyll shrubs as toyon and ceanothus formed a rich understory. We know from fossil evidence that Madro-Tertiary sclerophyll vegetation arrived in California long before the Ice Age and, by roughly 26 million years ago, dominated the interior of southern California. The coast at that time was enjoying higher humidity, and a more mesophytic combination of palm, oak, closed-cone pines, and trees of the laurel family took advantage of the more equable climate.

Responding to the fluctuations of temperature and precipitation as the glacial masses advanced and retreated, the mesophytic conifer forests of Arcto-Tertiary origin moved down in elevation and south or up in altitude and north, but the greatest change took place after the close of the Ice Age. Though summer drought, induced by cooling sea surface temperatures and a strengthening Pacific High that confined warm-season hurricanes to more southerly latitudes, had been established before the continental ice sheets accumulated, it is only after their demise that the Mediterranean climate fully developed in California. In the subsequent warming up and drying out, the sclerophyll species that withdrew to southern California during the preceding cooler period regained former territory to the north and even expanded. The cone-bearing forests encroaching on the lowlands went back to high mountain retreats or were confined to the coastal strip. It was as though two great hands were at work, one keeping the Arcto-Tertiary elements on the cooler and moister mountain chains and along the shore, the other shoving the summer drought adapters north and west from their interior and southern bases. Eventually, all of these forces at work—geological, climatic, and biological—sorted out, shifted, and shuffled the species a generous nature had put at their disposal.

A number of forms with a wide tolerance range for many climatic and environmental variations continue their universality. Various types of currant, ceanothus, and manzanitas flourish almost all over the state. Each of these three generic groups has representative species at timberline and on the sea-coast, and from desert hills to redwood groves. Other genera, however, have restricted distributions. The big tree grows only between certain elevations on the western slope of the south and central Sierra. Those with more rigid requirements remained in places where conditions were congenial or died out. The dry climate species of the central outer Coast Ranges survived only in battlements unassailable by the wet climate types. They settled on the sandy barrens, the steeper, often unstable slopes, dry exposures, and infertile serpentines. Among the more successful were those having tolerances for conditions avoided by other species: soil hyperacidity or alkalinity, mineral deficiencies, and so forth. Unique endurance features are the mainstay of their defense.

As conditions became drier along the coast, those needing moisture either retreated to the northern third of the state where rainfall was more dependable or kept to the higher elevations, north-facing slopes, fog zones, areas of seepage, and drainage bottoms. Escaping the turbulence of changing times, the relicts stayed behind in hospitable niches—the refuges so numerous in the broken, climatically complicated country of coastal California. They remain conservative, cut-off, the diehards of the plant world. How does this explain the star-billed eight?

The closed-cone pines remained in ramparts where they successfully withstood competition through the years. The knobcones keep to sterile sand deposits and serpentines or to the exposed and southward-facing slopes of the inner ranges and foothills. These are conditions many trees cannot tolerate. Bishop pines cope with infertile sites such as Mendocino County's white beds and the diatomaceous shale substrate of San Luis Obispo County, but seemingly only under favorable climatic conditions. Where they grow naturally, bishop and Monterey pines are restricted to maritime regions. Temperature ranges are small, summer fogs are frequent, and precipitation is sufficient for their needs.

Recent evidence indicates that all three—with their much-disputed cousin, the island pine of California's offshore islands and possibly a few mainland sites—now occur in remnant or relict stands of a widespread closed-cone pine forest of ancestral species. Presumably this ancient forest—Madro-Tertiary in origin—flourished in a mild climate similar to the coastal conditions required by bishop and Monterey pines which continue to hold their own on climatically suitable if edaphically difficult sites. The three fire pines have not hybridized with each other to any great extent. Bishop and Monterey pine live side by side in several places, and though some hybridization occurs in the contact zone, in general they keep their identities distinct. Apparently, this is because they shed their pollen at different times. Bishop pine has a slightly more northern distribution pattern than its occasional neighbor and is therefore somewhat winter dormant. It sheds its pollen in April; whereas Monterey pine, restricted to the gentler climate of maritime midlatitudes, sheds its pollen in February. Obviously, the two species cannot pollinate each other's cones. This is a striking example of seasonal isolation which is just as efficient as geographic isolation in keeping species from merging genetically. There is evidence, too, that Monterey pine seems to take the better soils, leaving the poorer for its relative.

The cypresses have more or less the same story. Each species, long evolved from a common ancestor covering a great deal of territory in its time, has established residence in very specialized kinds of environment. There is indication, however, that their ecological amplitudes are narrow and diseases such as cypress canker play havoc with any experimental attempts, man-made or natural, for establishment elsewhere. The different Monterey and Gowen cypress habitats point this up nicely. Dr. S. Carlquist of Rancho Santa Ana Botanic Garden has come to the conclusion that a combination of fog, granitic substrate, and salt spray confines the Monterey cypress in its homeland to sea-bluff sites. Any attempt to move out of this narrow ecological niche dooms it to canker infection. In a way it has, as Dr. Carlquist says, "painted itself into a corner." Through overspecialization it may carry the seeds of its own destruction.

On the other hand, the Monterey pine, so restricted in California, is one of the most widely planted trees in the world and is constantly used in afforestation and reforestation projects. Huge plantations in temperate regions of South Africa, Australia, and New Zealand testify to its vigor. In these locations it grows tall and tapered, as classic a conifer as one could ask, when protected and away from wind harassment.

It must not be inferred that all endemics are relicts, left-behinds from ancient epochs. As we shall see in a later chapter, California is rich in newcomers, species originating from a

number of evolutionary processes, for instance, mutation—
the abrupt appearance of a new trait caused by genetic change.
The new trait is perpetuated with the help of isolation, geographic or otherwise. Any isolated area, such as an island, is
favorable to the production of speciated endemics. Mutant
species, unable to spread, remain imprisoned. The crossbreed-
ing of such "sports" gives rise to more diversification, particularly where there is a variety of ecological niches to accommodate them. For example, the ancestral pair of Darwin's finches
gave rise to a whole congress of new types in the Galapagos
Islands, all still finches but each species distinguished by its
own special bill shape which evolved through adaptation to
the feeding requirements of a particular ecological niche.

In this very important aspect, the California Floristic Province is an island, isolated by the sea to the west, deserts to the
east and south, and colder temperatures to the north. In addition, the province is a veritable archipelago of smaller "islands"
isolated by soil differences, exposure face, elevational changes,
broad and narrow climatic patterns, and other physical features of the environment. Not only does this mean tremendous opportunities for the evolution of new endemics but also
strongholds for the relict species. Here are all kinds of opportunities for outpost positions. Though many species with wide
ecological amplitudes, or tolerances, continue to have widespread distributions, those with limiting requirements remain
in pocket environments where conditions are favorable to their
needs. One community, mixed evergreen forest, is a collection
of remnant species from both northern (Arcto-Tertiary) and
southern (Madro-Tertiary) elements. It is a compromise, a
transitional assemblage frequently found between a moist
community—the humid coniferous forest—and a drier one—
chaparral or grassland.

The aged pines of Steinbeck's tale may well have their own
stories to tell: the demise of less fortunate relatives, the hardships of being paisanos, countrymen, native Californians who
have weathered many ghost-ridden, moon-haunted hours
through the long slow nights of geological time.

Redwoods near Bull Creek

6. The Tall Forest

Many visitors to California redwood groves are depressed at first by the dark and somber dignity of the forest, particularly in rainy or cloudy weather. On bright days in spring and summer, however, the groves have color resources of their own. The pink petals of oxalis (redwood-sorrel) open tiny whorls among shamrock-shaped leaves. Sword ferns arch green fronds over log and root. Orange-bellied water dogs paddle about in the clear shallow pools of the streams and rivers draining the coastal slopes, and the banks above are brocaded with five-finger and maidenhair fern. As the early sun burns through the morning mist, long shafts of light touch the flattened fanlike foliage with silver fire. In autumn the leaves of the vine maple blaze coal-red through the shadows of the understory.

A relict like the fire pines, the redwood belongs to California, except for a 14-mile (22 km.) extension into Oregon. In a state which boasts of eighteen coniferous endemics, two have such outstanding features that they are the best known California trees. The coastal species—*Sequoia sempervirens,* or redwood—is the world's tallest tree, and its mountain relative—*Sequoiadendron giganteum,* or big tree—has the largest base circumference. Both have enviable records of longevity. The tallest redwood was discovered only recently. For years Founders Tree near Dyerville in Humboldt County had this distinction, but its 364 feet (109 m.) have been overtopped by a giant 367 + (110 + m.) feet tall. Once on privately owned land near Orick in Humboldt County, it and several others almost as tall are protected in Redwood National Park. However, the distinguishing feature is not the unusual loftiness of several individuals but that the species as a whole is characterized by great height. Records have been claimed for Douglas-fir and Australian eucalypts, but none standing today can match the redwoods. Big trees, whose sheer mass is most impressive, cannot come near their coastal relatives in height; too often their tops have been lightning blasted. But they outdo the redwoods when it comes to age. Though 2,200 years of life, a coastal record, are venerable indeed, much longer lives have been noted for the big trees; however, these have been bested by the bristlecone pines of the White Mountains in eastern California and other Great Basin ranges.

Though the largest groves and most magnificent stands are in the three northernmost coastal counties of the state, redwoods occur as far south as southern Monterey County where little groups cluster in canyons opening out to the sea. At one time, they were part of the forest cover on most of the coastal hills from Santa Cruz north, but logging has removed them from many of their former habitats. The northern part of their range extends farther east than does the southern portion, which is confined to the western flanks and valleys of the outer Coast Ranges.

The beauty of their forests, their great height and long lives, their hardiness and the quality and durability of their lumber have put these giants into a very special category. They evoke a kind of reverence accorded no other American tree. Their groves have been called temples and their spires cathedrallike; every writer describing them is lavish with vocabulary borrowed from church architecture. But our task is to go beyond description and attempt to account for their lingering presence along the northern coast. There is fossil evidence that *Sequoia* and related genera were widespread over much of the northern hemisphere following the heyday of the dinosaurs. They flourished as part of the Arcto-Tertiary flora, the great plant group that thrived in the mild humid climate then prevalent far to the north. The family, Taxodiaceae, in which this genus is placed includes the baldcypress of the southeastern United States and Mexico, *Cryptomeria* of Japan, and a relict relative of the sequoia discovered just after the close of World War II, the deciduous dawn redwood of China. California's two famed trees are not wholly alone in the world, ancient and isolated though they are.

If redwoods have died out elsewhere but continue to thrive in the coastal mountains, there must be some explanation why this is so, particularly since they have peculiarities. Their seedlings rarely survive in soils rich in the humus of undisturbed forest floors; fungi present in such soils are harmful to their roots. Instead they do well only on newly exposed soils where duff has been removed by fire or some other disturbance, or on recently deposited silt. A layer of topsoil is soon built, however, by decomposing needle drop. Redwoods as a species are relatively tolerant of shade. Seedlings apparently require full or partial sunlight; yet well-established youngsters flourish in the shade of the forest's interwoven canopy. This is not to say that the crowded trees do not respond to thinning. The increased light, nutrients, and moisture made available to the remaining trees result in growth spurts reflected by wider year rings of woody tissue.

One generally accepted characteristic of redwoods is their restriction to the fog belt of maritime central and northern California. Not only are the climatic conditions here most closely akin to the mild temperatures and humidity of the ancient Tertiary epoch, but redwoods, like all plants with foliage, lose water from their leaves by evaporation. The almost daily summer fogs are of inestimable value in reducing such water loss as they increase air humidity and decrease temperatures. An additional requirement limits the species. It does not fare well in soils having less than 18 percent available soil moisture in August, the critical month in California's dry summer climate. Fog drip contributes surprisingly large amounts of moisture to soil during the dry season, up to 12 inches (30 cm.), it has been demonstrated, in parts of the northern coast. The same study confirmed the presence of important nutrients in fog drip that were collected either as air-borne substances or from deposits on the leaf surface. In any case, they help enrich the soil under the trees.

Despite its special needs, the genus *Sequoia* had tolerances enabling it to compete successfully with newcomer species. These began intruding when the climate settled down to summer drought and greater temperature ranges, seasonally and regionally. Such conifers as the cypresses and knobcone pine, whose close allies, if not the same species, are recorded from this period, are better adapted to a dry climate than the mesophytic redwood. Conversely, wet-climate species—Sitka spruce, grand fir, Port Orford cedar, and canoe, or western red, cedar—are descendents of old cronies from Arcto-Tertiary days. They are important elements of the Pacific Northwest rainforest from which redwood is absent north of latitude forty-two degrees. They cannot endure any prolonged summer drought, and though they mingle with redwoods up in Del Norte and Humboldt counties in a mixed-conifer forest, only grand fir and western hemlock, another conifer of mesic sites, appear as far south as coastal Sonoma County. Redwood has a well-defined climatic niche—too summer-dry for strong representation of many north coastal conifers but damp enough to edge out xerophytic species that are held to the drier pockets of these corrugated mountains.

All through its range, redwood is part of the coastal landscape. Its edaphic and climatic needs concentrate the species in canyon bottoms, along river flats, on north-facing slopes, and where ocean fog is a dependable summer visitor. Though we have stressed the importance of a maritime climate for sequoia, it is seldom found right on the coastline itself. It does not take kindly to salt spray or salt-burdened sea wind. A buffer strip of coastal scrub and prairie, closed-cone pine and cypress forest, and headland thickets of Douglas-fir, Sitka spruce, and beach pine takes command of the immediate coast from Mendocino County northward. Anywhere from 1 to 10 miles (1.6–16.1 km.) inland, redwood forest assumes authority, sharing it with lowland (grand) fir at its seaward edge as far south as near Fort Ross and Douglas-fir throughout much of its range. In this northwestern corner of California western hemlock occasionally joins them, particularly on moist lower slopes. Just as redwood leaves the exposed shoreline bluffs to their typical residents, it avoids both serpentine, allowing the intrusion of western white, Jeffrey, and knobcone pines, and the highly acid podzolic soils with their typical closed-cone pines and cypresses. Douglas-fir and Port Orford cedar also cope with serpentine and other related soils that are basic as opposed to acidic in nature, the latter tree chiefly on moister sites. Two other conifers we usually associate with the Sierra Nevada and the southern mountains—sugar pine and incense cedar—infiltrate the redwood domain and they also occur with yellow pine and white fir at higher elevations on the inner ranges of the northern coast.

Like pieces of shag rug surrounded by healthy house plants, grassy glades open out amid the conifers. Where natural as opposed to man-induced, they are usually on clay soil, often somewhat alkaline, or basic. Hardpans have developed in several prairie soil types of the redwood region, confining moisture to shallow depths. Patches of chaparral perch on their characteristic thin soils, steep slopes, and south-facing exposures. Toward the inner edge, where the ocean's mild influence is less and precipitation decreases, the moisture-requiring conifers fade out, and elements of the mixed evergreen forest that have been such faithful companions throughout the north coast coniferous forest gain ascendancy. Finally, they too give way to the increasing drought and the seasonally more extreme temperatures of the Great Valley where oak woodland opens vistas of rolling, tree-dotted terrain.

We should pause here to appreciate the northern ranges of California a bit more fully, in particular the Klamath Mountains balanced on the border between the California Floristic Province and the more humid coniferous forests of the Pacific Northwest. The tidiness of the repeated topographic patterns of outer and inner Coast Range breaks into a confusing welter of stream-furrowed mountains from the coast to Mount Shasta. The Klamath Mountains include several principal ranges—the Siskiyou Mountains that curve from eastern Del Norte County into northern Siskiyou County and southern Josephine County of Oregon, the Marble and Salmon mountains to the south of the Siskiyous, and the Trinity Mountains of southern Siskiyou County, northern Trinity County, and western Shasta County. The section of this range known as the Trinity Alps contains some of the taller peaks, over 8,900 feet (2,700 m.), and has the sharply eroded terrain of past glaciation, which also attacked higher portions of other areas in the Klamath Mountains.

The region is distinguished by having the southernmost extensions of such representatives of the great Pacific Northwest rainforest as Alaska and Port Orford cedars and silver and noble fir. (Western red cedar, lowland [grand] fir, western hemlock, and Sitka spruce continue south into the northern Coast Range.) It also has small relict populations of two other trees better known to us in the Rockies and other western ranges. They are Engelmann spruce and the timberline subalpine fir, the presence of which was only confirmed in 1969. Like so many subregions of California it has its endemics. One of the most interesting is weeping spruce that, though locally common, is now found nowhere else outside the Klamath Mountains. It is a tree of higher elevations, 7,500 feet (2,250 m.) and above, and typically dominates north-facing slopes and rocky ridges. Other trees of the higher altitudes include red fir (Shasta variety); lodgepole, white-bark, and foxtail pines; and mountain hemlock.

Serpentine soils are frequently encountered in the Klamath ranges and support characteristic species, among them a number of regional endemics such as serpentine arnica, a bright yellow bloomer in the sunflower family, and shortlobe paintbrush. A most intriguing species, the insectivorous California pitcher plant, is confined to sphagnum bogs in southern Oregon, the Klamath Mountains, and the northern Sierra.

South of Sonoma County sequoia is less an element of a larger coniferous forest complex and more a series of isolated groves in the coastal hill mosaic with scrub, grassy balds, chaparral, closed-cone pine forest, and mixed and broadleaf evergreen forests claiming characteristic homesites. The last-mentioned types of vegetation are typically transitional between the humid redwood groves and drier vegetation types and often form buffer stands between the two extremes. Man, however, has greatly interfered with these natural patterns because of the high commercial value of redwood timber.

A number of features of endurance help offset the requirements of redwood. Like the fire pines, it is adapted to fire. Not only do its seeds flourish in the bare soil left by fire, but it root-sprouts and trunk-sprouts as well. Sprouting is the characteristic method of propagation where the soils are rich in humus or in heavily shaded areas where seedlings probably would not survive. Rings or straight rows of saplings are typical features of all the Pacific Northwest rainforests. So-called nurse trees are downed logs which are fertile substrate for seedlings growing like well-behaved schoolchildren in line on the upper surface of the decaying trunk. More typical of redwood are the circles of young trees which started as sprouts around a burned or injured parent tree. Fire usually is not fatal, however. Thick, fireproof, nonresinous bark; wood of high moisture content; and a humid environment limit its destructive ravages. Most burn scars heal over in time, and trees whose foliage and side branches have been destroyed may re-sprout as fire columns. The new shoots project from dormant buds as bushy twigs all along the trunk.

One might say that the coast redwood seems disaster-proof, up to a point. Floods, short of the rare catastrophes that under-

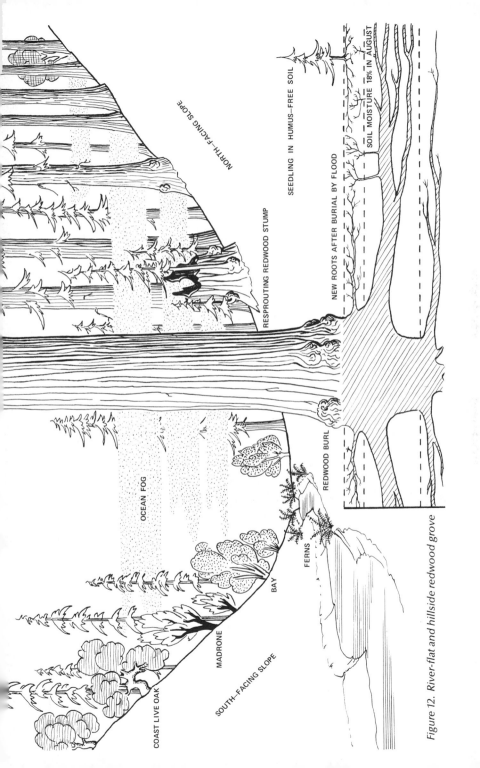

Figure 12. River-flat and hillside redwood grove

COAST LIVE OAK

MADRONE

BAY

FERNS

SOUTH-FACING SLOPE

OCEAN FOG

REDWOOD BURL

NORTH-FACING SLOPE

RESPROUTING REDWOOD STUMP

SEEDLING IN HUMUS-FREE SOIL

NEW ROOTS AFTER BURIAL BY FLOOD

SOIL MOISTURE 18% IN AUGUST

cut roots and topple trees, add silt to its substrate, encouraging seedlings and even invigorating the mature stands. The finest groves are on alluvial flats. They not only survive the low oxygen levels of flooded soils, but extend up to the new soil surface vertically oriented temporary roots from the old roots. Shortly after, they begin to spread horizontal root networks from newly buried portions of their trunks. The giants of alluvial terrain characteristically have several such whorled systems from each successive flood.

Cut or burn them, and seedlings and sprouts soon form thickets of vigorous growth. Insects and decay rarely trouble them because of chemicals in the thick bark. Though high winds can fell them as they have shallow root systems, they are considered by foresters to be relatively wind-firm. Diehards they are, in their fog-frequented, wind-sheltered canyons or hillsides, when they have sufficient soil moisture to tide them over the summer season. Foresters have referred to them as "disaster climax forests," meaning that if totally protected from the rejuvenating effects of near calamity the species would sooner or later suffer the consequences of its vigorous nature and degenerate under the decadence of soft living. Regeneration of the forest occurs only when new plants become established to replace the dead and dying. As noted above, sprouts grow from injured roots and boles, and seedlings thrive when fire or flood prepares the seedbed and opens the forest to fresh growth. It appears that the older a stand becomes, the more it is prone to extensive damage and destruction, with rejuvenation taking place less readily. Some researchers judge that a 300-year-old grove is already entering senescence with accompanying loss of vigor.

Sequoia sometimes grows in pure stands, more often with other trees. Douglas-fir is probably the most common coniferous companion to redwood throughout its range. It has an extremely wide amplitude, for it thrives in the wetness of the Olympic Peninsula rainforest as well as on the drier slopes of western mountain ranges and is the most common conifer of the broadleaf evergreen forest. Requiring the same conditions for seedling health, bare mineral soil and sunlight, Douglas-fir is strongly represented in redwood forests. But as it does not stump-sprout and is susceptible to death from fire and flood, its success as a potential competitor is somewhat limited. It is also relatively unresistant to insect damage. Two less frequently encountered cone bearers, California nutmeg, an endemic, and western yew which has a wider range, are found in redwood country. They look somewhat alike in having sprays of large flat needles, but nutmeg has hard berrylike fruits which keep it from being a typical cone bearer. It is often classified as a semiconifer.

Several shade-tolerant members of the broad-sclerophyll forest comprise a by-no-means ubiquitous understory and also grow at grove edge. Tanoak, California bay, madroño, giant chinquapin, and in some areas live oak, black oak, and Garry oak share the light filtering down through the crown canopy. So hungry are some individual trees of these species for light that they angle out over stream beds or trails, become off-balance, topple over, and then continue to send up branches growing to the light at right angles to the horizontal trunk.

Numerous shrubs fill out a second underlayer: rhododendron, hazelnut, dogwood, ceanothus, poison oak, salal, huckleberry, Oregon grape, wax myrtle, and various berries. Western azaleas are shiny-leafed bushes with fragrant gold-and-white blossoms. The startling flame-red fruits of the western burning bush smolder by trail or path. Looking like a giant stalk of celery, spikenard, one of the herbaceous ginsengs, looms 10 feet (3 m.) tall and seems taken straight from a tropical jungle. Many of the old-growth cathedral groves lack these understories except for shade-tolerant ground cover plants, and only an occasional vine maple or redwood sapling brings the tracery of foliage to eye level.

The herb layer is characteristically rich with ferns, spore-bearing plants whose antecedents have flourished since before dinosaur times. Sword, chain, and wood ferns spray out like small green fountains by pathside, on fallen timber, and at the bases of trees and stumps. Epiphytic ferns, mosses, and club mosses grow in a green plush over branches and root tangles, reminiscent of a tropical cloud forest where epiphytes cover every inch of woody tissue. Bracken often spreads between the boles of the forest. Lady ferns are streamside and nod under the impact of drops tossed from the little cascades of coastal brooks.

Except in openings such as in meadows, along stream courses, and by trail and roadside, the wildflowers of the redwoods are often inconspicuous. The blossoms of Solomon's seal, woodland star, sugar scoop, and alum root glow like small white sparks in the trailside shadows. Red clintonia has a long stem supporting a top-heavy cluster of rosy bells. Alaska fringe cups have delicate pink-edged puffs along slender stalks. Wild ginger, buttercups and violets, trillium and other members of the lily family appear in the springtime woods drying out from the rains of winter.

As in all California's coast and foothill country, trees growing along the river bottoms and beside the larger streams are often somewhat different from those occurring slightly higher. Few redwood trees are at river edge. Their place is taken by riparian (streamside) vegetation which includes many species also found along interior river courses: boxelder, cottonwood, willow, white alder, dogwood, and big-leaf maple. One such species, red alder, is typically coastal and is never found very far inland. Individual trees of the broadleaf and coniferous evergreen forests drop down to the stream bank here and there.

A generalization often made about redwoods is that one seldom sees animal life deep in their mature groves. One may look and listen in vain for signs of birds and mammals other than *Homo sapiens*. When by oneself the silence seems to have small sounds of its own. It is as though by listening hard enough one could hear the multiplying cells, the flowing sap, the stretching roots—the countless processes going on and on in these great trees, and around them, too, for a redwood forest is not quite the zoological desert it is often assumed to be. It is an ecosystem in its own right; and though animals such as black-tailed deer come and go in their constant quest for browse, many others are at home in these shadowed stands.

Steller's jays are the most easily recognized of several birds occurring in the dense foliage of coastal coniferous woods. Their cocky black crests, bright blue plumage, large size, and abrasive call are unmistakable. In a place where life seems to go about on hushed tiptoe, their boldness is refreshing. Any camp or picnic table will be under the surveillance of one or more of these friendly neighbors perched on a nearby limb, hoping to freeload off some generous visitor. Sit on a comfortable trailside log and watch quietly. Brown creepers and pygmy nuthatches will resume their appraisal of the insect population, apparently never stopping to rest during daylight hours, constantly pattering up and down the massive trunks and along the larger boughs. Chestnut-backed chickadees are on the same quest and work over the needled foliage. They often hang upsidedown as they probe with their bills into likely places. A large robin-like bird with a broad black *V* across its orange breast is the varied thrush. It moves about quietly under shrubs or sits on the lower limbs of trees. This thrush and the chickadee referred to above are two of the only six birds to nest in the north coniferous forest, according to one of the most informative books on the subject to be published in recent years, *The Birds of California,* by one of the state's finest ornithologists, Arnold Small (Collier Books, 1974). The others include the rufous hummingbird, whose male is an incomparable little jewel with his "backwards" collar of Mandarin red, and its equally attractive near-relative, Allen's hummingbird whose back is green rather than brownish red. The other two nesters are about as different in appearance and behavior as two birds can be. One is the chickenlike blue grouse, which spends most of its time foraging on the ground for berries, nuts, and such or sitting huddled on the branch of usually a coniferous tree. The other is the Vaux swift, the Porsche of wild winged traffic, elegantly darting here and there in search of insects, but returning to earth to nest in hollow trees.

Additional avian residents of the dense north coastal woods are winter wrens which flit in and out of root tangles and rest occasionally to pour out the rivulets of song so typical of wrens. Golden-crowned kinglets flutter through the masses of limb and leaf pausing only to pick up a tasty insect. Hairy and the imposing pileated woodpeckers work away at their respective forges—the pounding of the latter is distinctively loud and slow.

Though mammals are harder to find in these dark groves, one species, the Roosevelt elk, has almost become a symbol of the northern redwoods. No doubt this is because of the fine herd maintained at Prairie Creek State Park in Humboldt County. Not mammals of the dark forest only, they browse their way in the more open glades and meadows, feeding on the vine maples and shrubs. Closely related to the Rocky Mountain elk, this particular subspecies is restricted to the humid forests of the Pacific Northwest. The Olympic elk of Walt

Disney fame belongs to the same group. Many of the parks in Washington's rainforest are supposedly kept open by the browsing of the elk, for they spend the winter there when the higher ranges are snowbound.

At the other extreme in size is the Trowbridge shrew, a tiny fellow whose insect prey may be almost as large as the captor and whose runways tunnel the duff. Two kinds of chipmunks, Sonoma and yellow-cheeked, are residents; and the western gray squirrel of the oak groves is also at home in coniferous forests. One would suppose the gray squirrel to be in severe competition with the agile chickaree or Douglas squirrel, but the latter's diet of cones and nuts is very different from that of its acorn-eating cousin. Chickarees often nest in woodpecker holes small enough to prevent entry by the larger carnivores, such as bobcats and mountain lions, and too high for gray foxes and skunks.

One of the most intriguing, if rarely seen, animals of the redwoods is the mountain beaver. It is not related to the true beaver except that it too is a rodent. Looking like an outsized gopher, it lives in a system of tunnels whose entrances are screened over with brushy cover, berry patches, fern fronds, salal, and the like. Plants make up its diet which includes needles and leaves. It digs efficiently, and its task is made that much easier when it chooses to construct its tunnel maze in the damp earth of streamside, which it often does.

The many creeks, moist places, and rivers of the redwood country are home to amphibians of more than passing interest. The rosy-hued *Ensatina* and the ocelot-spotted giant salamander are common, as are several newts and other salamanders frequenting this damp habitat. *Ensatina* keeps undercover much of the time, in rodent burrows and hollow logs, under leaf litter, and in other hidden places. The giant salamander apparently prefers being close to water, for it seldom goes far from stream or creek. On occasion, however, it takes to climbing tree trunks.

Other oddities of the sequoia woods are the large banana slugs, shell-less land gastropods unable to live in drier environments or expose themselves to the direct sun for too long a time. Any desiccation of their mucus-covered skin would be fatal. They ooze about on the duff, feeding on vegetation and litter.

As with all biotic communities, the redwoods have their

share of animals that feed on each other. Owls and the giant salamanders watch for amphibians, small reptiles, and rodents such as red tree and deer mice. Various insectivorous birds, shrews, and smaller salamanders hunt tiny game. Raccoons forage about in their favorite streamside haunts for frogs and other water dwellers including the young of fish such as steelhead and cutthroat trout and salmon which begin mature life by spawning in these coastal rivers. Regardless of the species discussed above, these great groves, it is true, do not support the animal life so rich in many other communities. Lack of variety in diet, scarcity of grass seeds, and the absence of sheltering cover, particularly in the old-growth stands that are so impressive and dramatic, help account for the paucity of both individuals and species.

Very little is written about redwoods without serious concern for their future. We know they are some of the most valuable timber resources, and provision must be made for their most efficient utilization. Aesthetically we may deplore the ugly scars and slash piles of their harvesting, but we will not be able to prevent this major industry from operating in these coastal forests. Nor should we wish to stop its activities entirely. The wood is too useful and of too fine a quality for abandoning sequoia as a timber crop. Wise forestry practices should ensure a continuing supply from maturing second growth.

Be that as it may, we are the custodians of one of the world's most wonderful natural heritages, the proud old-growth redwood forests. Through the activities of various conservation groups, the American people have had the foresight to set aside a number of the virgin stands which invariably call forth wonder and admiration from all who come to stand at the feet of these great giants. Not too much is left of the privately owned "cathedral nave" forest, and its acreage gets smaller each month as the lumber companies continue their felling.

A major victory in the battle for their conservation was won in 1968, when Congress passed an act creating a 58,000-acre (23,490 hectares) national park in the Redwood Creek area of Humboldt County and in Del Norte County's Mill Creek section. Soon after the park's establishment it was realized that the original boundaries were at best inadequate. They would have to be expanded to protect adjoining watershed and remaining old-growth redwoods not as yet logged. Forty-eight thousand acres (19,440 hectares) were added to the Redwood Creek unit in 1978, but the Mill Creek section needs expansion as well. Such organizations as Save the Redwood League are currently raising funds for such acquisitions. The three neighboring state redwood parks—Prairie Creek, Del Norte Coast, and Jedediah Smith—were at one time to be transferred to the National Park Service for management, but so far the state has declined to relinquish control. There is no doubt that the state has done an excellent job of taking care of the twenty-nine coast redwood parks, many of which have been enlarged since their establishment.

Over fifty years of unflagging effort are at last bearing fruit. The finest remaining specimens will be protected from the logger's chain saws. There is much question, however, about the possible long-term effects of complete protection. Many foresters and ecologists are doubting the wisdom of such a procedure. The total absence of fire and flood may bring about an eventual loss of vigor and even their demise, allowing competitive species such as tanoak and Douglas-fir to replace the redwood stands. We need to know much more about their behavior and life history before we can accurately prognosticate their future. It may be that we will have to counteract the results of our interference with the processes of nature by further, but enlightened, interference.

Valley Oaks, Agoura

7. Woodpeckers in Oak Trees

Time itself seems to yawn and take a nap in the long golden hours of a foothill summer day. Bees hum in the straw-dry grass, dipping into the curl-rimmed saucers of white and russet mariposa lilies, hovering among the purple trumpets of harvest brodiaea, both late bloomers and heralds of summer in the oak-dotted parks of the foothills. Scrub jays answer each other from thickets of buckeye and other brushy growth. Yellow-billed magpies swoop onto fence posts, ready for flight into nearby oaks on the hillside. Digger pines sift the sunlight through their sparse foliage.

Little country roads pursue circuitous routes, here reaching around grassy slopes, tawny-brown in late June, there keeping company with drought-shrunken streams or hanging onto steep-sided roadcuts.

If one pulls off on many of these narrow tracks fenced by aging posts and the ubiquitous barbed wire, he should soon become acquainted with one of California's most typical foothill residents, the acorn woodpecker. His shrill JACK-A *jack-a jack-a* has all the forthrightness of a football coach giving hell to a losing team. With scalloped white-and-black flight he nips from tree to fence post and back again with a seemingly endless source of energy. His red cap glimmers back to the nape of his neck, and the white and ebony cowl around his face frames the pale circle of his eye.

Watching a *carpentero,* as he was called by the early Spanish settlers, fitting acorns into holes he has drilled for the purpose is an instructive experience. He positions the acorn, tip end first; then he drives it in with a few hard whacks until it is flush with the surface. His drum major costume becomes him as he clings to the side of the tree, head back, eyes alert, and feet and tail firmly braced.

Once central California slides down the eastern slope of the outer coastal mountains it buckles into the accordion pleats of the middle and inner Coast Ranges. Though the interior ridges surrounding San Francisco Bay and the western Delta are influenced by the sea and its foggy winds, our transect at last is moving away from maritime California. Summers are hotter and of longer duration; winters are colder; and rainfall averages drop considerably in many places. However, most of the biotic communities to which the reader has already been introduced remain familiar landscapes—chaparral, mixed and broadleaf evergreen forest, streamside vegetation, and fire pines and cypresses—but with variations. This inland mosaic is somewhat different from its maritime counterpart. Several new dominant species and three new communities must be added: northern oak woodland, foothill woodland, and savanna. Not that these are absent from the outer Coast Ranges—quite the contrary—but since they are best developed in the interior, it seemed advisable to leave them for this chapter. One community disappears, the coast redwood with its dark dignity—except for some isolated stands in Napa County. The coastal closed-cone pines and cypresses must also be left on their picturesque bluffs and headlands. Some features are essentially the same in both the mild humid coast and the drier, more extreme interior. Chaparral still covers many south-facing slopes and steeper crests with its rough homespun. Live oaks, bay, buckeye, and madroño thicken on north-facing slopes and mingle with the typical trees of canyon bottoms—willow, alder, cottonwood, and big-leaf maple. For the most part, a casual glance reveals little that is different from the ranges neighboring the sea. Closer inspection, however, discloses some deviation. The grassy balds, which summer-bronze ridgetops and hillsides, have many species more representative of interior grasslands than coastal prairie, and a number of shrubs with which we have become so familiar are absent. Salal, blue blossom ceanothus, and wax myrtle, for example, are gone and will not reappear. Though present on the inner Coast Ranges either north or south of the Bay Area, or both, other mesophytic shrubs and trees such as ninebark, tanoak, California nutmeg, western yew, and Douglas-fir are missing from Mount Diablo and Mount Hamilton but reoccur on the Sierran slope. Yet many members of the chaparral are as common here as they were on the more humid coast: toyon, hollyleaf cherry, chamise, poison oak, silk tassel bush, coffeeberry, redberry, mountain mahogany, and scrub oak.

Two outstanding species of the coastal sage scrub of the southern half of the state—black sage and California, or wild, buckwheat—range as far north as Mount Hamilton. Together with California sagebrush and bush monkeyflower, they form a thin cover on the drier hills of the Diablo Range. All are subshrubs; and two, sagebrush and black sage, are partly deciduous in summer, an adaptation nicely designed to meet the acute water stress these plants must undergo in the drier months. During the hottest time of the year this sage scrub community has a very different appearance from the northern coastal scrub which is thick with bracken and sword fern, umbels of many kinds, and berry brambles. The half-dead-appearing vegetation of the dry interior hills looks as though dried twigs have been thrust willy-nilly into the inhospitable soil. As in the southern ranges, elements of sage scrub are often temporary, moving in after fire and then giving way to the reinvading chaparral or forest.

In place of the mesophytic conifers, drought-resistant species now enter the landscape. Frequently encountered in the interior of the southern half of the state, though it occasionally appears on seaward slopes, Coulter pine occurs as far north as Mount Diablo. Not only is it distinguished for being one of the state's native sons, it has the world's heaviest cone; specimens 18 inches (46 cm.) long and weighing up to 9 or 10 pounds (4 – 4.5 kg.) have been collected. They have thick, coarse, clawlike scales. Unlike the gaunt and somewhat starved-looking digger pine, Coulter pine, though also a xerophytic species, has a prosperous, well-fed and well-watered air about it, particularly on better sites. Plants of the chaparral such as squaw bush, manzanita, redberry, and poison oak frequently consort with it, and small live oaks are not uncommon companions.

Knobcone pines keep to their serpentines and other infertile sites, associating with Jeffrey pine, on occasion, and other drought-tolerant shrubs and trees. Yellow pines have a spotty distribution in the coastal portion of the transect. From the Santa Lucia Mountains south of Monterey, they skip to sandy badlands in the Santa Cruz Mountains, go on to two rather confined localities on Mount Hamilton, and become more prevalent on the inner ranges in Napa and Sonoma counties to the north.

Sargent cypress has a widely scattered distribution in the interior, appearing casually on Mount Hamilton and reaching south to Santa Barbara County and north to Mendocino County. Another resident of serpentine soils in the inner Coast Ranges is MacNab cypress. It and Sargent cypress are the only two California species whose ranges overlap, though it appears that MacNab cypress keeps to higher slopes. It is also the only cypress to "complete the horseshoe," that is, it begins in Sonoma County, continues in the hilly country around Shasta Lake, and is scattered in the foothills of the northern Sierra Nevada south to Nevada County on a variety of soil types, many of them poor. California juniper is new to the transect. Very drought-resistant, it is usually a shrub, but it can achieve a height of roughly 33 feet (10 m.), becoming the westernmost tree-size species of its genus in North America. One can find it on canyon slopes of eastern Mount Hamilton, on rocky outcrops on Mount Diablo, and follow it north to Tehama County, east to the Sierra Nevada foothills, and south to numerous lower mountain slopes of southern California. Mingling with pinyon and Great Basin sagebrush, it pushes a piece of the arid interior as far west as Ventura County. It is widespread through the inner Coast Ranges of central California, often consorting with scrubby oaks.

The most typical conifer of hot-summer California slopes is the digger pine—that awkward, off-balance excuse for a shade tree with its thin, long-needled foliage. It shares a derogatory and undeserved name with a group of California Indians who did much more than dig. They wove some of the world's most beautiful basketry, a type of craftsmanship that has never been surpassed. Their namesake tree is for the most part confined to the foothills and ranges surrounding the Great Valley from 100 to roughly 6,000 feet (30–1,800 m.) in elevation. They filter west, however, to sea-facing bluffs in southern Monterey County and confront the desert interior in Kern County and on the Modoc Plateau. Truly a Californian, it does not grow in Oregon and is rare south of the Tehachapis, though a stand near Gorman in northern Los Angeles County extends east for some distance. Because it frequently accompanies the deciduous blue oak, one of the more drought-tolerant trees of the interior, this partnership is often referred to as the digger pine-blue oak association of the foothill woodland. In general, the characteristic conifer of this community is a lanky and unappreciated tree. Nevertheless, it has a remarkable ability to withstand conditions imposed by the hot, interior, summer-dry hills. Infrequent on deep, fine-grained valley soils, its typical substrates vary from the coarse alluvium of foothill riverine beds to serpentine and rocky slopes on both sides of the Great Valley. One of the most drought-enduring pines, its light gray, drooping needles reflect much desiccating sunlight, and evaporative surfaces are reduced because of the sparse foliage.

Though there are parklike sites in the foothill woodlands where one receives the impression of a random scattering of trees whose canopies seldom touch, there is considerable variation in density of cover. In places, the predominant blue oaks combine with live oaks, digger pines, and assorted drought-adapted shrubs and small trees in fairly open stands with a rich carpet of grass and other light-encouraged herbaceous growth. North-facing slopes, on the other hand, often support heavy thickets of various oaks and trees and shrubs of the mixed evergreen forest with little or no grassy layer. Digger pines occasionally sprawl in thin groves up through tangles of wiry chaparral. Elsewhere, diggers and blue oaks grow together on undulating slopes, which in early spring look as though they are carefully tended golf fairways.

Savanna is the driest of the three community types we are discussing here, but for a community of trees the foothill woodland is also one of the less well-watered California habitats. Rainfall ranges from 15 to as high as 40 inches (38–102 cm.); but long, hot, dry summers cancel out many of the benefits of the increased precipitation of more favorable sites. Its identifying species are blue oak, digger pine, and, to some extent, valley oak, and their distribution determines the limits of foothill woodland. By and large, it is confined to the "bathtub ring" around the Great Valley with minor incursions into the outer Coast Ranges and low passes east and south of the southern Sierran slope. This pleasing, gentle landscape with its happy combination of silky grass and handsome trees lounges between the mesophytic forest at its upper edges and the xerophytic savanna, grassland, or scrub of lower elevations. Chaparral is often a ragged belt separating woodland and forest.

Northern oak woodland (to distinguish it from southern oak woodland of Santa Barbara County and south) enjoys an annual rainfall of from 25 to 40 inches (64–102 cm.). Like an ambitious politician, its characteristic tree, the deciduous Garry, or Oregon, oak seeks widespread support. It displaces blue oak, elbowing it off to poorer soils and drier habitats, while it associates with digger pine and other foothill woodland constituents in the valleys and surrounding low terraces of the inner North Coast Ranges and Klamath Mountains. Elsewhere in the same region it meets with tanoak, madroño, Douglas-fir, and other cronies of the mixed evergreen forest. On its own it takes command of both ridgetops and wide valley floors in performances rivaling similar valley oak groves to the south. This relatively mesophytic oak widens its base by venturing into the rocky volcanic soils of Siskiyou County with yellow and Jeffrey pines and western juniper, that hard-bitten old campaigner of timberline and dry plateaus. Though rare,

Garry oak pushes as far south as the Santa Cruz Mountains in coastal California and in the Sierra Nevada, often in shrub form, to the Tehachapis. Unlike California trees of more modest aspirations, it is a candidate for international recognition—it is the only oak species in western Canada (British Columbia). One more community disengages itself from the vegetation mosaic of the inner Coast Ranges. This is savanna, a term commonly used for the tree-dotted stretches of the drier tropics. In California, it is the transitional community between the woodlands of the hills and the grasslands of the broader valleys. Where the original trees still stand, they are fewer in number and more widely spaced than those of the woodlands proper. For the most part they are valley oaks, with blue oaks and interior live oaks making an occasional appearance, as do buckeye and a few xerophytic shrubs clinging to footholds on roadcuts and rockier places. Where the trees cluster in arroyos and along stream courses, they are often joined by riparian vegetation typical of the dry interior. Characteristically, these sparsely wooded lands flow down out of the forest and scrub of the higher crests, slopes, and canyons of the Coast Ranges. Driving to Vacaville or to Tracy via Livermore, you can quickly note the dark mounds of the upper brush and tree-blanketed hills, and see how these separate into freckled slopes giving way in turn to cultivated fields, range, and residential tracts with an occasional old valley oak left standing here and there.

California's oaks are almost as exceptional as its pines. Approximately sixteen (the number differs with each expert) species of *Quercus* (oak) occur here in contrast to Arizona's thirteen (again, more or less), and only three are shared with our southernmost neighbor state—holly-leaf oak, desert scrub oak, and canyon live, or golden cup, oak. The last species is also found as far north as central Oregon, as is black oak; and Garry oak, noted above, continues through the northwest into British Columbia. Thus, the California Floristic Province can claim the remaining eleven species for its own. The tree forms endemic to the province are coast and interior live oaks and valley, Engelmann, blue, island, and MacDonald oaks. The last two are found on the Channel Islands. The shrub types are huckleberry, deer, scrub, and leather, a species confined largely to serpentine soils. (Serpentine, incidentally, has been officially designated as California's state mineral—a distinction for one of the state's most infertile soil types.) A number of oak species, particularly those that are evergreen, do well on xeric sites inasmuch as they occur in arid regions of California and Arizona. Not only are they deep-rooted, their foliage has many drought-resisting features. A number of species suffer extensive damage from fire because of thin bark and other vulnerable features, but each of California's oaks has developed strategies to cope with this ever-present threat, including the ability to sprout from branches or the base of the trunk, or both.

The genus tends to hybridize with ease, and species intergrade with bewildering complexity. For this reason it is often difficult to determine a specimen's exact status, particularly one of the shrubbier forms. They may be dwarfs of generally larger types, examples of true scrub forms, or hybrids of shrubby species.

Because they are so much a part of this general area of the state and vary considerably in their habitat tolerances and preferences as well as appearance and behavior, it might be useful to discuss each species of tree oaks of the midlatitude Coast Ranges in some detail. We shall segregate them in three commonly used subgroups (subgenera)—white, black-red, and intermediate. The first is so designated because the bark of white oaks is usually light gray or brown in color, black oaks have dark brown or blackish trunks, and intermediate species are a lighter grayish brown, reflecting the transitional character of this small subgenus. There are additional differences, some of which are apparent only to the trained observer. Others are more obvious. White oak acorns mature in a year; the other two subgroups, with one or two exceptions, require two years for maturation. The inner surface of the acorn shell is definitely hairy in the black oak group whereas white oak acorns lack this characteristic. Intermediate oaks may or may not have hairs on the interior of the acorn, depending upon the species. Black and intermediate oaks have leaves with pointed lobes or teeth, and white oaks usually have rounded lobes on their foliage. All three subgroups have both shrub and tree forms, and black and white oaks include evergreen as well as deciduous species.

Though frequent hybridization is typical of the genus and has long been a taxonomic problem, as far as is known, natural crosses occur only within the subgroup—white oaks hybridize with other white oaks—and the same is true for the other sub-genera. One fairly common hybrid California oak is the result of a cross between desert scrub oak and blue oak and is designated *Quercus* X *alvordiana* (the X refers to its hybrid position). It is a highly variable shrub or small tree, extending through the inner Coast Ranges from San Benito County to northern Los Angeles and southeastern Kern counties. Recent studies disclose a fascinating adjustment to local conditions. Where investigated, the plant was shrubby on dry southwest-facing hillsides and had desert scrub oak characteristics whereas on more protected northeast-facing slopes, types closer to blue oak developed.

The White Oak Subgroup

Valley oak *(Quercus lobata)*. This is the most impressive local tree of the oak group for sheer size and patriarchal demeanor. It bends its huge limbs over such diverse understories as shopping centers and chicken runs, where allowed to remain. A deciduous species, in wintertime it looks as though it had finally succumbed to insect infestation or drought. But after a month or so of springtime warmth, it leafs into great spreading crowns that bless the hot interior valleys with cool dense shade. Though found as high as 5,600 feet (1,680 m.) in the mountain complex east of Mount Pinos in Ventura County, for the most part valley oak is confined to deep, often fine-grained soils of valley floors and low rolling hills from 200 to 4,000 feet (60–1,200 m.). From the Pit River (Shasta County) south it extends the length of the lower Sierra slope to Kern County, graces the hills of western Los Angeles County, and continues north in the Coast Ranges to Mendocino County. The lovely grass-carpeted parklike groves we so often associate with this tree, the largest of all the American oaks, are best developed on alluvial terraces or in broad valleys. These oaks are also well represented in riverine woodlands, notably in the Great Valley. Because of their lowland inclinations it has been assumed that they must utilize shallow water tables, but a number of upland valley oak savannas thrive on ridgetops, at times surrounded by Coulter pine and coast live oak, less mesophytic trees. It is presumed that the wide spacing of the oaks in these sites diminishes competition for the moisture present in moderately deep soils. The binomial name refers to the lobes scalloping the leaf edges; thus, the foliage resembles that of the eastern white oak; indeed, valley oaks are frequently called California white oaks.

Blue oak *(Quercus douglasii).* Primarily it is a tree of the foothills. It rarely occurs above 4,000 feet (1,200 m.) or near the ocean, the exceptions being southern Monterey and Santa Barbara counties where a few groups come within several miles (10–12 km.) of the coast. Along with digger pine, blue oak is the indicative tree of the foothill woodland in the interior of the Coast Ranges from Santa Barbara County northward to Mendocino County. It continues in the hilly country south and east of Lake Shasta to form an unbroken belt down the entire lower Sierran slope and nips into the northwestern corner of Los Angeles County and southern Kern County, completing the ring of woodland around the Central Valley. Three other drought-tolerant conifers are local components—pinyon in Kern County, linking hands, as it were, with the stocky woodland trees of the American Southwest, California juniper in the inner Coast Ranges and Sierran-Cascade foothills to Shasta County, and western juniper in eastern Shasta County, where blue oak woodland has established an odd little colony far to the east of its main range. The common name of blue oak refers to the leaf color, though at times the bluish haze on the deciduous foliage is less apparent. Then there may be difficulty in distinguishing it from neighboring valley oaks; but in general the leaf is less lobed and smaller in size. Blue oaks seldom become as large as valley oaks, and they rarely venture out onto the broader floors where the latter is king. Though they integrate with California buckeye, toyon, holly-leafed cherry, and other xerophytic trees and shrubs, they often occur in pure parklike stands, particularly in savannas edging the floor of the Central Valley. On north-facing slopes they may crowd together, and the canopies touch and intermingle; elsewhere in drier places the trees dissociate from each other. Clumps are not uncommon and are usually the result of stump-sprouting, following fire. At best, they are broad-spreading, good-looking trees and welcome providers of shade on a hot summer day. Blue oak is one of the more drought-adapted deciduous oaks and tolerant of hardships in general. It is commonly found on rocky soils and infertile disruptions of mixed evergreen forest. Where it associates with interior live oak, the latter often leaves the south-facing slopes to blue oak and claims more mesic hillsides for itself, though there is evidence that both species tap into ground water where it is available. The canopy effect, as it is called, has been noted by a number of observers. The herbaceous cover is somewhat different in composition, taller, and more luxuriant under blue oak trees. Estimates have been made that vegetation production increases by 15 to over 100 percent. It also remains greener for a longer period of time. Presumably, this is because of a significant increase in nutrients from decayed leaf litter and manure from resting livestock and other animals, resulting in richer soils with a higher water-retaining capacity. Shade from the tree probably aids in prolonging subsurface soil moisture as well.

The other California members of the white oak subgroup are leather, scrub, desert scrub, Engelmann (or mesa), Garry, and deer oak. The last species is of special interest because it is the only far western representative of chestnut oaks, a small group whose leaves resemble those of chestnuts, trees that, along with oaks, are in the beech family. The other species are either in eastern North America or Asia. Confined to southern Oregon and adjacent counties in northern California, it has a wide range of ecological tolerance. It occurs in the shrub layer of mesic mountain forests as well as in the brushy cover of warm, dry, south-facing slopes. Apparently it also accommodates serpentine substrates. Deer oak is another one of the endemic relicts that make the Klamath and other ranges of northern California so intriguing.

The Black Oak Subgroup

Coast Live Oak (*Quercus agrifolia*). As its common name implies, it is almost completely restricted to the Coast Ranges from Sonoma County to Santa Barbara County. From Ventura County south it is widespread at low elevations on the seaward sides of the Transverse and Peninsular Ranges and occasionally occurs on hills adjacent to the coast. Like Garry oak it has its roots in many camps. Along with bishop pine, coyotebrush, and coffeeberry, it stabilizes old beach dunes in Monterey

County and is one of the most common associates of mixed hardwood forest in moist canyons, on north-facing hillsides, and other favorable sites. In early summer the bright green of California buckeye contrasts nicely with the deep green of the live oak in dry gullies and other less mesic places where they grow together. It mingles in some areas with blue oak, but more often the latter, a less mesophytic species, is relegated to south-facing slopes or drier interior habitats. Despite its sociability with other species it can be the lone arboreal contender for sandy soils of cool coastal hills, or it clusters in groves that separate the brush and grassland of lower coastward slopes from the redwood stands of higher hillsides and canyons. Inland from the sea, coast live oak does very well on alluvial terraces, presumably with the help of a high water table, and, though not strictly riparian, it frequently consorts with typical streamside trees such as willow and sycamore. Like zealous assistants, shrubs such as toyon, poison oak, and snowberry crowd under their patrons in dense shady groves. In more xeric habitats or where soils determine, grass is companion. Coast live oak is considered an evergreen as it does not shed all of its leaves at one time, but many old leaves are discarded when new foliage is produced in spring. The young leaves are a glistening, rich green in contrast to older leaves which are darker and somewhat curled under around the edges. Both young and old foliage has the sheen, crispness, and shape of holly leaves, prickles and all. Where the atmosphere has sufficient humidity, coastal oaks are often hung with "grandfather beards" of *Usnea* and *Ramalina*, pendant lichens.

Interior Live Oak *(Quercus wislizenii).* In appearance, it is much like its coastal counterpart, but its leaves are generally more leathery, less curled, brighter green, and shiny on both surfaces. There is a major difference in behavior. Though both are black oaks, the acorns of the interior live oak take two years to mature, and those of coast live oak require only one. The best way to tell them apart is by geographical ranges. The interior species enters foothill woodland on the mountains of northern Santa Barbara County and is scattered in the middle and inner Coast Ranges to continue east across the foothills of the upper Sacramento Valley and south along the Sierran slope. A shrubby variety extends the range in chaparral from the Tehachapi Mountains southward to northern Baja California. Apparently, coast live oak requires more summer soil moisture than its interior counterpart, and the two species are seldom in direct contact. Where they overlap, such as on Mount Diablo, coast live oak may claim the moister seaward slopes and canyons while interior live oak copes with drier inland sites. In the same way, the coastal species usurps the stream banks, and the inland species is left with neighboring rocky slopes. With this in mind, it is interesting to note that the interior oak has successfully invaded what is usually thought to be the territory of the coastal oak. It has been reported that interior live oak is one of the common understory trees in redwood forests in the Santa Cruz and Santa Lucia mountains. In the warmer inland valleys and surrounding hills it may contribute to valley oak savanna and associate with another woodland colleague, blue oak. It tends, however, to sprout-clump around rocky outcrops or to keep to north-facing slopes at higher elevations, often mingling with canyon live oak. Where the grassy cover is replaced by chaparral, interior live oak is frequently joined by digger pine in a sparse woodland, in which the isolated trees appear like harassed adults supervising a crowd of restless children. The shrub variety of the species is common in chaparral throughout the Coast Ranges where it often forms thickets on the tops and sides of summits along with small canyon live oaks and California bay. Other dense patches lie just below the forests of higher elevations. Where the groves are more open, the character and individuality of the tree's rounded masses are quite apparent.

Hybrids between this species and coast live oak are more common than formerly believed, particularly in the northern part of their overlapping ranges. Apparently this is the result of the convergence of two once widely separated species because of changing climatic conditions prior to and during the Ice Age.

California Black Oak (*Quercus kelloggii*). This species with its brilliantly green, deeply cut deciduous leaves is certainly one of the most beautiful of its group. It is quite extensive in the mixed evergreen forest, often on dry uplands and interior hills, from the Santa Lucia Mountains to the northern Coast Ranges and the Klamath-Shasta region where it is represented in northern oak woodland and mountain conifer forest. In the Sierra Nevada black oak is most frequently encountered with yellow pine in a broad elevational range extending from the upper borders of chaparral and foothill woodland to the white fir forest. It is a drought-resistant species and is established with Jeffrey pine in dry sagebrush-pungent alluvial slopes of eastern Lassen County as well as in a number of canyons on the eastern slope of the Sierra. Like canyon live oak, in southern California it tends to stay on north-facing slopes and higher elevations with Coulter, Jeffrey, and yellow pines and white fir. Where conditions are favorable, it may be quite large in size, but it is not as impressive as valley oaks of venerable age. Black oaks appear to thrive in a variety of environments, from scant-soiled rocky slopes to deep-loamed valley floors, if well drained. They vary from pure stands where competing vegetation has been removed by fire or other disturbance, allowing the vigorous growth of sprouts, to association with pines and other trees of the mixed forests where they commonly occur.

The Intermediate Oak Subgroup

Canyon Live, or Golden Cup, Oak *(Quercus chrysolepis).* With still a third name, maul oak, this is one of the more widely distributed species, ranging from Oregon down into Baja California, and extending into Arizona and possibly beyond. It is present on all the major mountain ranges of California, with the exception of the White Mountains, and it occurs on the New York Mountains of the eastern Mojave Desert. It is the consummate strategist of all our oaks, gaining footholds, precarious as they may be, in such wide-ranging natural communities as cypress groves, redwood forest, mixed evergreen forest, chaparral, riparian woodland, foothill woodland, Coulter pine forest, yellow pine and white fir forests, and even pinyon and juniper woodland of high desert ranges. It typically occurs on canyon floors, sometimes in narrow gullies, and often on rocky terraces where it seems about to lose its footing and topple to the depths below. The phrases used in ecological literature are quite forthright about the severity of some of its homegrounds: "driest, discontinuous rocky soils of steep canyon sides" and "steep southwesterly slopes with rock mulch soil." These oaks must have the hardihood of seasoned old campaigners to take on the rigors of such precincts. Extreme environmental conditions appear to hold only for the northernmost part of the state where summer drought is less demanding. It prefers more mesic sites such as north-facing slopes and sheltered ravines in central and southern California. Frequently following stream courses up from foothill woodland to higher elevations, it breaks into coniferous forest on less favorable sites or is part of the broadleaf understory. Canyon live oak may be just another diligent member of its community, joining tanoak, madroño, and California bay, for example, on shadier slopes, but it is often a dominant species as well.

There is great variation in leaf shape. The younger ones are often sharply spined; but older leaves, which persist the longest of the three evergreen tree oaks of the transect as they take from three to four years before dropping, are usually toothless. Distinguishing characteristics useful to the amateur naturalist are the color and thickness of the acorn cup. Though occasionally thin, it is more commonly heavy, woody, and of a golden color, hence one of its common names.

Canyon live oak is the only tree in its subgroup; the others are shrubs, three of which occur in California—holly-leaf, huckleberry, and island oaks. MacDonald oak, the other species thought to be endemic to the Channel Islands, is now considered a hybrid between valley oak and scrub oak, and evidently it occurs in a few mainland sites as well.

Tanoak, or Tanbark Oak (*Lithocarpus densiflora*). This is the last species to be discussed here. It is a handsome nondeciduous tree of the mixed evergreen, redwood, and Douglas-fir forests, not a true oak. Instead of flat scales its acorn cups look as if covered with patches of brown Turkish toweling. With the exception of some stands in the central and northern Sierra Nevada and in the Mount Shasta area, tanoak is a Coast Range tree from western Ventura County northward. It is not quite as versatile as some of the oaks in the same communities though its habitats vary from moist river terraces to drier slopes where yellow pine is comfortable. From Marin County south, tanoak is a major component of redwood border forest along with madroño and coast or canyon live oak. The foliage, often larger and more spear-point-shaped than that of live oaks, when new is woolly in texture and delicately pink, changing to light golden-green before full maturity.

Though fire and man have been as active here as in the outer hills, climate and edaphic conditions, in general, account for these rolling parks, and for their inclusion in the natural landscapes of California. Where rainfall averages 10 inches (25 cm.) or below, plants of the chaparral usually fail to compete with more xerophytic scrub and herbaceous species. Much of the extreme eastern inner range country, where the foothills flatten out beneath the floor of the Central Valley, experiences even less than 10 inches (25 cm.) of annual precipitation because of rainshadow. Large portions of the woodland communities enjoy more rainfall, however, particularly those at higher elevations. Of great importance is the long summer drought with the added complication of high temperatures during the dry season. Additional factors too are at work—soil particle size, the presence of impervious hardpans and claypans, compaction of grassy root masses—which lead us to a close examination of the herbaceous partners of the trees which are such outstanding features of this gentle and charming landscape, and to discussion of how the trees themselves fare so well where many smaller woody species do not intrude.

The highly drought-resistant features of grasses are of prime significance in their sharing of this marginal environment, particularly the annuals, either native to California or introduced from elsewhere. By and large, they grow more quickly than the perennial grass species, which, though having drought-adapted features of their own, were driven from their home territories (see Chapter 8) around midpoint of the last century. Rapid growth enables grass to use the available moisture of spring before it disappears under the powerful rays of the summer sun. The original bunchgrasses, of long residence in the foothills, included such species as needlegrasses, blue wildrye, various bromes, melicgrass, and deergrass. They were replaced by fast-growing annuals—soft chess, foxtail fescue, wild oats, and the like—opportunistic species able to mature quickly and head out before the harsh heat of summer.

The soils of the interior valleys and hillsides also influence vegetation cover. Valley and terrace soils generally are accumulations of residual material washed down from higher areas. Certain types of parent rock such as shale tend to produce soils with a high clay content. When wet, the finer particles act as glue. Such soils become heavy; runoff is accelerated, and water fails to penetrate to any depth. In addition, soils of this nature often develop a hardpan close to the surface. This impervious layer tends to concentrate moisture at or just below the soil surface, resulting in water puddling and deoxygenation during the rainy season and rapid dryoff during drought. The optimum growth period, therefore, is limited to a narrow time span between saturation and dehydration. Quick-growing grasses and forbs are remarkably adapted to just such a situation. They make the most of the few wet weeks allowed to them before they succumb and leave seeds or underground plant parts from which they sprout when the rainy season returns.

What of the trees? Unlike the shallow- and fibrous-rooted grasses, they can exploit deeper sources of moisture with long, woody roots. Even so, the valley oaks tend to remain close to riverways or where the water table is high. Blue oaks, though winter deciduous, are slightly sclerophyllous and benefit from this protection. In years of unusually severe water stress they have recourse to a drastic though very effective adaptive maneuver—they drop their leaves in late summer, discarding their food-making but, unfortunately, water-losing equipment, to opt for early dormancy. Live oaks share the xerophytic characteristics of sclerophylls, but there is evidence that coast live oaks frequently rely on shallow water tables as well. In one study area in the Sierran foothills it was noted that both blue oak and interior live oak had roots long enough to reach pockets of water roughly 33 to 66 feet (10–20 m.) deep in fractured bedrock. One effective means of successfully sharing a meager water supply is wide spacing: the drier the site, the fewer the trees competing for the available moisture. As the rainfall averages decrease on descent to the floor of the Central Valley, the point is reached where trees cannot exist at all, with the exception of valley oaks and riparian species that depend on underground or surface water sources. Out on the rolling plains, grass and its partner forbs reign supreme or did until irrigation inaugurated the drastic changes which have so altered many interior hills and valleys.

As for the distribution of chaparral within the realm of the drier woodlands, there are numerous islands of brush throughout the interior hills, and brush species sometimes form a dense understory beneath the trees in more mesic sites. Low rainfall in the savanna precludes much brush growth, however, and it is rarely found on the lower approaches to the Great Valley. When chaparral occupies isolated patches within the oak groves, most probably edaphic conditions differ from those of the open woodland. Sclerophyll shrubs depend, not so much on surface water, as do the grasses, but on moisture sources in lower horizons and buried in bedrock but accessible to vigorously probing roots. Clay accumulations in dense subsoils of terrace and valley floor would prevent such root development. The shallow-soiled, well-drained, xeric hillsides and ridges with pockets of bedrock water remaining long after the onset of summer drought seem to be the natural home of brushlands, unless fire or man has interfered. Deep, well-drained soils with adequate water throughout the drier months can accommodate heavy woodland and forest. Even the steeper slopes of the inner Coast Ranges from Mount Hamilton north can be clothed with such vegetation if edaphic and exposure conditions are favorable.

Several additional factors are also active in maintaining more open landscapes. Root and stem masses of grass are sometimes so compacted that seeds of woody species cannot penetrate them or reach the soil beneath. If they were successful in germinating, chances are that the quick-sprouting grasses would soon deprive them of water during the short growing season. For many prairies this is a possible perpetuating factor. Another influence is fire, destroying the seedlings of woody species but with little long-term effect on the grasses which readily renew themselves the following spring. The older trees of open woodlands seldom undergo serious damage as grass fires are relatively "cool" and, in the absence of brush, quickly burn out. Furthermore, most oaks stump-sprout. Unless severely injured by repeated fires or browsing animals, they eventually return to their former prominence. Stock and wildlife cropping, referred to above, is the third factor controlling the maintenance of open country.

These are lively communities, particularly in spring. Canyon oak and California hairstreak butterflies emerge from pupae, ready to lay eggs from which will come larval forms feeding mainly on oak leaves. California sister, silver blue, and tailed copper are the other common butterflies of the oak woodlands, bright flashes against the newly green hills.

Trees and grass offer more than food to their animal associates. The herbaceous cover provides shade and shelter for jack rabbits and many kinds of wild mice. The oaks serve as observation posts for hawks and other predators, and are rich sources of food for the acorn eaters—magpies, scrub jays, mule deer, tree squirrels, and band-tailed pigeons among them. The attractive pink-fronted Lewis' woodpecker, western bluebirds, plain titmice, and black-headed grosbeaks call and carol, hunt and probe for insects or seeds.

During the last ten years or so increasing use, particularly by ornithologists, is being made of the term *guild*—"a group of species that exploit the same class of environmental resources in a similar way." Though closely related species may be part of a guild, feeding and other habits are the definitive factors that determine membership. A foliage-gleaning guild has been described for an oak woodland on the Hastings Natural History Reservation in Monterey County. The diet of its birds largely consists of insects and other arthropods found on oak foliage. The blue-gray gnatcatcher, warbling vireo, orange-crowned warbler, plain titmouse, and Hutton's vireo are the principal members of the guild during the breeding season. Though the guild loses the first three species to migration, the last two are permanent residents, and they are joined by ruby-crowned kinglets and yellow-rumped warblers in the winter months. Both seasons, the birds of the guild avoid undue competition with each other as each species has its preferred food and foraging tactics. About 60 percent of the warbling vireo's diet, for example, is comprised of insects in the moth and butterfly order, which contributes only 6 percent of the food of the plain titmouse.

Two bird inhabitants of the woodlands have quite complex relationships with their arboreal neighbors. The acorn woodpecker feeds on their acorns but not to the point of preventing their replacement. Because it prefers the more easily penetrated wood of dead trees or limbs, it usually does not damage living healthy trees with its hole-drilling activities. The scrub jay may even enter into a mutually beneficial association when he buries the acorns in the ground, unconsciously taking the role of a competent nurseryman as he places them in the substrate most suitable for their germination, mineral soil under duff. This activity is possibly of much value to the oaks, for their acorns without such aid often come to rest in tangles of dry grass stems where germination is improbable. The oaks feed the jays and the jays plant the oaks, a most useful relationship. Both birds use the trees for nest sites. The woodpecker excavates holes in dead trunks and branches; the jay uses living trees for support and to harvest the twigs as nest material.

Speaking of acorn woodpeckers, let us digress for a moment to appreciate a rather remarkable bird. Although it has some unusual patterns of behavior, described below, it shares many of the features distinguishing the group as a whole. Its tail is used as a brace. Bent at an angle and propped against the surface of whatever the woodpecker is climbing, it serves to support the bird as it hitches along. Like the rest of its tribe, the acorn woodpecker can drill into bark and wood with speed and strength that seem almost power-tooled. Not only is the cranium unusually thick for birds in general, but spongy tissue takes up the pounding jar of hole boring. Most woodpeckers have a long tongue which fits into a sheath around the back of the skull. When extended, it projects some distance in front of the bill and serves to capture grubs living in bark and other tree tissue. Bristles on the tongue assist in the process of grub capture. Many authorities feel that the larvae which frequently infest acorns are the principal target. Others are certain that the woodpecker is primarily after the contents of the acorns themselves. Regardless, this particular species depends on acorns as an important food source, though it chases flying insects and eats significant quantities of sap which it gathers from holes drilled for this purpose.

One attribute distinguishing this species from other woodpeckers, indeed, from many other birds as well, is a pronounced type of colonial behavior. It is social to the degree that it excavates large nesting holes for the communal tending of eggs and young. Any adult bird in the colony will feed any fledgling regardless of its parentage. Presumably, mates and food are shared in the same relaxed fashion. A well-developed colony is the place to look for the classic acorn storage places, trunks of dead or aged trees, fence posts, and wire poles, often so full of holes and acorns that one can hardly see the wood between.

Such tight interaction between organisms of the same species is not too common, but close relationships between organisms of different species in a community are frequent. When there is an intimate association between two or more dissimilar species, this is commonly spoken of as symbiosis. The term includes three basic types of such a relationship with gradients from one to the other so that there is often no abrupt shift or hard line drawn between them. They are commensalism, mutualism, and parasitism. The first implies that one organism lives with another, deriving benefit from the relationship but without injury to the partner. The second, as the word indicates, means benefit to both organisms and danger to none. The third is more sinister; one organism lives at the expense of another, even to the point occasionally of killing its host.

The woodlands of the foothills have many examples of all three symbiotic relationships, including degrees of each. Such variations in degree often reflect incomplete knowledge on our part of the exact relationship. It is difficult to know whether a certain interaction, or "coaction" as it is sometimes termed, is parasitic or semiparasitic when there are little data on the relationship involved.

The insect world is one of highly developed parasitism. In the foothills, bot flies prey on chipmunks, ground squirrels, and wood rats. Aphids suck plant juices and in turn are utilized by braconid wasps. Other sucking insects include several oak pit scales, whose injection of poisonous saliva into the bark can cause serious damage, and immature crown white flies which encrust oak leaves. Oak moths defoliate their host as do tent caterpillars, whereas the larvae of western sycamore borers and oak twig girdlers bore through the bark to the living tissue beneath. The acorns are the target for the larval forms of the filbertworm, a moth, and the California acorn weevil, in the beetle group. Gall insects are among the most fascinating of the oak-grove parasites. Small organisms known as cynipid wasps are gall makers; each species, usually restricted to one type of tree, chemically activates the host plant so that it develops a distinct form of gall. The story is by no means simple. Two generations are involved. Female wasps oviposit their eggs on leaf buds, young twigs or acorns, unopened catkins, and the like. The eggs hatch into larvae which feed on the plant tissue and make an irritating substance which stimulates the

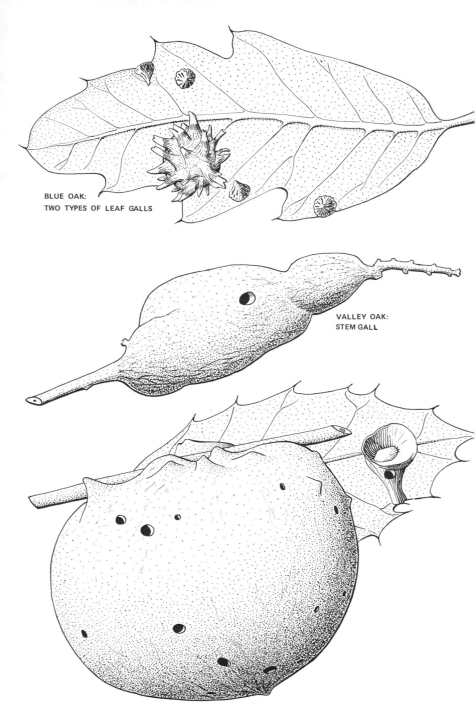

BLUE OAK:
TWO TYPES OF LEAF GALLS

VALLEY OAK:
STEM GALL

Figure 13. Several types of oak galls

INTERIOR LIVE OAK:
ALTERNATE GENERATIONS OF SAME SPECIES OF GALL WASP PRODUCED TH
VERY DIFFERENT STEM AND LEAF GALLS

tree into producing galls. The round feather-light brown pro-tuberances, or "apples," scattered on scrub or tree oaks are familiar to most of us (see Figure 13). They are really benign tumors in that large numbers of wasp attacks would be necessary to harm an oak seedling. Only female wasps develop in the large round galls which are sources of food as well as shelter. When the temperatures of spring force the oaks to bud, the wasps emerge and lay their eggs on leaf buds. Another set of galls is produced, and these are often bizarre in color and shape. Some are shiny little pink blobs bristling with antennae like the stalked eyes of snails. Others look like tiny champagne glasses. The larvae of these galls are of both sexes. When adult they mate, and the females complete the cycle by laying eggs that will hatch into "apple" gall-making larvae again.

Not only do the wasps feed on the galls; bees, woodpeckers, and ants also enjoy the sweet substance exuded from some of them. Guests, often other cynipid wasps, share the table with the original inhabitants. Both guest and host wasps are parasitized by a very pretty little iridescent blue-green chalcid wasp which, disdainful of the gall itself, feeds directly on the tiny creatures within.

Where life has spectra and range, from grass stems to oak trees, from wasps to woodpeckers, the network of its patterns is complex in structure and rich in detail. Things live on things that live on things, combining and recombining in innumerable symbiotic associations, spinning out food webs and energy chains that reflect the great diversity life has enjoyed in Californian hills.

Sycamores, Lobo Canyon, Santa Monica Mountains

8. Riverlands

No natural landscapes of California have been so altered by man as its bottomlands. The grass-rich stretches of the great Central Valley are, for the most part, lost to orchards and vineyards, cotton and alfalfa fields. Many miles of curving green ribbon along its water courses have been eradicated, replaced by the sterile concrete of flood control and navigation channels. Most of the tule marshes of the Delta country are now neatly diked rice paddies. On the freeway between San Francisco Bay and Sacramento one forgets that this was once wild land with golden beaver going about their industrious ways and great blue herons on guard with that watchful immobility so peculiarly their own. To recreate this world of slough, bank, and riverway takes more than the simple listing of what can be recalled, or guessed, was there. It needs imagination coupled with a persistent searching for the last few remnants of the original river country. It means that the bait-and-beer shacks and houseboats, and the ocean freighters and bridges must retreat from consciousness, if one is to evoke the past. Instead, walk as the Indians did on game trails through the riverine undergrowth, where silence and birdsong are complementary.

In a way, those times were harder for the Great Valley. It was alternately soaked and shriveled as the floods of spring were followed by the hot winds of summer. Then the valley knew a seasonal pattern it will never experience again as long as man controls the rivers flowing into it. Enterprising as always, the first white men to arrive here knew a good thing when they saw it, and the valley did not disappoint them. It is one of the richest pieces of agricultural land in the world today, blessed with good climate, rich soil, and an irrigation potential unequaled in the West.

To those interested in the natural landscapes of California, the Central Valley of Indian days would have been far more fascinating than it is now. None, not even the most enthusiastic sugar-beet farmer, can seriously claim that State Highway 99 from Bakersfield to Sacramento is one of California's great scenic highways. Little towns once broke the monotony of the two-lane highway back in the 1930s; but bypassed as they are by the multilaned throughway, they almost escape notice.

Two hundred years ago, the valley had many features that would have been most attractive to naturalists, professional and amateur alike: great shallow lakes in the southern end with staggering numbers of waterfowl and other birds, the many rivers flowing from the Sierran slope, and the network of woodland bordering these streams with tangles of welcome green during the warmth of summer. The Delta, where the two great river systems, the San Joaquin and the Sacramento, meet to flow out through Suisun Bay to the Golden Gate, was a vast complex of basin and island, natural levee and slough. Its marshes were host to birdlife that must have numbered in the millions, particularly in the season of migration. Roads then would have connected a series of cool shaded oases bordering riverbeds or skirted sloughs and lakes teeming with wild creatures making the valley their home.

But history brought its changes; and after the discovery of gold in the Sierra foothills it was but a matter of time until the great potential of this flat-floored topographical oddity was recognized. The last noun is used advisedly, for the Great Valley is unique in the mountainous West. There is no other flat area of comparable size west of the Rockies. Elsewhere any level terrain, such as Oregon's Willamette Valley, is either much smaller or broken by intruding hills. Any good relief map of the United States will show California's Central Valley to be an outstanding feature. Geologically, it is simple. It is merely a trough between the Coast Ranges and the Sierra Nevada, filled with thousands of feet of alluvium washed down from the surrounding mountains. Lying in the rainshadow of the Coast Ranges, the valley has a rainfall which varies from between 30 and 40 inches (76–102 cm.) near Redding to less than 7 inches (18 cm.) south of Bakersfield. Most of it is relatively dry, and its rivers are like the fingers of beneficent gods to the farmers living here. These streams ensure an underground water supply from artesian wells, and impounded behind dams, they become power and water resources without parallel in California.

The four southernmost streams, the Kern, Tule, Kaweah, and southern distributaries of the Kings, are not part of the San Joaquin river system; but irrigation has altered the original drainage patterns to some extent. Prior to reclamation measures, these rivers fed two lakes, Tulare and Buena Vista, locked in a basin by the huge alluvial fan which the Kings River system built during ages of eroding the Sierra Nevada.

The fifth of these southern Sierra streams, the San Joaquin, flows west until, deflected by the broad, alluvial plain fronting the inner Coast Range, it turns northward. The next five rivers—Merced, Tuolumne, Stanislaus, Mokelumne, and Cosumnes—feed one by one, at right angles, into the main, northward-flowing stream.

In the northern end of the Central Valley, the American, Feather, and Yuba rivers join the Sacramento which flows due south from the junction of the Pit and McCloud near the base of Mount Shasta.

There are but one or two permanent tributaries to either the Sacramento or San Joaquin rivers reaching them from the west. The detritus deposits of the few intermittent creeks are small compared with the great fans on the flanks of the Sierra. As the valley dips slightly to the west, the rivers all run to within sight of the inner Coast Range foothills before entering the main north- and south-flowing channels. Each of these major tributaries has its own delta. Collectively, in conjunction with the main bodies of the San Joaquin and Sacramento, they lace the west-central valley floor with veinlike systems of branching and rebranching channels and islands of higher land between.

Marshy areas were common in much of the valley before agricultural reclamation. A number of federal and state wildlife refuges have been established in these once vast wetlands and are hardly more than grainfields periodically and deliberately flooded. There are places, however, such as San Luis Island near Los Baños, where one can still see old slough channels, margined with woodlands, and shallow basins.

Near the confluence of the two great rivers, the land grades into several levels: the upper floor on eroded alluvial surfaces, the floodplain which is covered in times of high water, and seven basins—Butte, Marysville, Colusa, Sutter, American, Yolo, Sacramento—which lie between natural levees (known technically as *the* riverlands) and the higher levels. So-called islands are smaller land segments in the delta formed by the two rivers. Before agricultural development they were, for the most part, extensive marshland. This last landscape will be discussed in Chapter 9, and Chapter 10 will describe grasslands characteristic of the higher plains. In this chapter the primary concern is with the natural levees which, when undisturbed, support communities of towering woodland of a very special type. Such streamside vegetation has been given the name of riparian, a term in frequent use throughout these three chapters. Because it is so much like corresponding riverine woodlands in tropical savannas, or grasslands, it could be referred to as "gallery forest," though this term is often used to describe the riparian woods of the tropics.

The levees are banks of flood-borne sediments some 5 to 20 feet (1.5–6 m.) above the streambed and are up to 10 miles (16 km.) in width. Where both levees and vegetation have remained undisturbed, a heavily wooded landscape borders the river, with more open groves where the levees slope down to the neighboring floodplains. The meandering rivers are often muddy and sluggish, leaving C-shaped sloughs called oxbows where the river has abandoned its meanders in efforts to straighten its course. A gradient of a dozen or so feet (3.6 m.) separates sea level from midcourse out on the valley floor. Too slow to carry rocks, unless in flood, their floors and banks are composed of silt, sand, and gravel. Bars detach themselves from streamflow and are bare or covered with such quick-growing plants as mule fat, whose long limber stems bend with the swifter currents of flood time. During high water, the vertical banks erode into chunks which fall into the stream.

Riparian vegetation is often rampant in growth. Some of the temptation to refer to it as gallery forest is inspired by its junglelike appearance, particularly in summer when wild grape and clematis hang in thick green curtains reminiscent of the lianas in rainforest clearings. Unless one follows trails it is almost impossible to penetrate such profligacy of plant life. Not only are the trees so crowded that the foliage of one merges with that of its neighbor without interruption, but also the underlayers are savage conglomerations of fallen limbs and other debris, berry vines, wild rose snarls, poison oak patches, rank herbaceous growth, and saplings. Away from the river, the woods usually open out into more parklike stands.

It is still possible to find groves of well-developed riparian growth in certain state parks such as Caswell on the Stanislaus near Manteca, and Colusa which edges the Sacramento River 80 miles (129 km.) to the north. Here, as well as on private land, individual trees and thickets remain to give some idea of the overwhelming nature of this lowland arboreal landscape and its special character. Most of the trees of the riparian woodland (some authorities prefer to call it forest because of its density) are confined to this streamside environment or other areas of plentiful subsurface moisture. Cottonwoods and willows are the dominant trees at river edge, joined by Oregon ash, box-elder, and California black walnut on lower terraces and gravel bars that are more or less firmly in place. Though valley oaks and sycamores are components of the riparian community, they are typical of higher terraces, and the oaks thin out to less dense woodlands away from the immediate vicinity of the river. Live oaks, bay, buckeye, and white alder make appearances, particularly where streams course through the foothills. Many shrubs find themselves at home in such a favorable habitat: buttonbush, honeysuckle, snowberry, elderberry, and smaller forms of dogwood. Among the herbaceous and semi-woody plants, most of them perennial, are two considered most unwelcome by human visitors, poison oak and nettle, and three burdened with names that are singularly awkward— mule fat, the introduced horehound, and mugwort. The last, by the way, is an *Artemisia* (wormwood and sagebrush) and has the typical pungent odor of this genus. It is frequently bound with tangles of the orange string-stem parasite, dodder. All five have tall, shaggy-leaved stems in these densely shaded groves, and three—horehound, mugwort, and nettle—are nitrophiles. They are restricted to fertile soils rich in nitrogen, which are typical substrates of the community. Grass is but occasional and, where it does occur, has the long stems of shade-tolerant species. One of the relatively few annuals—a habit less suited to this lush environment where warm season moisture is seldom lacking—is the California hibiscus. This rare and handsome species with its crimson-centered flowers is restricted to wet places in the delta regions and northward to Butte County.

No place is less typical of California. One can almost expect to see the fireflies of a midwestern summer evening when the hot wind of the great valley rattles the leaves of the cottonwoods and catches back the drapery of wild vines falling from the richly embossed canopy overhead. California's familiar

evergreen natives—madroño, bay, digger pine, and the like—
are missing on the bottomlands, and the observant visitor can
make the acquaintance of a new assemblage of trees, all of
them winter deciduous. This alone is unique behavior for
much of the vegetation of the state, but there are even more
unusual features. Not only do the same or kindred species occur widely throughout the West, but all are related to well-established broadleaf species of the East.

Most of the eastern tree groups are left behind when entering the Rocky Mountains. The West has no native elms,
beeches, basswoods, or hickories, for example. The East, in
turn, cannot claim California bay or madroño, tanoak or Douglas-fir. It is an intriguing question: What is this woodland doing
here, with its deciduous oaks, its sycamore, willows, walnut,
ash, alder, boxelder, and cottonwoods—all with large, bright
green, water-lavish leaves, all with kin in Ohio, Tennessee, and
Arkansas?

Habitat provides the main clue—streambank. The deep
silty or gravelly loam soils are fertile for a number of reasons.
Subject though they are to annual runoff from snow melt, it is
short-lived, and for the rest of the year the soils of the higher
terraces are well drained, enriched by the flood-borne rock
particles and organic debris. Abundant decaying litter is the
source of additional nutrients. Furthermore, this is the one
California environment in which the plants do not have to allow for summer drought or aridity in general. Permanent
groundwater makes evergreenness less useful. There is no advantage in having foliage ready and waiting to make use of the
unreliable coincidence of spring warmth and sufficient moisture. There *is* usefulness in dormancy during the cold season.
Not only are the winter temperatures lower in the great valley
than they are on the coast, they also last longer. The lowlands
and foothills of the upper Sacramento Valley can expect frost
for six months of the year. In contrast to coastal scrub with its
average winter low temperatures of 35° F. to 40° F. (1.7°–4.4° C.)
these interior woodlands may experience average lows of 32° F.
to 38° F. (0°–3.3° C.); and dips down to 15° F. (−9.4° C.) can
occur. Long weeks of near-freezing tule or ground fogs intensify the winter chill. Rapid radiation of the earth's heat during
long winter nights cools the air below dew point. Condensation results, and dense, persistent fog blankets the valley floor
with cold, clammy mist.

Since cold air is heavy, it drains downhill and along canyon floors opening into the great valley. Bottomlands often have lower temperatures than the surrounding hills and ridges. Moreover, any winding, narrow foothill gully will be partly shaded for much of the low-sun winter day, and north-trending canyons may have little or no solar radiation. Thus four features account for local pockets of colder air: northward aspect, steep and shaded gully sides, gravity, and interior or continental-type temperature extremes. Dormancy in this period has possible survival value for trees able to depend on summer warmth *and* water, a most unusual natural combination in California. No wonder that these types, left over from ancient landscapes and unadjusted to the climate of the rest of the state, remain only in river-edge refuges where local conditions resemble those of Mississippi bayous. Boxelder, alder, ash, and certain willows are surmised to remain from the Arcto-Tertiary geoflora, the mixed conifer and hardwood forest widespread in what was then a mild and humid Northwest, whereas sycamore, Fremont cottonwood, and other willows are remnants of the semidry woodlands of the ancient Southwest and northern Mexico. As the climate became increasingly summer-dry and cooler, the trees such as magnolia, pecan, and elm that we know today from the eastern hardwood forests of North America disappeared from California, leaving only a few species now confined to riparian and other environments with permanent groundwater. Lush as they appear in all their summer splendor, our river-border forests are but impoverished scraps of much larger and richer forest and woodland communities.

For all of the environmental factors encouraging riparian growth, there are some negative features as well. River flow, particularly in flood, causes siltation, bank erosion, sandbar shift, and inundation which, if prolonged, will eventually kill most trees and shrubs. To counter these potentially destructive threats, streamside plants are vigorous sprouters from roots, trunks, branches, and even twigs. Regrowth is but a matter of time though the parent vegetation was uprooted, split apart, or otherwise injured.

To further facilitate reproduction, both the pollen and seeds of most riparian plants are readily dispersed by wind. They have numerous devices that can take advantage of the upstream and downstream drafts occurring daily in many riverine habitats. Cottonwood seeds are given additional buoyancy by attached tufts of cottony hair. Big-leaf maple and boxelder seeds are winged for increased aerodynamic efficiency.

In its natural state, the riverbank community is startlingly isolated. The gradation from grassland to tree grove is about as abrupt as that from street curb to lawn edge, particularly now when so many of the valley oaks formerly dotting the floodplains have been cut down. Transitions from one biotic community to another are termed ecotones. In most instances, it is a zone containing various elements of both vegetation types, but it often has certain features of its own. For example, the mixed evergreen forest of the hills—Douglas-fir, tanoak, madroño, bay—is transitional temporally as well as ecologically. It came into being during the confrontation of the two great Tertiary floras, Arcto- (northern) and Madro- (southern) and has elements of both. Today it is transitional, in other words, an ecotone between the mesophytic redwoods and the xerophytic brush or grasslands.

An ecotone, or meeting place of two communities, is likely to be rich in animal life. This "edge effect," as it is called, results from two habitats offering resources to shared populations; for example, one may provide shelter and the other food. There are inner and outer edges for both strips of woodland bordering a stream, making four altogether—two riverbed-grove ecotones, one on each bank, and two grove-grassland transitions. The outer ecotonal zones may be widened when forbs and grasses form an understory under extensive oak groves as at Caswell State Park. From another point of view, there are three habitats: the river itself, woodlands, and the surrounding prairie. Figure 14 illustrates what could be a typical habitat combination along the lower San Joaquin River.

Many animals use two or all three communities, though some confine most of their activities to just one. A kingfisher may choose a limb of a sycamore tree for a perching site but will restrict the business of food-getting to the river. A family of raccoons may hunt for crayfish in a slough, hide in a tree-trunk hole, and raid a farmer's orchard in one twenty-four-hour period. Aquatic insects, on the other hand, tend to remain in water or near it. Some, like dragonflies and damselflies, are water dwellers during the nymphal or immature stages, but as adults are flying predators. They usually are not far from water, however, and often pause to rest on some half-immersed log or

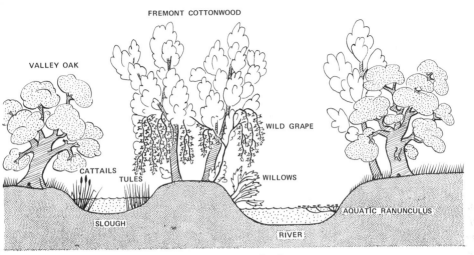

Figure 14. Riparian vegetation in the Central Valley

aquatic plant. Water striders, back swimmers, and water boat-men rarely leave their aquatic home at any stage of their development.

Tent caterpillars and boxelder bugs, which utilize certain species of riparian trees, pay little or no attention to the river. The former weave webby shrouds filled with a nerve-unsettling mess of wiggling larvae feeding off the imprisoned leaves of such trees as cottonwoods. Whole branches can be defoliated by the voracious caterpillars. Attracted by the rich riparian vegetation and its food resources, many other insects are common—butterflies, day-flying moths, wasps, and bees among them. Such a wealth of insect life in turn attracts their feeders. Aquatic insect species are sought by the native and introduced fish of these lowland rivers—carp, squawfish and other local minnows, bass, bullhead, bluegill, and perch. Even though dams prevent their free access to the higher interior streams, salmon, steelhead trout, and lampreys regularly use the Sacramento and San Joaquin riverways for spawning.

Flying insects are not only taken by the leaping fish such as trout but by insectivorous birds that find these riverine groves good hunting grounds. The deciduous habit of much of the vegetation encourages heavy use by summer visitors as well as the year-around residents. Wilson's and yellow warblers, yellowthroat and chat flit and flutter from tree to tree searching for insects that are abundant because of the many sources of food supplied by the rich plant life. Bell's vireos and willow flycatchers are equally active. Downy woodpeckers tip-tap their way through the riveredge strip of trees. Flickers call from snags, and the rare yellow-billed cuckoos are seldom seen anywhere else. Bewick's and house wrens find the environment to their liking, and many knotholes have wrens' nests. Swainson's thrushes are shy and usually prefer to remain in plant cover whereas western bluebirds take advantage of the edge effect, perching on tree limbs when surveying more open country for insect food. Each high snag seems to have a watchful avian predator—white-tailed kites and Cooper's, redtailed, and red-shouldered hawks. They watch for movements of basking lizards or adventurous rodents. Great horned and long-eared owls take their places at night. Where the shrub and herbaceous growth is rich, seed-eaters such as goldfinches, song sparrows, black-headed and blue grosbeaks, and towhees are constantly at work. "Bullock's" and hooded orioles hang their nests in cottonwoods and willows and are exquisite flashes of orange and black against the peridot green of the canopy.

In the backwaters of sloughs, western pond turtles look like suspended lumps as they float, nose out, just under the quiet surface. Tiger and California slender salamanders frequent banks and pockets of moist earth or debris. Being insect feeders in part, their riverine life should satisfy any tastes they have for such a diet. Though raccoons and the once plentiful golden beaver never stray too far from the river edge, gray foxes, cottontails, coyotes, jack rabbits, and striped skunks travel back and forth from river to grassland or, to be more accurate, to the farmfields of the present time. Not only is a variety of food available for herbivore and carnivore alike, but cover is handy in these dense thickets. The shade afforded by riparian growth is most welcome in the heat of the day. Small rodents such as harvest and deer mice tend to stay close to seed-rich areas for food; many of the ground layer tangles are tunneled with their runways. Moles find the silty soil easy to excavate, and duskyfooted woodrats are very much at home in all the litter and debris from profuse plant life.

At one time, golden beaver, a variant of the well-known aquatic mammal, were plentiful in the Central Valley. Today they are controlled to the point of occasional occurrence. Unlike their mountain-dwelling relatives, they rarely build lodges but prefer to dig dens in the banks lining slough and stream. For this reason they are also called bank beaver. When they do construct lodges they use tules as well as the boughs and mud commonly associated with the efforts of these intriguing rodents. They feed on the bark of riparian trees as well as other available vegetative material such as tules or even suitable food from planted crops. Though they seldom build dams in these lowland streams, their activities have resulted in damage to irrigation installations. They are considered a nuisance, and the valley is one of the few places in North America where beaver may be taken at any time if the person wishing to do so can provide proof of damage and has a permit.

When fall nudges summer out of the way, these woodlands imitate, somewhat timidly, the color sequence of their eastern counterparts. The cottonwoods and willows turn butter yellow, and their leaves drift down onto levee tops and floodplains. The foliage of valley oaks bronzes before it drops. Boxelder and ash leaves become light tan and look as fragile as charred paper. Then the sycamores expose trunks of mottled cream and white and massive boughs which bend and angle in all directions. Tufts of mistletoe are obvious now, unscreened by summer's canopy. The rain-gray skies of February wrap the bare twigs and branches in their own kind of melancholy. Juncos may pick in the more open glades, but the rich lushness of summer with its counterpoint of bird chorus seems very far away. Fourth of July picnics in the oak groves seem as unlikely as Roman orgies until April opens silky green leaf buds, and warblers return to the willows. Seasonal California tells a special kind of story in her riverlands.

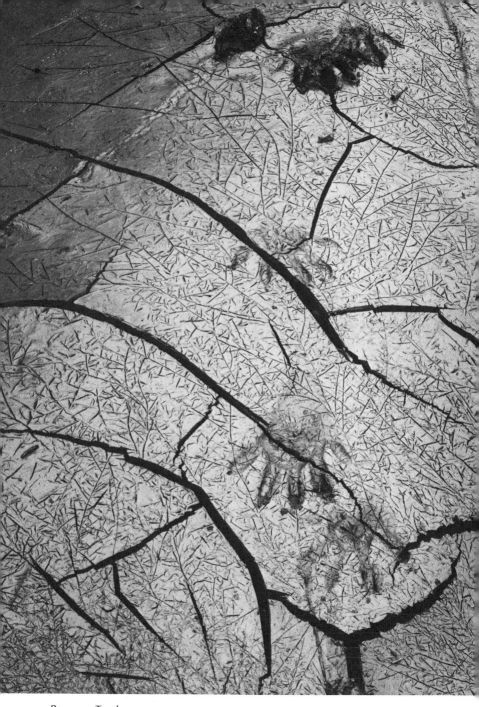

Raccoon Tracks

9. Red-Winged Blackbird

He clung to the swaying tule, his left foot higher than his right. Through binoculars both legs looked like thin, dried twigs bent at sharp angles, particularly where his feet grabbed the stem in little knobby-cornered rectangles. Above his slender underpinnings, he was ebony and red. As he swung in the cool wind of a May morning, he flicked his tail and displayed the flame-bright shoulder patches that have given him his name. From time to time he clipped a short, crisp chirp. Then a dark gray female flew overhead and settled on the branch of a nearby willow tree. He immediately hunched his shoulders, bowed his head; and as the epaulets opened into elegant scarlet puffs, he flung out that ringing *kon-ka-reeeee!* that is the marshland's carillon of spring.

The couple was not alone. All around, black and red wings dropped to the tule and cattail thickets or rose to take off for fields and trees bordering the slough. The clucks and the calls, the comings and goings were those of busy, sociable creatures, flocking with their own kind in a habitat of their preference. Red-winged blackbirds have rather rigid requirements for nesting places, and they seldom choose any other environment than freshwater marshes, rich in the sedges, cattails, and reeds they need for shelter and nesting material.

Wet or damp places are not uncommon features of the earth's surface. In fiction, the three words, *bog, swamp,* and *marsh,* are used casually, often synonymously, along with terms inherited from dramatic fiction indigenous to the British Isles: fen, heath, and moor, where countless lovers have had misadventures in forbidding, treacherous, and often mucky wastelands symbolic of death. Many aquatic habitats, however, have a wealth of life. Though evolution has destined numerous species to arid environments, every living cell, plant or animal, is a microscopic puddle in which the genetic material determining what we are is suspended in what could be called the liquid of life. Water in some form or another is absolutely necessary in the life cycle of every living organism.

Most aquatic habitats are potentially rich in living things. This is true of the sea and its littoral, and of the bays and sloughs of the saltwater world. Freshwater environments, such as swamps, bogs, and marshes, share this wealth. Though these words are often used interchangeably, they have definite and separate meanings. A freshwater marsh usually has shallow water clogged with dense masses of sedges, cattails, rushes, reeds, and other types of aquatic herbaceous vegetation. Pools of open water are commonly present unless plant material has accumulated to the extent of crowding them out. Bogs have a unique vegetation characteristic of poorly drained lakes and ponds. Sphagnum moss and other plants coagulate in floating masses or islets which sometimes loosely cover the entire water surface. Plants of the heather family are often present as they tolerate the cold, acid, waterlogged, and peaty soils characteristic of the true bog. Swamps are distinguished from marshes in that they have shrubs and trees, though they also may have vegetation typical of the other two environments. All three have two features in common which differentiate them from the freshwater habitats typical of streams and rivers. They have abundant, conspicuous plant life and have standing rather than running water.

California has few true bogs, as they tend to be confined to northern latitudes and the once-glaciated midcontinental states around the Great Lakes. A cooler climate seems to be a requisite of their formation, but a number of small pitcher plant bogs are located in the northern part of the state. Swamps are plentiful in the American South with its water-soaked baldcypress groves. Though some swamps occur in California—along the riverways of the lower Colorado River, in the delta of the Sacramento and San Joaquin rivers, and elsewhere—most of the state's native trees requiring large amounts of water are riparian in habitat. They grow in edge forests along the banks of rivers and streams where the substrate may be damp, but not covered with water except during floods. However, marshes are, or were, numerous in the Delta, up north in the Klamath country, and in coastal and interior drainages where water slows down and accumulates.

Although we tend to employ the words *river, creek, brook,*

lake, pond, and *pool* as loosely as the three we have just discussed, they have usefully different meanings. River, creek, and brook imply running water. The first is the largest of these three landscape features; the last is the smallest. Within a region of uniform climate they frequently share the same biota, that is, the inventory of living species found in any one community. Among the factors determining the biotic composition of California's stream environments are amount of brackishness (significant in the lower Delta), water temperature, seasonal fluctuation, rate of flow, and, in recent times, degree of pollution. Cold and rapid streams contain more dissolved oxygen than those that are warm and slow. Consequently, aquatic organisms requiring ample supplies of this gas are limited to life in fast, cool water. California's sluggish lowland rivers are not well aerated. They are akin to marshes in the biota they support and, indeed, are often paternal to such soggy places— sloughs formed from water cut off in oxbows or spread in overflow basins. The word *stream,* incidentally, refers to any flow of water of any size.

Lakes, ponds, and pools are bodies of standing water, and like the terms for running water indicate a size range. They intergrade with other wetland environments. Intermittent streams dry into puddles that eventually disappear until the next wet season and are related to a special type of pool, springtime or vernal—"hog wallows," as they are sometimes called in the Central Valley. The biota of these evanescent pools, saline or fresh, depends on its ability to exist in some manner through the dry season. Permanent ponds and lakes, though these may be involved in a long-term successional change from a wet habitat to a dry one, have stable communities that change little from year to year. They are found in lowland sloughs where river water spreads into a sink or basin and in higher country where they are often the heritage of lava flow obstruction or where cirques scooped out by glacial action and other natural depressions collect down-draining water. Lowland lakes often have extensive marshlike or swampy areas around their borders and in bays and inlets.

After the initial open water phase, invasion by marsh vegetation begins, and chances are that time will gradually close out any remaining pool-like areas as living plants and their dead debris enlarge the ever-growing clumps and brakes. Man interrupts the process when he drains marshland, accomplishing in one year what would take nature centuries to do, that is, change it from wet land to dry.

The Delta and its bewildering waterways have their special terms—bypass, cutoff, cut, wasteway, slough, sink, tract, island, canal, river, channel, dike, levee, and aqueduct. The first settlers added their anxieties and needs to these words—Little Potato Slough, Whiskey Slough, Bacon Island, Disappointment Slough, Hope Trace, and Poverty Road. No doubt life, property, and economy were all somewhat precarious in the sometimes drowned, sometimes desiccated bottomlands until control from levees and dams imposed the dependability so necessary to the farmers of the Delta.

Before these reclamation efforts, there were many square miles of tule-choked marsh. When the problems were removed so was much of this wetland which, when drained, made an excellent place for crops. Today only a few sloughs and a basin or two still resound with the calls of red-winged blackbirds. Most of the original wetlands are now rice or produce fields, spreading out in tidy rectangles enclosed by dikes. If one really hunts for the last remnants of the marshes, one can find them: around Trapper's Slough west of Stockton, in Butte Sink, along the Yolo and Sutter bypasses, and in the quiet little side waters here and there, the cattails still grow tall and release their seeds to the westerly winds of the Antioch Gap. Look for these small watery worlds. Stand, perhaps, on a dike in the Gray Lodge Wildlife Area where a wealth of wildfowl pauses on migratory wanderings along the Pacific flyway to glean in croplands planted for its benefit. Or watch quietly beside some riverside pond. One can become an observer of life as rich as that of a tide pool, but often as unobtrusive as that of a decaying log in a lodgepole pine forest. Most of the organisms of a marsh go about their business hidden under the water surface or in the tangled screen of its vegetation.

The similarities of fresh or brackish water environments to the salt marshes and tidelands of the sea are apparent upon observation of their biota. Once again we meet plankton at one end of the size range, and birds and the larger fish at the other, with all manner of intermediate-size organisms in between—crustaceans, molluscs, worms, coelenterates, sponges, and bryozoans among them. Salinity fluctuates from place to place, and tidal rise and fall occurs some distance upstream from Suisun Bay; but there are major differences. No great tidal surge brings food and oxygen to marsh dwellers. In compensation, they do not have to undergo the risk of low-tide exposure and desiccation, though flood and drought are possible risks. Insects reach an importance they never have in tide pools; on the other hand, molluscs are seldom found in large numbers in most freshwater habitats, but there are exceptions such as the alien Manila clam whose success in colonizing California's inland waters is phenomenal.

Every body of quiet standing water, salt or fresh, demands several basic adjustments on the part of its residents. In the first place, they must adapt themselves to inadequate oxygen. There are several reasons why marshes may lack this essential element. Running water aerates itself as it tumbles around boulders, down rocky stretches, or over waterfalls. A major source of oxygen in water is plant life. In the process of photosynthesis, oxygen is released. The tiny primitive organisms—bacteria, fungi, and the like—responsible for the decomposition of the dead material on the floor of the marsh have no green bodies, or chloroplasts; therefore, they do not photosynthesize. They use oxygen in the process of respiration, as do most living things, but they do not liberate it. Instead, they release methane or marsh gas. The green plants, on the other hand, present in the aquatic environment add to the available store of oxygen. In addition, some of this element is absorbed directly from the contact surface between air and water; in general, however, it is scarce in these stagnant, often warm pools. As the temperature of water rises, its oxygen-holding capacity decreases.

As a result, marsh dwellers have developed many ingenious ways to make sure they obtain enough oxygen. Giant water bugs, the formidable "toebiters," and a number of aquatic beetles capture air from the surface of the pond, forming bubbles they wear like silver cloaks or trap under wing covers. For many of the beetles the original oxygen in their tiny portable "tanks" is augmented by additional amounts diffused into the bubble from the surrounding water. Riffle beetles depend upon the oxygen from a blanket of air caught in tiny hairs on their bodies. As well as using air chambers, back swimmers ease up to the surface and head down, thrust their abdomens to the air which enters and diffuses through their suspended bodies. Immature forms of many of these creatures as well as damselflies, caddisflies, and other aquatic insects have external gills located on segments of the abdomen or at its end which absorb oxygen. Some are leaflike; others are collections of tiny, sometimes branching tufts. A few species such as the predaceous water beetles have caudal (tail-end) breathing pores, which they raise to the water surface. Many aquatic insects have a number of successive larval forms, the most immature of which are in themselves large gills as they absorb oxygen cutaneously, that is, directly through the cuticle. Dragonfly nymphs have internal gills that draw water into the rectum and expel it. In addition, this means of respiration is also a form of jet propulsion and affords the tiny animal a means of moving about. Mosquito wrigglers have breathing pores at the tip of snorklelike breathing tubes that they frequently extend up to the water surface. Fish must also adjust; and those, like trout, needing a great amount of dissolved oxygen keep to streams where it is plentiful. Sluggish stream fish such as carp are often surface gulpers, and tadpoles have the same habit. They must begin early in adjusting to life out of water.

Green plants also need oxygen for respiratory activity. Fortunately, it is a product of photosynthesis, and many marsh plants have air spaces in their stems to store a surplus for future use. Aquatic plants have made many adjustments to their habitat. Floating species have air pockets scattered through the tissues of their leaves and stems for buoyancy. As water screens out solar radiation, submerged plants must cope with the diminished supply of light. Their stems and leaves have thin "skins," that is, little or no cuticle, and the gas exchange necessary to photosynthesis and respiration can take place directly and readily from water to plant and vice versa. The chloroplasts, or food-making green bodies, are concentrated in or just under the surface tissue to make the most efficient use of their unique ability. Many amphibious plants simultaneously grow two types of leaves which differ markedly in appearance. Those that are submerged are finely divided to provide more surfaces through which gas exchange can take place. Those reaching to the air are coarser, and the leaf pores or stomata are more numerous on upper surfaces of floating foliage. Emergent vegetation—tules and other bulrushes, cattails, reeds—is confined to shallow margins and hummocks as much of the individual plant is usually above water. Moisture is abundant in the substrate, making large root systems unnecessary. The stems often have connected air chambers assisting the transport of gases to the submerged portion of the plants.

Rank, coarse growth of such vegetation clutters the edges around open water, along with witch-caldron brews of thick green pond scum (filamentous algae), sheets of duckweed and the unrelated duckweed fern, and attractive islets of such flowering plants as smartweed, yellow waterweed, marsh pennywort, curly-leafed dock, and arrowhead. Small jungles of interwoven stems and matted leaves discourage mammalian predators and baffle avian enemies of nesting birds. Marsh wrens, rails, bitterns, and red-winged and yellow-headed blackbirds rely on the shelter afforded by the tangled vegetation. Even such sharp-eyed predators as marsh hawks, watching with interest the progress of the breeding season, find nest raiding difficult in the concealing marsh plant cover. Western and eared grebes and coots sometimes scorn such screening and use the plentiful plant material to build small floating masses on which they lay their eggs out in more open water.

Whistling swans and various geese—Canada, white-fronted, and snow—are winter gleaners in the grainfields and crop lands fringing many of the Delta marshes. As they are visitors, they need food, not nesting cover. A number of ducks are commonly or occasionally resident here and make good use of the diversity of diet and nest site in the wetland habitat, among them, mallards, gadwalls, redheads, and ruddies. The first two are dabblers, utilizing mostly plant food, but both may take to neighboring crop fields for further foraging. The last two are divers and feed at or near the bottom of the pond for the plant food that makes up the bulk of their diet.

Blue-winged and cinnamon teal are summer guests, though the latter is increasingly a year-round resident; but pintail, American widgeon, and green-winged teal settle in the marshes of the Central Valley during the cooler months, often in impressive numbers. Startled from their quiet feeding, they wing past by the thousandfold, riffling across the pink-and-gray of a winter's dawn or the freshly laundered sky left by a solstitial storm.

Most of the shorebirds with which we have become acquainted earlier in the book visit the inland marshes: greater yellowlegs, avocets, stilts, sandpipers, long-billed curlews, egrets, and black-crowned night, green, and great blue herons. White-faced ibis, gallinules, and Virginia rails are partial to screening thickets of cattails, tules, and other emergent marsh vegetation for nest site and material.

Underwater plant material provides concealment or anchor base for fish, insect, and snail eggs; pupa cases; various types of larvae and nymphs; molluscs; and crustaceans such as crayfish. Stems, root masses, submerged leaves, and the undersides of floating leaves offer attachment sites and shelter, protecting numerous small residents of the marsh.

Many aquatic insects, adult and immature forms alike, are strongly predaceous, quick to hunt down and attack any suitable prey. Dragonflies and damselflies, for all their gauze-winged elegance, are "hawking" as they hover over ponds and other quiet water. Such varying aquatic forms as back swimmers, water striders, and creeping water bugs are all classified as true bugs which also includes the fearsome-looking toebiter, giant of its family. Much of the group is aggressive, assaulting all possible victims unfortunate enough to come to its attention. One diving beetle actually feeds on small fish.

A marsh and its surrounding feeding grounds form an ecosystem. The creatures found in it, with the exception of bird and terrestrial insect visitors, remain within its borders and seldom venture beyond. Energy, the capacity for performance, once it enters the marsh, cycles from the various plant producers to and through the consumers of the habitat's characteristic food webs.

All the energy powering the biotic world originates from the sun. Plants are the conversion factories changing solar energy to chemical energy through the remarkable process of photosynthesis. Such diverse forms as huge trees and single-celled green algae share this ability. One of the milestones of evolutionary history is the amazing capacity to use the energy of sunlight and, through chlorophyll, combine certain basic chemical elements into nutritious material. Not only useful for the food needs of the plant, these nutrients are basic for all the animal kingdom's energy requirements. Unlike plants, animals cannot directly utilize solar energy. They depend on food to power the activities of life. Food chains spin into food webs that enmesh the living world through interdependencies without number. As the initial "chunks" of solar energy, captured in leaf, root, seed, stem, and flower, are ingested into the bodies of the first order consumers, or herbivores, part of this energy is used to build and repair animal tissue, part is discarded through elimination, but part of it is burned through activity and dissipated as heat. When the herbivores are consumed in turn by second order consumers, or carnivores, more of the initial solar energy escapes as heat, though the efficiency of energy transfer increases with each step away from the plant base. So it goes until the last of the original energy is used by decomposers, as they in turn break up what matter is left into basic chemicals needed by plants. It is a remarkable

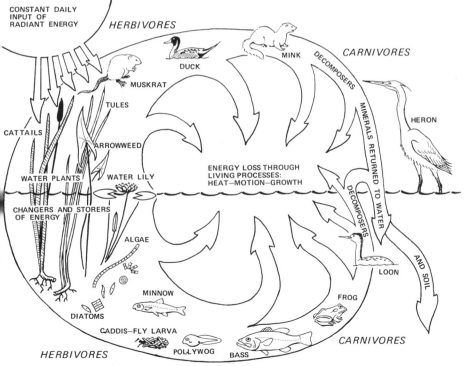

Figure 15. Typical freshwater marsh energy flow patterns

cycle; none of the matter is really lost. At the end of what may be a long journey, the final organisms of decay sift back to the earth the basic nutrients needed for the nourishment of plants which then resurrect it in the form of their own tissue.

Energy flow routes, through food webs, are not too difficult to discover in the microcosm of a marsh. Some of the chains begin with worms, snails, and immature insects cleaning microscopic algae from submerged rocks and logs. Comparable to the marine environment, one-celled algal forms—diatoms and the like—are present in the waters of the marsh. Protozoa and other microscopic animals comprise zooplankton, also a food source. Many plankton feeders have developed devices to strain out the tiny organisms on which they feed. Fresh or decaying plant life of larger size is eagerly sought by such diverse forms as ducks and insect larvae. Occupying important positions in marshland food chains, rotifers, daphnia, copepods, ostracods, molluscs, and insects enlarge the menu for predaceous species. These include fish, freshwater jellyfish, amphibians, carnivorous insects (including immature forms), shorebirds, and waterfowl. Many marsh residents are omnivorous and eat anything from tadpoles to pond slime, arrowweed tubers (also called duck potatoes) to caddisfly larvae. The ubiquitous coot is one of such feeders, as, on a smaller scale, is the water boatman which ingests and grinds up tiny organisms, plant and animal, in the ooze on which it feeds. Scavengers are common in the wetlands. Debris feeders—sandfly larvae, crayfish, worms, amphipods, etc.—grab the last morsels before the decomposers reduce them to elemental ingredients.

As the potential energy within the last plankton meal of a hapless rotifer is transferred to its captor and on through successive and inevitable food chains, each progressive marshland consumer uses its share until all that remain of carcass and wastes are basic substances. They can only be reassembled by the indirect energy of sunlight acting on carbon, hydrogen, and oxygen pulled into plants of the wetlands and creating new food through the catalytic agency of chlorophyll.

It is no wonder that a marsh, with all its generosity of food sources, is a community rich in animal residents. It rings with bird calls and the sonorous honk of bullfrogs. Marsh hawks (northern harriers) hover, hoping for a garter snake, but make do with a dragonfly. Wrens clutch bobbing tule stems, eyes alert for damselflies. Pools mirror grebes, ducks, and coots feeding, clucking, swimming with that effortless-appearing ease behind clumps of cattails as aesthetically pleasing as though arranged by some artful human hand. Wilson's snipe and greater yellowlegs work over the mud, exposed where a pond is slowly shrinking under the summer sun, for small crustaceans and insects. Feet resting on dimpled pockets in the water surface, water striders dart about with incredible agility, hunting for any small animals they can capture, including others of their own kind. Red-winged blackbirds have many neighbors, large and small, which by the simple act of living, open their own accounts in the energy-nutrient bank and withdraw from them until death. What remains of them is transferred to other accounts in an endless cycling of resources.

Annual Grasses, Conejo Valley

10. California's Kansas

It must have been a living sea—brilliantly green in April and richly tawny in August as the glinting grass bounced back the sun. Early travelers marveled at the vast flat floor of the Great Valley, its *tulares* alive with wild birds and its rivers wandering through hedgerow woodlands. But most probably they viewed with keenest interest and speculation the great wind-riffled prairies. Only three vegetation communities originally occurred here; and their distribution was dependent on the available moisture. The riverlands with their dense riparian woods and navigable streams were both useful and trouble-some to the first settlers. One could hunt the animals seeking shelter in the rank vegetation, cut down trees for construction or firewood, and use the waterways for transport; but the sloughs and channels imposed barriers to both foot and stock traffic, especially during the wet season. The marshes were, except for duck and geese hunting, largely useless. Indeed, their soggy interiors forced the slow travel of the day into wide detours. During the runoff, much of the valley was a flooded wasteland that denied permanent use and settlement.

The prairies were something else again, particularly those on higher ground which, in normal years, stood above the flooded bottomlands. They were covered, for the most part, with perennial bunchgrasses which quickened and died in a seasonal rhythm changed but little since the present climate regime took over from that of the Pleistocene. The green of spring is followed by the gold of summer. In the open rangelands of the Central Valley this sequence of color is as inflexible as the tidal timeclock of the sea. In spite of the problems posed by such pronounced seasonal changes, the white man recognized the promise of the grasslands. The original prairie, which has now all but disappeared, contributed an undisputedly important chapter to the story of the state's agricultural growth.

The title chosen for this chapter implies a comparison of California prairies with those of the Great Plains. There are resemblances and differences. Both regions were originally quite similar in appearance and in type of vegetation, and they owe their grasslands to low and often undependable rainfall. The regions are dissimilar in cold season temperature averages and the time and length of the growing season. The Great Plains experience far more severe winters than does the Central Valley. Blizzards and freezes characterize their cold months; whereas lowland California rarely has a temperature drop lower than 25° F. ($-3.8°$ C.), and such a period of chill does not last for any length of time. The midcontinental states enjoy summer rainfall, however, and California's Great Valley seldom does, except for a very occasional thunderstorm. Such conditions mean that the period of dormancy—when the plants die, leaving seeds, nascent shoots, or underground root masses—is almost reversed. Late spring and summer is the growing season for Kansas, late winter to midspring for this part of California. Dissimilarities of growth habit are also apparent. The Central Valley has a number of indigenous annuals in contrast to the paucity of such types in the Great Plains, but it lacks the abundance of sod-forming species so typical of the latter region. Instead, the valley's perennial grasses are bunchgrasses. The shoots begin at the basal nodes and extend up within the hollow sheaths of old dried stems. Sod formers have underground rhizomes—modified shoots from which both roots and leafy stems develop. Both regions relax in fall, one in preparation for a winter of bitter cold, the other for the first warm days after the onslaught of the autumnal rains. The perennial grasses are ready to spring into action and take advantage of favorable temperatures and available moisture, sparse though it might be.

The climatic and edaphic features that regulate much of the other rangeland in low-elevation coastside (as opposed to desertside) California also controlled the original valley prairies. The oak-pine woodlands with their carpeting understory of grass, the balds and *potreros* (Spanish for pasture) of the coastal hills, as well as what remains of the range in the Great Valley must bow to the commands of sun and rain, soil and slope face. The rules have not changed though foothill and valley grasslands have undergone profound alterations since white men entered the region. Not only have thousands of acres (hectares) been turned over to agricultural pursuits, it is no exaggeration to say also that most original native grasses of low-altitude California have been replaced by immigrant species. This successful invasion is one of the most striking examples of its kind to be found anywhere. Aside from the deliberate introduction of agricultural and urban development, no other plant community in western North America has changed so much, over such large areas, and in so short a period of time. Forests and brushlands, after fire or commercial removal, tend to return to their former composition, if left alone. But California's grasslands will never again look as they did before the great "catastrophe" of civilization's arrival. Too many aggressive newcomer plants have settled down and are doing very well in their adopted land. Though some of the alien grasses and forbs were deliberately introduced from southern Europe and elsewhere, most appeared accidentally. Mixed with crop seed or straw packing, caught in the hair or wool of imported livestock, or dropped from their feed or in their wastes, the seeds of the foreign annuals found a fertile land and a familiar climate.

How did the invading species achieve their spectacular victory? Many factors contributed to the ease of the rout. The native perennial bunchgrasses do not cover the ground completely, but they leave small patches of bare soil between their clumps which are open to invasion. Besides needing dependable soil moisture for optimum production, they do not recover well from heavy and continuous grazing. This is especially true if springtime foliage is removed before it has time to manufacture enough food to replace reserves used in making the season's new growth. When these grasses are cropped and crippled, water and nutriment demands are much reduced. Invading herbaceous species benefit from the increased supply of these essentials. Perennials also grow more slowly than do the vigorous annual species.

Curiously enough, the first grasses to benefit from the impact of the white man's coming were California's own annuals. They took advantage of the plight of the perennials, now heavily besieged. Through remote eras of time, the bunchgrasses had provided fodder and feed for the many herbivorous animals—ruminants such as elk and antelope, rodents, lagomorphs, and even insects—but they had never been subjected to the trampling and concentrated grazing of large herds of domestic livestock. Most animals prefer the more palatable perennials over the often less nutritious annuals. During the mission and rancho years of California history, overgrazing, particularly in the coastal areas, thinned the ranks of the bunchgrasses, enlarging the bare spaces that were already present because of the growth habit of these species. Ready for invasion into the disturbed areas were both the native annuals such as sixweeks fescue and the aggressive newcomers.

By the 1850s immigrant species were expanding into the Central Valley, though at that time its perennial grasses were suffering comparatively little damage as the number of livestock was still rather small. A drought lasting into the 1860s, however, followed by a large increase in cattle and sheep so weakened the remaining natives that the immigrant species took command. The weedier types—wild oats, soft chess, ripgut, nitgrass, and silver hairgrass along with wild mustard and filaree—marched into abandoned wheat and other crop fields, overburdened pasturage, and the periodically drought-stricken rangeland.

Annual grasses have much that contributes to their pioneering and opportunistic qualities. They react immediately to reviving rains and produce numerous seeds even under adverse circumstances. Many of them, such as goatgrass and mouse barley, are poor forage as they dry out quickly, are rough in texture, and have barbs or other objectionable features harmful to stock. The less desirable species escape the pressure to which the preferred types are subjected, allowing the former to spread to new terrain. Grazing, incidentally, is by no means always damaging. Light use actually stimulates the plants and during drought may prove of value. When they are kept small by casual cropping they need less water which, however, is then available for tarweed and less desirable plants. Even moderate use at the wrong time may destroy reproductive tissue before the seeds are set and thus slow the annual recovery rate.

The needlegrasses, melicgrass, wildryes, bluegrasses, deergrass, and perennial bromes with their long graceful stems growing from roots and the compact mats of vegetative material from previous years have retreated from the fields of the Great Valley. With them went many of the animals and other plants which, in adjusting to each other by the laws of communal living, had succeeded in creating an extensive and flourishing community. Though it appeared to be stable, and its species were those well adapted to conditions of soil and climate, the inherent weaknesses of its dominant plants and white man's fatal advent compounded its doom. What lowland prai-

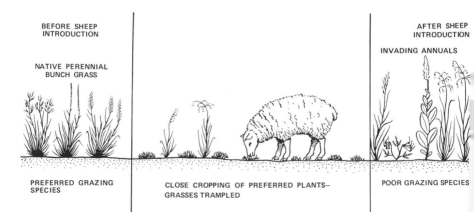

Figure 16. History of alien grass invasion in interior prairie

rie remains in the vast tracts of peach groves, grape vineyards, alfalfa, and sugar beets is a poor kind of thing—too small in size, or too alkaline for other than a few specially adapted species, or bristling with sock-infesting foxtails.

Such tenacious barbs on the seeds of many of the invading grasses proved of no uncertain value in the spreading of their populations. Some of the attributes of weedy plants are unique types of seed dispersal. The early settlers did not plow the range and sow it to filaree. All they did was to bring it here, and the spirally twisted hairs at the ends of its seeds saw to its distribution. They curl and uncurl with changes in air moisture. Such motion propels the seeds along the ground until suitable germination sites are encountered. Seeds with barbs or hooks are dispersed by the animals to which they become attached. Tumbleweed, another obnoxious import from Europe, rolls with any breeze, scattering its seeds as it literally sails along. No doubt dandelion is prevalent in gardens and lawns because of the tiny parasols of its seeds which are wind-wafted for considerable distances. There are so many devices to ensure ease of dispersion that one would think that species without such special adaptations of this sort would never get a chance to replace themselves. But fortunately for the less adventurous plants, other features of the environment have their influences as well; and in the end, it is those types which best balance their tolerances and their needs that remain members of the community.

There were three variations from the monotony of the seemingly endless rangeland, two seasonal and one edaphic. Winter rain and springtime warmth not only awakened the grasses, but encouraged in many places a rich floral display. The rosy owl's clover, pale yellow cream cup, bird's-eye gilia, popcorn flower, lavender thistle sage, blue lupine, and sunlit poppy were first to bloom, followed by such bulbs as blue dicks, blue-eyed-grass, harvest brodiaea, and mariposa lilies. To this day, where rangeland still rises above the crops of the valley floor, wild flower fields are visited by thousands of enthusiasts in nostalgic search for the remnants of what must have been a Persian rug of color.

Certain curious patterns of wildflowers in what are called "hog wallows," or vernal pools, have attracted much botanical attention. They are small depressions in which rainwater collects. As the pool evaporates, concentric rings or garlands of certain annual forbs and grasses succeed each other until the last plants on the now hard, cracked clay floor of the pool succumb to summer drought. Though such springtime pools occur in Riverside and San Diego counties and in suitable places in the Coast Ranges, most are found in either old or new alluvial terraces on both sides of the Great Valley, but particularly on the east. They also occur on volcanic areas of Tehama and Shasta counties and in southern Oregon. As summer drought is a prerequisite for their development, one would assume that they would be a feature of all regions of Mediterranean climate, and apparently vernal pools are found elsewhere in Mediterranean Europe and South Africa.

Groups of pools are often separated by small hillocks called mima mounds (after similar mounds in southeastern Washington). Speculation about their origin ranges from activity by extinct giant pocket gophers to expansion of subsurface clay beds, but no one theory has yet been accepted as the correct explanation for mima mound formation. Other conclusions about these unique wetlands are undisputed. All have impervious clay- or hardpans or rock horizons that trap water in the depressions for varying amounts of time, depending upon the size of the pool and other conditions. Some remain full from the first generous storms to late spring; others are full only intermittently and dry soon after each rain. According to one authority, those that are wet only for a day or two at a time should be called hog wallows.

Wild oats, poppies, lupines, and other annuals typical of valley grassland surround the pools, but from the moist margins down to the submerged or muddy bottom a sequence of more or less amphibious species appears in response to such environmental factors as depth of water, length of inundation, and the pH and temperature of soil and water. Many plants such as the elegantly blue-blossomed *Downingia* and a number of the aptly named popcorn flowers germinate and remain as seedlings under water and then flower after the surface moisture is receding or has disappeared. Others like water starwort and spike rush complete their life cycle while still in standing water.

To come unexpectedly upon one of these spring-fresh pools is an enchanting experience. One sees it only from one point in time and must guess what was there before and what will come after. Typically one would see garlands of goldfields, brilliantly yellow against the newly verdant grassland, cream-colored Johnny tuck, and lacy masses of meadowfoam around the upper edges followed by white rings of popcorn flower at lower zones as it can tolerate longer periods of inundation. The most startling display is that of the *Downingia*—of the lobelia family. They often fill the center of the depression in pools of blue that replace the reflected sky of the now receded water. Conditions vary from pool to pool and season to season and with them corresponding fluctuations in succession patterns.

The flora of California's vernal pools is a special assortment of about 200 species that are either restricted to or are associated with this particular habitat. Most are annuals, and a surprising 91 percent are natives in contrast to the highly foreign nature of the adjacent grassland. Sixty-nine percent are endemic to the California Floristic Province, reflecting the islandlike isolation of the pool environment as well as its unique demands. One such genus is *Orcuttia,* a rare and unusual grass with six species that are confined to vernal pools. In contrast to the amphibious plants discussed above, *Orcuttia* sprouts in late spring after the pond's water has begun to evaporate and continues its life cycle rooted in the mud of the drying pool bed. It has physical and behavioral characteristics setting it apart from most of the other California grasses—its fruits (seeds) must be immersed in watery mud for several months preceding germination—and it has been speculated that *Orcuttia* and a close relative, *Neostapfia,* are old genera that developed on the edges of the ancient shallow inland sea that once filled portions of the Great Valley prior to the Ice Age.

Like many other California landscapes, vernal pools are threatened by human encroachment, a tragic fate considering the uniqueness of both the environment and its plant life. One set of pools near Pixley in the southern San Joaquin Valley has been declared a research reserve by The Nature Conservancy, a private organization that is also attempting to acquire other pools in the state. A number of other groups are also trying to preserve remaining pool sites, but it is feared that recreational misuse, housing tracts, and projected roads will destroy these fascinating places. *Orcuttia* and other vernal pool endemics have been declared endangered species.

Where the substrate is heavy with salts and other solutes to which is given the name "alkali," only certain plants will grow.

They must be able to compensate for a potential reversal of osmosis or fatal wilting will take place. Two native perennial grasses, alkali sacaton and salt grass, still thrive in these sinks. Apparently, few newcomers could successfully compete under such ecologically severe conditions. Other alkali-tolerant plants are also present—various saltbushes, pickleweeds, and other goosefoots, particularly in the southern end of the Central Valley.

The nutritious grasslands of the world are the homes of most of the great herds of herbivores. This is certainly true in Africa where zebra and antelope such as wildebeest congregate so impressively. It was equally true in the Great Plains, though the buffalo was the only large grazer of any appreciable numbers remaining when the white man entered its domain. Two grazing ruminants took advantage of the valley prairie, tule elk and pronghorn antelope. The former, the smallest type of its genus in the New World, is exclusively Californian. The only other elk native to the state is the Roosevelt, and it is the same as the Olympic elk of the Pacific Northwest. Members of the deer family, all North American elk belong to the genus *Cervus*, which includes the red "deer" of Europe. Only the western hemisphere has what we refer to as deer, or *Odocoileus*. The rest of the world's "deer" are other genera, though in all fairness, the Old World could say that it has the true deer, since it named them such first, and the western hemisphere has something else. Be that as it may, the tule elk suffered greatly during the conversion to agriculture and the consequent disappearance of the valley grassland. Legend has it that the subspecies was reduced to two individuals, a kind of Noah's Ark predicament. Through the efforts of conservationists, however, the animal has increased numerically. Several dozen are kept in a small state reserve near Buttonwillow, in the southern San Joaquin Valley, some are scattered about in zoos, and another 300 roam in the Owens Valley, subject to controlled hunting. Additional herds have recently been established elsewhere in the state.

The story of the pronghorn is much different. It has largely disappeared from California except for a restricted range in the northeastern part of the state. It occurs, however, in many places in the rangeland West and does not seem to be threatened with extinction, as is the tule elk. Not a member of the deer group at all, it is the only remaining species of its family. Nor does it have much connection with the Old World antelopes, though its pretty markings bear some resemblance to those of the graceful wanderers of the African plains. A major difference is in the horns. Pronghorn antelope have a permanent bony core which is not discarded though the outer covering is lost once a year. African antelopes never lose any part of their horns, but keep them for life.

There were and still are numerous grazers among the smaller animals of the valley plains. Many rodents share a liking for grass and other prairie plants, this species preferring one part or type, that species other plant materials. The San Joaquin kangaroo rat feeds largely on the seeds of wild oats and bromes. Meadow mice rely on herbaceous shoots, leaves, and roots, but also include seeds and even bark. The nocturnal harvest and pocket mice are primarily seed eaters, sharing their bounty with the seed-harvesting birds—goldfinches, linnets, sparrows, and the like. Gophers eat juicy stems, roots, and foliage, pulling them down into their burrows and runways.

Evidently there has been an upsurge of gophers since the great change in grassland composition. Lloyd G. Ingles, in *Mammals of the Pacific States* (Stanford University Press, 1965), estimates that up to thirty individuals of this species can be found in just one acre of valley grazing land. Though its numbers appear to be on the increase, owing to the elimination of many of its predators through government control, poisoning campaigns are causing many other rodent populations to diminish rapidly.

Jack rabbits, or black-tailed hares, technically not rodents but lagomorphs, are unparticular about their menu; and they browse and graze through brushy patches, and in grassland and crop field alike. California ground squirrels are the short-tailed, heavy-bodied little fellows one sees sunning themselves by the entryways to their burrows or darting back and forth on the dirt shoulders of valley and foothill roads. Like the jacks they have a wide range of food interest, and readily raid farmlands for nuts, fruit, and greenstuffs, as well as making use of what native vegetation is provided. They, too, have been the victims of an extermination campaign, not only because of the crop damage they inflict, but because they have been proven to be carriers of fleas responsible for outbreaks of bubonic plague.

Grasshopper mice, as their name implies, rely heavily on insects, a rather unusual departure from the feeding habits of most of their relatives. Their stomachs are specially equipped to digest the chiton-covered fare. Deer mice also take insects, relying on them in the spring and reverting to seeds in the fall. These last two species could be said to be useful to the farmer in helping him get rid of such pests, in contrast to the rodents whose feeding activities are harmful. Many types of rodent behavior are beneficial, however. Their burrowing breaks up and aerates the soil. Nor should one ignore the value of their nitrogenous wastes.

In areas where there is such pronounced seasonality as in the California grasslands, its creatures must adapt to these great annual rhythms, particularly in regard to available diet. When green feed is present in spring, those who prefer it feast on it. After the summer drought has cured the grassy cover to hay, which still retains some nutritious material, many forbs remain juicy for a longer period of time. Soon, however, they succumb to the relentless heat of the valley summer. Then the seeds, now mature, are wonderful sources of food owing to their concentrated nutrients. Other nourishing plant sources are harvested. On investigation, the tightly rolled leaves of the bunchgrass in one of the few patches of original prairie still remaining proved to contain some green material, even in mid-August, as the curling decreased the amount of evaporative surface and retarded dry-out. Since the coming of agriculture, most of the herbivorous dwellers of the grasslands have not neglected to take advantage of the succulent results of irrigation and farming, though, as we have already noted, such supplementation of the natural summer diet has led to the endangerment of some of the species.

The role of insects in grassland is not to be underestimated. They take their toll of vegetation, and it has been proved that ants, crickets, and grasshoppers are responsible for the destruction of much herbaceous material. Harvester ants are common in range areas. Their mounds are often in the centers of bare patches as large as fifteen feet across. Not only do they consume the vegetation cleared in such circles, but they also transport seeds from the nearby forbs and grasses into their underground homes.

As in all natural communities, there are checks and balances operating in the prairie to prevent the unrestrained growth of any one of its populations. When the herbivores multiply to the point of threatening the food supply, carnivores help control the burgeoning numbers. Burrowing owls, American kestrels, red-tailed hawks, and shrikes victimize plentiful rodents, while nighthawks, kingbirds, meadowlarks, and horned larks take advantage of insect increase. Coyotes, badgers, and kit foxes are on the prowl along the numerous trails cutting through the grassy plain for plump mice and ground squirrels. Coachwhips, long-nosed snakes, kingsnakes, and gopher snakes wind through the sparser cover and along the little grass-walled trails, as ready as the predatory birds and mammals for a chance-encountered meal.

To escape both the summer heat and their enemies, many rodents—kangaroo rats and deer mice, for example—conceal themselves in underground burrows and confine their foraging activities to the friendlier hours of darkness. Deprived of the shelter of shrubby thickets, some animals, jack rabbits among them, make use of the matted grass stems. They hollow out forms where they crouch quietly away from the pitilessly bright sun of the open country.

Midsummer was the beginning of hard times for the original California prairie. A few bees stirred over the straw-stiff grass. Rodent activity slowed down, as the babies were now grown and able to fend for themselves. On the floors of the vernal pools the *Orcuttia* grass was exploiting the last moisture of the cracking floor, and the spadefoot and western toads had already escaped the desiccating drought by estivating, that is, they burrowed underground and entered a state of torpor, or deep sleep of a low metabolic rate, to conserve energy, moisture, and body weight during this time of scarce food and drying heat. Some of the snails of the pool habitat also estivated by migrating down into the muddy floor, while crustaceans such as fairy and clam shrimp oversummered in the form of drought-resistant egg stages. The flying aquatic insects such as water boatmen and water beetles left for wetter places as the surface water disappeared. The Santa Cruz long-toed sala-mander (now an endangered species as it is confined to only four vernal sites in Santa Cruz County) spent the summer in mammal burrows in the nearby chaparral. Some of the preda-tors of both grassland and pool habitat left to look for better hunting grounds up in the foothills.

September was the month when the true carrying capacity of the range could be judged. This is the amount of wildlife the prairie could support during its most critical season. Then the biomass, which is the totality of all the organisms within the community, still present during the lean days of early fall indi-cated the tremendous productivity of the prairie. Though many of its ordinarily day-active creatures spent longer peri-ods of time within their underground passageways than they did in spring, they ventured out in the cooler hours to look for unclaimed seeds or an overlooked juicy stem, or to find the nearest water. Hawks soared in the pale blue sky, watching for a stray ground squirrel. Vultures gathered for the inevitable toll of drought upon April's crop of offspring. But much of it was waiting. Toads slept deep in their cozy pockets; and seed and shoot rested in readiness for the first gray clouds to linger over the parched distances.

Owl's Clover, Kern County

11. Where the Diggings Were

The Indians of the Sierran foothills had no notion that they were literally sitting on a gold mine. If they did note the stray shiny specks in creek beds and in the gravelly rubble of canyon floors, they most probably dismissed them as useless. In the simple routines involved in living at subsistence level, only the patently useful objects and materials were of significance—obsidian for arrowheads, willow bark for baskets, acorns for food, and deer hides for clothing. On the other hand, ornaments such as beads and certain shells were much prized. It runs as a universal thread through man's diverse culture patterns that some objects, intrinsically of merely ornamental or decorative worth, become symbols of wealth and hence valued media of exchange. Among the many types of small shells so plentiful on the California coast, the pale purple olivellas would seem to be usable for adornment but not much else. If, however, a tribe had fostered a tradition that a kind of small purple shell was exchangeable on a rough unit basis for useful or otherwise desirable objects, olivellas were wealth.

Gold, by and large, is nothing more than olivella value on a huge scale, and the Indians of 1849 must have quickly realized why their ancient homelands were being overrun by hordes of frantic gold seekers. It must have been harder for these gentle people to understand the violence, greed, outlawry, and chaos of the camps which were scattered like proliferating cells over the foothills of the Mother Lode.

There is no denying that a miner's life was hard. Not only were the diggings on recently established frontier and every necessity or convenience in limited supply, mining itself was grinding physical labor. For many of those who came to find gold, however, the task of getting to California was the worst part of the whole experience. The long arduous journey overland or the even longer and more difficult passages over the Isthmus of Panama, through the Straits of Magellan, or around the Horn were harrowing to the point of causing modern readers of history to wonder how the lure of gold could have been strong enough to induce thousands of men to undertake such perilous adventures. Though many of the forty-niners would have vigorously denied it, the Mother Lode was not the worst place in the world for mining gold. Alaska and the high Rockies were far less friendly to their exploiters. Indeed, the foothills, rough and canyon cut though they often are, must have appeared to be hospitable and friendly country to many who had struggled over the barren alkali flats of the sagebrush country or faced the formidable dangers of a High Sierra winter. The summers may be warm at these low elevations, 200 to 3,000 feet (60–900 m.), but the winters are comparatively mild. Snow rarely troubled the men of the diggings, and when it did it quickly melted off. Wood and water were plentiful for domestic use and for mining equipment and procedures. Civilization, if one can call it that, was not far away, and roads soon connected the main mining centers with Sacramento and San Francisco. Food, though expensive, was available from the ranches and farms of the Great Valley. The monotonous meals of salt pork and beans were supplemented by game of many kinds. Hunting was a common pastime between the chores of minding sluice boxes and blasting out ore.

As they clambered up the ravines looking for telltale veins and placer deposits or rode into Hangtown and Volcano over links in the chain of dusty tracks that connected the camps, were most men aware of the beauty of the hills that had so long held in trust their treasure? Did they come to love the richly cascading rivers and streams that not only could be harnessed into ditches and flumes to wash through rockers and long toms, but could rinse out a man's laundry and quiet the thirst of a hangover? Did they note the effects of the seasons on the landscape, the wealth of young grass and wildflowers in May which become a special kind of gold in August?

No doubt many did, and perhaps even remarked to the more understanding of their pick-ax wielding companions their admiration of a land so blessed with beauty. It is safe to surmise that much speculation took place on how nature formed the precious metal they had come so far to find. Much of it was just that, unfortunately—speculation. Accurate geological knowledge of the Sierra Nevada, missing in Gold Rush days, has been painstakingly gathered for many years by survey teams and other experts, first on foot and horseback and later by motor vehicle. Though these efforts have helped uncover many clues to the story of this great mountain range, some puzzles are still unsolved. It appears that we do not yet know just how the lode came into existence.

Geologic evidence points to a series of events that began about 150 million years ago in the Mesozoic (dinosaur) era. Marine sediments and volcanic material had been deposited in the general region of what we know as the Sierra Nevada for countless ages prior to this time. During the Mesozoic, while the dinosaurs still roamed the earth, the North American continental plate drifted northwestward, bringing it into contact with the eastern edge of the Pacific plate. During the collision the ancient sedimentary and volcanic rocks were subjected to tremendous heat and pressure that fractured, folded, and even altered them into somewhat different types of rock (a process called metamorphism). Other rock was melted completely into massive quantities of magma that cooled to become the white granite so characteristic of the range. Solutions from this molten mass filled the cracks and faults of the metamorphosed rock and formed veins of quartz containing gold and other minerals.

Through the succeeding eons additional pulses of magma intruded into the granitic core, which continued to rise, exposing itself to erosion. During the end of the Mesozoic era and the beginning of the Tertiary period erosion continued until the ore bodies themselves were subject to weathering and decay. The climate at that time was warm and humid, and the temperature and rainfall patterns resembled those of the present-day Deep South.

The weathered, eroding veins lost much of their precious metal to the streams of that period. If there had been any miners grubstaking during the Eocene, the second epoch of the Tertiary, they could have found the shiny nuggets easily, for the streams of that era were tapping the original ore-bearing veins as they flowed down the hills ancestral to the Sierra. Time and the great orogenic upheavals that fashion the foundations of the earth's landscapes conspired to hide California's treasure once again. Volcanic activity covered the hills with layers of ash, mud, tuff, and lava. At last a series of uplifts, in fairly recent (Pleistocene) times, thrust up the granite of the ancient batholith. A system of faults, 400 miles (644 km.) long, created a huge block, tilted so that the western slope is gradual and the eastern scarp face is steeply abrupt. Now, erosion once more could attack the concealing layers. The streams flowing down the long slope from the crest went to work, exposing the ancient Eocene stream beds with their placer deposits, washing the rubble into new drainage patterns, and cutting into the veins themselves—the real Mother Lode.

No doubt, most forty-niners were aware of the more noticeable natural features of what they considered their temporary home. They knew of higher ridges and peaks to the east. They realized that their creeks and rivers were the offspring of snow fields in the rugged back country. They were aware that certain trees had certain uses. The soft wood of conifers was more easily worked, but some of the broad-leaved species—oaks, for instance—had harder, more durable wood. They may have heard rumors about huge trees a hundred feet around at the base. They discovered wild berries, and some probably learned that wild onions added flavor to back-of-the-stove stews. They relished the venison from deer browsing through the open glades and certainly heard many a tale of harrowing escapes from grizzly bears that lived in the thickets of the lower Sierra before their extinction around 1920. A few lonely souls probably made pets of white-footed mice, coons, or ringtails (these normally shy nocturnal carnivores were so useful in keeping rodents in check that they earned the nickname "miners' cats"). If so, they joined the ranks of those to whom the companionship of wild creatures is a rare and wonderful thing. Yet how astonished they would have been if they could have known that in a short century, there would be more people seeking recreation and outdoor experiences on the Sierran slope than there were living in California in 1849.

Like geologic investigations, those of the natural history of the state meant years of slow accumulation. Early research was mostly taxonomic in character, describing and naming the various types of flora and fauna. It was not until C. Hart Merriam, Joseph Grinnell, and others worked out a concept known as life zones that biologists took a somewhat different look at natural environments. They began to see that these occurred consistently under certain climatic conditions. The life-zone concept proved most useful in that it stressed the correlation between latitude, elevation, and life associations and provided a simple means of establishing a common understanding of the major biotic regions of the West. Six major zones were identified, and they were named in accordance with the geographical areas in which corresponding plant-animal groupings were most characteristic. Since desert and scrub plants of North America are well represented in what is known as the Sonoran Desert, which includes the Colorado Desert, the two lower zones are called Lower Sonoran and Upper Sonoran. A Transition zone, identified by the occurrence of such trees as yellow pine, is usually found between the arid lowlands and the Canadian zone whose lodgepole pines and red firs are reminiscent of the great tracts of conifers in southern Canada. The Hudsonian zone occurs higher on mountain ranges, close to timberline, where conditions are like those met in the taiga around Hudson Bay. The highest of all is the Arctic-Alpine zone, and here life must adjust to as rigorous an environment as that of the Arctic tundra. In the Sierra the zones are plotted by the ranges of altitude (shown in Figure 17, p. 197).

Though we see references to these zones and current modifications in recent publications, for the most part the system has been found to be far too general and not definitive enough, particularly where there are so many exceptions as in the mountainous and climatically inconsistent West. A much more precise organization of habitat and life form is possible using the concept of natural communities. It is now standard to refer to a classification developed for California by two eminent botanists, Philip A. Munz and David D. Keck, based on dominant plant species. This community approach has been extremely useful for all ecological work, as it can be enlarged to include typical faunal representatives. Variations of the original Munz and Keck list have evolved, and this book, though it adheres quite closely to the basic twenty-nine as defined by their developers, has taken a few liberties.

In the Sierran foothills we return to three communities which have already been introduced—foothill woodland, chaparral, and riparian forest. For the most part, they show but little change from their counterparts to the west. One must travel higher on the range before new communities and new plants appear.

As would be expected, rainfall begins to increase a few hundred feet (90 m.) above the floor of the Central Valley, and the Sierran side enjoys a larger amount of precipitation in contrast to the lower rainfall at the same elevations in the inner coastal hills. There are many more permanent streams and rivers draining the Sierra than flow either east or west from the central Coast Ranges. Distance from the ameliorating influences of the sea has resulted in a climate more characteristically continental than maritime, and the winters are colder and the summers warmer than in coastal regions of comparable latitude and elevation.

These differences notwithstanding, one can wander through an oak-shaded meadow or drive by a patch of chaparral and find it difficult to tell from vegetation alone whether one is closer to the Golden Gate or to Yosemite Valley. The Sierra foothills have the same natural mosaics, the same mixed bag of brush, prairie, and woodland as the Coast Ranges around San Francisco Bay, but on a somewhat larger scale and, by and large, less interrupted by urbanization and intensive farming. This is ranching country still; and though livestock raising, recreation, logging, fire, and gold mining have left their distinctive traces, much of the land, particularly south of Yosemite, looks more serene, undisturbed and less harassed than its coastal counterpart.

Only in the lower foothills is the terrain gentle and unassuming. Grass-covered hills succeed each other, gradually increasing in elevation and ruggedness, until steep V-bottomed gullies and canyons begin to predominate. The miners knew these gulches and probably cursed their plunging and unstable slopes as they worked them over for their precious contents.

The open savannas of the Great Valley—or what is left of them—are spattered with dark dollops of shade as the valley oaks are joined by their foothill cousins, interior live oaks and blue oaks. Before man's influence, it is estimated that most of these rolling landscapes were thick with brush or trees, particularly on shaded or north-facing slopes. Where more mesic wooded areas remain, humus-rich, moist soils encourage many shade-tolerant, thin-leaved herbs and winter-deciduous shrubs. Similar in behavior to riparian trees, such shrubs as redbud and snowberry can experience leaf loss and bear the strain of complete spring refoliation if their substrates retain some moisture throughout the warm season. Except for a puzzling absence in Tulare and southern Fresno counties, digger pine joins interior live and blue oak, patrolling both brushy hillsides and grass-covered dips and rises. The hardy knobcone pines occupy rocky infertile sites such as outcroppings of serpentine. Golden cup (canyon live) oaks billow out from their canyon walls like small brown-green clouds.

Because of the importance of oak trees in the natural landscapes of California, the previous chapter that featured their woodlands stressed the various species and some of their climatic and edaphic requirements and preferences. Ecologists also discuss the foothill woodland complex in terms of phases—subtypes that are characterized by dominant species or topographic position. A brief discussion of the four phases follows as it summarizes and simplifies what can be a confusing amount of habitat detail. The valley oak phase includes both the savanna of the lower foothills and the denser groves of moist valley floors and river terraces. The blue oak phase constitutes a similar savanna of oaks that, though deciduous, are capable of coping with thin rocky soils because of long thirsty roots and drought-adjusted leaf drop. The interior live oak phase is more characteristic of higher elevations, becoming significant just below the conifer forest. It also tends to replace blue oak on north-facing slopes and claims rocky but subsurface moisture-filled outcrops. This phase also includes the shrubbier forms that mass in chaparrallike thickets. The north slope phase corresponds roughly to the mixed evergreen forest of the Coast Ranges. These cooler, more mesic sites often harbor dense growths of hollyleaf cherry, buckeye, California bay, toyon, live oaks, and redbud with scattered digger pine and at higher elevations adventurous black oaks, incense cedars, yellow pines, and white firs.

One plant often encountered in shady nooks of ravines or using other vegetation as support is pipevine, a California member of a family whose usual habitat is tropical. It is a woody-stemmed vine that hangs like a loosely woven coverlet over rock or shrub, behaving like other common foothill vines—wild grape and wild cucumber. The maroon flower is similar in shape to a curve-stemmed pipe. The upturned end of the tubular flower is constricted. Insects—small flies and the like—attracted to it by odor, and possibly for other reasons, can easily enter the opening; but tiny hairs, pointing downward, make escape almost impossible. They must wait until the hairs relax before they are released. Then they fly to another flower and, retrapped, pollinate it by means of the tiny grains adhering to them after contact with the stamens of the previously visited flower. Because of the structure of the flower and nature of its reproductive parts, the plant must be pollinated by insects. Though the flies are temporarily imprisoned, they flourish on a diet of nutritious pollen. Such interaction is another example of mutualism in the foothill world.

As in the Coast Ranges, open spaces between the scattered oaks hoard a springtime wealth, wildflowers flourishing with bright prodigality. In March and April, when valley and blue oaks are first leafing out, buttercups, yellow violets, and baby-blue-eyes are spread like needlepoint on the green of the awakening slopes. Fiddleneck, poppies, annual blue lupine, popcorn flower, owl's clover, and cream cup begin to spread blankets of color much as they do on the lower prairies of the Central Valley. May and early June are the best months for breathtaking displays in the higher foothills, well back on the Sierran slope. One soon learns to recognize the habitats which certain favorites prefer. Out in the grass of open, drier terraces and hillsides, look for mariposas, harvest brodiaea with its clusters of indigo trumpets, and its distant relative, golden star. Some of the most charming of the mariposa group are the nodding fairy lanterns. One is creamy white; another has three petals of pink satin curving together under sepals of maroon. They grow seemingly as well in the dry soils of roadside cliff edges as they do in the shade of taller brush and woodland. The latter environment is a good place to see Chinese houses, already described in Chapter 4, the red starbursts of California *Silene* or pink, and the coral circlets of wind poppy. Here, too, pale violet grass nut or Ithuriel's spear, another species of Brodiaea, is much at home. Farewell-to-spring masses pink and magenta on the shallow soils of rocky cliffs, and various members of the sunflower family are common along the road and in the field.

Though most perennial grasses such as needlegrasses, bluegrasses, and melicgrasses have retreated under the advance of the annuals, some pockets of the former remain here and there in the foothills. We have already discussed the disastrous results of preferential grazing on the perennial grasses of California (see p. 169 above). Here, as in the Great Valley, the annuals are now in almost complete control. Some, like foxtail fescue which thrives on shallow soils, are native. Others are introduced: soft chess, red and ripgut brome, slender oats, European fescue, and mouse barley. In summer the hills rise through the haze with such understatement that one often questions their presence. It is only when the road encounters the profile of a canyon or curves around an outcrop that the shimmering swells begin to have validity. The brush and arboreal communities of the foothills help sharpen the definition. Patches of chaparral lie about like discarded fur coats, moth-eaten in places where rock slides and other inhospitable soil conditions interrupt the cover. In spring pink sprays of redbud and the little yellow parasols along the branches of flannel bush are as colorful as the flowers of their herbaceous neighbors. Canyon floors can usually boast of permanent water, surface or underground; and once again we meet sycamore, alder, Oregon ash, willows, Fremont cottonwood, bay, and valley and live oaks with big-leaf maple and the first of the yellow pines, Douglas-firs, and incense cedars that have crept down from the great green wall of Sierra conifers.

The same influences responsible for the coastal mosaic operate here. Prairie spreads its wind-quickened grasses over the more gentle slopes and valley floors interrupted by oaks, digger pine, buckeye, and shrubs in light or heavy stands depending on edaphic conditions. North-facing hillsides and canyon bottoms support broadleaf deciduous or evergreen trees, mesophytic shrubs such as chokecherry, and adventurous conifers more characteristic of higher elevations. Thin-soiled and rocky ridges back in the foothills are often covered with chamise, manzanita, and other species typical of the dry chaparral. Serpentine sites, of which there are many in the metamorphosed rocks of the western Sierra, have their own characteristically adapted plant life. Where these outcrops occur, lush woodlands halt, and other abrupt changes in the vegetation pattern are not uncommon. In a region where thin soils frequently mantle hillsides and ridges, many serpentine soils are exceptionally shallow and look as though the bedrock was sprinkled with a few handfuls of gravel and left to itself. Here even brush, typical of many serpentine areas, thins out; and stunted annuals, many endemic to these pockets, grow sparsely. Digger pines make occasional appearances.

Much of the foothill belt has a soil mantle startlingly red in color, particularly when damp. In early spring the brilliant green of grass overlaying the vermillion of roadcut is a splendid contrast of color. These soils, often called lateritic because they resemble, in color and other ways, the tropical laterites, were derived from basic igneous rock such as andesite and basalt, and their sedimentary and metamorphic derivatives. Many specialists feel they are the result of long weathering. During this time, hundreds of thousands of years, many minerals were leached out, leaving high concentrations of iron oxide which account for their bright color. At low elevations on the Sierran slope where the precipitation is only moderate, even low, these soils are neutral to alkaline; when rainfall increases beyond a critical amount, they become acid. Characterized by a deficiency in phosphate, some plants cannot grow in them at all, but most of the trees and grasses of the woodland tolerate this condition. The brighter soils are usually less fertile than those on the brownish side. Brush is the typical cover of the more sterile sites.

Other edaphic variants control the vegetative cover. Near the town of Ione in Amador County are knolls of ancient sandstones and marine clays overtopped by several richly red, iron-cemented horizons and a surface crust of iron oxide. The sediments deposited so long ago were parent to soils that supported tropical and humid subtropical forests. At the same time they were exposed to the climatic barrage of weathering during which most of the minerals needed for plant growth were leached downward, leaving only iron and a special kind of clay called kaolin. The original soils were buried by additional sediments following their development, but erosion has uncovered these remnants from a very different kind of natural landscape, exposing what are now highly acid and infertile soils that only a few plants such as the endemic Ione manzanita and Ione wild buckwheat can tolerate. Other species are dwarfed—interior live oak and white-leaf manzanita, for example—and are indicative of a very inhospitable substrate.

Pine Hill in Eldorado County has quite a different geologic history. Its gabbro is one of many intrusions of plutonic rock associated with the crustal upheaval that resulted from the collision of the two continental plates described earlier in this chapter. The soils that developed from this parent rock are also acid, but not extraordinarily so. Moderately high in magnesian minerals, they resemble serpentine to the point where leather oak, usually considered a serpentine endemic, occurs on Pine Hill. One species of flannel bush, *Fremontodendron decumbens,* is restricted to this site alone. Other plants have also a very limited distribution, allowing them membership in the elite "rare species" list. Unfortunately, this particular knoll of great botanical interest and research value has attracted the attention of developers, and it is hoped that at least a portion of this rare assemblage can be preserved for future study. Shallow soils of low water-retaining ability mantling certain types of volcanic rock, such as andesite and tuff, are hostile to mesophytic growth and usually support grass with sparsely scattered oaks or brush. Limestone areas are scattered in a number of places on the Sierran slope. Soils derived from them are relatively infertile and unable to hold much water.

The enigmatic arbiter of California landscapes, fire, once again proves to be of great importance. J. R. Sweeney in an informative booklet, *The Responses of Vegetation to Fire* (University of California Press, 1956), makes several interesting points. On the foothill areas he studied, grasses seem to be slow starters. They do not become dominant until three or more years after a fire. Forbs are the typical plants during the first and second years. He maintains that the seeds which germinate the first season after the burn are already present and on the site during the blaze. How do seeds survive such an episode? Many plants germinate only after the seed coats have been heat treated or scarified. Lying dormant through the intervening years, they are the offspring of plants that last sprang up the first year after the previous fire. These fire types rarely appear the second year, as their seeds must wait for the same process that released their parent plants. Some remain secure under the effective insulation of soil. Just an inch or two will protect the more vulnerable seeds from destruction. Other species can sprout only when the duff is removed from the topsoil. They need bare mineral earth or ash to begin growth. According to Sweeney, this may be involved with the larger amount of oxygen present in such exposed soils. Increased fertility resulting from ash deposit is an additional factor, for fire releases nutrients captured in both debris and living tissue. Many brush seedlings take advantage of all these improved conditions, particularly those whose seeds require heat treatment; but quite a number die during the first year. Not only does competition from the light-requiring, pioneering herbaceous or subshrub intruders threaten them, but some have a hard time enduring summer drought when the exposed soils of the new burn are open to increased evaporation.

Fire plays a great role in determining the vegetation patterns of the coastal hills. Equally important in the western Sierra, here also it has established a partnership with topography and soil factors. Though chance and wind direction often determine a fire's path, observers have noted that rolling terrain burns less patchily than broken country, and southward-facing slopes are more fire-prone than moister north exposures.

It is often taken for granted that a fire holocaust means total disaster to the animal residents of a fire-hit community. This is not quite true though some animals do die. A fire does not mean total destruction; there are always islands of unburned vegetation and cooler sites, such as north-facing exposures and riparian bottomlands, which may escape complete ravagement though the fire is raging around them. No doubt some animals simply leave; a whiff of smoke and they are off. Many birds fly away immediately. Burrow-dwelling creatures are protected under as little as 5 inches (13 cm.) of soil. Animals hidden in deeper crannies and on rock outcrops have a good chance of survival. Hollow logs and gnarled and hole-ridden trunks also provide shelter. Grass fires, in particular, are relatively cool and quickly over. Temporary refuges, possibly inadequate during hotter fires, safely harbor many animals making use of them.

Though many animal populations decrease immediately after a blaze, some may even experience growth surges, especially seed eaters and grazers as the herbs take over. It has been long known to biologists that catastrophe often results in an increase in the number of offspring, and this feature alone helps to repopulate the burn. There are other positive features of fire. The newly opened brushlands provide more grazing and browsing opportunity. If islands of mesophytic vegetation are left, they attract animals from less sheltered neighboring areas. Predators are drawn by the newly opened hunting grounds and by the possible increase in prey populations.

Of these last there is usually a goodly number in an environment that furnishes grass and other seed-rich plants. In a bulletin published by the University of California College of Agriculture (no. 663, April 1942), various kinds of rodents and one rabbit are listed as being resident on the San Joaquin experimental range administered by the college. The food and nesting-site preferences of eleven species are examples of an ecological niche structure:

> The Merriam chipmunk is scarce and usually found in brushy ravines, where it depends largely on shrubby plants for food. The gray squirrel is likewise scarce. It usually stays in or near digger pines and lives on the pine seeds. The San Joaquin pocket mouse, present in a population of at least one to the acre in 1939, is a small species which subsists mainly on minute seeds. The California pocket mouse is rare. The harvest mouse is even less numerous, and is restricted to the larger swales which retain moisture through the dry season. The white-footed mouse is one of the commoner rodents, and was present in a population of at least one to the acre in the summer of 1939; it occurs mainly in open grassland. The brush mouse and the rock mouse are both common where there are rocks and brush thickets; populations were computed at several to the acre for both in the summer of 1939. The wood rat is partial to situations where there are large outcrops, brush thickets, or live oaks, where it may occur in a population of several to the acre, but it tends to avoid open grassland. Because it feeds mainly on leaves of shrubs and inner bark of twigs from oak and chaparral, it is unimportant as a forage destroyer but may compete with livestock for browse. The meadow mouse is scarce and confined to a small portion of the range, the large swale bottoms with permanent covering of thick vegetation, where the ground remains moist through the summer. The jackrabbit is rare on the range.

All these smaller animals compete with the larger wild herbivores and range livestock for the vegetation of the foothills and, as a result, are resented by ranchers and game management personnel. Not only do they compete for more palatable forage, they may damage extensive areas of rangeland by burrow networks. There is reason to suppose that they were partially responsible for less desirable weed species invading the prairies and savannas as they helped keep the vegetation thin and open to interlopers. These habits alone indicate that the presence of controlling predators such as hawks, owls, and coyotes is highly desirable, including the sharp-tailed snake which occurs in the oak-pine woodland of the Sierra and whose preferred food is slugs.

Green and gold and green again, nature's great brush washes color on color as the seasons come and go. At a casual glance, the hills of the lower Sierra appear almost as untroubled as they were before the forty-niners claimed their treasure, but this serenity is often rudely broken along the Mother Lode and major traffic routes. Man has done more than create unsightly piles of gravel residue from dredging operations and more than scarring the land with quarries and artificial badlands from hydraulic methods of placer mining. He is busy carving these gracious hills into vacation and retirement developments and is too often totally unconcerned about the mushrooming of shoddy business construction, out-of-place and in poor taste. He has ruthlessly thrust superhighways through tranquil little towns rich in Gold Rush history and scenic charm.

Lovely though these hills still are, they show in many ways that their beauty is fragile. They will remain lovely only if man allows them to, only if intelligent appreciation guides their destiny.

Fallen Sequoias, Sequoia National Park

12. The Great Green Wall

No unbreachable rampart such as that which often lines a tropical river, the coniferous forests of the Sierra Nevada—its Great Green Wall—are usually open and readily entered. There are exceptions. Close thickets of saplings are decided hindrances. Patches of manzanita or chinquapin can be difficult to negotiate, and mazes of fallen timber impede or stop progress entirely. On a sunny day the forest is cheerful and welcoming. Atomized by numberless yellow-green needles, sunlight spatters in golden sprays through the fanlike branches of firs or falls in heavier showers where the cover is broken. Screened in by the coniferous foliage, this zone of the Sierra has few vistas. The delights of trail and road at these elevations are immediate— a meadow bright with wildflowers, a blossoming dogwood, a stream cascading into pools of green champagne. Only on occasion does the forest give way to a wider sky, where domes and peaks, waterfalls and gorges disclose the granitic foundation.

Though the life-zone names for the vegetation belts of the Sierra are rarely used today, the obvious altitudinal zonation of its plant life has led to several similar systems but with more appropriate designations, many of them based on currently used names of natural communities. T. I. Storer and R. L. Usinger in *Sierra Nevada Natural History* (University of California Press, 1963; highly recommended as a guidebook) list Central Valley, foothill belt, yellow pine belt, lodgepole pine-red fir belt, subalpine belt, and alpine belt on the west slope and designate a Jeffrey pine belt, a sagebrush belt, and a southeast desert region on the east side of the range. Another classification separates western mountains into the grasslands of lower elevations, then foothill forest, montane forest, subalpine forest, and above timberline alpine tundra. The lower portion of the Great Green Wall is called the yellow pine belt or montane forest, depending on which system of nomenclature is preferred. It corresponds to Munz and Keck's yellow pine forest community, found roughly at elevations of 2,000 to 7,000 feet (600–2,100 m.) in the Sierra Nevada, and is named for one of its dominant species. An additional system of Sierran vegetation types is currently in much use. The yellow pine belt is referred to as the lower montane zone, and it includes two important forest types—yellow pine and white fir-mixed conifer. The yellow pine forest occurs from 1,000 to 6,000 feet (300–1,800 m.) in Eldorado County and northward and from 4,000 to 7,000 feet (1,200–2,100 m.) in the southern section. It is replaced by white fir-mixed conifer forest on mesic sites, particularly at higher elevations, and by Douglas-fir forest on north-facing slopes from Mariposa County northward. The closely related Jeffrey pine supplants yellow pine at its upper margins in dry places throughout much of the Sierran slope. Yellow pine is by no means missing from the white fir-dominated forest. It continues in drier situations along with other drought-tolerant trees such as incense cedar and black oak whereas sugar pine and, locally, big tree (giant sequoia) become important where soil moisture is more abundant during the summer months.

After the heat-burdened foothills, the first ranks of the coni-

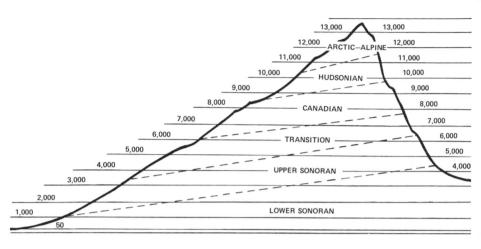

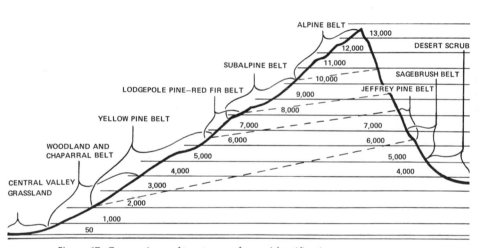

Figure 17. Comparison of two types of zone identification

fers seem almost exuberant with growth. Their abundance, rich variety, and differences in texture and color make traveling through these living canyons a most rewarding experience. One rightly surmises that such forests indicate an abundance of water, and in fact rainfall often exceeds 50 inches (127 cm.) a year. Progressing upward from the floor of the Great Valley, there is an average increase of 8 to 10 inches (20–25 cm.) of rain per 1,000 feet (300 m.). This continues to a midelevation maximum and then may slack off. For sugar pine to be as tall as 255 feet (76 m.) and giant sequoias over 300 feet (90 m.), not only must there be sufficient moisture, but the growing season must be fairly long and dependable enough so that life processes can continue unhindered for a good portion of the year. It averages from four to seven months depending on elevation, local conditions of relief, and degree of exposure. Growth periods of these durations are considerably shorter than any encountered so far, and they are further constricted by summer drought. Thundershowers notwithstanding, Sierran seasons reflect the general rainfall pattern of the state. Such dry conditions during the growth period plus cold winters that are by no means short have challenged native plants. Here again, evergreenness proves to have survival value; less energy is needed to activate already existing foliage during the first warm days of spring than to grow a whole new crop of leafy tissue.

Sierran forests are not without other defenses: snow and the character of the forest itself. If all the moisture fell as rain it would be far less beneficial to plant life. Snow functions as a reservoir, slowly releasing its meltwater, allowing it to sink into the soil. The more favorable sites retain soil moisture throughout the summer, and many streams are permanent, testifying to the reserves of water locked into snow banks. Moving up into the Great Green Wall, one enters country that expects winter snow. For the first time in our trek across California snow is important, something with which to reckon, not only because of its runoff potential and involvement with highway maintenance and winter sports. Snow acts like a blanket, for air trapped in tiny pockets between flakes is excellent insulation. Snow-covered plants are protected by this naturally fluffed quilt from wind and freezing temperatures of damaging degree.

It has been often said that forests make their own climates, which is surprisingly true. Though the overall climate pattern is the main determining factor, the forest itself contributes to its mesic environment. Shade and the presence of litter and humus decrease evaporation in upper soil levels. Wind is considerably less, and temperatures tend to be slightly cooler in summer and warmer in winter than in open fields. Not only shade but the daily evaporation of hundreds of gallons of water from the leaves of constituent trees increases the humidity.

Shading, the interception of direct sunlight, has profound influences on vegetation. In all but the densest forests, there is usually enough light for some photosynthesis, even at ground level. Leaves and boughs are twisted and swung by the wind, scattering sunflecks down through canopy and understory onto the lower layers. Light is diffused and reflected by shiny leaf surfaces, boulders, and the like. Nevertheless, reduced light is a feature of the forest floor and has a large role in a complex survival problem. Plants contending with low light intensities frequently have poorly developed root systems. It appears that young trees with meager roots find it difficult to compete successfully for soil moisture and nutrients with well-established trees possessing large vigorous roots. Thus many seedlings under a closed canopy die, not because of any inability to make sufficient food but because of their poor showing in the competitive struggle for water and nutrients.

In adjusting to the great range of light conditions in most natural communities, a number of adaptations to both sun and shade have evolved. Many plants are able to grow two types of leaves, depending on available illumination. Shade leaves are usually thinner and spongier, have thinner cuticle and fewer palisade cells, are larger in area, and have more openings or stomata, through which gas exchange takes place. Light can enter the food-making cells with greater ease; food production can be carried on more efficiently; and there is a larger amount of photosynthetic material to make use of the available light. These leaves, however, may wilt under strong sun and even die. Sun leaves, on the other hand, are smaller, more heavily cutinized, and have fewer openings. Such adaptable plants grow sun leaves when the site is open to the full sun and shade leaves when the conditions are in reverse. Many California conifers have the ability to inch along in the dim light as saplings, sprouting twigs with tufts of outsize or "shade-leaf" needles in what is termed a suppressed condition until released by the opening of the canopy because of tree fall or some other circumstance. Then they respond with great vigor to the increased sunlight. Tapered shape is also useful, allowing the longer branches of lower levels to receive a share of the light.

People developing an ecological point of view soon become aware of the structure of the white fir-mixed conifer community. The canopy, or overstory, is composed of dark pyramidal masses of needle leaves breaking into silver-green where new growth tips out. They are supported by trunks that hardly seem to taper and which are often girdled by tufted rows of brilliantly chartreuse staghorn lichen. The understory is composed of young conifers and a number of broadleaf trees, crowded in some places, scattered in others. Where streams work down gully and canyon floors, creek dogwood, white and mountain alder, black cottonwood, Oregon ash, big-leaf maple, various willows, and other moisture-requiring species encroach upon the coniferous ranks. In the canyon country of the lower Sierra vegetation is frequently missing from riverine areas where one would expect luxuriant growth. Periodic floods, with their pounding boulders and uprooted debris, sweep away any riparian plant life. Where some of the most strikingly handsome rivers of the range, such as the Merced and Kings, boil down steep walled canyons, their beds never support a large number of trees. They are too narrow and boulder choked, and have too little soil and too many floods.

Many of the understory trees of the white fir forest are old friends. They accompany Douglas-fir in what could be termed an impoverished extension of coastal mixed evergreen forest, poorer in that it lacks redwood and other impressive cone-bearing trees of the northern coast. Big-leaf maple and Pacific dogwood are near streamcourses or on shady slopes whereas madroño and tanoak accept a wider range of accommodation. Bay claims moist canyons throughout the lower montane zone. Two smaller conifers venture east of their coastal haunts— western yew, staying strictly to Calaveras County and north, and California nutmeg, clinging to cool moist outposts south to Tulare County. Canyon live oaks occur on dry ridges, steep rocky walls, talus slopes, and rock-strewn gully bottoms, and they are often found in isolated perches, as lonely as eagle nests. Black oaks are among the loveliest of deciduous trees. Their dark trunks and spreading masses of large glossy leaves are remindful of eastern hardwood forests with their wealth of oaks. When it first leafs out, no tree is a more charming introduction to spring; the velvety new growth is the color of a ripening peach. Though it is scattered throughout the yellow pine forest, apparently at ease in such xeric locations as dry open ridges, one occasionally sees impressive stands of this species. There are several noteworthy groves on the floor of Yosemite

Valley, evidently enjoying full sun which it seems to prefer through much of its life.

Each major level in the forest has its typical animal inhabitants. Some seldom shift from one to the other; whereas others move about freely while feeding, though they may prefer certain foliage and branch strata for nesting and shelter. Few mammals spend much of their time in the canopy layer. Chickarees, or pine squirrels, and flying squirrels are the exceptions. Several birds confine most of their food-searching activities to the treetops. Olive-sided flycatchers dart out for insect prey from observation posts high on the topmost snags or dead branches, pausing to whistle the "hick, *three* beers" so typical of the Sierra forests. Two nuthatches, red-breasted and pygmy, hunt through the higher portions of coniferous trees. The first keeps close to the top levels of trunk and main branch, while the second forages in the needle tufts at the tips of coniferous branches. A related species, the white-breasted nuthatch, is usually content to remain lower down.

Midheight levels have their characteristic flycatchers. The wood pewee is joined by the western flycatcher, one of five little gray fellows so indistinguishable individually, each is often referred to simply as an empidonax, the generic name for the group. Another bird of occasional flycatching habit, though of different family, is the Townsend's solitare. Active in the middle layers of foliage growth, it may consort with ruby-crowned kinglets, solitary vireos, and Nashville, yellow-rumped, and hermit warblers. Males of the last three species have bright yellow patches of color in contrast to gray, white, and black plumage elsewhere on their bodies. These small birds are gleaners, busily assessing twigs for insects, though many go after flies on occasion.

Two larger birds are occasionally seen at these elevations— band-tailed pigeons and Sierra (or sooty) grouse. The first species flocks in groups of a dozen or more and is the only native member of the dove group nesting regularly at such altitudes.

Understory occupants have two features of the environment to their advantage. The canopy overhead affords them protection from exposure to the elements as well as aerial predation. Their habitual distance above the ground keeps them well away from most four-footed enemies.

The amount and extent of shrub growth vary within the

Great Green Wall. Several important groups such as manzanita, *Ribes* (pronounced *rye-bees,* a genus that includes both currants and gooseberries), and ceanothus are represented in practically all of the zones of the Sierran slope. In general there are three major brush zones: foothill chaparral, midaltitude shrub growth, and montane or mountain chaparral of the lodgepole pine-red fir forests. A number of the brush species of lower elevations penetrate the coniferous ranks above, two being silk tassel and white-leaf manzanita. Chamise, various kinds of ceanothus, flannel bush, scrub oak, toyon, and their companions of the chaparral continue to buffer the hills between the rolling foothill woodlands of the piedmont and the forests of the Great Green Wall.

Within the lower montane zone, shrub cover varies. Where soils are poor or shallow, as on many rocky hillsides, or where the forest has been removed by fire, disease, or logging, bitter cherry, birch-leaf mountain mahogany, greenleaf manzanita, deer brush, and *Ribes* form ragged tracts. In time, most plants pioneering after a disturbance will be shaded out by the reestablished trees, though patches of common brush species appear sporadically under mature cover if it is not too dense. Bracken is another fire opportunist, but great expanses of it also occur under trees or in meadows, particularly on highly acid soils. Two species grow in extensive covers under uncrowded forests or on open slopes. One is a low-growing, spicy-odored shrub with featherlike leaves, known by the uncomplimentary name of mountain misery. The other, less common, is squaw mat, a dwarf ceanothus. Aside from the last three plants, shrubby growth under the conifers is irregular. Under heavy stands of yellow pine and white fir it may be completely absent, primarily because of shade. Some species flourish under moderate shade—thimbleberry, wild rose, mock orange, chokecherry, mountain snowberry, and spiraea. Others apparently need such mesic sites as stream banks or local surface seeps—western azalea, willows, hazelnut, creek dogwood, twinberry, and spice bush with its turkey red chrysanthemumlike flowers.

Montane chaparral consists primarily of pinemat and greenleaf manzanita, bush chinquapin, snow bush, Coville's ceanothus, bitter cherry, snowberry and huckleberry oak. It is characteristic in the upper montane zone and the upper edges of the yellow pine-white fir forests where it appears as understory or scattered about on granite slabs where deposits of soil are slowly building. It also congregates in small thickets or clings to rootholds in cracks or fissures. Hardier shrubs like tobacco brush—a large-leaved ceanothus—and various currants creep up to relatively high altitudes.

Many birds preferring riparian growth feeding niches are bright specks as they flash through the willows—Wilson's and yellow warblers, downy woodpeckers, and black-headed grosbeaks. Plainer birds such as warbling vireos, willow flycatchers, and the Swainson's thrush—a ground dweller—make use of the insect wealth of streamside environments. Out on the sunnier chaparral-covered slopes, fox sparrows and mountain quail comb through the brush. Dusky flycatchers "hawk" for insects in the air over open hillsides. Where the shrub and herbaceous layers are shaded by a forest canopy overhead, winter wrens dart through the tangles of twig and stem, pausing on the roots of upturned trees to twitch their tails or sing surprisingly noisy songs. MacGillivray's warblers also frequent thickets where cover and a variety of nest sites and food are available. The shrubs provide flowers, fruit, bark, and foliage for various appetites and attract insects which in turn bring those birds feeding on them.

Herbs are certainly not in short supply in the forest community. Like all their plant and animal neighbors they have their habitat preferences. Many penstemons, like the magenta Sierra pride, claim cracks in exposed bedrock holding but a thimbleful of soil. Stonecrops and even some drought-resistant ferns share such unlikely seeming homes. Other penstemons—the spectacular scarlet bugler and equally colorful species that are lavender, pink, and electric blue—join scarlet gilia, the satin-petaled blazing stars, Sierra iris, sometimes the color of weak tea, paintbrush, orange or yellow wallflowers, locoweeds, vetches, and lupines in hill and roadside gardens flourishing in July and early August. A handsome lupine is appropriately named the harlequin because of its bright pink and yellow blossoms. Where moisture lingers, near a spring or on a creek bank, one of California's few native orchids, rein orchid, thrusts up stalks along which tiny, delicately scented white flowers are arranged in tidy vertical rows. These are towered over by the elongated stems of monkshood, bleeding heart, red columbine, the spreading panicles of flowers of the carrot family such as swamp whitehead, wild onions with their ball-shaped blooms of delicate rose, and the brilliant scarlet monkeyflower.

Herbs are rare in heavily shaded, litter-floored woods, but they are not completely absent. Even though one knows they are to be expected, a clump of bright red snow plants, saprophytic members of the heather family, blazing up from the needle-littered floor is a delightful shock. Here, too, are the slender stalks of pine drops, wintergreen, and coralroot orchid, other saprophytes that also obtain food from decaying organic matter with the help of soil fungi. Such a strategy has obvious value where dim light precludes much photosynthesis, and relatively mild winter temperatures allow year-around fungal activity. In more open forest, where the humus is less thick, yellow-throated gilia, often called mustang-clover, spreads like a blanket of foothill flowers transplanted to these altitudes. In the deeper shade and on moister slopes, one may find miterwort, with its tiny circles cut from fragile green lace, and a small white-flowered relative, woodland star. Nor are grasses missing. Species of wildrye, needlegrass, squirreltail, bluegrass, fescue, brome, melicgrass, hairgrass, wheatgrass, and reedgrass grow in glades as well as in clearings and around the edges of wet meadows.

Scurrying about over the roots and between the stems of the plants of the forest community are avian ground dwellers— robins, dark-eyed juncoes, and chipping sparrows—usually going about the business of food-hunting on the shady floor. One such bird is relatively shy and, brown-backed with a spotted cream-colored breast and reddish tail, would probably escape attention but for its song. This is the ethereal fluting of the hermit thrush which rises to meet the first stars in a series of spaced, ascending phrases. It has a quality shared by few other sounds in nature, and it makes little difference to the listener that the singer may be merely reestablishing his territorial boundaries or is communicating with his mate. His song is of firs and pines darkening against the sundown sky.

Insects, earthworms, and other soil dwellers claiming the attention of robins and thrushes are also eagerly sought by shrews and moles. Seeds dropped from the foliage layers overhead are harvested by a host of small herbivorous mammals— chipmunks which take to shrub branches on occasion, golden-mantled ground squirrels, and brush and deer mice. Wood rats and gophers make use of the green vegetation usually found somewhere within foraging reach all summer long. The largest herbivorous mammal is the mule deer. Visitors often see one or more of these graceful animals in open glades or out in meadows, browsing or filing along wildlife trails. Many larger predators are more omnivorous than strictly carnivorous and rely upon plant augmentation of their diet in season, almost as much as they depend on animal prey. Coyotes, gray foxes, and those engaging pests, the black bears, scout for anything appealing to their appetites. The same is true for some of the smaller meat eaters—spotted and striped skunks, raccoons, and ringtails. Only weasels, martens, bobcats, the few remaining mountain lions, and the extremely rare wolverine on the Sierran slope are strictly carnivorous.

If one is fortunate, one can get a glimpse of California's most beautiful snake, the mountain king, as it winds through the duff of the forest floor. Though many people, particularly those from the East, react strongly in the negative to the striking combination of red, black, and cream because of its superficial resemblance to the poisonous coral snake, this handsome montane species is thoroughly harmless. Rattlesnakes, however, are a different story. One species, western rattlesnake, occurs throughout the Sierra, except in the higher elevations. The rubber boa is a reptile that looks much like a long, shiny, light-brown worm with its blunt tail and small size; it is one of the most gentle creatures in the world. Garter and gopher snakes are as frequent here as they are in other natural communities of California. Three types of lizards are common— fence, skink, and alligator. The last two apparently need more shaded and protected habitats than the first, which can often be seen sunning itself on rocks and stumps.

Many animals range widely through the forest. Owls and hawks soar over the canopy and keep watchful eyes for game below. They often perch on snags or rest in the upper branches for the same purpose. The spotted owl is partial to golden cup oak thickets. Bats seldom rest away from their accustomed roosting places but make use of the open foraging space, above the overstory and between the trees. Traveling up and down, either by flight or by working their way over trunks and branches, many birds utilize almost the entire length of the trees. Brown creepers and several woodpeckers—pileated, hairy, and white-headed—constantly check the bark of trees in their feeding rounds. Yellow-bellied sapsuckers, specialized woodpeckers, add nutritious sap to their insect diet.

The noisiest flitter is the crested jay. Though often encountered on the ground, it works up the trunk by hopping from branch to branch as if going up stairs. It is one of the most obvious birds of the Sierran slope, and one cannot spend a day in the white firs without making its blue-and-black acquaintance. Chickadees frequent many levels while inspecting foliage buds and needle clusters. The most colorful bird in California, the western tanager with its red head and yellow, black, and white body, often behaves in the same way as a flycatcher. It perches on snags and branch tips, swinging out like a little burst of flame to snatch insects while in flight. Two mammals have arboreal habits in these lofty forests. Gray squirrels, residents as well of the yellow pine forest, scamper across the duff, run up on boulders, and disappear into the lower limbs almost faster than the eye can follow their quick movements. Telltale patches of raw and bleeding sapwood where the bark has been gnawed away indicate porcupine damage. These slow-moving, formidable-appearing rodents account for the destruction and injury of thousands of trees yearly. Their sluggishness on the ground gives very little hint of their agility in climbing, particularly saplings or young trees whose lower branches are close to the forest floor.

Though most trees of the Great Green Wall are common to other parts of the West, one species is a famed native of California. This is the big tree or giant sequoia (now named *Sequoiadendron giganteum*) scattered in isolated groves throughout the middle elevations of the central Sierra from Tulare County to a very small isolated grove in Placer County, commonly on gentle slopes between valleys glaciated in the Ice Age. Restricted to deep soils having sufficient ground water through the summer as well as relatively mild winter temperatures, giant sequoias characteristically occupy south-facing slopes at the northern edge of their range and north-facing hillsides at the southern limit of their distribution. Like its coastal relative, the redwood, it is not only remarkably resistant to fire but, as we shall see, dependent upon it, particularly for reproduction. Big tree is protected by thick, nonresinous bark that contains large amounts of fire-retarding tannin, and its height and the short-lived nature of its lower branches keep the foliage canopy above destructive flames. Though it is no longer considered the oldest living thing, as the remarkable bristlecone pines of eastern California surpass them in age, big trees have enviable longevity records, and their 3,000 or so years are to be respected. They can claim title to being the largest plants on earth. They are not the tallest, for the coastal redwoods top them by several dozen feet (10 or so meters), but their girth and board footage elect them over their relatives for sheer size. Many individuals would be tall enough to rival their coastal cousins except that lightning has blasted away their tops. Even so, their fire scars heal over, and they maintain incredible vigor in spite of thousands of years of storm and wind. They are not easily destroyed, but their shallow spreading root mats give way when exposed by erosion. Then the giants topple to lie undecayed for centuries.

Seedlings rarely begin life on undisturbed sites. The seeds are too light in weight to penetrate the deep litter of the forest floor. The surface duff dries rapidly after the disappearance of winter's snow and at the end of showery intervals, and seeds falling into it usually desiccate and die. In spite of this serious obstacle to reproduction, a number of interrelated factors, some environmental and others programed into the tree's morphological characteristics, contribute to its survival as a species. For one, the tree is a prolific seed producer. It has been estimated that under optimum conditions over 20 million seeds may be released per 2.5 acres (1 hectare) per year. These conditions include fire, which not only destroys floor litter but whose heat hastens the opening of the cones. Like the cones of the fire pines, those of the giant sequoia are serotinous. They retain seed as long as they are still green, and, in the absence of other circumstances, natural browning is slow. It may take as long as twenty years for undisturbed cones to become dry enough to open by themselves. The individual tree, however, produces a large number of cones, and each year a certain percentage is ripe enough to open and release its seeds.

Fire is not the only environmental agent to hasten seed fall. Cones dropped by storm damage dry out and open, and recent research reveals that a longhorn beetle and a rodent, the Douglas tree squirrel, have positive roles in stimulating seed release. Although giant sequoias are thought to support a smaller amount of insect life than do most conifers of the area, over a hundred species use parts of the tree for one purpose or another, most of it more or less destructive. The larval forms of the longhorn beetle, however, are in the long run beneficial by their activity. They bore into the cone scales, causing them to dry and shrink. The damaged cones, fortuitously, it appears, open in late summer and fall when the danger of hot dry soils is less and fall precipitation is imminent.

The tree squirrel evidently prefers eating the green scales of big tree cones when it can get them. Not only does it cut and eat the cone in or near the tree; it also relies on caches of cones it stores for the winter months in the ground or thick duff. Deposits of seeds left because of the squirrel's dietary preferences are additional reproductive sources.

Fire benefits in other ways. Seedlings need sufficient amounts of soil moisture, a commodity particularly difficult to obtain during the dry summer months. Fire increases the wettability of the soil of the sequoia forest, in contrast to its effect on brushland soils, and allows easier penetration not only of the seed but of the roots of the ensuing seedling, which strive for subsurface water. (There is the usual other-side-of-the-coin: it also produces bare ground which can heat to temperatures lethal for the seed.) At any rate, the combination of fire and wetter-than-average winters appears to best promote big tree reproduction. If fire is excluded or suppressed, it is speculated that giant sequoias will cease to reproduce themselves to any great degree, and the resulting white fir-mixed conifer forest will gradually be deprived of one of its most memorable species.

Giant sequoia generally requires sunlight. Intermittent fires not only help remove species that are easily burn-damaged as well as those more shade-tolerant, but they also provide sunlit gaps in the forest cover. Tree fall is also locally important. It not only opens the canopy, but it produces by upheaval patches of bare mineral substrate and a supply of cones as seed reservoirs.

The other members of this coniferous royal court are no mean princelings. Each is a monarch in its own right in certain advantageous environments. Four species—white fir, sugar pine, yellow pine, and Douglas-fir—have individuals whose heights tower close to or over 200 feet (60 m.). In the face of such an impressive community, it seems difficult to accept the view that conifers, in general, have retreated in the advance of the recently evolved broadleaf trees. Though both the Sierran yellow pine belt and the coastal slopes of the Pacific Northwest have easygoing climates, elsewhere coniferous forests have been pushed to sites of adversity—dry highlands, subarctic muskeg, sandy lowlands, and infertile pockets. Cone-bearing trees have features that enable them to cope with numerous hardships. Some thrive in highly acid soils, intolerable to many plants, which are characteristic of cool, moist climates where humus accumulations decompose slowly in cold, poorly aerated soils, producing varied amounts of acid. Nutrients and fine particles, important in plant growth, are leached or washed down to lower levels along with basic salts, which, if remaining in the topsoil, would have neutralized its acidity. Certain plants of the heather family and conifers have adapted remarkably to such hostile circumstances and may even benefit from the reduced competition. The ability of the latter to live in very acid soils where other plants cannot compete may be a major factor contributing to their continued survival in the face of the aggressive broadleaf trees. Since their decaying needles contain acid which further aggravates the soil condition, the coniferous group must have been in danger of destroying itself. Becoming tolerant to soils high in acid, in which a partnership with root fungi plays no small part, was superb strategy on the part of a versatile, tenacious group of trees.

The pines are even sturdier members of a robust tribe. Many species of this hardy and flexible genus have taken on extremely rigorous environments. Some, like the closed-cone pines, flourish in regions subjected to frequent burns, germinating best in bare mineral soils and fire-adapting to the extent of producing offspring only when the cones open after exposure to sufficient heat. Many pines thrive in thin or coarse dry soils. In California, pines of the forest must live through the dry summers in an environment where the shade-limited root systems of young trees prevent them from competing successfully with older or better established neighbors for the scant soil moisture. How have the pines met these adversities? Head on, as it were, with a vitality apparently able to overcome all but the most rigorous conditions.

As a group they have long lateral roots, are xerophytic with many drought-resistant leaf features, and are high photosynthesizers, thus efficient in producing food. Moderately shade-tolerant while young, most require abundant sunlight in maturity and seldom close in dense ranks. One local exception is lodgepole pine, which is discussed in the next chapter.

To return to the important cone bearers of the Great Green Wall, we first take note of the tree giving its name to this vegetation zone, western yellow pine. This important lumber tree is also favored by light, regularly spaced ground fire. The thick bark is highly resistant to burning, though fire scars are common on the lower bases of many older trees. Fire is beneficial to the preparation of its seedbed, and it removes brush that if allowed to accumulate would provide fuel for a much hotter and more destructive blaze. It also discourages the entrance of shade-tolerant trees by keeping the groves thinned and open. Yellow pine is considered a shade-intolerant tree as normal growth is stunted by less than 40 percent of full sunlight. It appears, however, that saplings can accept some shade from overstory trees, but they respond well to the good fortune of increased light. Most stands of yellow pine are open and easily penetrated. The trees seldom crowd in on one another. Thick as incense, the pungently resinous pine-woods odor is best on a summer afternoon when warm winds sweep upslope and sing in the needles overhead.

Though great tracts of these pines are common throughout mid- and higher elevations in the West—notably near Flagstaff, Arizona—in much of the Sierra they are scattered here and there. They move into openings in the forest where tree fall gives them light, and they often cover larger areas that have been cleared by fire or that are exposed or relatively dry and unattractive to more mesophytic species. Strong, deep roots help the western yellow pine live in areas of comparatively low rainfall where one would expect more xerophytic growth. Quite often it is the harbinger of the great coniferous tracts of the Sierran slope, straggling along a foothill streamcourse or standing over the clustered oaks of a north-facing hillside. Where it keeps to itself in groves on upland flats, underbrush is usually scarce, and the litter is a springy layer of golden-brown needles broken by occasional carpets of mountain misery, squaw mat, bracken, grasses, and flowering forbs.

Jeffrey pine, its close relative, is usually distinguished by the vanilla odor of its bark, larger cone size, and the down-pointed rather than out-pointed scale spines. It has pushed to more extreme positions than yellow pine, the outposts of the western ranges. It occurs on serpentine and bald granite domes, in draws where cold air settles and on high exposed canyon walls from 5,000 to 6,000 feet (1,500–1,800 m.) on the northwestern Sierran slope and from 7,000 to 9,000 feet (2,100–2,700 m.) on the southwestern. More tolerant of a colder as well as drier climate, it skirts the yellow pine forest at its upper edges, where it mingles with white fir and incense cedar and ventures into the red fir-lodgepole pine forests of the upper montane zone.

Sugar pines are moderately shade-tolerant, and young trees do fairly well in the understory; but unless released in later life, they seldom grow large enough to dominate old-growth canopies. At full size their height is balanced by long slim branches held out like stiff straight arms at right angles to the trunk. Their tips are often pulled down by cones measuring up to two feet (.6 m.) in length, the longest of any conifer in the world. This species is less xerophytic than ponderosa or Jeffrey pine. Best growth occurs where precipitation rates range from 40 to 50 inches (102–127 cm.). Unlike many Sierran conifers, sugar pine appears to germinate as readily in duff as in bare soil. Besides the pines we have just discussed, the lower montane zone has other outstanding cone bearers.

Though very common in much of the mountainous West, the Douglas-fir is somewhat of an enigma; it does not seem to fit easily into any coniferous family. One of its Latin names, *Psuedotsuga taxifolia*, means "false hemlock with the leaves of a yew." It has been called Oregon pine and Douglas spruce as well as Douglas-fir. The last two common names refer to David Douglas, enthusiastic collector of botanical specimens in the palmy days of western exploration. It is unique, however, and has no close relationship to these other species except that it is a conifer with some characteristics very much its own. Unlike true firs, the cones hang down with bracts that are whimsical miniatures of mouse hindquarters, tails and all, tucked in between the scales. The needles are soft and two-ranked, spread like those of the coastal redwoods or drooped to give the pliant twig a weeping aspect. Apparently it needs more light than many other cone bearers, although seedlings seem to do best in some shade at first. Being only midtolerant of shade when older, other species that are more so, such as white fir and incense cedar, can crowd it out when it is weakened by too long a sojourn in the understory. Because its seedlings do well in exposed soils and thrive in the light shade of temporary cover, it is a fire or disaster pioneer. Pure stands of Douglas-fir can usually be attributed to some such opening of the forest. It requires more mesic sites such as north-facing slopes and moist, shady canyons in the drier parts of its range.

To many people, incense cedar looks like a small cousin of the big tree, with reddish bark and scalelike leaves. It has a much wider range and occurs in the northern Coast Ranges, the Klamath Mountains, the Sierra, and the mountains of southern Oregon, as well as in southern California. No near relation to the other western cedars—various cypresses, junipers, and other cone bearers given the common name of cedar (true cedars are Old World species)—it is, like the Douglas-fir, a member of a small but widespread genus. More shade-tolerant than Douglas-fir, it suppresses very well and can wait for years in dense thickets of saplings waiting release to the sun. Apparently it does not need as much soil moisture as many of its coniferous cohorts. It receives less than 20 inches (51 cm.) a year in many places where it grows.

One of the true firs, white fir (the genus *Abies*) is a close relative of its higher dwelling cousin, red fir. Both cones and needles, particularly those on the higher branches, thrust up from the branchlets with a jauntiness not found in most conifers. Aside from pine, it is usually one of the most recognized conifers as its saplings are the familiar "silvertip" Christmas trees so common in the West. They are quite shade-tolerant, and, like incense cedar, dense groves of these young trees are often encountered under light cover of yellow pines and other trees. Unlike the pines, however, white fir is prone to fire damage and needs a plentiful supply of soil moisture. It is at its best where annual precipitation rates range from 40 to 60 inches (102–152 cm.), commensurate with its elevational distribution in the Sierra Nevada of 4,000 to 7,000 feet (1,200–2,100 m.).

Life in a forest is no simple enterprise. For plants, five important factors help control distribution: soil type, moisture, temperature, wind, and light. Sandy soil, 5 inches (13 cm.) of rain, warm climate, gusty winds, and 360 days of bright sun create deserts. Deep loams, 50 inches (127 cm.) of rain, temperate climate, moderate winds, and 200 days of bright sun result in forests. Soils must not be neglected in any discussion of natural areas and their causative features. Their influence in determining the communities found on serpentines, in salt marshes, and on thin-soiled steep hillsides has already been discussed. It is time to consider the soil as such, and be introduced to its various properties. Without it and the moisture and minerals it holds we have a moon, a lifeless, ungenerous, sterile floor. With it, we enjoy the richness and diversification of the living world, dependent as it is on the often ignored vital cover beneath our feet.

Stated simply, soil is a mixture of air, water and its solutes, mineral particles from the parent bedrock, decaying organic matter, and organisms responsible for this decay. Nutrients may be present in cereal-dry or frozen soils, but they are unavailable to plants in these circumstances. To be at their best, soils should contain much organic matter decomposing under warm, moist, and aerated conditions. Then the organisms responsible for decay can easily break down the litter and reduce it to water-soluble elements and compounds which only then are readily assimilable by the living plants needing these chemicals for growth.

Soil specialists speak of this living "skin" in terms of horizons. The *O* horizons include fresh leaf drop and partially to completely decomposed matter. They rest on the *A* horizon, sometimes divided into an upper *A1* where decaying debris is mixed with mineral material, and a lower *A2*. This last is rather depleted because it is the zone of leaching. Water, pulled down by gravity, carries with it much of the organically derived nutrients from the upper layers and deposits them, with fine rock particles, in the *B* horizon lying below. Hardpans and claypans, impervious layers through which water cannot percolate, may consolidate here under grassland and other types of community. The *C* horizon, lower still, consists, for the most part, of partially weathered rock fragments, close to the bedrock from which the mineral particles are derived. Little organic matter is trapped here, and the soil profile passes into the *D* horizon. This is primarily bedrock and, generally, is uninvolved with the organic breakdown occurring above. Horizons may be missing or thin, depending on local circumstances.

The typical soils of the Sierran coniferous forests, at their best, are deep and hold water well. But they may be podzolic, that is, moderately to highly acid and unkindly to species not adapted to this chemical condition. Summer drought also complicates matters. Needles, twigs, and other organic material continue to accumulate, but dry soils, though warm in the summer months, further retard the decomposition of decay-resisting, acid humus. Thus the major agents of soil fertility, the living organisms responsible for soil enrichment—bacteria, earthworms, insects, and the like—are hampered by acidity, drought, and the nature of the plant litter itself. Needles contain large amounts of lignin, woody material that is slow to break down. Nevertheless, soil production continues, though at less than optimum pace. Snow meltwater reserves and occasional thunder showers contribute moisture, and nature has other devices as well. Bacteria, living commensally with roots of certain plants, notably the legumes, fix atmospheric nitrogen into compounds available to plants. Since this necessary substance is scarce, leachable, and often destroyed by fire and other disruptions of the natural community, agents able to transfer free nitrogen into water-soluble and easily absorbed soil substances are of tremendous value to neighboring plants. Vetches, lupine, and other wild legumes of the Sierra are very useful in this respect, and they are supplemented by nitrogen-fixing species of ceanothus and alder. More acid-tolerant than bacteria, fungi, discussed more fully below, have a very important role in the decay processes of coniferous forests and are responsible for decomposing large amounts of organic litter.

In spite of the efforts of these organisms, evergreen forests often have relatively poor soils. One has but to think of the nitrogenous reserves locked up in the great boles and foliage masses of coniferous forests to realize that not much nutriment is being returned to the soil. Local conditions vary. Decay and the replenishment of nitrogen are slower in the Great Green Wall than they are in the always warm, moist climate of the Amazonian rainforest with its broadleaf trees, but the process is faster on the western slopes of the Sierra than in the arid pinyon woodlands to the east. Throughout the summer-drought regions, nevertheless, what needle litter falls is not only resistant to decay but is protected from decomposition by the nature of both the climate and soils found in the habitat.

Fungi are key links in the chain of decay and soil build-up, and they play an immeasurably important part in the continuation of cone-bearing forests. Hyphae—microscopic filaments from such simple plants as mushrooms, toadstools, bracket fungi, and the like—are woven through the soil in an incredible fabric. Thousands of miles of these threadlike structures are estimated to live in each acre of forest soil. They digest the organic debris by the excretion of enzymes, freeing the elements and compounds so necessary for continued plant growth. Mycorrhizae are fungi that are engaged in mutually helpful symbiotic relationships with certain plants. The hyphae either surround the rootlets or enter them, in both cases making nitrogen compounds available to the partner plant. It is quite possible that the fungi prefer acid soils and condemn the trees to live in these unfriendly substrates. If so, they have certainly compensated for their choice of homesite by aiding in the liberation of vitally needed elements. There is evidence that fungi and certain algae resident in decaying logs are also nitrogen-fixers, providing an additional source of this valuable element.

The same organisms responsible for soil fertility are active in the disintegration of woody tissue. Fallen logs are reduced in time to the basic elements which were needed for their growth in the first place. Each is a small ecosystem, literally crawling with a life of its own. If you examine such a decaying log, you are likely to find centipedes and sow bugs curled in the dirt, perhaps startled by the unexpected light. There might be holes where carpenter bees have entered, and by lifting a portion of the loose bark, you can see where bark beetles have excavated their wandering, apparently aimless channels between sapwood and bark. Termites may have penetrated into the heart, and carpenter ants may have begun long galleries as circuitous as those of medieval castles. Probably part of the heartwood will be pithy and punklike because of fungi, those insatiate digesters which bind not only soil but fresh fallen wood with mats of mycelia that exude juices into the dead tissues. Where the wood is really rotten you can rub it to dust between your fingers. Here, skulking in tunnels, are the larvae of wood-boring beetles and flat bugs feeding on the fungus-riddled wood.

One type of decomposer succeeds another as the breakdown continues. While dead or discarded animal debris and wastes are being worked over by ants, carrion beetles, and

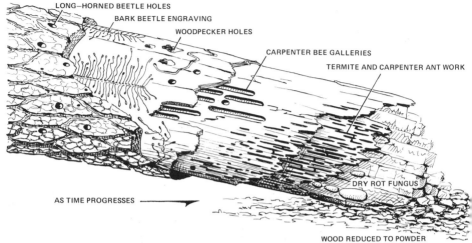

LONG—HORNED BEETLE HOLES
BARK BEETLE ENGRAVING
WOODPECKER HOLES
CARPENTER BEE GALLERIES
TERMITE AND CARPENTER ANT WORK
DRY ROT FUNGUS
AS TIME PROGRESSES
WOOD REDUCED TO POWDER

Figure 18. Reduction of fallen log to soil

flies, springtails and silverfish are ingesting dropped leaves and other dead herbaceous material. At the same time, bacteria and fungi are exploring these new additions to the litter of the forest floor. Softened by initial attacks, the humus attracts sow bugs, earthworms, and millipedes. The droppings of the decomposing insects and other small invertebrates are worked on in turn by still smaller organisms. The litter is constantly being reduced to particles that decrease in size as the process continues. Each stage results in the release of additional enriching substances. Finally everything has been removed from the picnic table. All that is left is inorganic matter. It remains in the soil, ready for use by another generation of plants and the succeeding consumers of the forest food web.

In time, even the stricken giants of the big trees, lying here so long without noticeable decay, will succumb to the forces of weather and decomposition. Nothing, once alive, can fully protect itself from eventually returning to the soil from which it came originally. Elements circle and recircle, occasionally caught in the life histories of various living things. It is entirely possible that each of us carries an atom of potassium or carbon once in the tissues of a tree fern of the Dinosaur Age or an ancient trilobite. Tens of thousands of years from now, other organisms will reuse the same basic materials life on earth has found indispensable for its growth and evolution.

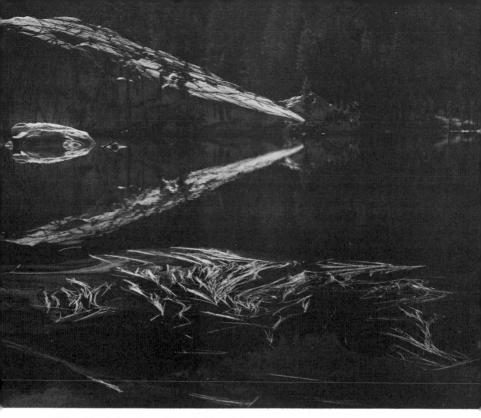

Wilbur May Lake, Sierra Nevada Mountains

13. Mountain Meadow

Mid-October is a good time to discover the responses of the high country—that above 7,000 feet (2,100 m.)—to approaching winter. The experience will be all the more delightful if you start your trip in the lowlands of the Great Valley, in Sacramento, for instance, as the temperature there will probably be in the seventies or eighties, and the watered lawns still green. The road up Carson Pass is an easy and excellent introduction to the Sierra Nevada. You will be spared the trucks of Highways 80 and 50 to the north and the speed of newly straightened roads in Yosemite further south.

At the outset, try to ignore the conifers or, at least, don't let their impressive ranks keep you from watching for the sometimes elusive deciduous trees and bushes. These are the color bearers, the rich bunting that decorates the solemn groves of needle-leaf trees. In the yellow pine forest, dogwood leaves slowly shift from deep green to reddish purple. At the beginning of the cold season, while the days are still warm, the transformation is barely noticeable. The centers of the large oval leaves first become tinted with magenta which finally spreads throughout the entire leaf. Branch follows branch in catching fire as frosty nights succeed each other. Then the foliage lightens in color to a rose-gold before dropping off entirely. Another colorful tree of mesic sites is big-leaf maple whose leaves burn with clear yellow or orange flame. Black oaks vary from golden-brown to russet, when backlighted by a sun now firmly in the southern sky. The elegance of their sharply scalloped leaves compensates for any lack of brilliance of hue. Of the many deciduous shrubs and woody vines in the foothills and lower slopes, poison oak and wild grape have the handsomest fall foliage. Both begin to flush rose-pink soon after Labor Day without waiting for temperatures to drop to freezing.

Ascending the Sierran slope, one sees but flares of color here and there—in a canyon, out on a brush-covered slope. Where are the masses of brilliance, the would-be rivals of the eastern hardwoods? Persist on to higher altitudes; and if you are fortunate in your timing, you will be properly overwhelmed. As the yellow pine and white fir forests give way to red firs and lodgepole pines, the long, conifered ramps of the range begin their break into the granite heartland, the basins and ridges of the High Sierra. The first true mountain meadows open into surrounding groves of pine and fir. Here, the quiet pools of autumn's shallow creeks reflect the slim fingers of willow leaves, the color of buttercups. Around the meadow edges, away from the marshy center, mountain blueberry spreads low-growing clumps of burgundy and cerise.

The meadow floors themselves are wondrous autumnal tapestries. Corn lilies, tall monocots that seem to have escaped from farms in Iowa, stand in golden shocks. Sedges and rushes run in streaks of russet through shining grass. But the glory of these meadows, the rocky benches around shores of alpine lakes, and wide upland slopes is the groves of aspen—the West's answer to New England's fall. Framed by peaks silvered with the year's first snow, reflected in lakes of gentian blue, flickering in a wind fresh out of a sky the color of the lakes, these tall, white-barked torches of orange-gold flame for a brief week or so of incandescence before dying out in the chill air of coming winter. They are at their best when they mingle with a few conifers. The contrast of smoldering silk and somber plush is startling and effective. For the most part, their neighbors are the pines and firs of the upper montane zone— red fir and Jeffrey, lodgepole, and silver (western white) pines, the last a relative of the sugar pine of lower altitudes.

Red fir interfingers with white fir at its lower limit of elevation, 6,000 feet (1,800 m.), meets and mingles with lodgepole pine at about 8,000 feet (2,400 m.), and finally gives way to subalpine forest at 9,000 feet (2,700 m.). Precipitation, almost entirely in the form of snow, ranges from 35 inches to an ample 65 inches (90–165 cm.). Sugar pine and incense cedar occasionally extend into the higher montane zone, Jeffrey pine keeps to its outposts, and mountain hemlock, particularly south of Yosemite National Park, consorts with lodgepole pine and red fir in sheltered, shady gullies. Silver pine, on the other hand, accepts dry, open rocky slopes. Because of the dense overstory, shrub growth is scattered, except for fire-created breaks, and for the most part consists of species common to montane chaparral—bush chinquapin, pinemat and greenleaf manzanita, bitter cherry, and snow and tobacco bush ceanothus. Huckleberry oak appears to tolerate relatively unfertile soils.

These high mountain meadows, with their handsome stands of aspen, have been called the jewels of the Sierra by that greatest of all mountaineering naturalists, John Muir. Tucked in walls of dark green needles, they spread out to the alpine sky. One rarely sees them below 6,000 feet (1,800 m.), except for such valley floors as Yosemite. Here, however, the vegetation is typically that of the yellow pine forest, and it has but few species representative of higher elevations.

Why are these moist open swales usually found in the upper montane zone or above? The answer is found in the circumstances of their birth which forecast their death as well, for most of these gemlike natural gardens are doomed to disappear from the Sierra in a process as inexorable as that of ice melt in a warm room. Their origins stem from glaciers that sculptured the range during the Ice Age. After the slow rise of the western slope, which culminates in the Sierran crest, the streams draining it were forced to reorient their channels in a westerly direction except at high elevations, where many tributaries continued to flow to the south or north before joining the major rivers. These reconstructed drainage ways were used by glaciers which the Sierra supported four times during the Pleistocene. Several ice fields were formed by the pressure of accumulating snow. Glaciers spread like great tongues from these masses, moving down such valleys as the Hetch Hetchy and Yosemite.

An active glacier alters considerably the landscapes under its control. It excavates a cirque, or rounded basin, at its head. Where several glaciers grind cirques at the base of a peak, it may be carved into a pyramidal mass known as a horn. Such spectacular relief features are frequently encountered in extensively glaciated mountainous country. As an ice cap or field spills over into moving glaciers, the terrain over which they pass is considerably modified by the shattering and grinding that marks their progress. V-shaped stream courses are widened into U-shaped valleys. Jointed or cracked surface rock is plucked from place and frozen into the ice mass. This captured rubble scrapes and scours the bedrock, which when already fractured by orogenic forces, is easily quarried. Pulled away, these pieces leave vertical cliffs like those lining Yosemite Valley, which at one time was filled with ice 3,000 feet (900 m.) thick. Tributary channels above the main glacial body become hanging valleys, left high but not dry when waterfalls plunge from them to the canyon below, as they often do.

In time, the climate warmed and the glaciers receded, leaving behind scattered boulders called erratics, often on patches of glacial polish (rock scraped to shiny smoothness by ice flow). Moraines are piles of rock discarded by the glaciers as they melted back up their valleys. Where, in their downward journey, they encountered unresisting rock, they carved basins. These became today's stream-connected lakes or their offspring, meadows. To accurately describe what is meant by that last phrase, a little time must be spent on a major ecological concept, succession.

It was early noted in the study of ecology that disturbed sites, if left alone, would revert to a former community well adapted to the environment and capable of replacing itself indefinitely. This stability is reflected in the term "climax community." Each stage in the transition to climax is characterized by certain plants and animals adapted to the conditions of that stage. This process has already been touched upon in relation to what takes place after fires have swept through some of California's biotic communities (see pp. 82ff.). The first stage is usually herbaceous growth. The second may be brush, which in turn is supplanted by re-invading trees or shrubs. They shade out or, in other ways, compete successfully with temporary species.

In contrast to this secondary succession, which follows destruction of the community, there are two types of succession known as primary, ecological history beginning in a sterile area with no previous plant or animal inhabitants. These processes operate over much longer periods of time and start with open bodies of water, on one hand, and bare rock faces, on the other. Though it may take thousands of years and gradual changes of substrate and organism, both of these environments will probably finally support a climax community. To bring it closer to home, in the far distant future both Lake Tenaya in Yosemite National Park and the rounded surface of nearby Polly Dome will disappear under climax vegetation, whatever it might be in that period of geologic time, unless human or other circumstances interfere. The stages of transition from water to land form a hydrosere, and from rock surface to soil, a xerosere. There is a tendency on the part of both to eventually become mesic, or moderately moist.

The High Sierra has many examples of both processes. As we have hinted, most of its mountain or alpine meadows are stages in successional history. As the great glaciers receded, they left behind chains of basins that quickly became lakes as they collected rainwater and meltwater. Many appear almost exactly as they did when deserted by their glaciers—clear, ice cold, rock-bedded, and almost devoid of nutrients, thus incapable of supporting much plankton or higher plant life. In places, the ice mass has so recently receded, it is but yesterday, geologically speaking, that it retrenched to higher sites. There are about seventy or so small glaciers left in the High Sierra. They are not the impressive rivers of ice we see in Alaska, on Mount Rainier, and in the Canadian Rockies, but glaciers all the same.

Other features of the environment keep high country lakes in youthful stages. Succession is slowed by rigorous climatic conditions precluding much plant activity. Because of their lofty positions, little sediment drains into them from surrounding rocky heights. They tend to remain clear blue and not very hospitable to living organisms. At lower altitudes or under more favorable conditions, the transformation from lake to meadow progresses at a faster rate. Slowing their pace as they enter quiet water, streams drop loads of detritus, building deltas and distributing sediment over the lake floor. Dead plankton and the remains of higher vegetation and aquatic animals augment the deposited debris. Typical plant species of Sierra lakes include pond scums, chara, and other algae, pond weeds, water lilies, or wocas with their yellow cups, arrowhead, aquatic buttercups, water starwort, and an astonishing little plant, bladderwort. The latter is one of the three carnivorous plants in California, all of which occur in areas low in nitrogen such as marshes and bogs. It grows in feather-leaved ganglions sprinkled with little beadlike bladders. These have trap doors at one end that are triggered to operate when tiny creatures such as minute crustaceans or newly hatched tadpoles swim close enough to spring them. If careless victims touch the sensitive bristles around the doors, the bladders open to suck them in, and they must surrender their nitrogen-rich little bodies for the benefit of the plant.

As the debris of dead organic material accumulates, and stream flow and runoff deposit additional sediment, the lake becomes shallower. Its edges tighten as plant life pushes out farther and farther into the shrinking pond. Sedges and rushes, several aquatic grasses, horsetails, and mosses, including sphagnum—of limited occurrence in the Sierra but still present—crowd together on the rim. These plants succumb to winter, and their dead leaves and stems enrich and build the soil, raising the pond's floor little by little. Fallen trees slowly decay in the chill, poorly aerated muck, but eventually they also contribute their remains. Now other plants, many of them showy wildflowers, tolerant of wet to damp substrates begin to homestead—corn lilies, paintbrushes of varying reddish hues, white violets, shooting stars with their small pink rockets, wild hollyhock, cranesbill, the charming purple lilies known as camas, wild iris, brilliant orange and maroon Sierra lilies, a number of white umbels, monkshood, and potentillas and buttercups as yellow as turned aspen leaves. Two flowers are so interesting they deserve more than places behind commas—green gentian and elephant's head. The first, cousin to blue gentians, also meadowland neighbors, rivals corn lilies in height. Pale green flowers, whose parts all seem at right angles to each other, grow in long rows next to the stout stem. Two species of elephant's head are picturesquely named for their rosy blossoms, exact miniatures of angry elephants with flaring ears and upraised trunk. In all but the dampest places, grasses take advantage of these open sites—needlegrass, blue-grass, trisetum, hairgrass, bluejoint, fescues, and ticklegrass.

Where the meadow slopes up to enter the surrounding forest, many wildflowers and shrubs are at home. The composites are represented by cone flowers, sneezeweed, and goldenrod. Forget-me-nots and their cousins, chiming bells, open pink and blue blossoms beside clumps of willow and fireweed. Some of the shrubs have flowers as colorful as the herbs. American laurel has clusters of small rosy cups; mountain pink currant bends sprays of flowerets over streambanks and other moist places. Blueberry, Labrador tea, snowberry, ceanothus, and red elderberry move onto better-drained soils, as do the trees. More tolerant of poorly drained soils, lodgepole pines step in front of their red fir associates. The youngsters of both species often show snow damage. A foot or so from the ground, the trunk suddenly bends at right angles and, with another sharp turn, straightens itself again. These "knees" indicate that snow, extremely heavy in the pine-fir belts, once burdened the sapling to the point where it almost broke under the pressure.

As the pond gives way to the encroaching meadow, it may become but a narrow slough, drying in late summer. If running water drains the swale, the meadow may continue, more or less, to be held at bay. Under both circumstances, however, the trees inch in, sapling by sapling, until every vestige of the old marsh has completely disappeared. Now forests of the two major climax species crowd out the herbs and shrubs and only a few of the latter remain.

Both red fir and lodgepole pine are best established on mineral soil, but the fir seedlings do well under shade and the tiny pines do not. A most interesting relationship in terms of fire history has developed because of this difference in shade tolerance. Large-size lodgepole pines that survive light fires are particularly susceptible to bark beetle invasion. Red firs can become established in the shade of the dying pines, but the pines cannot regenerate under these conditions. Where fire has destroyed the overstory, lodgepole pine seedlings readily take advantage of both increased light and improved seedbed, but the red firs soon establish themselves under the shade of the pine saplings and eventually overtop and kill them. The firs, however, require well-drained soils and leave to the lodgepole pines moist sites such as those near streams, around meadows and other places where the water table is close to the surface. There is evidence that these pines are remarkably versatile in terms of soil moisture. They can both increase their water intake and transpire at a much more rapid rate when on wet ground. On the other hand, dwarf forms of lodgepole pine pioneer the thin soils of glacier-scrubbed ridges and basins, extending its range to 11,000 feet (3,300 m.)—well above that of red fir.

Because of its germination and early growth requirements, lodgepole pine is a fire invader. Such behavior could be considered compensatory as burns are very destructive to its thin bark. The subspecies of the Rocky Mountains and intermountain ranges has serotinous, delayed-opening, cones, an additional insurance of successional status following fire. Most of the dense groves of lodgepole pine throughout the mountainous western interior are burn colonies. Packed together like matches in a box, the stand grows in unison, as it were, no one individual rising much higher than its peers. Self-pruning, the process whereby the lower branches of the trees die and are discarded when there is inadequate light under the canopy for efficient photosynthesis, keeps the boles of many tree species relatively free of snags. Lodgepoles, however, do not self-prune as efficiently as some other conifers. Looking into a dense stand, one is reminded of tangled lengths of heavy wire by the slim, bare branches hanging awkwardly from the trunk.

In the Rockies, shade tolerants such as subalpine fir and Engelmann spruce overtake the spindly lodgepoles and eventually cause their demise. In the Sierra, however, the pines appear to be holding their own and growing to impressive heights, except when red firs prove to be their nemesis because of blighting shade.

Throughout much of its range, quaking aspen is another fire

pioneer and takes over, when the field is opened, from underground suckers that remain from groves that sprang up after previous burns or other disturbances, including avalanches. Its blocky patches are notable features of meadows, shoulders, and subalpine slopes where underground moisture is at no great depth. Like most fire pioneers, it is very shade-intolerant and gives way, in time, to the dominant trees of the climax forest.

Meadows have their typical animal residents as well as visitors from the nearby forest—tanagers, white-crowned sparrows, hermit and yellow-rumped warblers, pileated, hairy and white-headed woodpeckers, olive-sided flycatchers, wood pewees, chickadees, red-breasted nuthatches, Townsend's solitaires, and fox sparrows.

Some birds are more or less confined to higher forest zones. Ruby-crowned kinglets give way to golden-crowned; Cassin's finches replace purple; and the Williamson's sapsucker and three-toed woodpeckers do not venture much below the lodgepole pine–red fir belt. The western bluebird of foothill fields is supplanted by mountain bluebirds, flashes of sky blue as they feed out in the swales. At the upper edge of the zone, Clark's nutcrackers take the place of crested jays. They are as noisy and cheeky but less colorful than their cousins. Several cone openers are active, pine grosbeaks and crossbills, found in coniferous boreal communities across the continent. Evening grosbeaks are striking with their gold, black, and white plumage. They forage either in trees or on the ground, looking for berries and seeds or nibbling succulent buds. Two owls hunt through forest and meadow alike—great horned and pygmy—looking for the many rodents and small animals making use of open, herb-covered terrain.

Snowshoe hares replace the black-tailed jacks of lower elevations. Though rarely seen, the intriguing patterns of their paw prints, a series of little blue-shadowed dimples in the snow, disclose their skill in negotiating deep drifts. Chickarees are actually more common here than in lower zones. This noisy, inquisitive arboreal squirrel leaves telltale caches of green unopened cones, pine bough tips, and piles of descaled cone cores throughout the woods where it is resident. Pine marten, several weasels, mountain coyote, the rare red fox, and black bear scout through the forest and along meadow trails.

The drier meadows are undermined with intricate tunnels.

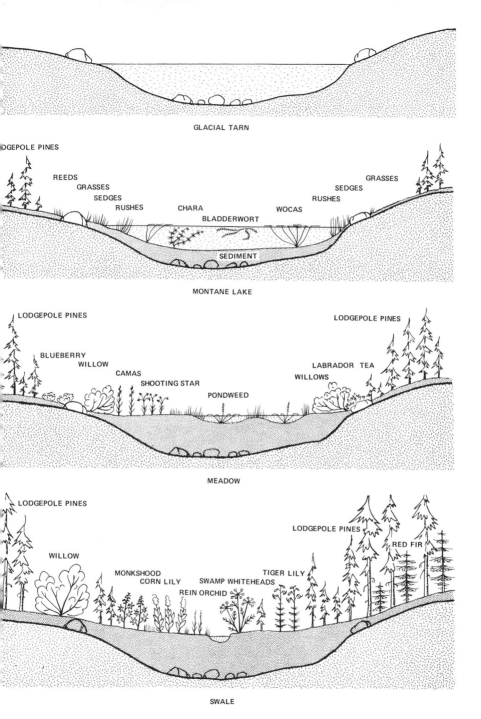

Figure 19. Stages in succession from lake to climax forest

Belding ground squirrels are the familiar picketpins of Tuolumne and Red's meadows, favorite campgrounds for many visitors. They are most engaging as they fold their paws on their plump little stomachs and, with backs as straight as fence posts, stare at their neighbors. Jumping mice and meadow mice use the tangled vegetation of damp meadow floors; pocket gophers tunnel the soft, easily worked soil even through the winter, leaving winding little mounds of dirt that settle out in the spring from where they were stored in the snow. Shrews often scurry through this convenient labyrinth of passageways or forage in the grassy mat. Vegetation is affected, to lesser or greater degree, by extensive small mammal excavation. Disturbance of soil, the accumulation of nitrogenous wastes, and the transporting of seeds and vegetative shoots would tend to rearrange the distributions of plants from patterns they might otherwise have adopted. One of the gaudiest of meadow dwellers is a tiny treefrog, strikingly marked with green, red, or yellow, and but an inch or two long. At the other end of the scale in size, mule deer often browse in these open places. One should watch for them in late afternoon or early morning.

Nowhere are streams more glorious than in the high country, running through flumes of white granite, churning in natural potholes, widening into perfect trout pools. If you are patient, you will be rewarded by acquaintanceship with one of the West's most unusual birds, the water ouzel or dipper. Rather plain in appearance—robin-sized and gray—it works its way along the stream, often stopping to perch on spray-wet rocks to bob up and down. It actually feeds right in the water, at times submerged, looking for the aquatic insects that form its diet.

Most high-country ponds, lakes, and streams have representatives of what may not be the most visually impressive but certainly has the potential of being the most annoyingly aggressive group of animals in the world—insects. Their numbers and representation vary with the differences between aquatic habitats. Timberline lakes in sterile bedrock or gravel-floored basins are almost lifeless. Too cold, too frozen much of the year to support much plankton or higher plant life, there is little food for the small crustaceans and herbivorous insects whose absence discourages not only predaceous insects but trout as well. Unless deliberately stocked, these lovely turquoise-hued lakes are the sources of much angling anguish as cast after cast proves fishless. California's state fish, the golden trout, was once confined to the Kern River drainage, but it now has been planted throughout much of the Sierra. Where lake-meadow succession has advanced to the stage of supporting both flourishing aquatic vegetation and well-developed shoreline growth, insect life crawls, flies, and swims into strategic positions in the local food web. Diving beetles, water pennies, water boatmen, and water striders are active predators, and the same is true for the immature forms of dragonflies and damselflies, the larvae of dobson- and alder-flies, and mosquitoes. Most mayfly nymphs, on the other hand, feed on algae and other types of plant material. A number of aquatic insects, stone-fly nymphs, for example, use both plant and animal material. By their eating habits they are capable of filling all kinds of intermediate positions, and their lack of dietary restriction is useful should circumstances curtail part of their food supply.

No current of water is much swifter than that of a rushing mountain stream. In many ways it is one of the most inhospitable aquatic environments, and few organisms can cope with its obstacles. Chill in temperature, often almost barren of any plant life, about the only feature in its favor is that it has a plentiful supply of oxygen. Only when it encounters restraining meadows or slows down to rest in pools or lakes can residents be complacent about its flow. To live in a swiftly flowing stream, one can either escape the relentless push by seeking shelter or develop ways to oppose the ever-present pressure. Streamlining, presenting as little resistant surface as possible to the current, is common among stream dwellers. Trout, other swift stream fish, and even some invertebrates such as certain nymphal mayflies have taken this tactic. Adult riffle beetles cling to roots with strong claws. Black fly larvae have suckers and hooks with which to anchor their bodies onto stream-swept rocks, and immature net-winged midges have suction discs for the same purpose. The adaptable caddisflies vary both food-capturing and protective devices. In swift water, several species construct nets to gather food supplies. Among those preferring not to do battle are some caddisflies which burrow into sandy floors. Others construct little cases out of gravel, plant material, and other bits and pieces, cementing the tapered little shelter with their own secretions. The case may be weighed down with heavier pebbles. Some crustaceans hide under protecting overhangs and in crannies, but many aquatic forms simply avoid the problem entirely and never tackle the hazards of the torrential flow.

Where the streams have helped build soil by depositing rock fragments on upland valley floors or where slopes have accumulated them on foundations of talus piles or bare incline, the high world supports forests of lodgepole pine, red fir, aspen, and hemlock. Elsewhere on this rolling, swelling granitic sea, among glacial erratics and scattered boulders, there are both lone individuals and clumps of high altitude conifers wherever they can gain a foothold; and the same is true for a number of shrubs—alpine gooseberry, alpine prickly currant, creeping penstemon, pinemat manzanita, huckleberry oak, and sagebrush, which slips in over the crest from its domain to the east. In places such subalpine species as Jeffrey, whitebark, and other timberline pines and the striking, red-barked mountain juniper appear to be growing right out of bedrock as their roots disappear into narrow cracks. Stunted lodgepole pines hang onto tiny patches of soil tucked in fissures or accumulated on the surface.

How does the process of soil manufacture start on the sterile substrate of bare rock? In other words, how does a xerosere develop? There are no cooperating streams to drop silt or gravel; seemingly, no plants add their decayed remains. There are, however, forces at work. Bare rock disintegrates into small particles by mechanical and chemical weathering. Freezing water caught in cracks or crevices expands and forces open such apertures and clefts. This action repeated over and over results in much broken and fractured rock. Heat from the powerful alpine sun performs the same task. Both work together to peel off slabs of granite, particularly where large, surfacing rock masses have expanded upon release from great subterranean pressure. This process is called exfoliation, and it has shaped the smooth bald domes so typical of the Sierra. Gravity pulls down the cracked-off debris and piles it into talus slopes, leaving the smaller particles, gravel, and the like, in heaps scattered about on ledges, in depressions, or packed at the bottom of open fractures. Meltwater and temporary springtime rivulets carry down eroded fragments and deposit them in catchment pockets.

At the same time, biological as well as geological processes are at work. Those primitive, long-suffering plants—rock lichens—manage to persist on their heat-baked, wind-blasted, bone-dry homesites, often covering whole cliff faces with a brilliant mosaic of marmalade orange, sulphur yellow, black, and gray. Incidentally, where there are seeps from cracks that intercept underground water flow, long black streaks on cliff walls are caused by algae. The steep side of Half Dome has excellent examples of this discoloration.

What follows is a description of what could be called the "classic" stages of a xerosere, now thought to be rare in the Sierra Nevada. Not only do chemicals released by the lichen aid in corroding the rock surface, its decaying tissues add organic material to soil particles slowly accumulating from the disintegrating rock beneath and fragments deposited by other means. Eventually, enough soil may collect to support mosses which thicken the tiny growing plot. They in turn decompose, and then a small bed is ready for pioneering hardy ferns, and grasses and other small flowering plants. The patch grows and may cover 9 or 10 square feet (1 sq. m.) and be several inches (10 cm.) thick unless a catastrophe removes it. A venturesome shrub takes root, then another, until the rock surface now supports a real thicket. Trees find foothold in the deepening soil and in convenient cracks in the parent rock below. Finally, all traces of the original surface become buried under the soil and litter; climax vegetation has arrived.

The more typical Sierran xerosere begins in clefts. As gravel grains and other debris gather in them, higher plants can take advantage of any water held by accumulating rock fragments, dead leaves, and other organic matter. Hardy grasses and forbs become established without having to wait for lichens and mosses to work on the substrate. Such colonies in time spread out mats of vegetation that slowly cover the adjacent bedrock. Even trees, though remaining dwarfed, can begin and continue growth in cracks whose meager soils are enriched by discarded plant litter. Other xeroseres originate in the shallow piles of weathered rock fragments accumulating in hollows and gullies. Herbaceous plants such as mountain jewel flower and the ground-hugging pussy paws colonize the little drifts until the soil is thick and rich enough to encourage taller herbs, then shrubs, and finally trees. The roots themselves actually aid in the disintegration of rock by releasing chemicals that form carbonic acid, an active agent in the weathering of limestone and other rocks with significant amounts of the mineral calcite.

Mountain meadows are more than the flower-bright expanses of burgeoning green so pleasing to summer visitors. They are gracious pauses in ecological time, hospitable to a number of diverse creatures and rewarding to plants requiring light and moisture, open as they are to the energizing warmth of the high country sun.

Sunrise, Sierra Nevada

14. The Bluest Sky

Two natural communities are found at elevations of 9,500 feet (2,850 m.) and above, and one of these, unlike the other biotic complexes of California, cannot be reached by ordinary car. The motor traveler can look above the highest outposts of subalpine forest to true alpine country from several road-traversed passes, but these rock-bastioned rims and slopes are aloof. They are reserved for hikers and trail riders willing to expend energy, time, and in many instances money. Even with limited resources of all three it is possible to venture into the alpine world on your own. You should have at least a full day, a snack, a map of the area that interests you, and tennis shoes or good boots that have been broken in.

There are many places in the Sierra where all you need allow is a day in which to ascend from your car to timberline and above, and return. The Saddlebag Lake-Tioga Pass area is a favorite as 2 miles (3 km.) in any upward direction will take you to one of the numerous rock fields above tree limit. At the head of Rock Creek a stiff but feasible 3-mile (5 km.) climb switchbacks up to Mono Pass. Several trails struggle above the Bishop Creek headwaters. On the other side of Minaret Summit, a vehicular crossing of the divide, the trails from Agnew Meadows quickly mount to spectacular alpine scenery via Shadow and Garnet lakes. From trail head at the Virginia Lakes is another short but sturdy 3-mile (5 km.) climb to Summit Pass. Sonora Pass, a motor highway, is rewarding; for only a mile or two up on each side of the summit, alpine gardens begin to carpet the rocky slopes.

Some clarification of terms is useful at this point. *Alpine* refers to mountain areas above timberline; *subalpine*, those at timberline or slightly below. *Timberline*, or *tree limit*, refers to the upper edge of tree growth. The two communities discussed in this chapter are subalpine forest and alpine fellfields. Timberline, actually an ecotone, occurs between the two, as the upper limit of the subalpine forest is the lower edge of the alpine zone. Tree limit is locally irregular and is roughly 10,500 feet (3,150 m.) in the Yosemite area, slightly higher south of the national park and lower to the north. There are a few localities in the Sierra where timberline is just about road level—Minaret Summit and Tioga and Sonora passes. These are the easiest places to become acquainted with the most typical timberline tree of the Sierra, whitebark pine.

Each of the vegetational zones of the range has characteristic pines adapted to certain climatic, edaphic, and topographical conditions. They extend from the thirsty slopes of foothill oak and digger pine to damp meadow floors ringed with the slender boles of invading lodgepole pine. Whitebark pine literally tops the group, with its lofty residence on many ranges throughout the mountainous West. At its lower limits in the Sierra it meets five other pines: Jeffrey, lodgepole, silver, limber, and foxtail. Two additional conifers—mountain juniper and mountain hemlock—have the necessary stamina to exist on these storm-battered heights. The first is often a loner, dominating granite ridges and other rocky exposures, or sharing them with curl-leaf mountain mahogany and pinyon. It also occurs with other subalpine conifers such as Jeffrey pine in open forests and patches of woodland throughout much of the High Sierra. A ruggedly good-looking tree, it copes with rocky balds and terraces where soil and moisture sources are scarce. The closely related western juniper (it and mountain juniper are subspecies of *Juniperus occidentalis*) is the arboreal companion of sagebrush in the arid Modoc country of northeastern California and throughout much of eastern Oregon. Some of the scattered distribution of mountain juniper can be attributed to the birds and mammals that feed on the nutritious fruits. Evidently this subspecies is so dependent upon this means of dissemination that its seeds will not germinate unless they pass through the digestive tract of some animal. They rarely grow taller than 50 feet (15 m.), and when fortunate enough to be in a sheltered location, they have stubby but up-right cinnamon red trunks. Where winter winds harry them, as on ridge tops, they are forced into the picturesque gnarling so typical of timberline trees. Hemlocks, on the other hand, are companionably shade-tolerant, and one seldom sees isolated individuals. They are among the most graceful of subalpine trees, and their supple, small-needled branches bend readily under snow drift. A heavy pack in the sapling stage accounts for off-balance clumps, or "knees," thrusting out at odd angles to the slope on which they are growing. In the southern part of their range they do best in protected basins and ravines, on cool shady slopes, and in canyons where snow drifts remain until full summer—sites that guarantee soil moisture sufficient for their needs.

Whitebark pines are capable of great endurance. On their hard-won castellations they do battle with an extremely severe climate and the scarce soils of glacier-scoured terrain. In growth habit they resemble no other western pines in that they often form multitrunked thickets no taller than large shrubs, particularly in the more exposed places. The white bark that gives them their name has a silvery luster rather than the chalky color of aspen, their meadowedge confederates. They are scattered about—on rocky shelves high on the sides of a pass and in hedgelike masses, often no more than several feet (1 m.) tall, on blizzard-blasted ridges above lakes and meadows. Unlike lodgepole pines they are not wet-footed but prefer well-drained sites. Until the days of lightweight air mattresses, hikers were advised to spread their bedrolls on springy piles of whitebark pine branches, but improved equipment and good high-country manners have discouraged this destructive practice.

Those traveling the trails that traverse the crestline ridges find their paths leading to lakes and meadows of unsurpassing loveliness. Nowhere in California is there more beauty crowded into each square foot of scenery. Willow-bordered brooks wander through verdant patches of sedge, rush, and grass, spreading into small spongy marshes or tightening into rills edged with flowers. Many of the same floral types found below recur here—elephant's head, lupines, groundsel, monkeyflowers, shooting star, columbine, paintbrush, buttercups, orchids, and gentians. But some, like sky pilot, are unique and seldom move down from their high homes. Small shrubs of the heather family grow on the same fringing terraces, particularly granite, where whitebark pine grows. The little magenta bowls of red mountain heather resemble those of a related shrub of high meadows, American laurel. Cassiope hangs elfin bells of pure white from tiny crimson star-point sepals. Sod-building sedges, spread out in coarse, compacted masses, or so-called dry meadows, are characteristic alpine dwellers.

The dwarfed plant cover above timberline has often been referred to as alpine tundra, not only because of its similarity to the treeless plains of the Arctic, but also because the two communities share a significant number of the same plants. Certain differences, however, distinguish the two types. Alpine tundra lacks the mosses and leafy lichens so abundant in the Far North; because of pronounced relief, its soils are better drained, and they are not underlain by extensive permafrost, or permanently frozen soil. The two environments also differ in the amounts of precipitation they receive and other climatic factors.

Many of the plants of both tundras are circumpolar, that is, distributed in Arctic regions around the North Pole on the North American and Eurasian continents and adjoining islands. There is evidence that these species probably evolved in the mountains of central Asia and were forced downslope by the increasingly cold temperatures of the early Pleistocene. Some could have traveled to the New World via the Bering Strait and other boreal land bridges that were becoming exposed as the continental glaciers continued to lock more and more water into their huge icy masses, lowering the ocean surface. Reaching the mountain ranges of the West, they migrated upslope and down as well as northward and southward as the glaciers retreated and advanced with the fluctuating climate. A number of species probably persisted in mountaintop refuges that were clear of the icefields below them. At the close of the last glacial period, the plants of the tundra, repeating journeys made several times in the past, clambered back to their alpine strongholds where the climate resembled that of the Arctic. By now they were both depleted because of the wear and tear of climatic change and enriched by numerous endemics that had developed in isolated pockets.

The many alpine plants also present in the Arctic are indicative of periodic contacts between the two areas. While some are confined to the boreal regions of the New World, the large majority are either circumpolar or have a more limited distribution with outposts, however, on both continents. The author has seen the diminutive pink, moss campion, in several widely separated locations—up on Trail Ridge in the Front Range's Rocky Mountain National Park on a bright July morning when "brown" rosy finches were feeding on a nearby snowbank, at midnight when the sun was crawling through fog shrouding Norway's North Cape, and on a mountain flank overlooking a magnificent glacier during a typical Alaskan downpour.

It has been estimated that roughly 40 percent of the tundra flora of Rocky Mountain National Park is circumpolar. In contrast, only about 20 percent of the alpine flora of the Sierra is found in the boreal world. This is not to intimate that the remaining 80 percent is unrelated to tundra floras. A number of genera are shared—*Gentiana, Saxifraga, Ranunculus, Polygonum, Juncus, Phlox,* and *Silene,* among others. The burgundy-red little succulent roseroot, Arctic pearlwort, alpine sorrel, willow herb, white Arctic draba, elephant's head, and shrubby cinquefoil are included in the list of plants found in the Sierra as well as the Rockies and the Far North. In addition the Sierra has many flowers that are almost identical to those farther east or north; they differ only in their specific status, and are similar in appearance—primrose, sky pilot, and alpine paintbrush are examples. But anyone who has memories of the gardens of the High Rockies with their exquisite one-inch tall clumps of unforgettably blue forget-me-not, moss campion, fairy primrose, goldenbloom saxifrage, and alp lilies no larger than a child's thimble will look for them in vain. Differences in floristic composition are not the only distinguishing features of the two alpine vegetations. Richly developed tundra with thicker soils is poorly represented in the High Sierra which has three basic alpine landscapes depending upon the region's overall climatic patterns. What we can call "characteristic" alpine—most closely resembling alpine tundra—is more common in the northern Sierra (and the southern Cascades and Klamath Mountains of northern California). It is typified by: (1) high annual precipitation, (2) some summer rainfall, (3) cool to cold temperatures, (4) deep snow, (5) dependably long growing season—with the exception of areas under persisting snow, (6) humus-rich soil with extensive development of sod, and (7) because of the abundance of water, a large number of moisture-requiring plants, many of which are circumpolar.

The second type is dominated by summer drought, and it occurs in the higher elevations of the central Sierra. Winters are very cold, but snow may vary from light to heavy. As the summers are warm and dry, the deep snow of the wetter winters extends the length of the subsequent growing season. Soils tend to be thinner than in the community type described above and do not display as many frost modifications. Mesic species are confined to moist sites.

The third type is found on the drier eastern slope of the Sierra and the southern part of the range. Termed alpine steppe, it is characterized by cold winters of light snowfall, hot summers relieved by occasional thunderstorms, dry infertile soils, and xeric vegetation.

There is great variability of individual sites within this broad wet-to-dry, climatically determined spectrum. The wetter areas include bogs and marshy places with peatlike acid soils; turf-floored meadows with abundant vegetation, where water is present throughout much of the summer; meltwatered slopes below snowbanks; and smaller seeps and rills. Drier sites, often with thin nonsoddy soils, range from dry meadows and scree and talus slopes to shallow catchments of gravel in rock crannies and exposed, boulder-scattered ridges and flats.

Many are free of snow in winter and, in consequence, suffer from the loss of its protective cover as well as a source of summer moisture. Plant cover is scattered and may be scarce.

Such variation from wet meadows to dry rock (or fell-) field provides a splendid example of the importance of locality—the often subtle differences between 1 square foot of rock field and those 10 yards or 10 miles away. Parent rock, amount and duration of snow cover, direction of slope face, wind exposure, soil depth, length of growing season, soil pH, altitude—the list is long of interactive variables that nudge a habitat to its place in the spectrum.

A recent study (summarized in Michael G. Barbour and Jack Major, eds., *Terrestrial Vegetation of California,* John Wiley, 1977, pp. 624–42) meticulously analyzed 188 stands in three geologically diverse areas of the central High Sierra in terms of substrate and water availability. For this one alpine region the research revealed nineteen plant communities (subcommunities of Philip A. Munz and David D. Keck's alpine fell-field in their *A California Flora,* University of California Press, 1963), each with its preferences for a certain set of substrate and moisture correlates. A few examples are in order.

Wet, peaty meadows on the marble substrates of Convict Basin are characterized by *Kobresia* (a member of the sedge family) and short-fruited willow, circumpolar species found nowhere else in California, and alpine meadow rue, also circumpolar but incidental elsewhere in the high altitude Sierra. Alpine shooting star, Lemmon paint brush, and Mount Rainier cinquefoil, typical representatives of very moist meadows on granite-derived soils, are much more limited in their distribution though more ubiquitous species also occur here. As for the poorly developed soils of dry places, snow draba, Great Basin buckwheat, and Clokey's daisy appear confined to marble in this area, and dense-leaved draba and Shockley's ivesia are part of the thin plant cover on granitic parent material. When moisture is sufficient to encourage intermediate, damp, but not wet, sod meadows, Mexican rush, western needlegrass, and alpine yarrow are marble-based species. In corresponding granitic meadows, Arctic willow, alpine aster, and alpine everlasting find footing.

A study by B. F. Chabot and W. D. Billings ("Origins and Ecology of the Sierran Alpine Flora," *Ecological Monographs,* vol.

42, no. 2 [Spring, 1972]) has such a succinct summary of vegetation patterns in the Mount Humphrey-Piute Pass area that it is worth quoting (circumpolar plants have asterisks):

> Vegetation on peaks and ridges above tree line consists generally of herbaceous perennial species of low stature, plants characteristically alpine in form. Typical of this group are *Phlox caespitosa* [carpet phlox], *Penstemon davidsonii* [creeping penstemon], *Ivesia pygmaea* [dwarf ivesia], *Ivesia lycopodioides* [clubmoss ivesia], *Draba lemmonii* [Lemmon's draba], *Arenaria nuttallii* [Nuttall's sandwort], *Carex hellerii* [Heller's sedge], *Eriogonum ochrocephalum* [ochre-flowered buckwheat], and *Potentilla brewerii* [Brewer's cinquefoil].
> . . . At higher elevations *Oxyria digyna** [alpine sorrel], *Polemonium eximium* [Sierra sky pilot], and *Hulsea algida* [alpine hulsea] are constant alpine members, restricted usually to soil pockets on talus slopes. Much of the present alpine area was once heavily glaciated so that bare rock is abundant and is a major determinant of plant-distribution patterns. The most luxuriant sites are along the snowbank runoff streams where *Dodecatheon Jeffreyi* [Jeffrey's shooting star], *Lewisia pygmaea* [pygmy bitterroot], and *Sedum rosea** [roseroot] are found. Soil pockets between boulders may be densely vegetated with *Juncus* [rush] and *Carex* [sedge] species, and others, more arid, support *Arenaria nuttallii* [Nuttall's sandwort], *Lupinus brewerii* [Brewer's lupine], and *Castilleja nana* [dwarf alpine paintbrush]. In many sites a thin, gravel veneer covering the rock surface produces a particularly arid habitat in late summer which may be devoid of all vascular plant species but *Calyptridium umbellatum* [pussy paws] and *Polygonum minimum* [dwarf knotweed]. The vegetation patterns in this southern Sierran alpine location indicate that water is limiting in many sites.

From this summary it is plain that the pieces of the alpine zone mosaic are just as diverse as those of the coastal hills but on a much smaller scale.

Such diversity notwithstanding, why are there noticeable dissimilarities between the alpine plant life of Colorado's Front Range, for instance, and the Sierra? Climate is an important part of the answer. The Rockies receive far more summer rainfall than the Sierra. It is an exceptional July day when one can roam up Colorado's Yankee Boy Basin in the San Juan Mountains, over Trail Ridge or Independence Pass without several showers falling in a twenty-four-hour period. A soil-plant pattern has consequently evolved. It was set in operation by the presence of abundant moisture during the growing season.

The more rain, the more plants, resulting in an increased supply of leaves, roots, and other remains that in turn deepened and enriched the soil. Summer precipitation has also made possible luxuriant herbaceous undergrowth at midelevations in the Rockies. Though at their best, Sierran wild flower gardens are impressive and colorful, sister ranges to the east have a superior display, with its famed blue columbine, coral tinted gilias, golden gaillardias, and violet harebells. Both floras have some species in common; but there is a flamboyance, a spendthrift air about the flowered banks and slopes of the Rockies, in sharp contrast to the parsimony of Sierran hillsides in the summer, except where streams and drying ponds provide a continuing source of water. It has been pointed out that these wild gardens have contributed many dwarf forms to the alpine plant life of the Rockies. Another process may have been in operation. It has been suggested that many of the tundra species now shunning Sierran heights were once present, and summer drought gradually forced their retreat, driving them out of an increasingly hostile environment. The nature of the terrain is also of consequence. Soil build-up is slow on the sharply eroded peaks and cliffs of this young range that also is separated climatically and physically from the Cascades to the north and the Rockies to the east.

Where then did it come from—this wild alpine garden with its hot pink primroses, sunflower-bright hulseas, and pennant blue-and-white lupines? Lush where nurtured by moisture, sparse where the soil is nothing but gravel, a sieve to water and poor in organic material.

As we have seen, by either eliminating some species or preventing others from venturing south, summer drought is in part responsible for the fact that only 19 percent of the Sierran flora also occurs in the Arctic and 38 percent is shared with the alpine Rocky Mountains. Drought, however, is but one circumstance that influenced the development of the Sierra's alpine plant mosaic.

Significant Sierran uplift had taken place by the end of the Pliocene, just prior to the beginning of the Ice Age. It is presumed that both boreal and cordilleran plant elements began migrating south into the rising ranges of California at the same time and continued into the Pleistocene. The Sierra Nevada was heavily glaciated during the Ice Age, much more so than the Rockies to the east as it immediately intercepted moisture-laden Pacific storms. Much plant life was destroyed at this time, but nunataks—peaks and ridges above the ice sheets—may have been both refuges and resettlement sources for plants adapted to both intense cold and a short growing season. But, as we have suggested, what the ice had not removed was now being threatened by a new danger. The intervening warm periods and postglacial heating up, combined as it was with increasing summer drought, evicted another segment of Arctic alpine species.

The boreal and cordilleran plants that remain are largely, but by no means entirely, confined to moist habitats in the northern part of the range where the alpine environment is most like that of tundra. Two exceptions are alpine sorrel, which is found in rocky, often moisture-poor places south to Mount San Jacinto in southern California, and alpine sandwort of like habitats and a range as far south as Inyo County. Donner and other passes that drop the mountain environment below timberline interrupt the continuity of alpine flora and reinforce climatic barriers to their southward expansion.

Although there is much to support the theory that the migration of cordilleran species was south from the Canadian Rockies along the backbone of the Cascade, Coast, and Sierra Nevada ranges, another viewpoint holds that Rocky Mountain species may have moved west, pioneering into and then spreading out from cold bogs scattered over the Great Basin. That interesting collection of circumpolar species in the Convict Basin with either limited distribution in or absence from the rest of California has been used as a case in point. Both points of view are in agreement that an important source of Sierran alpine plants is the Great Basin. In fact, lowlands on both sides of the Sierran crest contributed floras from which many alpine endemics evolved. Other localized species were derived from those hardy ancestors that hung in there through both Pleistocene cold and the subsequent burden of summer drought. Seventeen percent of the Sierra's alpine flora is endemic, and, as it is equipped to meet the environment's unique conditions of aridity, it successfully withstands competitive pressure by the moisture-requiring Arctic-alpine species. A few genera such as lupine and buckwheat have produced a large number of endemics, an enrichment that greatly benefited from the isolation of both individual habitats and the range itself. Another unique feature of the plant assemblage at the Sierra's high elevations is the relatively large number of annuals, most of which have pioneered from lower altitudes. In contrast, it appears that all but one of the alpine plants of the Rocky Mountains are perennial.

A ride over any one of the higher passes of the Sierra discloses what happens to trees on the approach to timberline. They are smaller in size and fewer in number, and at last give up entirely. Those at the highest elevations exhibit many characteristics common to tree limit. Some take advantage of microclimates, small environments in which features of relief provide localized modifications from the general climatic pattern. Favorable microhabitats are quite numerous in alpine regions: sheltered pockets behind rocky projections where storm winds hesitate on their wild journey across the crest, and slopes comparatively warmer than others because of down drainage of cold air. Southerly or westerly aspects have the advantage of direct sun during the warmer parts of the day. Snow provides its own series of microenvironments, some more helpful to plant growth, some less so. Where it lingers in crannies or on north- and east-facing hillsides, it can prevent vegetation entirely if it does not melt until late summer. Where there is too little protective snow cover and meager meltwater, plants are also discouraged. Where snow lies in a thick blanket ready to disappear into the soil at the first signs of summer, vegetation effectively escapes the terrible pair, winter wind and cold, and benefits from the replenished soil moisture. Temperatures may be much higher under insulating snow cover, and wind is practically nil. Many plants, including trees, cannot live through the blizzards of an alpine winter without this friendly quilt. On the drier high east face of the range tree growth appears to be best near places where heavy snow accumulates, providing dependable sources of moisture during the summer.

Aside from the "knees" described earlier, abundant snow is responsible for other types of injury or damage ranging from broken branches to widespread destruction by avalanche. Backpackers in the high country may notice unsightly masses of brown, dead needles that look glued together on the lower branches of lodgepole pine and other trees of timberline. They are caused by a fungus, encouraged by the humidity within the snow pack, that invades the branches when they are forced into contact with the ground by the weight of thick snow. Solifluction, though often associated with permafrost, also takes place on bedrock. Saturated and lubricated from snowmelt, the unstable soil eases downslope, piling into little hillocks that may cradle tiny ponds. Such creep continues until plant life is established.

The German language has contributed a useful word, *krummholz*, which means "crooked wood." It refers to the stunted, contorted trees of timberline. One study has made clear that the depth of the average winter snow cover determines the height of *krummholz* trees. Branches venturing growth above its shelter are menaced by both the desiccating effects of wind and the blast of its tiny frozen projectiles. A little searching and one can find examples of this process carried to an interesting degree. Look for a boulder, perhaps not more than a foot (.30 m.) high. You might find a little hedge of whitebark pine extending back behind it. At one time, a seedling took advantage of the protection afforded by the rock, and as it continued growth it was compelled by the driving winds to creep close to the earth, taking advantage of snow cover. As it elongated horizontally rather than vertically, it also established new roots here and there.

Occasionally one will see trunks that are bravely tall, considering their winter ordeal. Very commonly the branches on the upper part of the tree will be permanently pointed in one direction, giving rise to the term *flagging*. It is easy to guess the direction of the prevailing wind, as the side of the trunk meeting it head on is bare of limbs or foliage. Though there may be some training by wind, much flagging is due to dehydration and the consequent killing of twigs attempting growth on the windward side. In contrast, the lower limbs are often fully foliaged, protected as they are by snow. Ice and snow bombardment are also responsible for the damaged tissue. Compaction is another adjustment to cold and strong wind. Though unprotected tips of shoots are subject to wind shear, lateral or side buds form densely crowded masses pruned back to stiff hedgelike clumps that can actually bear the weight of heavy objects. When leaders, topmost twigs, project above the snow cover, they are often doomed to be killed by both chill and dehydration. Die-back or the death of most of the tree, leaving a minimum amount of foliage and bark to continue food making and transport, is another adjustment to the harsh environment.

The trees and shrubs of timberline have other causes for stuntedness and dwarfing. Thin, gravelly soils, low in organic material, do not hold moisture well; in addition, at this altitude they are generally cold. Summers are short as well as cool at these elevations. Temperatures can drop below freezing any night of the year, and during winter they close down for eight or nine months of intense cold that rarely rises above frost. But for snowmelt and the only too occasional summer shower, it is an arid world as well. Not only is cold air dry, water in the form of ice is as unabsorbable by plants as the iron in a railroad track; only solutions can penetrate cell membranes. Little rain falls in the Sierra during summer, and the first precipitation of the rainy season will probably be in the form of light autumnal snow. If it melts, it is but a brief interruption of a long drought for any timberline tree not fortunate enough to grow by a wet meadow. From September to late May, moisture is either scarce or locked up as snow and ice kept below melting point by the frost of winter air. Even if soil temperatures reach above freezing, cold substrates tend to significantly lower the metabolic rates of the plants of the community, even in summer.

This leaves but one open course, dormancy. The woody plants of the heights follow the same routine as those of the chaparral, except for a shift of season. Most food manufacture and water transpiration cease during the fall. When spring finally returns, which may be as late as July, full activity is resumed once again though still hampered by chill and the drought that follows when the melting snows have disappeared. All in all, the shrubs and trees of timberline do not have the time or energy to grow much. Even their cells are small in comparison to trees of more temperate regions. Trees whose soil resources are restricted, such as those growing from bedrock cracks or in shallow gravel beds, are subject to additional stress.

How do they maintain their vigor and, as in the case of California's most famed timberline tree, the bristlecone pine, live to incredible ages? If they anchor themselves to wind-harried, often unstable footholds, they could be sending down long roots which penetrate to water and soil pockets deep in bedrock cracks. The evergreen habit again proves useful, for no new foliage need be produced each spring. Already present, it is ready to go to work. Another helpful adaptation is known as hardening. The cell sap gradually thickens in fall. As if anti-freeze was slowly being added, the freezing point is lowered which prevents frost injury to what would otherwise be vulnerable tissue.

What about the herbs, the most fragile highland denizens? Most of them are perennials, for annuals have several strikes against them in the game of alpine survival. The flowers may be left unpollinated or the plant killed by frost before the seeds can mature and disseminate. By being perennial, the plant does not have the liability of being forced to complete an entire life cycle, from seed to seed, as it were, in the short summer of the high country. It is assured of several years of life in which to produce successfully germinating seeds. At the onset of the growing season, new foliage quickly develops from energy provided by food-storing roots, bulbs, and other underground parts of the plant. Photosynthesis begins at once even though the temperatures may still be near freezing. A number of alpine species reproduce from rhizomes, underground fleshy stems, another stratagem that abrogates the need for seed. The thick sods formed by grasses, sedges, and rushes in high altitude meadows are the result of vegetative reproduction. Once the new leaves are established, flowers quickly open from buds that were formed in the previous season or even two years back. Such rapid development promotes the probability that seeds will be set and scattered before the arrival of winter. Flowers even precede leaf production in a few snowbank species.

Several basic plant shapes and adaptive devices, admirably suited to the alpine world, have evolved. Some huddle in little wind-resistant sofa-cushion humps. Few leaves and, in some species, few stems extend above the sheltering compaction. Cushion buckwheat bulges up in tiny silver-leaved tufts so solid in mass that one can stand on them. Other plant pillows are phloxes, cushion-cress and the related comb draba, Sierra podistera, and alpine sandwort.

Because closeness to the earth's surface is so desirable, many species are mat plants. They have not only shortened their stems but have also spread out, flattening themselves to the sun-warmed soil. High Sierran examples include Coville's phlox and carpet clover. Plants like pussy paws and Lobb's buckwheat have basal leaf rosettes that serve the same purpose. Several dwarf species, about as big as buttons, include a tiny bitterroot, pygmy ivesia, an alpine willow, and an alpine aster. These miniature plants use a minimal amount of water, time, and energy in producing just enough leaf and stem to grow and support reproductive parts.

Succulence is as useful here as it is in lower arid environments. One of the loveliest alpine plants is roseroot. It belongs to the stone crop group, a family known for its thick, juicy, wax-coated leaves and stems. Woolly leaves also deter water loss, primarily because the tiny hairs reduce heat build-up in the leaf. Several composites, among them silver mat and the striking hulsea, or alpine gold, have stems and leaves covered with a hairy coat that also serves to protect the plants from wind and cold. Long taproots help anchor some alpine plants in high wind as well as seek subsurface moisture. A number of species, however, seem to rely on no one set of adaptive features for survival in this harrowing environment. They bloom with all the aplomb and arrogance of less harassed relatives but usually within protected crannies and between large sheltering rocks—rock fringe (a richly carmine relation of willow herb), Sierra primrose, alpine columbine, and showy polemonium, close cousin to sky pilot. Plant life above the rock fields is mainly comprised of lichens, those stalwart associations of algae and fungi that seem to defy all climatic regulation.

The animals of timberline and above are equally ingenious in coping with their inhospitable home. By their winter habits they can be roughly classified into migrants, sleepers, and cautious but courageous actives. When mountain sheep were more abundant than they are now, their yearly exodus down to winter range must have been impressive. Those still living in the Sierra continue the process and leave the high slopes where they have been feeding when the first snows presage the onslaught of winter. They slowly but steadily move down into friendlier climes. The deer of the Sierra, though no rock hoppers, also descend to less snowbound regions. The most typical alpine birds, "gray-crowned" rosy finches, forsake their fell-field summer quarters. They too seek the warmer sun and more easily obtained food of the lower levels.

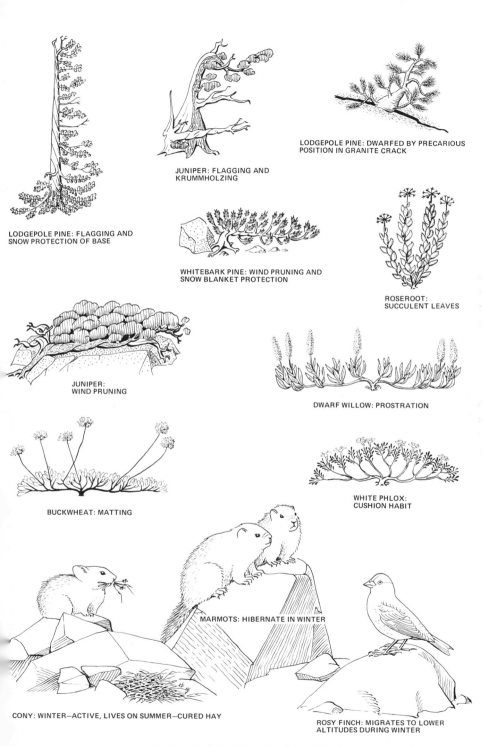

LODGEPOLE PINE: FLAGGING AND
SNOW PROTECTION OF BASE

JUNIPER: FLAGGING AND
KRUMMHOLZING

LODGEPOLE PINE: DWARFED BY PRECARIOUS
POSITION IN GRANITE CRACK

WHITEBARK PINE: WIND PRUNING AND
SNOW BLANKET PROTECTION

ROSEROOT:
SUCCULENT LEAVES

JUNIPER:
WIND PRUNING

DWARF WILLOW: PROSTRATION

BUCKWHEAT: MATTING

WHITE PHLOX:
CUSHION HABIT

MARMOTS: HIBERNATE IN WINTER

CONY: WINTER—ACTIVE, LIVES ON SUMMER—CURED HAY

ROSY FINCH: MIGRATES TO LOWER
ALTITUDES DURING WINTER

Figure 20. Adaptations to alpine climate

Most alpine rodents sleep through the worst months; they include ground squirrels, various mice, alpine chipmunks, and marmots, roly-poly plump and plumy-tailed fellows of grizzled russet that sit sentinel on rocks and outcrops of the high country. During true hibernation, body temperatures lower considerably, and the animal falls into deep sleep. Though it may wake on occasion, for the most part it is in torpor, and its slowed rate of metabolism and cessation of most activity place little drain on its food resources, the fat accumulated during the summer.

One small creature, the pika (cony or little chief hare) of the rabbit group is the winter resident whose life habits provoke surprise. No migrant or hibernator, it goes about its business during the short weeks of summer, gathering herbaceous material growing close to the rock pile home. It is one of the delights of the alpine trail to see these little gray ghosts, about the size of a teen-age rat, tailless and with ears as round as buttons, scurrying between meadow and rock refuge with loads of "hay" in their mouths. Hay it is, for they spread it to dry and cure, and then add it to the piles each cony jealously accumulates in preparation for winter. When it finally descends, they move about in runways, feeding on the crops of summer and protected from blizzard and frost alike in their scree-slope home. Pocket gophers are also active through most of the winter, excavating tunnels in the surface earth and snow to reach vegetation or caches of food buried beneath winter's cover.

Few people have spent much time at timberline in the Sierran winter. We can only surmise what it must be like: gale-force winds hurling snow across crests and peaks; cold that could sting an exposed cheek to frozen whiteness in a matter of minutes; and days when the screaming stops and the snow, packed in stream head basins, lies smooth and unrumpled under the bluest sky.

Owens Valley in Storm

15. The Other Side of the Mountain

The vast area on the eastern edge of the Sierra looks inland, not to the sea, the presence of which, even at timberline, considerably influences the natural landscapes explored so far. True, many winter storms from the ocean climb over the Sierran crest and move east to die or join those moving south from Canada or north from the Gulf of Mexico. But there is a transparency, a plate glass quality, to the atmosphere in these high interior rangelands seldom experienced near the coast. Distances no longer disappear behind blue gauze. They thrust up hills and mesas and lay down lakes and valleys that keep their details out to the horizon itself. Left behind are thirteen of the communities so far discussed. On the other side of the mountain, there are instead eight new communities, as well as variations of six already introduced.

Many Californians live some distance from the sea and may visit the beach, if at all, only once or twice a year; but still it is customary to speak of "coastal" fogs and "sea" breezes throughout a large portion of the state. Winter storms "come in from the ocean," and there is general awareness that the sun finally goes to rest beneath the waves of the Pacific. Now at the top of 9,941-foot (2,982 m.) Tioga Pass, a frequently used entryway to the eastern Sierra slope, it is as though another ocean pulls imaginations toward sunrise skies. What lies before the visitor is that great inland sea of mountain and valley, the basin-and-range province of the interior West.

Central California's small slice of it actually belongs to a major subdivision, the Great Basin. Not a lowland at all, though its name gives that impression, most of its floor is well above 3,000 feet (900 m.) in elevation. It is so called because it has few outlets to the sea and is rimmed by high plateaus and ranges except at the extreme northwestern corner, which is partially drained by the Klamath and Pit rivers. It is really a complex of basins or sinks in which collected runoff either settles in permanent lakes, disappears into natural underground reservoirs, or evaporates into the desert air leaving the alkali-bedded dry lakes so typical of the region.

Those with standing water, in the main, are remnants of once much larger lakes, inheritors of the pluvial wealth of the Pleistocene. Great Salt Lake is one of the much shrunken offspring of Lake Bonneville. Pyramid Lake in Nevada is what is left of ancient Lake Lahonton; and Mono Lake, which we will explore more thoroughly later, is also a leftover. All three lakes have terraces of former shores which are easily identified.

Each sink is a valley between ranges that, chopping the surface of the Great Basin like storm waves in the open sea, rise 3,000 to 4,000 feet (900–1,200 m.) above the basin floor. A few ranges reach impressive heights. White Pine Mountains, Wheeler Peak, Grant Range, Charleston Peak, the Ruby Mountains in Nevada and California's Inyo-White ranges and Panamints all top 11,000 feet (3,300 m.) in altitude.

Any relief map of the Great Basin will give a fair idea of the topographical complexity of the region. On such maps, Nevada looks as if someone had filled a pint Mason jar with caterpillars and dropped them, aligning them so that they were all crawling, roughly parallel, either north or south. Though some ranges amount to nothing more than bumps on the horizon, most are respectable in size and unique for their universality of trend. Like the Sierra Nevada, they are fault blocks, upthrust masses of rock—sedimentary, metamorphic, and igneous with extruded volcanic material here and there—along cracks caused by the stretching and thinning of the earth's crust in this region. Huge cones of detritus flank the bases of these ranges. Where they coalesce, they form alluvial skirts completely surrounding inner sinks.

This corrugated landscape, covering thousands of square miles (kilometers), could be presumed to have as varied a group of biotic communities as its relief features. Uniformity of climate, however, precludes the richness of natural scene common to most of California. To be sure, there are modifications owing to altitude, latitude, slope face, and drainage patterns; but much of it is characterized by the presence of one plant type which we now meet for the first time, Great Basin sagebrush. Preliminary acquaintance has been made with some of its relatives—coastal and beach sagebrush, mugwort, and alpine sagebrush, *Artemisia rothrockii*—but this is the book's first encounter with what may very well be the most abundant shrub in the West.

Traveling down from the top of Tioga Pass, one may not notice its quiet intrusion and, therefore, not truly realize its ubiquitous character until the road has dropped 1,000 feet (300 m.) or so on the east side of the divide. The rapid eastern descent of roughly 3,000 feet (900 m.) progresses with almost tobogganlike speed in contrast to the leisurely journey up the western slope. One can arrive at the foot of the range in less than a half an hour because of the nature of the eastern face. This is the escarpment along which movements occur that lift the Sierra from its heart-rock base.

Leaving the last of the alpine lakes, an artificially controlled but handsome body of water just east of the pass, those who are accustomed to the white granite of much of the High Sierra may well be surprised at the colorful slopes above. Extensive alpine areas of rust, buff, and yellow, brilliantly hued, typify the presence of metamorphic rocks. While wandering over some of the byroads in the vicinity of Mono Lake, visitors can note evidence of recent vulcanism, another feature of the eastern slope.

To return to the vegetation, if you have not had the opportunity to appreciate the dignity and charm of mountain juniper, here is your chance. They can be seen on each side of Lee Vining Canyon, perched on their exposed sites. Several patches of dwarf juniper blotch the upper walls of the canyon head, just below the rim. Before the road was straightened and widened, tiny seeps encouraged charming gardens where rein orchid, monkeyflower, monkshood, red columbine, horsetails, and other streamside plants found congenial little environments. Aspen sprawled every which way among the currant bushes that were beginning to stabilize the scree slides of this precipitous terrain. But bulldozers rule the age. Now the winding little road with its breathtaking turnouts and heartstopping curves, its miniature gardens and thickets of willow has yielded to a broad highway whose building has all but obliterated the flowered nooks and crannies, the tiny cascades and waterfalls by roadside.

The steep, semibarren cliffs of timberline follow the road down until the shrubs of the Great Basin begin to crowd onto the more gentle slopes of the lower canyon. Aspen, understoried by sagebrush, makes use of the long, easy sweeps; Jeffrey pine and white fir thicken by the stream that tumbles to the bottom of the gorge. Quite suddenly, the canyon floor widens out to several large meadows, verdant in early summer with aspen, grasses, sedges, rushes, and scraps of flag iris as blue as alpine ponds. Many of the canyons opening out from the escarpment were glaciated in the Pleistocene; and small lateral, recessional, and terminal moraines still block their mouths to some extent. They are not difficult to spot if you look for dikelike ridges of boulders and rock fragments over and along which the roads penetrating the canyons must travel. The Lee Vining Ranger Station is located on one of these moraines.

Once out on U.S. Highway 395, the Great Basin with its sagebrush is firmly in command. By no means is this dominant shrub the only woody plant of the region. Climate, edaphic conditions, and other ecological controls limit its occurrence.

Such circumstances are apparent approaching Mono Lake. Since it is highly saline, only such salt-tolerant plants as stinkweed and salt and alkaligrass approach the edge of this pale blue inland sea except where freshwater trickles into it. Several weedy goosefoots, a salt-tolerant family in general, have managed to establish colonies on the encrusted white mud surrounding the lake. Away from the lake edge the wet alkaline flats are replaced by brackish or freshwater marshy areas where cattails and bulrushes cluster over patches of desert buttercup and seep spring monkeyflower. The author has seen willows, dock, grasses, sedges, rushes, goldenrod, and even wild roses and blue flag iris clumps growing along concentric lines of hardened minerals, which mark old shorelines.

Mono Lake's brininess is the result of its geologic history. During the Ice Age, a much larger body of water, Lake Russell, covered most of the Mono Basin. Its ancient terraces can still be seen 600 to 700 feet (180–210 m.) above the present surface. As it evaporated, its salts were concentrated, and today it is a veritable soup of different substances. The two most important aquatic invertebrates in the highly saline water of the lake are brine shrimp and brine flies whose larvae were used by the Piute Indians as food and items of trade. The flies occur in such abundance that they gather along the shallows in living knots, which burst apart when disturbed and then quickly reform. Many shorebirds visit this inland sea—avocets, plovers, and several sandpipers among them. The three most numerous species are the California gull and northern and Wilson's phalaropes, whose habit of endless, rapid circling in place appears on the verge of dementia. Such seemingly pointless activity, however, is useful in that it keeps the water in motion and the pupal and larval stages of brine flies, on which they feed, easier to find. The gulls, on the other hand, feed mostly on brine shrimp. In this way, the three most populous species have neatly divided the food resources available to them, avoiding intense competition for any one item. A number of ducks such as pintail, green-winged teal, and shoveler and one of the largest seasonal concentrations of eared grebes in western North America also make use of the abundance of food. On the south shore of the lake, dozens of tufa towers are scattered. These grotesque structures, sometimes 15 feet (4.5 m.) or more in height, occur where freshwater seeps flow into the lake. Because of the action of calcareous algae, the calcium in the lake precipitates wherever it encounters freshwater.

The volcanic history of the area is evident everywhere. Lava and pumice floor the basin in many places, raising sections of it into tablelands often over 8,000 feet (2,400 m.) in elevation. Though the lake itself has two small island craters, one of the most notable features of the region's vulcanism is the group of small volcanoes known as the Mono Craters. South of the lake, they are inner cores of obsidian covered with pumice. Other craters, lava flows, hot springs, pumice flats, and cliffs of volcanic glass are indicative of the activity that is estimated by some to have ended but 500 years ago. On the north side of the lake, groves of cottonwood and huge willows, carpeted with grass, are green oases where streams flow down from the Sierra to partially replenish the slowly shrinking lake. (Recent steps by the Los Angeles Department of Water and Power to increase its intake of water from the High Sierra by diverting streams that formerly drained into Mono Lake are seriously threatening its future and that of its biota.) One such set of trickles spreads little marshes along the western shore. Yellow-headed and red-winged blackbirds use the cover provided by tules and cattails and call out their ringing cries from snags of willows shading these wet places.

If one drives south the road dips and rises, undulating over moraine deposits, foothill spurs, volcanic tablelands, drainage channels, and basin bottoms. Looking west to the Sierran escarpment, faceted by the numerous canyons eroded into its face, one can begin to understand why the interior side of the range is so different from the Pacific slope. Not only does its precipitousness give the kind of dramatic and spectacular scenery seldom seen at 6,500 feet (1,950 m.) on the western side, but tree zones are much less obvious on the eastern face. The brush-covered slopes, sheer walls, and scree jumbles are barren of much arboreal growth, though strands of such vegetation wind down gullies and canyons where water and deeper soils allow more mesophytic trees and shrubs. Riparian growth here amid sparsely covered terrain is even more evident than it is in the foothills of the Great Valley. Decidedly this is the edge of a desert, a high, cold desert, to be sure, but a desert all the same where there is only enough rainfall, from 5 to 15 inches (13–38 cm.) a year, to support low shrubs and scattered stands of drought-resistant trees. Contrast this scrubby growth to the Great Green Wall at 6,500 feet (1,950 m.) on the other side with its annual precipitation of 40 or more inches (102 cm.). Where stream flow or higher altitude provides enough moisture, there are many but not all of the conifers of the western slope—lodgepole, silver, and Jeffrey pines, white fir, and a few groves of yellow pine and red fir in certain restricted localities. In the streamside growth, a very handsome tree, water birch, is frequently conspicuous. Though it does occur on the Pacific side of the range, it is not too common; almost any stream on the east face, however, is bordered by this relation of the well-known paper birch of northern woods. Various willows, black and, more rarely, Fremont cottonwood, and aspen are its usual companions.

Where the stream courses of the escarpment widen into upland valleys containing lakes, as those on the June Lake Loop, in the Mammoth Lakes, Virginia Lakes, Convict Lake, and at the head of Bishop Creek, coniferous forests are more extensive, particularly on shady slopes. One can imagine himself back at Tuolumne Meadows or on the road to Glacier Point. High at road end in the more accessible canyons (many have mining roads that, though narrow, steep, switchbacked, and dirt, are negotiable by ordinary car) where trailheads promise high-country adventures, several trees approach timberline—whitebark pine, mountain hemlock, lodgepole pine, red fir, mountain juniper, and two mentioned casually before, limber and foxtail pines. Though both of the latter are confined to the high country in the central and southern Sierra, foxtail pine, a California native, occurs at lower altitudes in the Klamath Mountains and the Yolla Bolly group. Apparently it thrives, with the help of deep, extensive roots, in thin, well-drained soils on granite slopes, forming open groves of straight-trunked trees. Limber pine has a much wider distribution. It extends from southern California to the Rockies. Both have stiff, short-needled foliage covering the flexible stems like coarse fur. Foxtail pine appears to be more numerous on the west side of the divide whereas limber pine is more common on the east. It is a drought-tolerant conifer, at home on steep, dry, rocky slopes whose thin soils are poor in nutrients.

Jeffrey pine and mountain juniper continue to be important coniferous trees throughout the eastern slope of the Sierra, though the latter species, apparently more tolerant of cold than the pine, joins subalpine forest at higher elevations. In places an intricate forest-woodland-scrub mosaic has emerged, controlled by substrate and exposure. Mountain juniper and curl-leaf mountain mahogany, almost treelike in size and stance, persevere in scattered woodlands on exposed granite outcrops whereas Jeffrey pine forest, which usually includes some white fir and mountain juniper, claims less precipitous terrain or fraternizes with aspen where underground moisture is sufficient. Shrub growth varies from the mountain snowberry and tobacco bush of more heavily wooded ridges and slopes to the sagebrush and bitterbrush cover of open, less broken country.

At about 7,500 to 8,000 feet (2,250–2,400 m.) one-needled pinyon, another species new to the transect, begins an intrusion that though unobtrusive at first increases in importance as the elevation drops and becomes a woodland of its own. Understoried by sagebrush, rabbitbrush, and bitterbrush, it extends east from the lower slopes of the Sierran face to ridges here and there in the rolling terrain surrounding the Mono Basin. In these uplands a typical vegetation pattern has developed. Large sagebrush bushes command the deep-soiled valley floors, smaller plants of the same species mingle with pinyon on the lower slopes of surrounding hills, and Jeffrey pine occupies higher elevations or more mesic sites with open spicy-scented forests. Many shrubs of the dry hillsides move in under both Jeffrey and pinyon—buckwheat, manzanita, ceanothus, service berry, granite gilia, Mormon tea, desert peach, and wild currant. A broken line of contact wavers across the upland-basin complex north, east, and south of Mono Lake. This marks the shift from mountain juniper to Utah juniper, a smaller species of lower elevation and much wider range. Though one-needled pinyon merges with mountain juniper to the west on the Sierran slope and is partner with Utah juniper in a jointly shared woodland toward the Nevada border, it remains exclusive of both species throughout much of its distribution in California. There is considerable Utah juniper woodland in the Mono Lake area. Some of it occupies alluvial terraces in the northern part of the basin, and small groves occur in the hills southeast of the lake. Mountain juniper has homesteaded on Glass Mountain northeast of Crowley Lake and, though sporadic east of the Sierra, does occur in small populations in the Inyo and White mountains.

Here and there in this largely volcanic region, pumice flats, patches of barren volcanic debris, are being invaded by trees and shrubs just beginning their encroachment. Water drains down quickly through the porous rocky surface; consequently it is quite dry and cannot support much vegetation. Ecological succession will encourage soil building in toward the hearts of these sterile pockets, and forest or shrublands will eventually cover them.

Flowers are about as abundant here on the drier side of the Sierra as they are to the west. Early summer offers displays of prickly poppy (like perfectly poached eggs with their large white petals and brilliantly yellow centers), pink penstemons, scarlet bugler, evening primroses, scarlet gilia, mariposa lilies, and lupine. In late summer, rabbitbrush, a gorgeous plant despite its unflattering specific name which means "nauseating," lines the highways and clusters in clumps between the sagebrush with a striking combination of golden flowers and silver-green foliage.

Some of the same factors or related ones enforcing tree limit at high altitudes are at work here, where the trees of the eastern face finally yield to the scrubs and woodlands of the Great Basin. Even the hardier trees such as Jeffrey pine and mountain juniper cannot live below this ecotone, with the exception of riparian sites and a few isolated upland islands. The primary factor precluding tree growth is scanty precipitation, the effect of which on the habitat may be intensified by low winter temperatures, thin soils, and strong winds, potentially difficult conditions in themselves.

Where organisms attempt life in a marginal area, the hazards to which they can succumb are greatly multiplied. Take, for instance, Jeffrey pines, the last tall trees encountered if one travels east over the Mono Basin. What were all the circumstances that governed the establishment of the groves in the first place, and what are the possible threats to both individual and stand? The most important influence operating in natural communities is chance. It certainly plays a determining role in the distribution of organisms whose introduction to an area depends largely on the happenstance of their presence close enough to permit colonization of the new territory. Having entered, if they do, their continued presence, or ensuing disappearance, rests on environmental factors and the tolerance ranges of the species for these factors. Chance, however, continues to maintain its grip. Its cold impartiality has no regard for the effect of such circumstances on the well-being of the community. An unusually hard winter, a decade of drought, or a summer of fire, and no Jeffrey pines may be left to propagate. In 1936–1937, intense cold killed many young pines on the east side of the Sierra. Many mature trees live through such catastrophes, but cone-producing buds are often destroyed. Insect damage, destruction by larger animals, and fungal infestation of cone-bearing tissue also interfere with seed production.

In common with most species of the genus, the cones of Jeffrey pine take two years to develop. There are many hazards for the slowly growing cones—storms, fire, and hungry chickarees, crossbills, and the larvae of insects such as cone beetles (actually a fly) and pinecone moths. If fate allows, the cones will ripen and open to drop their seeds. Then the crop is attacked by hordes of ground-feeding birds and rodents anxious to fatten themselves for migration or hibernation, though many rodents aid dissemination by hoarding forgotten or never fully exploited caches. If the seeds escape destruction, fate still has the upper hand. They may fail to germinate because of lack of moisture or by falling on bare rock and other unsuitable substrates where they desiccate or decompose.

If all these hurdles are successfully passed, and the pine seed remains viable, it will burst one warm day when the ground is moist, and a tiny sprout will work up through the soil, living on the stored nutriment within the seed itself. After roots begin to penetrate the soil and the first few needles start photosynthesis, it is still at the mercy of its environment and chance. Intense frost and drought will always threaten it. Fire is never improbable. Winds and flood may topple it. Other plants could prove more competitive for soil moisture and minerals. Nutrients may be lacking as well as beneficial soil organisms. Cutworm attack is possible. Shade may doom its initial efforts. If they crop it, browsing and grazing animals will make very short work of its tiny attempt to live, and their hoofs can prove as destructive. If, almost miraculously, it escapes these fates and continues life to full maturity, its enemies seem to multiply. Porcupines, excellent climbers despite their clumsiness on the ground, eat its outer bark and destroy its food- and water-conducting tissue. Lightning plays around it during the summer months. Winds shriek past in winter. Man himself judges it for potential timber harvest or may cut it down to build roads, homes, or resorts.

Even if it escapes all these disasters, at some time an irreversible process will begin, and the end result is finally death. Mistletoe often begins the trend. This semiparasitic pest weakens the tree and prepares it for invasion by bark and other beetles, needleminers, flat-headed borers, and weevils. Roots damaged by rot and other fungi are open to additional attack. One of the rusts, also a fungus, infects the limbs of Jeffrey pine, while Oregon pine engraver, a beetle, confines its activities to the tops of mature trees.

One of the most deadly rusts is white pine blister rust which has a complex life history. Brought unwittingly from Europe, it found a remarkable set of biotic circumstances allowing it to flourish in the Great Green Wall. It requires two hosts for its existence, shrubs of the genus *Ribes* (currants and gooseberries) and pines of the white pine group—sugar, silver, whitebark, foxtail, and limber. Alternating between the two hosts, it has spiraled out until it threatens most of the white pines in the range. After parasitizing a pine, where the fungus invades a vital layer of tissue just under the bark to live off the tree, it produces sacs that release rust-colored spores into the air. Some spores infect leaves of *Ribes* plants and after several months and stages of spore reproduction, a final spore is released which returns the infecting fungus to needles of other white pines, and the cycle continues. Control of this disease is managed mainly by eradicating the *Ribes* clumps within the vicinity of infected white pines.

Every conifer in the Sierra is threatened by some type of fungus or insect damage, though some species such as the big tree are remarkably resistant. Even Jeffrey pines have chemicals in their sap and tissues which aid in their defense against infection. Sooner or later, however, all the individual trees in the range will succumb; then the various processes of soil making will contribute to their disintegration, reducing their remains to basic materials only then ready for chance to assign them to another living plant.

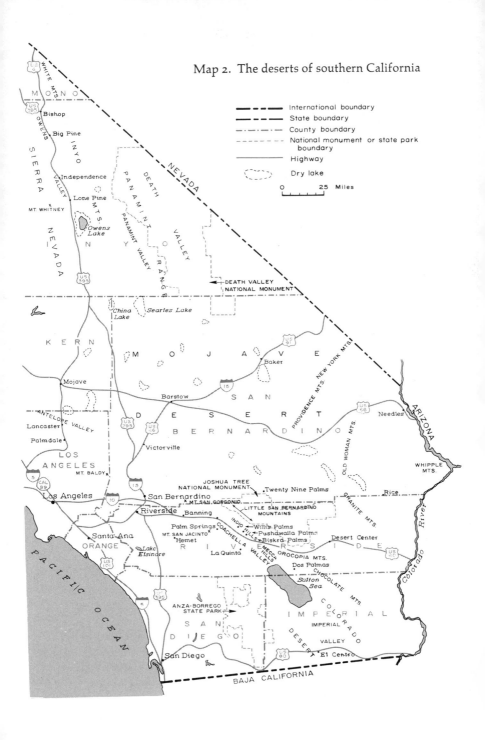

Map 2. The deserts of southern California

International boundary
State boundary
County boundary
National monument or state park boundary
Highway
Dry lake

0   25   Miles

Detail, Limber Pine

16. The Short Forests

Owens Valley is hot in the summer—undeniably, forthrightly hot. By nine o'clock of a July morning the already apathetic breeze is almost too bored to continue; and the mercury has soared to 90° F. (32° C.), even under the cottonwoods and poplars holding back the worst of the sun. When the clouds are large and thick enough for thunder showers, the rain only adds humidity to the ovenlike atmosphere of this great, walled-in trench, a topographical feature known as a graben or valley dropped between two parallel faults—in this case, those responsible for the Sierra Nevada to the west and the Inyo and White mountains which border the valley to the east. Such a term, however, conveys little impression of this part of California, one of the most spectacular rises of land anywhere in the country. Driving from Lone Pine to Bishop on a bright, cold December morning when fresh snow has sugared the Sierran crest, and the willow stems are cranberry red down in the bottomlands, one sees the valley at its best—that magnificent western wall of cream-colored granite rising full into the low winter sun. The candle-flame yellow of Lombardy poplars and cottonwoods traces the creekways draining the pediments, and the shadowy outline of the Inyo-Whites breaks the eastern horizon.

One can enter Owens Valley from the north on two major routes: along the foot of the Sierra and down Sherwin Grade from Crowley Lake via U.S. Highway 395, or on U.S. Highway 6, coming into California from Nevada a few miles east of Benton and following its own valley between the White Mountains and the uplands that tip into Mono Basin. A connecting road, State Highway 120, takes off from Benton Station to the northwest over an undulating plateau and, rounding the Mono Craters, cuts into U.S. Highway 395 just south of Lee Vining. Regardless of the route chosen, U.S. Highway 395 or State Highway 120-U.S. Highway 6, the traveler, dropping from the central High Sierra, invariably passes from aspen and Jeffrey pine, through stands of pinyon, and crosses long alluvial, scrub-covered slopes to the valley floor with its winding riparian corridors of rich summer green.

Though State Highway 120 is the longer, less traveled route, it is an interesting introduction to a new type of mosaic, that of the Great Basin, with its own set of climatic and edaphic characteristics with which we made acquaintance in the last chapter. Once the Mono Craters are to the west, the Sierra, a dominating feature throughout much of eastern California, somehow becomes less important. On the threshold of this vast interior realm of ranges and basins, one leaves behind the stands of white fir and sugar pine which thrived so well at the same elevations to the west. The rainshadow of the Sierra continues to operate far to the east, just as the influence of what is termed a continental climatic regime is felt as far west as the Sierra's eastern slope. Summers are warm, at middle and low altitudes, and winters are cold. Precipitation is much less than that of comparable elevations on the western Sierra, ranging from 8 to 20 inches (20–51 cm.) and falling mostly in the form of snow. Summer showers, nevertheless, can be expected, but there is much variation in number and intensity from year to year. It is a harsh climate, but very seasonal—a wonderful region for homesick easterners to visit when they complain of the climatic placidity of coastal California.

This lack of climatic coddling is much in evidence as one drives over the uplands southeast from Mono Lake. Much of the way is across the gray-green monotony of rolling, sagebrush-covered plains, modified by three vegetational interruptions.

1. Where rocky outcrops push up like rubble heaps, pinyon, juniper, desert or curl-leaf mountain mahogany, and even occasional Jeffrey pines suddenly appear in a dark green rash, in striking contrast to the quiet colors of the sagebrush slopes. Once again, broken bedrock and probing roots enable larger vegetative forms to compete successfully for their share of water. Sagebrush sometimes continues into these outposts as understory to the taller plants. There is some evidence that the trees of the rocky islands are protected from range fires by their isolation.

2. Many brushy slopes have streaks of olive green where bitterbrush—browse species highly preferred by stock and ruminant wildlife—has intruded into the almost solid sagebrush cover. Antelope bitterbrush has a wide range in northeastern California, and desert bitterbrush is common in much of the arid portion of the southern part of the state. Both species overlap in Mono and Inyo counties. Though often found in an intermixture, antelope bitterbrush also occurs in relatively pure stands, pioneering on recently deposited volcanic material, roadcuts, and mud flows. Both species appear to require porous, well-drained, coarse-textured soils whereas some species of sagebrush are tolerant of heavier soils. Antelope bitterbrush recovers very slowly after fire as it tends to stem-sprout less readily than the desert species.

3. Depressions and drainage ways, scattered over the tableland, nurture pockets of plants characteristic of more mesic environments, particularly where water is

more or less present the year around. Unexpected little ponds are delightful in this arid landscape, with their grasses, sedges, rushes, willows, and other moisture-requiring species.

By the time one has reached the long, straight stretch of road between Benton Station and Bishop, sagebrush, the constant companion since the top of Tioga Pass, has given way to another major scrub community, characterized by certain species loosely termed "scale bushes." Not only are their pale leaves usually covered with small scales, but their fruiting stalks often look like collections of fish scales glued along a central stem as each carpel is enclosed between two flaky bracts. There is a surprising variety of color among the scale bushes, their relations, and associates, in foliage as well as fruit bracts and flowers. Such differences are often subtle, to be sure; but an aware eye can see attractive notes of rust red, rose, gray, pink, tan, and various pale greens and lavenders blending in a pastel-tinted tapestry when seen from the window of a speeding car.

Once on the floor of the Owens Valley itself, the mountains to the east provide an introductory lesson in Great Basin ecology. The Inyo and White mountain ranges are fairly typical of the larger range or range complexes of this inland region. They are somewhat higher in elevation (White Mountain Peak is over 14,000 feet—4,200 m.), are closer to the Pacific Ocean, and may have suffered more of man's disruptive influences than sister ranges to the east; but they demonstrate the outstanding vegetational theme of the arid west: zonation. This is the striking feature of the mountains of the Great Basin. We encounter comparable altitudinal belts on the western Sierra, but the impact is less pronounced as one progresses up through conifer forests that seem all-of-a-piece to the uninitiated. It is only when one learns to tell the typical species apart that the various belts can be distinguished; they intergrade with few sharply defined boundaries.

The zones of vegetation are quite obvious on the western slope of the White Mountains, as the indicative species differ noticeably in appearance, given a little study. Their occurrence results from the same physical condition that produces vegetational shifts on the Sierra: adiabatic cooling. For each gain in altitude of 1,000 feet, the temperature drops roughly 3.2° F.

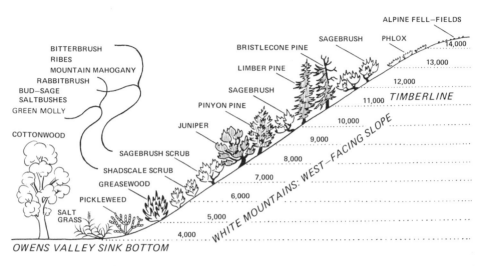

Figure 21. Altitudinal zonation on the White Mountains

(0.6° C. per 100 m.). Such cooling affects storms managing to overreach the heights of the Sierra, and there is consequent buildup of rainfall on the upper slopes of the White Mountains. The gradual decrease of temperature also influences plant cover.

Sagebrush, so extensive and ubiquitous, is the integrating background, the matrix, as some botanists term it, for many plant patterns superimposed on it by climatic and edaphic variation. It is absent, or nearly so, from only two Great Basin communities; but it is a prominent member of the others. From basin floor to the lower edges of alpine rock fields—where, however, there are modifications such as an edaphically influenced and spotty distribution in the bristlecone-limber pine stands of the White Mountains—sagebrush is as domineering a plant group as one will meet anywhere.

Because of its major role in the biota of the Great Basin, the group deserves a more detailed account and description than we have given it so far. It belongs to the genus *Artemisia* in the sunflower or composite family, though its inconspicuous, almost insignificant flowers are hardly what the botanically unsophisticated would consider typical of the family. Other members of the genus have already been introduced—the rank-growing mugwort of riparian sites, the feather-foliaged beach sagewort, and the subshrub, California sagebush, of coastal scrubs. Outriders of a near relation and look-alike of Great Basin sagebrush, Rothrock or alpine sagebrush, drift over the Sierran divide down into the subalpine forest zone of the western slope. At this point we are confronted with a taxonomic puzzle that has plagued many botanists. Should the last plant and the dozen or so other closely related sagebrushes really be separated into species, or should most of them be considered varieties or subspecies instead? Like the oaks, they cross easily, which confuses the picture considerably. Current thinking has divided them; those listed below occur in California along with their approximate distribution and ecological limitations.

1. *Artemisia tridentata* (Great Basin, basin, big, or common sagebrush) extends north to Canada, east to and beyond the Rocky Mountains, and down into Baja California. It is one of the larger species, ranging to 15 feet (4.5 m.) in height in better sites. Though it has a relatively wide tolerance for many edaphic conditions, as it is found in dry areas and moist, in valleys and on mountain slopes, in alkaline as well as nonalkaline situations, in pumice-rich soils and in sand, it does best in deep, well-drained soils and sheltered locations. There are several subspecies which seem to exhibit locational preferences, one of which, *vaseyana* or mountain big sagebrush, is restricted to higher elevations, as implied by its common name. Both it and Rothrock sagebrush occur in the High Sierra.

2. *Artemisia bigelovii* (flat sagebrush) is scattered throughout the Southwest from Colorado and Texas to California at altitudes of from 3,000 to 5,000 feet (900–1,500 m.). This is a very drought-resistant, small or dwarf shrub, well suited to drier sites.

3. *Artemisia nova* (dwarf sagebrush) ranges from 5,000 to 8,000 feet (1,500–2,400 m.) through the West, from Montana south to California and northern Arizona. In its darker form it is relatively easy to distinguish from other sagebrushes. Evidently it is a species that does well on shallow, gravel soils and limestone substrates.

4. *Artemisia arbuscula* (black sagebrush) is another dwarf species, and it grows from 5,000 to 9,500 feet (1,500– 2,850 m.), and from Washington south to California and east to northern Utah. It homesteads where many other species of sagebrush do not, on shallow, stony sites that are often alkaline in nature. On certain heavy clay soils known as scab flats, low sagebrush endures a period of meltwater flooding. The flats become shallow lakes, and the substrate is deficient in oxygen, a stressful condition for most plants.

5. *Artemisia rothrockii* (Rothrock or alpine sagebrush) is a low-growing shrub which seems at home in high mountains (up to 11,000 feet—3,300 m.) from the Sierra to Wyoming and Colorado.

6. *Artemisia cana* (silver or hoary sagebrush) has a wide distribution in dry meadows. It also tolerates seasonally saturated clay soils and occurs from southern Canada south to California and east to Colorado.

Few readers will worry much about differentiating between these six species in the field. The best that can be done here is to note the large forms and the dwarf types, those that can take alkaline and other less fertile sites, the forms characteristically found in high mountains, and those that occur at lower levels. In general their appearance is much the same. They all have aromatic silver-gray-green leaves of small size, decidedly three-toothed in some species, in others less so. The foliage typically bursts from gnarled woody trunklets in attractive tufts. In flowering season dozens of straight-stemmed stalks thrust up from the leaf masses and bear minute blossoms. Sagebrush is at its best during or just after a rain. The colors deepen slightly, and the world seems suspended in rich, pungent odor.

Other shrubs are by no means excluded from the sagebrush scrub (or steppe) community. Buffaloberry, bitterbrush, several *Ribes*, mountain mahogany, cotton thorn, and Mormon tea are common associates. Two other shrubs deserve additional description. One is blackbrush, so named because its gray bark tends to become black with age. A spiny member of the rose family, it is a monotypic genus, that is, there is only one species of this plant. It is confined to the Southwest, where it appears to prefer rocky or alluvial soils, and it is transitional between the cool and warm deserts. It consorts with Great Basin sagebrush at the upper limits of its distribution and descends to creosote bush scrub at roughly 4,000 feet (1,200 m.). Commonly found with it are bud-sage, turpentine broom, and winter fat. The other is rabbitbrush. Blooming in late summer, this striking plant is a flamboyant harbinger of the autumnal colors one can expect from the higher elevations of the Sierra and Great Basin mountains. It is often found growing between clumps of sagebrush, particularly on disturbed soils. It invades newly heaped roadside gravel piles and recently flooded sandy washes. Somewhat subshrubby, it quickly covers such areas with great bouquets of sunny color. Another composite, goldenbush, is almost as richly yellow. Herbs such as paintbrush, penstemon, blazing star, lupine, locoweed, Brewer's and other monkeyflowers, buckwheat, and many perennial as well as annual grasses flourish throughout the scrub unless the cover is too dense. The grass companions are often clues to the amount of moisture available at particular sagebrush sites as some species require more water and others less. Additionally, they are indicative of certain edaphic circumstances, for example, desert needlegrass is typical of sandy areas while basin wildrye commonly occurs on soils derived from volcanic ash.

From the discussion of the interior sagebrushes, it is apparent that the group, as a whole, has the capacity to live over much of the intermountain West. Given certain limitations and compensating tolerances, both of which vary from species to species, it may be found alone or with other shrubs, and as understory to most of the trees of the region. It reaches from chill mountain heights to hot valley floors; from moist, streamside sites to dry, thin-soiled slopes; from alkali clays to lithosols (literally, rock soils). In common with most other shrubs of the arid West, it has certain features which enable it to struggle along under adverse conditions, yet to thrive where the environment is genial. Small size and light color, due to white hairs on the leaves, suggest drought resistance. Long and extensive root systems aid in the search for water. Hence its universality within certain limits discussed below.

In recent years, the sagebrush group has enlarged its territory at the expense of the perennial grasses, which formerly were in favorable balance. Stock and wildlife forage preferences are of great importance. Sagebrush with its stiff twigs and small aromatic leaves is less palatable than grass. Though it is browsed when tastier food is scarce, it is usually left alone. Overgrazing and, according to some investigators, frequent range fires proved a two-headed nemesis for much of the Great Basin's better range, weakening the bunchgrasses—wheatgrasses, wildryes, Indian ricegrass, fescue, and a number of needlegrasses—that for thousands of years had lived compatibly with the sagebrushes. They grew between the shrubs and under the taller plants until forced out of the range by grazing and fire stress. Introduced annuals such as cheatgrass brome and Russian thistle (tumbleweed) took advantage of the vacuum. As they can use the skimpy, shallow soil moisture untapped by the sagebrushes, they managed to establish a working relationship with the dominant shrub, which also took advantage of its weakened ex-partners and enlarged its territory. Ranchers, in an attempt to return the range to its former productivity, have begun to destroy many acres of sagebrush by deep ploughing, fire, herbicides, and other means. Actually, the Great Basin bunchgrass species have suffered less, by and large, than those of the Central Valley and surrounding foothills. It is still possible to find good representations of them, here and there.

Sagebrush may be considered undesirable by stockmen, but the community shelters many animals using its thickets for cover and its resources for food. Several are completely dependent on it, and are found nowhere else. The sage hen, related to sooty (blue), ruffed, spruce, and sharp-tailed grouse, is peculiar to sagebrush plains. Though it has a smaller distribution than the others, it is the largest of the American grouse. Cock-of-the-plains is another name for the bird that boasts a courtship behavior considered to be the most spectacular of the group. In spring the strutting grounds echo with the drumming of the males. They inflate the air sacs of their necks and, spreading their pointed tail feathers and stiffly positioning their wings, they strut jerkily, producing a variety of sounds that have been compared to rusty pumps or cracking whips, depending on the observer. Undoubtedly they are well suited to their environment. Not only does their mottled plumage blend well with the quiet colors of their habitat, but they are one of the few animals that live almost exclusively on the leaves of sagebrush, augumented by occasional insects, fruits, and shoots of other plants, particularly locoweed, wild vetch, and goldenrod.

Another bird whose streaked front and gray-brown back fit it nicely into shrubby cover is the sage thrasher. Smaller than its cousins, it appears to alternate, as they do, between insects, when they are plentiful, and seeds at their time of ripening. Many sparrows find these open, rolling plains with their grasses and other seed-producing plants a desirable habitat—vesper, black-throated, black-chinned, song, Brewer's, and savanna. One species is confined to sagebrush, Bell's or sage sparrow. It forages between the bushes, using the tops of them for lookout posts and scurrying to safety under their cover when disturbed. The green-tailed towhee is smaller than the brown or rufous-sided towhees of the foothill brushlands. With its white and gray streaked face, reddish cap, and green tail, it blends well with the delicate shades of its habitat. Searching for prey, poorwills, prairie falcons, Swainson's hawks, and ravens drift back and forth over these gray-clad uplands. Great horned and burrowing owls are alert for the many rodents common to the sagebrush steppe. Shrikes are plentiful here and watch for grasshoppers and other large insects, and gray flycatchers, birds partial to Great Basin habitats, look for smaller prey.

Many mammals of the sagebrush plains—chipmunks, including the least, typically a resident of the region, and antelope ground squirrels—are day active, but at nightfall numerous nocturnal species trade places with them, taking over feeding sites vacated by diurnal forms. Great Basin and other kangaroo rats, the dark kangaroo mouse, wood rats, and several white-footed and pocket mice, one of which is restricted to the Great Basin, rely on seeds and fruit gathered in the darker hours. Jack rabbits are abundant, and pygmy rabbits, engaging little creatures somewhat smaller than the average house cat, rely on sagebrush to the point where it is thought to be almost exclusively their source of food. The sagebrush vole (meadow mouse) is another animal limited to the steppe interior. Shorter and smaller-tailed than most of its relatives (none of which is distinguished by long, graceful tails), it is also the most "desertized." It lives on any green stuff it can find and needs no other source of moisture than that present in the food it eats. Elaborate runways are the hallmarks of this little creature, and by remaining hidden in them a good part of the time, it escapes being dinner for coyotes, gray foxes, badgers, and other predators of the arid steppe. Numerous amphibians and reptiles forage here as well, including locally prominent species and subspecies such as the sagebrush (a fence) lizard, Great Basin gopher snake, and Great Basin spadefoot toad.

Almost unchallenged, sagebrush rules from alluvial slopes that apron the high-desert ranges to timberline and even above. Four factors, however, control its lower limits: temperature, rainfall, salinity, and soil structure. With the approach of warmer, drier climatic conditions, shadscale scrub frequently shares a broad ecotone with sagebrush and then supplants it. This rather desiccated-appearing cover of shrubs is remarkably uniform in size and appearance, considering the many families represented here. Not only tolerant of the so-called alkali soils characteristic of the floors and lower sides of the platterlike basins that abound in the region, it is very xerophytic with many of the adaptive features such as small, light-colored, hairy or scaly leaves, and extensive roots common to plants of arid regions. Wide spacing between shrubs is the result of intense root competition for soil moisture. Where rainfall drops below 7 inches (18 cm.) and both summer and winter temperatures are higher than those of the sagebrush steppe, these small, stiff, often spiny bushes, many of them goosefoots, are spread thinly over the lower alluvial slopes and basins. One genus, *Atriplex*, contains the scale bushes—shadscale, lensscale, and wingscale—for one of which this community is named. Another common name for the genus is saltbush, reflecting its ability to tolerate saline soils, though it appears that its drought-resistant features are of even greater significance.

In the western Great Basin several edaphically controlled associations of plants differentiate out of the matrix of shadscale scrub. Shadscale and the distantly related little greasewood dominate an association occupying well-drained soils that are low to moderately alkaline and not conspicuously saline. It is common on the bajadas, the coalesced alluvial fans that surround a desert playa or dry lake bed. Other important goosefoots are spiny hopsage and green molly, and the composites contribute broom snakeweed and horsebrush, names intriguingly zoological. Cotton thorn and boxthorn testify to the general spininess of the shadscale community, a feature of bud-sage, another sagebrush that is very common to the shadscale scrub. Its Latinized name, *Artemisia spinescens,* is indicative of its bristly character, a decided departure from the growth habit of its relatives. Its position in the shadscale landscape and away from the other sagebrushes emphasizes the eclectic nature of the genus throughout the Great Basin. Mormon tea and several small cacti, such as dwarf cholla and old man prickly pear, add variety of texture and, because of the cactus flowers, seasonal color and charm.

The ever-commanding goosefoots provide change in occasional islandlike masses of winter fat whose pale foliage is also highly palatable to deer as well as livestock. Apparently it has broad range of tolerance for both soil salinity and moisture. Nevada dalea, a species of a typical desert shrub genus, appears to be limited to stabilized sand dunes whose soils are relatively salt free and low in alkalinity. It is joined by many of the same shrubs that are companion to shadscale and little greasewood. Indian ricegrass is present throughout most of the bajada scrub, as wind-teased and fine-textured as a horse's tail.

Though some of the desert sagebrushes can stand soils that are moderately to heavily alkali, for the most part they need well-drained substrates that are not conspicuously saline. The shadscales and their neighbors, on the other hand, appear to thrive where salts are present in moderate concentrations. Desert pavement, a stony surface often found in arid regions, is rare in sagebrush areas, but frequently occurs in the shadscale community. Soils vary from sandy gravels to heavy clays, and hardpans occasionally occur. Considering that climatic drought is reinforced by edaphic conditions of soil salinity, resulting in physiological drought, it is not surprising that these little shrubs often look as though they were crafted from cornflakes.

Taking one of the many dirt roads crisscrossing the floor of Owens Valley south of Bishop, one encounters sooner or later the other scrub community of the steppe interior which replaces sagebrush—alkali sink. Where the water table is high in arid regions, capillary rise brings up dissolved material. Evaporation concentrates the minerals accumulating on the surface because of this upward pull, and those deposited by water draining off surrounding hillsides. Many basins in this landlocked region have playas, permanent or transient lakes, floored with minerals collecting through the thousands of years during and since the Ice Age. Trapped here because of the absence of sea-destined drainage, there has not been sufficient rainfall to leach these solutes below subsurface depths. Such collections are widely but somewhat incorrectly termed "alkalis." They may be alkaline, that is basic in nature, but many of these accumulations are on the neutral side. Strongly alkaline substrates are infertile for numerous species, just as highly acid soils discourage many plants. However, whether alkaline or not, the major reason for barren playa floors is the salts concentrated here. One highly alkaline soil is the infertile black alkali. A high percentage of sodium on clay particles not only results in alkalinity, but this soil type is very saline, as well.

After heavy rains, the heart of the sink is underwater for intervals ranging from days to weeks. Eventually, however, the water evaporates and the center dries out completely. Then mineral-impregnated surface clays are split by crisscrossing cracks. Such substrates are often underlain by claypans or other impervious layers. They concentrate the standing water, high in solutes, in shallow depths at and just below the surface. Such a combination of features is disastrous to any plant life, and the central portions of most sinks are quite sterile. American deserts have many mineralized basin floors scattered between their ranges: Bonneville Salt Flats, Death Valley's Devil's Golf Course, and numerous places where commercial mining of the more valuable minerals has been undertaken, such as Owens Lake at the southern end of Owens Valley and Searles Lake in the Mojave Desert. Though most are usually dry, mirages playing over these white expanses give them the appearance of reflecting water.

Around playa edges or in the moist heavy soils of salty sumps, such as those in Owens Valley, big greasewood makes its appearance, usually in company with other salt-tolerant goosefoots such as spiny hopsage and shadscale. Where, finally, permanently wet soil is encountered, these plants give way to the same succulent types met in the coastal salt marshes—pickleweed, with its fat little green "sausages" tightly strung together, and a look-alike, iodine bush, which seems to prefer a somewhat less wet substrate. One can find desert blite, related to the coastal sea blite, along with desert salt grass, a close cousin of the salt grass of tidal flats. Alkaligrass and alkali sacaton, other grasses frequently found in these sinks, and rushes, sedges, and bulrushes, tolerant of brackish water, fill out the tangles of growth which, having adjusted to a potentially inimical environment, can take good advantage of that desert rarity, a permanent water source. Like the seaside halophytes, they have made physiological and anatomical changes which protect them from the water loss threatened by reversal of the normal osmotic process and function well despite an unusually high salt content in their cell sap.

One other community literally graces the floor of the Owens Valley, the riparian woodlands of welcome shade lining what is left of the Owens River and its tributaries. Up on the pediments or fans above the valley bottom, running water allows conifers such as Jeffrey pine to invade lower elevations. On the floor itself, willows and cottonwoods are the principal streamside trees along with locusts, poplars, and other alien trees introduced by early settlers. High in these verdant tunnels, "Bullock's" orioles, Wilson's and yellow warblers, blackheaded grosbeaks, and several flycatchers find the food resources of the green arcades particularly rich. The whole valley is a birder's paradise. Black-billed magpies perch on every fence post, and no lawn is complete without a contingent of cocky robins.

As the warm season progresses, spring wildflowers—apricot mallow, evening primrose, and desert dandelion—give way to those of summer, particularly where irrigation augments the natural water sources. Prince's plume waves golden tufts in the hot breeze. The fences are so rich with bee plant, that a solid lavender wall may line the roads. When mixed with sunflowers, the effect is that of unending floral arrangements of unabashed color.

Several valleys to the east of the Owens Valley exhibit much the same patterns of vegetation: barren playa floors surrounded by salt sink vegetation that eventually gives way to shadscale scrub. They are sufficiently low in elevation so that some of the northernmost stands of creosote bush scrub tongue up from southern deserts into Saline Valley, Panamint Valley, and one of the most well-known desert depressions, Death Valley. This scrub intergrades with shadscale scrub on lower bajada slopes and allows intrusions of blackbrush and Great Basin sagebrush at higher elevations. All of these valleys have rampart ranges high enough to permit coniferous growth—pinyon on the Grapevine Mountains, east of Scotty's Castle, and the White, Inyo, and Panamint mountains, west of Death Valley. Bristlecone and limber pines are timberline residents on the last three ranges.

If a giant roller coaster could be built (only hypothetically, of course) from Mount Whitney to the floor of Death Valley, it would be an exhilarating as well as instructive ride indeed— from the chill wind of alpine rock fields to the saltbush and cottonwoods along the Owens River, up to timberline again on the Inyo-White ranges, and down to the hot salt sink in the lower Saline Valley, up to the bristlecones of the Panamint Range, and down to the blindingly white saline barrens of the Devil's Golf Course. When? Perhaps one should choose a time in May when snow is reluctant to leave the high draws and basins, the sky is willow plate blue and white, and the spring's bounty of wildflowers continues to be generous. Then our ride could linger over the most impressive display of the mandarin-red Kennedy mariposa lily that the author has ever seen. They brightened a canyon hillside high on the eastern slopes of the Inyo Mountains, just north of a spring where one of California's few stands of netleaf hackberry shades a spring-fed oasis. As imagination costs nothing, we could construct our roller coaster to swing south for a glimpse of the ferns of Darwin Falls across the Coso Range, east of Olancha. Since imagination can also be optimistic, we could hope that late rains have extended the fields of California poppy, Mojave aster, desert dandelion, apricot mallow, and desert-sunflower that spring-quicken the broad washes and lower bajadas of Death Valley.

As our roller coaster ride can only be imagined, to appreciate the vegetational zoning on the slopes of Great Basin ranges, take the drive from Big Pine to Westgard Pass and turn left to the bristlecone pine reserve high in the White Mountains. The shadscale scrub begins admitting a few sagebrush scrub species, and towards late summer, rabbitbrush flourishes in golden splendor. Suddenly, upward there are no more scale bushes.

Sagebrush is king again, but it does not rule alone for long. It begins to share its reign first with Utah juniper on the upper slopes of bajadas or gently rolling uplands and then with pinyon on steeper hillsides. Where the now-improved road to the White Mountain bristlecone pine forest departs from the main road through the pass, one could be deep in Arizona and expect to see a Navajo hogan tucked in the grove of small trees at the fossil trail turnout. This is one corner of California that should be elsewhere. The dwarfed forest somehow doesn't seem to really belong here, though climatically it has every right to be present. The tree-screened hills should widen out to the mesas and buttes of the Indian country, for this is their kind of natural landscape—pinyons and Utah junipers in their own dry, pitch-scented air. In California, only along the eastern base of the central Sierra and the western outliers of the mountains of the Great Basin can one find this tail-end extension of the coniferous woodlands of the Southwest.

What strange little trees they are. They have none of the grandeur of their taller relatives, nor the scarred dignity of the old fellows of timberline. Though young junipers are typically conical, and some mature individuals branch from the base in full-bottomed plumpness, many are grotesquely twisted, with tufts of foliage at the ends of posturing branches. Pinyons sometimes open out in canopies surprisingly wide for so short a trunk. On close inspection, it is simple to tell apart the two main species. Pinyons have needles (one, two, or four to a bundle depending on species), and junipers have scales for leaves. It is somewhat more difficult to distinguish between them from a distance. The pines seem a little on the blue side, the junipers slightly more yellow, but both have gray tints which darken on far hillsides so that the trees appear almost black. In the southern part of the state, California juniper is the semidesert companion of pinyon; however, it often occurs alone, particularly at low elevations. Utah juniper, on the other hand, is rarely without its associate though both species can and do grow in relatively pure stands, undiluted by each other.

The zone occupied by this coniferous woodland receives more moisture than those of the two Great Basin scrubs. Higher in elevation—5,000 to 8,000 feet (1,500–2,400 m.)—its rainfall averages from 12 to 20 inches (30–51 cm.). The trees have the deep-spreading roots typical of semidesert woodland, and the scattered spacing is indicative of active competition between individuals of the stand. They often avoid basin floors or the lower skirts of alluvial slopes. Like the shrubs of the chaparral, they seem to be most at home on shallow-soiled, rocky, hill and mesa sides where long roots can effectively probe for underground water. Yet they make a scattered appearance on the ochre and vermillion sands of the Navajo country, indicating a wide amplitude of substrate tolerance. Topography influences their distribution. At lower elevations on the west face of the White Mountains, the more mesic north exposures have well-developed pinyon-juniper woodlands, while the southern exposures are characterized by shrubs of the sagebrush zone. The woodland is also missing from soils of certain rock formations, for example, Wyman sandstone where big sagebrush dominates instead. In the more sheltered and moist areas, the trees are tall and crowded so that one has the feeling of a real though dwarfed forest rather than a woodland.

Through it all runs a tide of sagebrush, lapping up against rocky pinnacles, flowing out over tree-dotted ridges and across rolling plains. There is moisture enough to go around, it seems, and many plants of the sagebrush scrub have joined the community—mountain mahogany, bitterbrush, desert sweet, blue sage with its little bright purple balls of flowers, goldenbush, spiny phlox, desert peach, snakeweed, desert snowberry, several cacti, and Mormon tea. The last genus has a wide distribution throughout the arid West, true as well for various buckwheats which range from the soft-tinted monotony of the shadscale scrub to the timberline forest we shall visit shortly. The herbaceous layer features a surprisingly large number of perennial grass species, considering their fate in many areas of California, and numerous bright-hued wildflowers—penstemons, paintbrush, and lupine.

Birds work back and forth through the little forest, but the general aridity and lack of variation in plant cover limit the number of species usually found here. Many birds active in the coniferous forests of the Sierra also use the woodland. White-breasted nuthatches, chickadees, and black-throated gray warblers are not uncommon. Hairy woodpeckers are seen frequently, and one bird is very characteristic of the coniferous woodland, the pinyon jay. As its name indicates, it is seldom found elsewhere. It is a social bird. One cannot be long in this short forest without hearing peculiar angry-catlike calls as the flocks wing by. They are much duller in color than scrub or crested jays. The plumage is mostly dark gray with a faint blue wash over the wings and back.

A mutualistic relationship has developed between the jay and this small pine so characteristic of these dry woodlands. Unlike many pine seeds, the nuts of pinyons are unwinged, dropping in the fall directly under the parent tree. By harvesting the oil-rich seeds and burying them in the ground for future use, the jays not only ensure a food supply for themselves, but those they do not recover are given a better chance to germinate when the moist soils of spring warm up under the strengthening sun. When they are left scattered and unprotected on the woodland floor, the increasingly high temperatures may prove lethal for the sprouting seeds.

A large number of rodents have settled here—golden mantled ground squirrels, several chipmunks, pocket gophers, Great Basin kangaroo rats, porcupines, wood rats, and mice of many species. Though named for one of the dominant trees of the woodland, pinyon mice also live in the foothills bordering the Central Valley. They belong to the deer mouse group and have its characteristic white feet, large ears, and lightly haired tail. The larger mammals of the sagebrush scrub—mule deer and pronghorn antelope, among them—continue to accompany it where it slips in as understory in the coniferous woodland. Coyotes, gray foxes, bobcats, and mountain lions use the cover provided by brush and tree as they search for their prey.

Above 9,000 feet (2,700 m.), pinyon and juniper open their ranks and finally give way. The road now winds through sagebrush scrub, which has retaken full command. As the vegetation cover decreases in height, sudden views shape themselves. The Sierra looms to the west, and steep canyons drop on all sides. The intimacy of the woodland has been replaced by wide horizons uncluttered by trees. But not for long.

At 10,000 feet (3,000 m.), the first limber pines descend to road level, and the visitor enters the most amazing forest in the West. Many of the trees here were living when the pyramids of Egypt were being built—and look like pieces of driftwood. Not a few Californians felt a sense of loss when it was discovered that the superb groves of giant sequoias had lost the privilege of claiming the oldest living organisms to collections of battered snags, no more than 30 feet (9 m.) tall, high on some barren ridges hardly anyone had ever seen before, that is, until the photographers arrived. Any camera enthusiast can tell you that the big trees are tough subjects. They are just too large, too straight, and too much a part of a heavy forest to make exciting pictures. But those bristlecone pines! They are among the world's most photogenic trees, half the time resembling something else. Those with imagination can see a host of figures—tragic, joyous, pensive, pleading. Trees they may be, but there is something unique here. No other timberline area, where grotesquely twisted trees are to be expected, approaches it for wonder.

Aside from the fantasy and charm of their shapes, color sings out from both environment and tree. An intensely blue sky mates with soils as white as chalk in places. The exposed wood varies from cream to gold through rich brown. The seed cones are deep purple-brown, and the staminate, or pollen, cones a lovely rosy red. Plants underfoot range from the delicate pink and white of Coville's phlox, to the purple alpine spring locoweed, and the bright yellow circles of alpine flames and other goldenbushes; from lavender dwarf alpine daisy, to rosy everlasting, and the rich blue of western flax.

Though bristlecone and limber pines associate with each other in many places throughout this subalpine forest, limber pine descends to slightly lower elevations than does its coniferous companion, which in turn ascends to elevations above those tolerated by limber pine. As we shall see, both tend to shun certain soil types in favor of others. They look a good deal alike, but limber pine needles tend to tuft the ends of the supple branches, whereas those of the bristlecone pine grow in a bottle-brush effect, and are much stiffer in manner. The cones differ as well, since the bristles at the tips of the scales are a sure means of identifying the more famed species.

The story of their discovery is one of the fascinations of the forest. Though bristlecone pines were known to grow on the White Mountains and other ranges of the Great Basin and the southern Rocky Mountains, they had never aroused much interest until a scientist happened to drill deep within their boles in an effort to learn more of the climatic past of the Southwest. He was looking for trees, living and dead, which would enable him to extend the tree-ring story back to dates as yet unreached at that time. Certain trees are more sensitive to climate than others, that is, they react pronouncedly to variations in rainfall and temperature, with corresponding variations in the width of their annual rings. By correlating a series of tree-ring patterns, gathered from all over the Southwest, scientists were beginning to discover fluctuations in climate that had taken place in the prehistoric past. To Dr. Edmund Schulman's surprise, not only did he come across a bonanza that was destined to extend the tree-ring series to cover 6,000 years, but he found he had discovered the oldest living plants, and in one of the most cruel timberline areas of the West at that.

At 11,600 feet (3,480 m.), their upper limit, on a rainshadowed range receiving roughly 12 inches (30 cm.) of annual precipitation, hammered by gale-force winds sweeping unhindered over the high plateaus, with a growing season measured in weeks and substrates that vary widely in their fertility, it is amazing that trees are here at all. One would think, under these circumstances, that the bristlecone pines would claim the better soils and thus account for their occurrence *and* their almost unbelievable longevity. Not at all. On the White Mountains, they are usually confined to dolomite, a very light-colored type of carbonate rock that is related to limestone, also found in the area. It weathers into shallow lithosols, or rock soils, alkaline in nature, and low in the important minerals potassium and phosphorus. Looking across at bristlecone pine-covered slopes—and there are many for they are not restricted to the two best-known groves—the edaphic story of this fantastic landscape is clearly told. In fact, it is a classic example of the soil control of community distribution. Where the ground is white indicating a dolomite substrate, the bristlecones are scattered about in open groves. Where granite occurs, limber pine joins the bristlecones, particularly on north-facing and other moister sites. It is accompanied by Great Basin sagebrush, littleleaf cream bush, and other plants uncommon on dolomite substrates. It should not be implied that undergrowth is missing from bristlecone pine-dominated forests. Low sagebrush is present, usually near noncarbonate rock contacts; in addition, dolomite supports Indian ricegrass, and other perennial grasses, herbs such as those described above, rabbitbrush, golden currant, and mountain mahogany. The latter species is also particularly common on south-facing slopes, including granitic substrates, and on steep slopes of scree and other unstable rock. On sandstone, both pines are much less in evidence, but Great Basin sagebrush dominates, joined by the shrubby desert sweet and granite gilia with silvery lupine, sulfur flower, and other herbs.

The dolomite of the White Mountains has many properties distinctly discouraging to plants. It reflects light and heat because of its color and, therefore, is cooler in temperature—a distinct disadvantage to alpine plants. Not only does it erode into thin lithosols, but calcium carbonate crusts are typical. Low fertility and high alkalinity are additional undesirable features for most plants. On the other hand, those able to grow under such adverse edaphic conditions suffer little competition from those avoiding it, and here is much of the reason for the natural landscapes of timberline in the White Mountains. Species such as low sagebrush that need plentiful amounts of potassium or phosphorus cannot possibly compete with bristlecone pine on dolomite, but sagebrushes are strong contestants on better soils. They push the pines back to their infertile strongholds where they do well despite the soil's poor mineral content.

The pines are so remarkably adjusted to tree-limit hardships and infertile dolomite outcrops that they live the longest of any plants in the world. The dense wood is made of small insect- and decay-resistant cells. This lignification is partly responsible for the slow decomposition rate of dead tissue and accounts for the litter of "driftwood," rich resource of tree-ring data that has pushed back our knowledge of past climates to a span of thousands of years. The needles tend to remain for decades on trees in poorer sites, thus maintaining photosynthetic capacity without having to drain energy sources during times of severe stress.

Another important adaptation is the ability of the bristlecone pine to maintain metabolic equilibrium with available water. Though photosynthetic activity drops sharply during cold-season dormancy, respiration continues well into late winter, depleting stored food reserves. The growing season is too short and the amount of available moisture too small to allow the trees to both store food for winter survival and produce much woody tissue, accounting, in part at least, for their slow rate of growth. In addition, much of an older bristlecone pine is dead—beautifully and aesthetically dead, but dead all the same. Many of the trees, particularly those on more exposed sites, have but one or two foliated branches connected to the roots by a thin strip of living bark that carries the necessary ingredients of life up and down the trunk. The dead bark is scoured off by storm and sand blast, exposing the lovely wind-polished wood beneath. The bare branches slowly erode to picturesque snags, and old exposed roots writhe with appropriate gestures.

The Patriarch Grove, the higher of the two most commonly visited areas, is the archetype of such a landscape. Though many trees are still quite heavily needled, some with multiple trunks supporting thrifty, well-foliaged branches, the gently sloping plain could have inspired Salvadore Dali to his most extravagantly creative moods. A large number of the trees look as though they had been stripped clean, sawed off at the base, placed in position by some giant hand, and then carefully rearranged for best effect. Many of them lean slightly which gives them the look of being purposefully organized. Probably no other living landscape so much resembles an art gallery.

Driving higher—and it is possible to do so if your car can take it—the pines are left behind. Low-growing sagebrush and other high elevation shrublets and cushion plants are once again unchallenged. How consistent the sagebrush group has been, giving way only when soils proved so difficult it could not compete with better adapted vegetation. It has encompassed two short forests, besides creating one itself, where optimum conditions allow the largest of the species to grow tall in fine disregard for the rigors of the surrounding desert. It has played host to countless creatures dependent on its food and shelter. It has been gracious to bright flowering species enlivening its quiet green. It is, regardless of its extent and ubiquity, a favorite desert shrub to those who love its wide gray distances, reaching for the sky.

Palm Canyon, Palm Springs

17. Wash and Oasis

Deserts may be cold—Antarctic—or hot—southern Sahara—but only the sterile wastes of the highest mountains equal them in the hostility of their environment. In some respects, the deserts of California are more alive than many comparable regions of the world. A brief description of the earth's climate complex may be useful here, not only in an attempt to explain the why of deserts, in general, but to compare the dry regions of the state with other deserts elsewhere. Leaving out the polar deserts, plagued by generally low temperatures and scant precipitation throughout the year and long, dark, bitter winters, most true desert regions are semitropical, occurring roughly between the latitudes of fifteen and forty degrees on either side of the equator. They occupy zones of calm descending air between the trade winds, on one side, and the storm-bearing westerlies, on the other. Having lost moisture before and during its descent, such air is usually dry and sponges up water vapor rather than releasing it. Huge high-pressure cells are common meteorological features of these latitudes. They divert storms that might have drifted in from adjacent rainier regions and sit, more or less permanently, over large areas, further reinforcing the scanty precipitation regime.

Certain localized conditions may intensify patterns of aridity. When moist air flow is generally from one direction, intervening mountain ranges block advancing storms and rob them of their moisture. Rainshadow accounts for the great deserts of Africa or the Middle East only in part, but it definitely influences many local areas. It is very influential in the climatic spectra of the Pacific states. It even operates as far north as western Canada, whose mountains are directly in the path of storms moving across the continent from the Gulf of Alaska. The lee sides of British Columbia's coastal mountains and the Rockies are much drier than those to the windward. Distance from the sea, major source of atmospheric moisture, is an additional cause of aridity in areas deep within land masses.

For considerable distances along the western edges of most continents, cold currents upwell, chilling the local onshore winds and condensing their meager moisture. Fog, not rain, results, and it may modify the immediate natural landscape to a significant degree, particularly in terms of plants able to benefit directly from the increased atmospheric humidity. Patches of withered, shriveled cactus, apparently enduring prolonged drought, grow on bluffs overlooking Baja California's Pacific shore. Yet they are tufted with tatters of epiphytic lichen. Of little use to the cactus, the frequent coastal fogs have permitted flourishing growth of plant types characteristically at home in mist-wrapped forests atop the Santa Cruz Mountains, just south of San Francisco.

We should not imply, when we speak of zones of subtropical calm, that winds are absent from desert lands. On the contrary, strong wind, usually of a local nature, is a feature of desert climates. Unhindered, it sweeps through passes, down draws, and over dunes and bleak plains, further drying the already thirsty landscape. Nor is rain impossible. Thunderstorms, generated by warm-season convection air turbulence, account for spotty but often torrential downpours. Where deserts are peripheral to regions of greater rainfall, the highs occasionally break down, particularly when the world's climate belts have shifted because of the change of season. During summer, surges of humid tropical air slide northward, bringing rain squalls to the Southwest. Conversely, winter storms from higher latitudes occasionally ride down across the Mexican border, with welcome precipitation for northern Baja California and Sonora.

The closer an area is to the equator, the milder the winters become. Deserts of low elevation and latitude rarely experience severe winters, but they all blister under truly torrid summer temperatures. At their worst, arid regions are very hostile environments, with a pattern of extremely meager and erratically distributed precipitation, low humidity, gusty local winds, many hot days, and intense insolation. Marked diurnal temperature fluctuations are characteristic of regions of low humidity. Air moisture not only retards absorption of solar heat by ground surfaces but slows the loss of this warmth to the upper atmosphere. Where such buffering is absent, air temperatures soar and descend with little hindrance.

The arid lands of the North American continent are semi-tropical or southern temperate, occurring for the most part in the dry latitudes, slightly below or within 20 degrees north of the Tropic of Cancer. They are dominated by a rainshadow extending east from the Coast Ranges and the Sierra-Cascade mountain chain. Though isolated from the sea by this mountain barrier, they receive occasional gifts of moisture from the Pacific Ocean, and the gulfs of California and Mexico to the south and southeast.

Two conspicuous desert types are distinguishable, cool and warm. Sagebrush plains are typical of the colder arid lands and extend as far north as the Frazer Valley of British Columbia. Locally shadscale scrub first infiltrates and then takes over on descent to warmer and drier environments; but in general, the key indication of the Southwest's variant of warm deserts is the presence of creosote bush, a shrub as characteristic of this type of arid landscape as sagebrush is of cooler drought-bound regions.

Confining our discussion to California and its neighboring states, it is customary to refer to high and low deserts. Altitude is a determinant of prime importance. We might go a step further and individualize three types: high, middle, and low. The first is California's portion of the Great Basin, roughly over 4,000 feet (1,200 m.) in altitude and dominated by big sagebrush. The middle desert approximates the Mojave, from the western end of the Antelope Valley northeast to a basin-and-range complex that includes Death Valley and south to what is an admittedly arbitrary boundary, the Riverside County line; the altitude ranges from below sea level in Death Valley to 4,500 feet (1,350 m.). Average annual rainfall is from 4 to 15 inches (10−38 cm.) and mostly occurs in winter, varying from place to place and year to year. Over much of the middle desert, summer temperatures of 95° to 100° F. (35°−38° C.) can be expected, and night frost is common throughout the winter months. The third type drops from 2,000 feet (600 m.) to below sea level and comprises the Colorado Desert, California's part of the Sonoran Desert which extends east into Arizona and south into Mexico. Summer temperatures are often considerably higher than on the Mojave. Rainfall averages are somewhat lower (1 to 5 inches—2.5−13 cm.) and are extremely variable. Its topographic barriers are decisive only on the west and north. The Coast Ranges of southern California swing east from the ocean in the vicinity of Santa Barbara and, with the exception of a few passes, form an unbroken wall until they pivot around Mount San Gorgonio and thrust south to the Mexican border. The east-west trending mountains are termed the Transverse Ranges, and they are one of the few that show such marked departure from the usual direction of most of our continental ranges. Those extending south of Mount San Jacinto, partner peak to the taller San Gorgonio (Old Grayback) on the other side of the pass, are called the Peninsular Ranges as they form the backbone of northern Baja California. They are the relief features that not only bound but help account for the Colorado Desert to the east. Extensions of the Transverse Ranges, the Little San Bernardino and Eagle mountains, divide the Mojave from the Colorado Desert. East of these ranges there is no topographical boundary separating the two deserts. Though each has typical floristic components, tongues of low desert plant life lick into some southern sections of the Mojave. In general, the colder winters of the middle desert deter many species of the Colorado from establishing themselves farther north.

For the most part, rainfall increases as one goes north to the Great Basin or higher in altitude. The eastern portions of both low and middle desert are at the edge of the summer rainfall pattern of the intermountain West. What winter storms escape past the capturing peaks of the Coast Ranges and Sierra Nevada are supplemented by summer showers from moist air masses from the south and east. These storms, though local in nature, influence the structure of the plant communities of the eastern edge to some degree, and they occur as far west as Palmdale in the Mojave, and Palm Springs in the lee of Mount San Jacinto. It is normal for southwestern deserts to receive some rain during the warmer months; however, it is very undependable and localized and usually arrives in deluges with flash floods and high runoff because of the scanty vegetative cover.

On both sides of the mountains that abut the deserts to the west, many of the natural communities have been modified and their species rearranged to a bewildering degree. Alder thickets are small jungles along Whitewater Creek, which drains the desert side of Mount San Gorgonio. Brittle bush, one of the common plants of the lower deserts, drifts as far west as Lake Elsinore, only several dozen miles (kilometers) from the ocean. Great Basin sagebrush and digger pines are unlikely companions at the heads of desert canyons in the southern Sierra. California juniper, chamise, coast live oak, and cholla cactus, distinctive members of four different natural communities, are closely associated in Big Tujunga Wash, a major drainage system of the Los Angeles Basin. Another anomalous extension has found its way to the Coast Ranges, southwest of Bakersfield. Sagebrush, Mormon tea, pinyon, and rabbitbrush—all typical plants of the Great Basin—are but a short distance from the sea. Driving through this landscape on the winding road that skirts Mount Pinos and runs west to the Cuyama Valley, one can scarcely believe that the ocean is but 25 or so air miles (40+ km.) away.

The Mojave Desert itself is a meeting ground for many different floristic elements. A number of plants characteristic of northern Arizona are present in many of the mountains in the eastern part of the desert. Cliff rose, little-leaf palo verde, Apache plume, desert scrub oak, smooth menodora and single-leaf ash—the last are two of California's few representatives of the olive family—have made their way here perhaps because of increased summer precipitation. To the south a small number of saguaro cacti have ventured across the Colorado River. A fairly large grove occurs in the Whipple Mountains west of Parker Dam, and another stand is scattered from the Palo Verde Mountains south to Laguna Dam. A clue to the comparative lack of giant saguaros in California may be the paucity of so-called "nurse trees," arboreal desert species such as palo verde, whose shade prevents the overheating of the young cacti. Their abundance in Arizona is coincidental with the larger number of such trees in the summer rainfall deserts to the east.

From the north, big sagebrush, desert bitterbrush, and blackbrush have wandered down in broad gray and charcoal stripes along the flanks of the ranges on the deserts' western borders, ecotonal between the arid scrubs below and the pinyon-dominated woodlands above. Where the low desert intergrades with the middle in the eastern part of southern California, smoke trees and ocotillo have crept up from their usual haunts. Two native palm oases, on the north side of the Little San Bernardinos, are far from similar communities in the Colorado Desert to the south.

There are many instances of east and west, north and south meeting quite compatibly in the mountains of eastern Kern and Los Angeles counties. The southern Sierra, the Tehachapis, the Coast Ranges, and the Mojave Desert all come together in a welter of canyon and ridge. In addition to the unusual associations already mentioned, we find other interesting and peculiar assortments. Valley oaks, of all things, have crept through the Tehachapi Pass to the desert edge where they grow with Joshua trees and cacti. This and other odd combinations have been noted by Ernest Twisselmann in his *Flora of Kern County* (University of San Francisco, 1967), a very useful guide to the biotic communities as well as the plants of this ecotonal zone. He points out that quite a number of species commonly thought exclusive to the Pacific slope have leaked over to the desert—for instance, Chinese houses, California poppy *(Eschscholzia californica),* and owl's clover. In fact, one of the places in which one can still see profuse displays of the last two wildflowers is on the west side of the Antelope Valley where Joshua trees once formed thick groves. Low passes, ranges of moderate elevation, and a climate of fairly uniform aridity permit such strange floristic goings-on. In the central Sierra, the montane barrier is too high for this commingling.

The Mojave and the Colorado deserts share a matrix plant which not only ties the two areas together ecologically, but serves to give the sere plains a uniform appearance. Creosote bush is so well adapted to its arid home that it dominates the flora almost as undisputedly as big sagebrush, fellow tyrant to the north. With various cacti and a number of other shrubs— pygmy cedar, sweetbush, cheese bush, brittle bush, desert trumpet and other members of the buckwheat family, bursage, Mormon tea, desert (box) thorns, bladder sage, and indigo bush, it covers thousands of square miles (square kilometers) in a sparse scrub. Like sagebrush, it tolerates moderately saline soils, and it yields to interruptions, determined by substratal and climatic modifications. Though not as corrugated as the Great Basin, the Mojave Desert has its share of sink and mountain topography with characteristic zonation. Most of the ranges are fault-block in origin, but several extinct volcanoes and associated lava flows are intriguing relief features east of Barstow.

Components of the shadscale scrub occur sporadically over the desert plains. Not only does the community begin to exert itself as such where the soils become increasingly alkaline around the edges of playas, south of the Great Basin, it is often found on steep, rocky slopes of exceptional aridity. Though most shrubs of the shadscale scrub that we encountered in the Great Basin also occur in the Mojave Desert, most of them stop short of extensive appearance in the Colorado Desert. Greasewood, shadscale, and winter fat are among the species that are confined to the northern deserts. On the other hand, allscale and desert holly, another scalebush that is named for its handsome creamy green, deeply toothed leaves, are largely missing from the Great Basin.

Several authorities prefer to divide the alkali sink vegetation of the southern deserts into two scrubs, a xerophytic saltbush type on dry soils and a halophytic group on moist to wet substrates. In the Mojave Desert a typical sequence would find allscale, shadscale, and desert holly on dry, no more than moderately salty soils on the lower slopes of bajadas, giving way to halophytic scrub around dry lake beds, in sinks, or near seeps where the surface water is highly mineralized. The entrance of Parry saltbush and inkweed to the saltbush scrub is indicative of higher soil salinity. On the edge of the playa where the concentration of minerals increases, combinations of the more salt-tolerant species of the xerophytic scrub occur with big greasewood, desert salt grass, wingscale, lenscale, rusty molly, and iodine bush, often on little mounds of fine-grained soil a few inches (centimeters) above the floor of the salt pan. Mesquite groves can be expected where underground moisture is sufficient for these richly green-leafed and water-using plants, and bulrushes and cattails flourish where standing water, even though brackish, is available.

A playa assemblage in the Colorado Desert is much poorer in species. Allscale, lenscale, wingscale, and mesquite may be prominent members of saltbush scrub, and inkweed and iodine bush characterize damp saline soils around, for example, the edges of the Salton Sea.

Out on the upper plains surrounding both the isolated sinks and ranges like flecks of dark foam on a tawny sea, creosote bush and its associates are ubiquitous. Here and there this cover breaks, and other desert plants are given the opportunity to challenge the monopoly of the reigning species. A famed plant of the Mojave, Joshua tree, is largely confined to upper alluvial slopes, between the creosote scrub of the plains and the pinyon stands of higher elevations. Instead of replacing creosote bush, it thrusts up through the scrub, much like digger pine towering over a hillside of chaparral. A smaller relative, Mojave yucca, is widespread over the intermediate elevations of the desert for which it is named. It is not restricted to this region, however, as it is scattered down through the eastern Peninsular Ranges. Much less branched than its arboreal relation, it is similar in appearance because of its clusters of white flowers at the end of spike-leaved stalks.

The smaller hills, some almost buried in their own broken bones, as it were, show little or no plant zonation. Steeper faces of exposed and weathering bedrock are almost barren, but gentler slopes carry the shrubs common to the surrounding landscape. The taller mountains such as the Kingston Range and the New York Mountains and those flanking the deserts to the west have routed down, at altitudes from 3,000 to 6,000 feet (900–1,800 m.), southern extensions of plant types familiar from the short forests—rabbitbrush, cotton thorn, blue sage, horsebrush, sagebrush, pinyon, and Utah juniper. Above this zone, montane conifers—yellow and Jeffrey pine, white fir, and lodgepole pine—form islands of cool green on the Transverse and Peninsular ranges, overlooking the hot plains below. The highest peaks of these mountains reach to timberline with stands of limber pine 9,000 feet (2,700 m.) and above. In the eastern Mojave three ranges—New York Mountains, Clark Mountain, and Kingston Range—are tall enough to allow relict groves of white fir that have persisted from wetter times. Some of the stands are in north-facing canyons where they benefit from ameliorated solar exposure.

Just as certain species are typical of the Colorado Desert, there are several whose distribution is centered in the Mojave. Both common and Latinized names indicate this geographical pattern: *Mojavea* or ghost flower, Mojave sage, Mojave aster, Mojave dalea which is related to indigo bush, Mojave yucca, Mojave monkeyflower, and Mojave prickly pear cactus. One of the most outstanding wildflowers of the middle desert is the eye-striking Kennedy mariposa lily of Chinese red. Its little cups of flame usually sit close to the ground on short stems surrounded by several green-gray, slim, elongated leaves. When the winter rains have been good, the Mojave has as lavish a wildflower show as the Colorado. Many species occur on both deserts, but a few are more characteristic of the Mojave:

thistle sage—an exquisite flower that looks like bouquets of tiny lavender orchids—broad gilia with its little rosy trumpets, pennyroyal, and desert paintbrush. Desert candle or squaw cabbage is an oddity that once seen is seldom forgotten. Its inflated yellow-green stems look as though the plant had swallowed golf balls and are topped with absurd little tufts of purple flowers.

The Colorado Desert is much smaller in size than the Mojave. It has two quite distinct sections—a large trough to the west and a chunk of basin-and-range topography to the east. The northern part of the trough is called the Coachella Valley, cupped between two upturned hands whose thumbs are the Peninsular Ranges to the west and the Chocolate-Orocopia Mountains to the east. The bent-up fingertips are the Little San Bernardino and Eagle mountains on the north. In the gap, where the two palms are joined, lies the landlocked Salton Sea, the last in a series of lakes that periodically flooded this low-lying area because of overflow from the Colorado River. This large lake is a prime but problem recreation area for water-hungry sports enthusiasts. For a time, irrigation drainoff threatened to raise its surface until seaside resorts would be inundated. Now, constant evaporation is concentrating its dissolved minerals. Soon the water will be so briny that nothing will be able to live in it, and the fish population will disappear.

Below the Salton Sea, in the southern extension of the trough or the Imperial Valley, intensive truck farming is possible because of deep silt soil, level land, year-around mild temperatures, and availability of irrigation water. To the west of this rich valley, the Anza-Borrego, a desert-within-a-desert, is a tangle of much eroded badlands, plains, and steep canyons complicating the eastern base of the mountains in back of San Diego. In this broken country close to the Mexican border, one can find several plants that one would expect only in northern Mexico or southern Arizona. Desert apricot has worked as far north as the Cajon Pass area in southwestern San Bernardino County. The Anza-Borrego country lays claim to fairy duster with its delicate puffs of pink and an arboreal oddity, the elephant tree. One of several species called by this name, it is a *Bursera* and belongs to the torchwood family, which has few nontropical members. Like many desert trees, it is a bit peculiar in appearance, with branches tapering rapidly to resemble the trunk of an elephant. They are covered with white, papery bark which, when injured, exudes a blood-red juice. The tiny leaves do little to improve the looks of this short, stiff-jointed tree, which—while fairly common in Baja California, Sonora, and the mountains of the extreme southern part of Arizona—in California is restricted to one small grove near Fish Creek in San Diego County. A number of shrubs more commonly encountered on the Arizona desert have pushed as far west as the mountains east of the Salton Sea—gray thorn, California snakewood, and crucifixion thorn (*Koeberlinia spinosa*—several other prickly shrubs have the same common name), among them.

The eastern Colorado Desert looks much like the Mojave, and it is difficult to delimit the two areas. The same gaunt hills stand as though freshly quarried amid the chips of their shaping. The wide plains between them gradually lower in altitude, dropping steadily to about 300 feet (90 m.) above sea level at the Colorado River, which is now little more than a canal between reservoirs. There are few playas in the Colorado Desert, but many sand dunes. Excellent examples of this type of terrain run parallel to the Coachella Canal, on the east side of the Imperial Valley.

From the highway, the battered mountains look inhospitable to anything but the few desert shrubs that have footholds on their scarred flanks. But they hold surprises. The desert can be both a verdant garden and as barren as an airport runway, depending on season and substrate. Not all spring seasons have good wildflower shows. Rain must be adequate and correctly spaced for the maximum display. One 4-inch (10 cm.) cloudburst in September does not equal four storms bringing one inch each, several weeks apart, from late November through February. The more rain the better, of course, but timing is almost as important as amount. When there have been heavy, widespread, soaking rains and the desert is at the height of bloom, the highways push through masses of flowers lining the road on each side. Large white birdcage evening primroses, like little moons, gleam over variegated carpets of deep rose sand verbenas, sunny desert dandelion, desert marigold, coreopsis, and less showy composites. Where desert pavement is encountered, the display ends abruptly, and only occasional flowering annuals and the dropped blossoms of the undaunted creosote bush, little golden windmills, brighten the hard, rock-mosaic surface. If the winter rains have been kind, on the road that takes off to the hamlet of Rice from the main Los Angeles-Phoenix highway it is possible to see one of the queens of the desert, the wild "Easter lily," a miniature of the commercial lily of Eastertide. Though they are usually but a foot or so (30 cm.) high with five or six blossoms, they can grow to 5 or 6 feet (1.5–1.8 m.) tall and continue bearing flowers along this towering stem.

A few miles (kilometers) east of Indio, turn south via State Highway 195 for a quick look into Box Canyon. On the alluvium of the upper wash, springtime annuals may be sparse but still thick enough to be impressive. Here the outstanding plant is ocotillo, at this season tipped with flaming red flowers and green with new leaves. Decked with such rich colors, it is quite different from its fit-only-for-kindling appearance during the rest of the year. Desert plant oddities are by no means uncommon, but this shrub is still one of the most peculiar in appearance—bundles of needle-spined, whiplike rods tied together at one end and thrust into the soil.

Where the wash sides steepen to cliffs, arboreal forms, though rare in much of the California desert, either cluster in webby thickets against the gorge walls or string out along the gravel bars of the canyon floor. Box Canyon has some excellent specimens of these trees as do a number of canyons in the Colorado Desert. They are largely absent from the Mojave Desert because of colder winters and the lack of summer rain. Palo verde, ironwood, and desert willow (not a true willow but a member of a large tropical family) all grow to small tree size. When fully flowered, each is alive with color and bees. The first is a cloud of yellow, and the other two are pink, the last species having sprays of large trumpet-shaped blossoms. They are joined by the charming but aggressively spined smoke tree whose filmy gray contrasts with the harsh desert landscape. Other small trees frequently encountered here include mesquite and catclaw, a true acacia. They are related and both have fuzzy caterpillar inflorescences of pale yellow. Chuparosa or beloperone, a stiff little shrub with tubular scarlet flowers, is an inhabitant of the wash community and is much visited by the hummingbirds for the nectar obtainable from its blossoms.

After good winter rains, wild gardens brighten the wash floor and lower slopes—apricot mallow, clumps of coral tinted bells arranged along bending stems; fivespot, a graceless name for little pink bowls as fragile looking as Dresden china; yellow cups and other evening primroses; desert bells, a richly purple-blue phacelia; silk-sheened blazing stars; and ghost flowers.

Many desert annual plants, typified by extremely small size, are referred to as "belly plants" as that is the portion of one's anatomy on which one must rest in order to see them at close hand. Some common wildflowers of this group are *Eriophylum* (a tiny bouquet of yellow flowers), calico plant, rattlesnake weed (its milky juice places it in the euphorb group, distant cousin to Africa's great candelabrum trees), Bigelow monkey-flower, desert star, and nama, a magenta blotch on the gravel as though wine had been spilled and had congealed.

Jeep tracks wind up any wash wide enough to permit them. When they are forced to stop by deepening sand or enclosing boulders, foot trails take over, some almost indiscernible, and meander up the canyon. The paths that follow the floor often require hopping and clambering up steep staircases of large boulders, a strenuous type of exercise if one is out of condition. One can also skirt the gully rims on none-too-obvious trails that tack back and forth across the hill faces. Both above and below, one can see that water is the sculptor of these desert ranges, scarce though it is at times. It has tossed down the chunks of rock, large and small, littering the canyon bed, cut the great *V* the hiker is ascending, and created cliffs for miniature waterfalls when their streams are flowing.

Hillside vegetation often differs from that of the gully floor. On the rim sides grow cacti and low, scant, and often prickly shrubs—ratany, goatnut (Colorado Desert and east and south), Mormon tea, turpentine broom, bladder sage (largely Mojave Desert), and desert almond. There may be squaw bush, on an east-facing slope in the shade of a rocky prominence, and many species that have straggled up from the fan slopes below such as brittle bush and indigo bush. In such rocky areas south of Palm Springs, century plants are common. They begin to bud in early spring, thrusting up from thick, needle-tipped leaves giant asparaguslike stems which later break into clusters of rich yellow blossoms. Nolina, also in the agave family along with yuccas, has a similar growth form, but its stalks bear elongate puffs of creamy white. Cacti are forever underfoot, as any desert hiker knows. Fishhook and young barrel cacti tuck into the rocky hillside like small spine-covered boulders.

The canyon floor has protected crannies—under overhangs and against boulders—which shelter numerous plants. Apricot mallows and phacelias, four-o'clocks and bladderpod spray out lavishly. The last is also widespread on coastal bluffs and hillsides in southern California and is a member of the caper family. It has distended, swollen-looking seed pods, hence its name. It is a frequent shrub of the sand patches, level places between the boulder clutches where mesquite, catclaw, palo verde, and desert willow continue to find foothold. In most desert hillside canyons, rim trail and gully staircase gradually converge. Continuing still higher, they often lead to the most dramatic living feature of the Colorado Desert, a lush oasis, complete with springs, in the heart of a lifeless-looking, seemingly barren desert range. A number of these groves of welcome green shade not only have wild palms but true willows, cottonwoods, and cascading masses of pink and gold stream orchids in late April or May. To come unawares on such rich vegetation is a memorable experience, one which often leads to speculation about desert plant growth in general. Among the many questions often raised are why do plants even occur in the desert at all and where did they come from? It seems to be universal that where conditions are not so severe as to preclude all possible plant life, enough species will adapt, in one way or another, so that a true community exists: congregations of plants and animals that can live even under ruggedly adverse circumstances. Only on polar ice fields, the most unstable parts of large shifting sand dunes, the hearts of alkali playas, the few really rainless deserts, ocean depths, the punishing heights of the tallest mountains, and uncongealed lava flows is plant life in some permanent form virtually impossible.

As for their history, the deserts of southern California and the Southwest developed recently, presumably after the close of the Ice Age. By this time the elevation of both the Transverse and Peninsular ranges was effectively blocking winter storms, depriving areas to the east of these mountains of significant amounts of precipitation. Temperature ranges also became more extreme. As noted in Chapter 5, all of California experienced a cooling and drying trend throughout the Tertiary, the five epochs between the Dinosaur and the Ice ages. A succession of vegetative types evolved, each of which reflected broad changes in rainfall and temperature patterns.

Tropical savanna and dry tropic forest, such as that now typical of the Pacific side of southern Mexico, were widespread throughout the region during the Cretaceous, the final period of the Dinosaur Age. Ancient forms of magnolia, palm, tree fern, sycamore, baldcypress, and trees related to the present-day Norfolk Island pine (an *Araucaria,* a genus of several primitive conifers now confined to the Southern Hemisphere) were clustered thickly along stream courses or spread out in more open forests on drier slopes. Such growth, luxuriant in contrast to today's sere hills and plains, was possible because of ample rainfall, up to 50 inches (127 cm.), at least. It appears that there was some cool season drought, but the overall precipitation was sufficient to support abundant tree growth.

Relatively warm temperatures and high rainfall continued after the close of the Dinosaur Age. Fossil remains provide evidence that elements now present in the midaltitude tropical forests of southern Mexico—*Cordia,* sweet gum, avocado, cycad, wild fig, etc.—were well represented in what was to become desert at least until the first (Paleocene) epoch of the Tertiary. These components also contributed to the temperate rainforest then well established from central California northward.

By the fourth (Miocene) epoch rainfall had appreciably diminished (20 to 25 inches—51 to 64 cm.), and winters continued dry and mild. Dense evergreen forest grew only along waterways and in canyon bottoms. Elsewhere smaller, dry-season deciduous trees, dry tropical scrub (thorn forest), and oak-conifer woodland, much resembling the lowland and foothill vegetation mosaic of what is now the Mexican state of Sinaloa, dominated drier sites. Drought-adapted elements of the Madro-Tertiary geoflora had appeared long before this, however. As early as the second (Eocene) epoch the forebears of both sclerophyll woodland (for example, oak and madroño) and scrub (ceanothus) had been established in rainshadows, on south-facing and thin-soiled slopes, and other dry localities present in even that relatively well-watered time. Dry tropical scrub, a community with a number of xerophytic species (acacias, etc.) emerged roughly at the same time and under the same circumstances.

Precipitation continued to decrease and summer temperatures increased until the late Tertiary (Pliocene epoch). Though oak-conifer woodland and dry tropical scrub occupied much of the region, semidesert vegetation, which had been evolving on the driest sites since well before the Pliocene, became more important. The Pleistocene (Ice Age) brought many changes. The broad rhythms of glacial surge and retreat were reflected in pluvial wealth and paucity. During the last glaciopluvial period elements of subalpine forest such as bristlecone and limber pine covered most of the Great Basin, and pinyon-juniper woodland was widespread in the Mojave. Nonetheless, locally dry environments served as refuges for the more drought-adapted plants which waited, biding their time as it were, for the lean years ahead.

As postglacial aridity increased many of the dry tropical scrub and semidesert plants that formerly enriched the various floras of the region were restricted to either higher elevations or to southern Arizona, western Texas, and northern Mexico where summer rainfall is more dependable. The desert scrubs of California, as we know them today, are much impoverished. They are derived mainly from the dry tropical forest and scrubs once so prevalent and in part from the sclerophyllous vegetation ancestral to present-day chaparral and woodland. Indeed, a number of genera—*Rhus, Garrya,* and *Cercocarpus*—occur in both coastal and desert habitats.

Geological history also accounts for the differences in plant life between California's two warmer deserts. During the early part of the Pleistocene, the Mojave was elevated, lowering temperatures and thus removing many dry tropical forest elements of the ancient assemblage. To this day such species as palo verde, ironwood, and ocotillo are largely confined to the lower desert. Instead, representatives of the Great Basin scrubs such as big sagebrush and desert bitterbrush were left in the Mojave Desert at suitable altitudes.

About eighty-five species can be considered endemic to the California deserts. The list is longer if one includes the twenty-five or more species that are more or less confined to the Death Valley area. According to Peter H. Raven and Daniel I. Axelrod (the dean of American paleobotanists) in their excellent little publication, *Origin and Relationships of the California Floras* (University of California Press, 1977), the Inyo-Death Valley region is an important center of endemism. At least three new genera—*Gilmania* (goldcarpet), *Dedeckera* (July gold), and *Swallenea* (Eureka dunegrass)—have been discovered here, and, who knows, with patient searching some other small plants could prove different enough from their relatives to boost them into taxonomic designations of their own.

Desert plants can be categorized according to several primary types of growth behavior. There are as many versions of such organizing as there are naturalists who think them up. For simplicity we use three: those whose way of life announces that water is available the year around; those that retire from active metabolism during adverse conditions; and those that continue to struggle along. To put it another way, plants living in a desert are either water users, ephemerals, or drought-adapted perennials. The first two have made the fewest changes in response to their demanding environments. Where water is permanent—along mountain-draining or spring-source streams, around seeps and pools, and in the vicinity of the larger rivers such as the Colorado (or near present-day irrigation ditches)—waterside growth common to other parts of California and the Southwest is much at home. In moist soils where the water table is at no great depth, willows and cottonwoods, though not typical desert plants, are joined by mesquite, catclaw, and tamarix, a pink-plumed, salt-tolerant tree originally from the Near East. Reeds, seep willow, arrowweed, sedges, and various rushes are in the damper places, and tules and cattails where open water is constantly present. In areas of salinity and heavy mineralization, resident species are essentially halophytic. Salt grass and alkali sacaton are commonly found in such habitats. Shrubs such as saltbushes and inkweed are frequently found in the transitions between the oasis and the drier desert.

The oasis plant that deserves star status is the native fan palm. A relict of once much larger distribution and wetter climate, it has maintained precarious membership in the flora of the Colorado Desert. Two oases, however, are at the southern edge of the Mojave Desert, slightly misplaced. One very striking group remains in Arizona—Kofa Palms. Both the fan palm and a good-looking relative, the blue palm, are present in large numbers in deep canyons of northern Baja California. For the most part, fan palms are restricted to areas of permanent surface or subsurface water. Many groves are located in canyons on the flanks of the mountains to the west and north of the Coachella and Imperial valleys. Palm Canyon, for which Palm Springs is named, is one of these oases. Several small groups are in open desert where seeps and pools occur, such as Seven Palms, Dos Palmas, and Twentynine Palms, the latter being one of the two north of the Colorado Desert. A group of groves is strung along the base of the Indio Hills, whose south face is a scarp created by one branch of the San Andreas Fault which splits east of Pearblossom into two great cracks. One runs just north of San Bernardino and divides into a complex of smaller faults near Banning, recombining as one fault east of the Salton Sea; the other drops south near Hemet and slices down through the Anza-Borrego country, west of the Imperial Valley. At various points along the Indio Hills, groves of wild palms dot the otherwise almost barren slopes. Thousand Palms, Pushawalla, Biskra, Willis, Macomber, and a number of other oases draw on moisture sources where the water table has been forced to the surface by the fault. Though accumulations of salt are frequently found on the soil under the palms, accounting for the presence of alkali sacaton and other salt-tolerant plants, the water in their root zone is relatively free of salinity. Unfortunately, the thick masses of dead leaves are highly flammable. Escaped campfires and even deliberate vandalism have sent these thatch-burdened old fellows up in flames, blackening the trunks and destroying the undergrowth. Most palms, however, eventually grow new foliage and even benefit from the removal of the understory with which they must compete for the limited supply of water.

In the pastel-tinted Mecca Hills, cut through by Box Canyon, a much dissected landscape cradles several little oases, including one that is a gem, Hidden Springs. They are difficult to reach now as the aqueduct has cut off vehicular access. Hiking to them is adventurous but rewarding. Water erosion in these soft rocks, mostly mudstone and conglomerate, has carved out labyrinths of winding, steep-walled, narrow passageways, some in permanent shade, where dry waterfalls, tunnels, and alcoves crawl about in secret-dungeon complexity. Palm hunting in this odd geological pocket of the California desert is even more of a challenge as corridors narrow, and one must edge sidewise past sharp-rocked walls; or they widen out to charming canyons, often surprisingly thick with desert vegetation.

Camping in a canyon oasis has its own delights. Then one can catch memory-enriching details that a hurried visit usually misses: the golden hue of both surrounding rocks and palms in the light of late winter afternoon; the dry rustle of the fronds in the endless desert wind; the skirts of dead leaves that from a distance have the color and texture of the basketry made by the Indians that once lived in these oases; the faint smell of alkali which sometimes encrusts the ground with white crystals; the fruiting stalks hanging down from the masses of huge accordion-pleated palm leaves, heavy with sweet but tiny dates; and the sheer splendor of the palms themselves, towering into the blue sky, hemmed in but never dominated by the crags that rise around them.

When dates drop from the palms, these sugary morsels are eagerly sought by coyotes, carnivores with extremely wide food choices; they appear to eat almost anything edible, with the exception of grass and leafy material in general. Their footprints are often seen in the soft earth around springs and along desert streams. Among other mammals one can hope to glimpse in the vicinity of oases, particularly those in canyons away from the desert floor, are mule deer and bighorn sheep. The latter is the desert variety of an ungulate occurring in mountain areas from Canada to Mexico. True sheep, they browse on Mojave yucca and the leaves of many shrubs and small trees. One of the most fascinating experiences desert mountains can offer is the chance of observing a group of bighorns stepping, Indian file, along a game trail led by a ewe. Sheep, used to following their mothers while young, continue the habit of remaining behind a female leader when mature. Observation chances are best near waterholes, as these animals must drink regularly.

A number of such waterholes and streams in California's deserts are populated by a group of small fish that are rapidly becoming famous as the focus of controversy regarding land use—the pupfish. Conservationists are determined to preserve them as, biologically, they are of high significance. These tiny aquatic organisms tell the story of evolution as convincingly as Darwin's finches. Ranchers, however, protest they need the water that supplies their habitats for irrigation and other uses.

Though cyprinodons, or pupfish, are the best known, several other genera occur in our deserts—killifish, in the same family as pupfish, speckled dace, chub, and suckers. They are distributed from Fish Slough north of Bishop in the Owens River drainage to creeks draining into the Salton Sea (there are a few populations in the Arizona desert as well). The most controversial sites are in Ash Meadows, east of the Armagosa River and just over the Nevada state line.

During the Pleistocene, interconnecting systems of glacier- and rain-fed rivers and lakes developed in the Great Basin and Mojave Desert. It is most likely that the Colorado River to the east and south and the Columbia River to the north were eventually in contact. Fish could move with relative ease from one basin, and most probably one system, to another. As the ice fields retreated and the climate became warmer and drier, some lakes disappeared and others were reduced in size. The streams suffered the same fate. Huge underground reservoirs, however, have persisted from those water-rich times and supply the springs in Ash Meadows as well as other nearby surface water features.

The springs and small streams of the Death Valley area are isolated remnants of a much more extensive Pleistocene drainage system. The forebears of the modern forms of pupfish and the related killifish were confined to these remaining habitats, many of them environmentally extreme in terms of salinity and temperature. From these ancestral forms eleven distinct types of pupfish and five kinds of killifish have evolved, each restricted to particular sites. Some such as the Salt Creek pupfish have a wide range of tolerance for harsh conditions of heat, cold, and mineralization, and, in addition, they depend on a number of behavioral stratagems to mitigate these conditions. Others like the Saratoga Springs pupfish are confined to stable, much less extreme environments.

The Devil's Hole pupfish in Ash Meadows, Nevada, is distinguished by being one of the most restricted vertebrate species in the world. Not only the entire population but the whole species was restricted to one section of a large limestone cave. Unfortunately, agricultural development in the area continues to threaten this remarkable little fish. Pumping water from the underground aquifer supplying Devil's Hole has lowered the water level in the cave, exposing the shelf needed by the pupfish for food-finding and spawning. Recently legal activity on behalf of the species has resulted in regulation of pumping, and its habitat has been stabilized. An additional colony has been established near Hoover Dam.

Though the Mojave chub and the Owens pupfish have been placed on the endangered species list because of such threats to their environment, another situation is proving a serious menace to the desert pupfish that live in pools near the rim of the Salton Sea. Several exotic fish including mosquitofish, the sailfin molly, and Zill's cichlid have been introduced, the latter purposely to control aquatic weeds. Some of these foreign species are competitors for food, and others are possible predators. Certainly a double-edged biological sword threatens this little creature.

A number of reptiles are typical of arid rocky hillsides. Collared, and desert and granite spiny lizards sun themselves on exposed boulder surfaces which they desert for protected niches when they are startled. California's largest lizard, the chuckwalla, is, without exception, a rock dweller. Though much of its body is black or gray, individual color variations of red and yellow are not uncommon on its back and tail. "Chucks" are vegetation eaters, a habit not common in the lizard world. Thus they make good pets as they are easy to feed. But catching one is not too simple. They appear to be lethargic and slow-moving, but they are wary and elude their would-be captors by resorting to strategy. They escape into small crevices, and when cornered by threatening hands or capture devices, they inflate themselves, wedging in so that it is almost impossible to pull them out.

Black-tailed gnatcatchers, Gambel's quail, black-chinned sparrows, and ladder-backed woodpeckers are year-around residents of an oasis environment. In summer, blue grosbeaks, hooded orioles, and even a few pairs of vermillion flycatchers seek either insect or plant food, depending on their tastes. Along the Colorado River, brick-red summer tanagers work through the cottonwoods, west of their usual territory. In spring, chats, yellowthroats, and Wilson's and yellow warblers pause in their favorite habitat before going on to riparian woodlands north and west. White-crowned, Lincoln's, and chipping sparrows take their places in winter.

To return to the story of plant survival in this arid region, the ephemerals are short-lived annuals carrying dormancy to an advanced degree. They are, strictly speaking, alive as plants only a few weeks to several months of the year; they remain in seed form, needing neither water nor the ability to make food for indefinite periods of time. When rain occurs, some, but by no means all, will germinate and grow a tiny tuft of foliage and stem. Whether they succeed in producing spectacular wildflowers depends on the ensuing weather. In dry years, plants remain stunted and, at best, grow only a blossom or two. In optimum years, when the desert as a whole receives a great deal of well-spaced rain, then blooms the showy display. A large number of plants and seeds, however, are harvested by rodents and birds. Regardless of weather fluctuation, most of these plants have the characteristic juicy stems and green leaves of water wasters. Quite a number do have some moisture-conserving features—hairy or sticky foliage, small size, and so forth—but in general the ephemerals behave as though moisture were plentiful, as it may be for the short span of their life. If all goes well, the mature plants live long enough to drop seeds that will wait through the long sleep until the next growing season. Though most of the annuals of the California deserts are winter germinators, there is sufficient summer rainfall for the sporadic appearance of a number of summer annuals such as chinch weed, a pleasingly scented, yellow-flowered composite. The diversity and density of warm season growth definitely increases as one approaches the heart of the summer rainfall deserts in southern Arizona. The author has seen spreads of summerpoppy and desert marigold south of Phoenix in mid-August that rival many of the better springtime displays in the Coachella Valley. Research has shown that the substrate as well as precipitation patterns influence the distribution of desert annual plants. Some, such as birdcage evening primrose, prefer sandy soils, and others such as pebbly pincushion are more plentiful on stony slopes. A similar way of life holds true for plants such as the desert Easter and mariposa lilies, whose bulbs are safely underground throughout the dry months. The seasonal herbaceous cover is by no means beneficial to surrounding shrubs. It uses much of the surface moisture which would otherwise be available to perennial species.

Finally we come to the plants that survive the long, parched, wind-harried days between rains, not relying on permanent water nor restricted to the extreme dormancy of seed form. There are many ways to resist dehydration, nevertheless, and most drought-enduring plants combine several features and include the following.

1. Succulence. Such species have the ability to store water in fleshy tissue, cacti in stems and agaves and the much smaller stonecrops in leaves. The epidermis of such

plants is often heavily cutinized, drought-proofed, as it were, and as a rule they are shallow-rooted, taking up the surface moisture of even light showers to enrich their internal reservoirs. They have a remarkable ability to shrink and pucker during the seemingly endless months of drought, only to swell in corpulence when the rains finally return.

2. Deep or extensive roots. Many shrubs of desert hillsides and washes have root systems that are much larger than the tufts of foliage they support. Like those of chaparral plants, they probe for moisture sources within fractured bedrock or an accessible water table.

3. Leaf structure and seasonal growth patterns. As we have already noted, metabolism, the processes involved in the maintenance of life, uses and spends water.

Water balance—moisture loss equivalent to moisture intake—is essential for all plants if they are to continue growth. In the case of annuals, once seed has been dropped and water balance is no longer important, the plants wilt and die. Perennial species, shrubs, trees, and so forth, are out-of-step with such simple rhythms. Tenacious of life, they have modified to cope with the desert's most stern control, the limiting factor of water deficiency.

Conditions vary, but each organism has sets of tolerance ranges within which it must function, or it will die. Such ranges have limits at both ends. When these are approached, the life of the organism is threatened. We tend to first think in terms of a lack of a requirement—too little water, too small an amount of oxygen—but the other end of the scale is also operative. There can be too much of any one thing, either a necessity or a nonessential. Extremes of any nature are potentially lethal; for life as we know it here on the planet Earth is restricted to a rather narrow spectra of conditions. Unprotected living tissue has very little tolerance to fire, intense and prolonged heat, cold, drought, and radical changes in the chemistry of individual environments.

For most desert perennials, water deficit is countered by a number of resistive measures, many having necessarily to do with foliage, where most water loss takes place. Some plants have discarded leaf tissue or reduced it to spines, and manufacture food with chlorophyll bodies in stems or in bark. Cacti are excellent examples of such modification though a number of tropical species do have leaves, and many desert species have small succulent leaves that persist if soil moisture is adequate. Spine-covered cacti, however, are probably most familiar to us. The function of the spines has been debated. There is evidence that the interlacing network provides enough shade so that the tough, leathery epidermis will not heat to damaging temperatures. Such speculation raises the whole interesting point of the reason for the abundance of thorny or spiny plants in desert regions. It has been suggested that, because of its scarcity, the edible vegetation growing here is the target of all the plant-eating animals, which are surprisingly numerous in arid regions. Thorniness may be a protective adaptation, discouraging intensive browsing.

Palo verde trees conduct limited photosynthesis in green bark on their trunks and branches throughout the year. However, it goes into high-gear food production for a short time each spring when it puts forth slim-leaved foliage which it drops at the start of the hot season. Smoke tree behaves in a like manner whereas brittle bush has an even more neatly adjusted drought-drop pattern. When water is readily available, leaves are larger and less capable of controlling moisture loss. As the dry season sets in, these more mesophytic leaves drop away, leaving smaller, more drought-resistant leaves. Under severe water stress, even these are discarded, and only the terminal buds, protected by a dense cover of hair, remain. Some photosynthesis is carried on in the sticklike branches of the ocotillo, but much of the plant's food-making is confined to times of leaf growth following rain. When bare of foliage it tends to reduce metabolic activity.

The evergreen plants that maintain year-around foliage have many features for water conservation and reduction of heat: hairiness, waxiness—which reduces moisture escape through the leaf cuticle—light color, and small size. Many species of arid lands are able to wilt and recover with little or no damage to the plant tissue, but most have the capacity to resist wilting though undergoing a high percentage of water loss. For some, the osmotic pressure within the cell continues to be high even under adverse circumstances. These plants apparently are both more efficient in absorbing soil moisture and limiting the loss of water vapor through transpiration. The stomata, or leaf pores through which this process takes place, may be sunken or protected in other ways, and they may remain open only for short periods of time or be capable of closing quickly, should the need arise. It appears, moreover, that when plant leaves have such water-conserving features as small size and thick cuticles, the tissue will not overheat even when the stomata are closed and the evaporative cooling that is a positive feature of transpiration is curtailed. For such plants metabolic activity, including food-making, is reduced, forcing them to be relatively unproductive and slow growing.

In certain desert species nature has compensated in an ingenious way. Photosynthesis for most plants proceeds along a certain chemical pathway. Recent research has disclosed two other routes, both of which use water very efficiently. One of them, the CAM group, is typical of succulents such as cacti and agaves. Carbon dioxide is assimilated during the night, and the first stable product is stored in the form of an organic acid, presumably within vacuoles, or large cell bodies. The completion of the photosynthetic process awaits the arrival of daylight. The advantage of this arrangement lies in the fact that transpiration or loss of water vapor is reduced as the stomata are open only during the cooler hours. In addition, succulent plants are able to utilize respiratory, that is, metabolically produced, carbon dioxide during the warm part of the day, decreasing the necessity for gas exchange and the unavoidable loss of water this entails.

Some desert shrubs have recourse to rather simple devices for coping with heat and aridity. Goatnut (jojoba) turns only the edges of its leaves to solar radiation. Sun strength hitting broadside is warmer and far more drying than that striking parallel to the surface. Others such as creosote bush have a whole array of expedients that allows existence in a harsh environment. This constant companion of most plants, in one place or another, of the warmer North American deserts deserves some discussion. Not as spectacular as a large blooming cactus nor as grotesquely fascinating as a Joshua tree, this ubiquitous shrub has a number of most interesting attributes; not the least of these is its distribution. Until very recently, most of the botanists interested in desert flora assumed that the creosote bush of our deserts was the same species as a similar shrub common to arid lands in Argentina and Chile. In other words, the plant so prevalent in both deserts was one and the same, *Larrea divaricata*, even though separated by a distance of some 4,000 miles (6,500+ km.) and such diverse vegetation as tropical rainforest and alpine cushion plants! Research, however, has shown that *divaricata* should be retained as the name for the South American species, and *tridentata* for the North American plant. Both are so closely related that they are considered semispecies, an amazing taxonomic kinship considering the distance between them.

As three other species of *Larrea* as well as a number of related genera also occur in tropical and semitropical South America, it is thought by many authorities that this continent is the place of origin for the genus. Additionally, there is no fossil evidence of ancestral forms of *Larrea* in North America. How did it travel north to become such a widespread and significant plant in our deserts? One possibility is by means of migrating birds such as killdeer and other plovers, some of which retain seeds in their gizzards for as long as a week. Most probably, creosote bush arrived as *divaricata* about 12,000 years ago and subsequently evolved into *tridentata* and its races.

Once here, a number of characteristics enabled the creosote bush to claim its sizable territory in the arid West—from Death Valley in central California to latitude twenty degrees in the Chihuahuan Desert of Mexico, from the west coast of Baja California to the Big Bend country of Texas. In common with many evergreen desert shrubs, it behaves like a mesophyte when sufficient soil moisture is available, readily transpiring to obtain the benefit of evaporative cooling. During drought such profligacy comes to an end, and a number of moisture-conserving leaf features such as small size, resinous coating, epidermal hair, and protective layers of palisade cells augment stomatal closing, the almost universal plant response to water deficit.

Root development is often controlled by the substrate. The system is shallow and extensively branched, particularly where calcium carbonate hardpans interfere with soil drainage. In deep sandy or rocky soils, both a taproot and spreading lateral roots take advantage of moisture at different depths.

Regardless of these structural and behavioral modifications

to contend with the desert's aridity and heat, creosote bush can become dehydrated. Nevertheless, when severe moisture stress forces such companion shrubs as ratany and thornbushes into dormancy, creosote bush has the remarkable ability to continue photosynthesis and cell production, on a limited basis. When stress becomes more severe, it resorts to other stratagems. Partial leaf drop, particularly of older, less resinous leaves, is initiated to further reduce transpiration, and finally these shrubs decrease the amount of water-losing leaf surface by dying back. One after another of the numerous stems comprising the adult bush drop their shriveled leaves and become lifeless twigs that in time will break off and collect as dead litter. Finally, only a few viable stems and leafy wisps remain, carrying on limited photosynthesis and barely maintaining life. But a good season or two brings remarkable changes. Though the really dead woody tissue cannot be revived, the living branches sprout fresh green leaf crops, and the plant begins rapidly growing new shoots. The ability to recover quickly, making the most of good fortune, is characteristic of most desert plants. Activity and then dormancy, of one degree or another, is the typical rhythmic pattern of nearly all perennials during the desert year.

There is much variation in the individual appearance of the shrub. Creosote bush may be small with lightly foliaged, wisplike stems that seem ready to be snapped away by the desert wind, or it may be tall and richly leaved, particularly where highway paving or large slabs of rock concentrate runoff. It ranges from roughly 5,000 feet (1,500 m.), where cooler winter temperatures limit its distribution, to below sea level. Down bajadas and broad silty washes, under Joshua trees and over bur-sage, the thin gray-green cover appears solid at the horizon but breaks at near distance in a reticulation of shrub and bare ground. As this meager blend of leaf and shade descends to the basin floor, it mingles with saltbushes and other members of the shadscale and alkali scrubs until the salinity, and what is probably of even more importance, the heavy soils typical of playas discourage its growth. Creosote bush apparently needs soils rich in oxygen.

The plant is both insect- and self-pollinated, but reproduction from seed is a risky business. Optimum conditions of temperature and soil moisture for germination do not occur every growing season. Seedling survival, as we shall see later, is chancy at best. Creosote bush has resorted to another common method of reproduction—vegetative, or cloning. Recent investigation of this process has revealed some startling information. Our scruffy, "desert rat" of a plant has a new claim to fame— age. As the young plant develops, the characteristic shape of creosote bush becomes apparent. The multiple branches grow up and out around a central "stem-crown." As drought comes and goes, the inner branches die, and new root and stem growth spreads away from the central crown. Eventually it, too, rots away, and the plant has developed into a clonal ring, a circle of individual, though genetically identical, shrubs. The years pass and they give way to younger satellite shrubs around the outer edge of the ring. The original stem-crown has completely gone, and a patch of soil has taken its place. As time moves on, the circle of shrubs expands, and the central bare area enlarges as well. Botanists have measured certain clones in the Mojave Desert whose open centers are 66 feet (20 m.) or more across. By comparing the size of the clone with rate of growth, and using other data, extraordinary ages have been determined. One clonal ring is estimated to be over 9,000 years old, making it, to date, the oldest known single organism. Unlike the bristlecone pine, it has not persisted as one individual plant, but as part of the original genetic make-up, renewed in each satellite or daughter shrub present in the clone.

For many desert shrubs, infancy is the time of greatest danger. They may sprout but fail to live through the following dry period. There are a number of plants, mostly wash dwellers, in which germination can be accomplished only if the impervious seed coat is scarified by abrasion. Scratching of this sort usually happens when the seeds are tumbled along during the floods that periodically rage through the washes. Presumably it allows the entry of water into the seed which dissolves substances that inhibit germination. At any rate, quantities of water sufficient to carry the seeds swiftly down a wash floor is a kind of guarantee that enough moisture will sink beneath the surface to foster the seedlings once they are started.

One of the first things that people notice, on becoming acquainted with desert vegetation, is the spacing between shrubs. In places, particularly in the drier parts of the Colorado Desert, it is so uniform as to seem almost deliberate, as if someone had

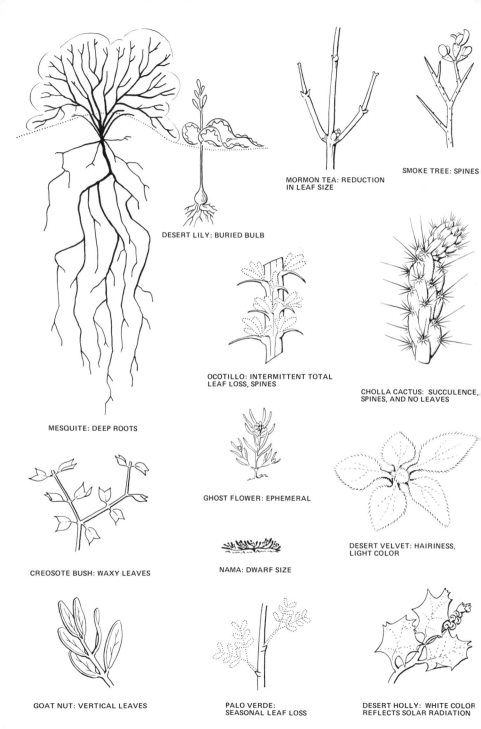

Figure 22. Adaptations to drought in desert plants

planted them a specified distance apart. Root competition for water effectively keeps plants separate. As each creosote bush has very widespread roots, the area it controls extends around it, much like a defended territory. There is much discussion about other mechanisms for accomplishing this spacing. Some scientists have proved the existence of certain toxic substances from leaf or root which discourage competition from too close neighbors. Whether this is true for such shrubs as creosote bush has not yet been generally accepted. Other factors may be of equal or more importance. The presence of water-repellent, light-textured soils under some creosote bushes has been cited as preventing the establishment of seedlings.

On the other side of the coin, most desert shrubs serve as nursemaids for the annuals taking advantage of the shade and protection afforded by their taller associates. In a region as rigorous as a desert, microclimates become particularly important. An overhanging rock, a sheltering bush or tree, a shaded cranny—these are fortuitous and fortunate circumstances providing habitats a little less xeric, where moisture remains somewhat longer than in more open environments. Any place that collects runoff favors vegetation. Highway pavement edges are classic examples. Hedgerowlike concentrations of plants flourish here because of the additional moisture draining off the highway. Sagebrush has been known to border roadways through arid stretches of shadscale scrub. It is also true of bases of "dry" waterfalls, edges of rock slabs, and other places where water, flowing off the nonporous surface, sinks into the waiting soil.

Life has not found deserts to be impossible places; however, there are secrets to survival here. A shrub can spend water when it is available, but it does so at its peril when moisture is in short supply. It is a way of life based on frugality, stamina, adaptability, and the premise that good fortune will come once in a while if life remains to take advantage of it.

Animal Tracks, Kelso Dunes

18. Sand Dune

When we first began our slow journey across California, we paused briefly in the coastal dunes. Their smooth flanks revealed an unsuspected traffic. Beachcombers other than human make their way over the sandy hummocks and leave behind telltale patterns that remain until wind or tide erases them. Then the clean page records a new set of encounters, travels, or adventures.

Desert sand dunes have even more story-telling potential. The number of possible plots and characters is almost endless, particularly in spring when the resident animals are joined by migrants, and the winter's pale green fuzz has suddenly sprouted into fields of wildflowers. Then the smaller sand hillocks, especially those with some vegetative cover, tell stories of remarkable complexity and detail. Their language may be difficult to understand, and only trained eyes can discover all they have to say. With a little curiosity, however, and reference books on California deserts—and there are several very helpful ones available—you should be able to spend a most entertaining morning reading a history that has its own surprises and excitement. Notice the word "morning." Though many desert animals are diurnal, equally many, if not more, are nocturnal. The best time to read a dune is right after dawn, before the wind has had a chance to rearrange the sandy surfaces.

Where can one find such a series of hummocks? Wherever there are sand and wind whose direction is fairly constant. In past years, a fine collection was just at the outskirts of La Quinta, now a high-priced piece of real estate southeast of Palm Springs. Much of the country around the upper end of the Salton Sea is sandy, and dunes may be found where urbanization and agriculture have not yet claimed them. These hummocks are the offspring of mountain and air current. Particles weathered from the surrounding ranges and brought down by the Whitewater River are buffeted by westerly winds channeled through the lower passes. Some dunes are large, such as those near Garnet, at one time an important station stop, but now only an offramp of a freeway that ignores the once omnipotent authority of the railroad. Most dunes are small, a dozen or so feet high, and from the air they look like arrested white caps in a sea of gravel.

All dunes result from local interruptions in the general wind flow patterns. When the wind is obstructed by rocks, plants, and even fence posts, it is forced to drop its load of sand grains, and a dune or series of dunes build up. There are many variations in dune appearance and behavior. Where the wind remains relatively constant in direction, eddies just below the crest on the leeside compel abrupt deposition of material. The windward flank has a gentle gradient, and the lee is steep. Sand like other erosional debris can accumulate on a slope pitch only until the angle of repose is reached. At that point, additional deposited material must roll down to the base. Thus dunes migrate with the prevailing wind as sand is transported from windward to leeward where it gathers at the foot, constantly encroaching on new territory. There are many instances of dunes invading forests and, after a few years, moving on to leave behind hundreds of destroyed trees. Crescent-shaped dunes usually occur in regions where the sand supply is small and prevailing winds are moderate in strength. The milder air currents sweep around rather than over the summit ridge and carry their burdens out to the tapering tips. Serpentine, or winding, and even star-shaped dunes have been described, all subject to the vagaries of the wind. Larger sand seas occur in many arid places of the world. There is an excellent example in the great Algodones Dunes area near Yuma, east of the Imperial Valley. Such expanses often bunch into elongate mounds roughly parallel to each other. At times, the sand surface is crinkled by ripple marks, thousands of tiny ridges that in early morning or late afternoon catch shadows in the troughlets separating them.

Not all dunes travel. Where winds seasonally reverse or are multidirectional, they tend to stay put. Vegetation often stabilizes the smaller ones, particularly those that have developed around an embedded plant. Many desert hummocks feature mesquite, a tree peculiarly adapted to remaining alive while sand accumulates around it. Both honey and screw-bean mesquite have extremely long roots. They tap the water table where it comes within fifty feet (15 m.) or so of the ground surface. In addition, these plants cope with clay soils periodically low in oxygen and mineralized. Hence they are strong contenders for riparian space. Before the lower Colorado River was channelized, unfortunately so, some contend, by the Corps of Army Engineers and the Bureau of Reclamation, thickets of willow, cottonwood, catclaw, tamarix, and mesquite massed on either side of the stream, sheltering much wildlife.

To those accustomed to this type of riverine growth, the clumps of mesquite decorating many local sand dunes seem to be venturing into unfriendly territory. Nothing is as dry as a sand dune—or so it would appear. There is more than meets the eye. The seedling began its career, perhaps, when wind had exposed moist soil or when rains were plentiful and the surface water sources at no great depth. As drifting sand piled up through the years, the mesquite grew with it, and its leafy top is all that is exposed. We see only a very small part of the entire tree. Below the sand surface, its bare and gnarled branches reach down to the trunk buried deep in the heart of the dune. This is why sand hill mesquite looks shrubbier than the tree forms we find in riparian sites. That it taps the water table is indicated by its behavior. It is winter-deciduous, a sure sign that moisture sources are available during the summer months.

Nowhere in California are there the large savannas of mesquite so typical of the relatively well-watered, semidesert plains of southern Arizona, New Mexico, and Texas, with their summer rains. Perhaps it is just as well, for the tree is proving quite a problem. Useful as it is for wood, fodder, browse, and shade, it is keenly competitive. When overgrazing weakens the perennial grass cover, mesquite moves in easily. Dunes forming around it also destroy valuable range. In common with many trees of desert wash and oasis, it is frequently host to a very fragrant plant, desert mistletoe. Unlike the leafier species such as that infesting cottonwoods or oak trees, it forms snarls of reddish-brown twinelike stems whose leaves are very little more than scales. Its points of attractiveness are limited to the translucent rosy berries and the odor of its inconspicuous little flowers, a combination of perfume and spice.

Other plants are not strange to dune environments, even those whose roots are unable to extend down to the water table. Almost all the rain received by sand sinks in; very little runs off. Though the surface dries quickly, giving the impression that the interior is moistureless, water is often present in the lower levels of the dunes long after the surrounding plains are sere. Four-winged saltbush frequently accompanies mesquite in the sand hills near the Salton Sea, but both yield to the halophytes, the only species able to contend with the saline soils edging the great playa.

Ricegrass takes to sandy soils as does big galleta, a gramineous species often found on dunes. Creosote bush and such relatively short-lived plants as Palmer coldenia, desert croton, and indigo bush find their way up on the unstable slopes. A number of annuals flood the hummocks with color when rains have been abundant—sand verbena (notice its rich, sweet smell), the large white birdcage evening primrose, desert-sunflower, and the little golden gilia, which though uncommon is not a real rarity. Sand food is another of the desert's oddities. Unlike other members of its family, the water leaf group, it is parasitic and looks like nothing more than a piece of fluffy wool that has escaped from an old comforter and has come to rest on the desert sand. If examined closely, the hairs are seen to cover a mass of purple flowers which are perched on top of a buried but edible fleshy stem, hence the peculiar name. It as well as several other species—desert buckwheat, giant Spanish needles, white-leafed sunflower, and Wiggins croton—if they occur elsewhere, are restricted, in California, to the Algodones Dunes. One genus and at least nine species of beetles are endemic to these dunes, making them high in ecological interest.

Where sand grains constitute a large part of the substrate, almost any bush or shrub encourages little drifts that pile up around it. For that matter, aeolian sand tends to gather in patches over most of the desert plains and washes. Dune, drift, patch, or even soft shoulder, if their particles are fine enough, traces of animal traffic will be imprinted on the surface, if only for a short while.

If one were to be suddenly dropped within the La Quinta dunes on some spring morning, with a bit of examination one could even backcast the weather. Very recent rain will have moistened the sand so that it feels damp to the touch. As sand is very absorbent, precipitation that occurred several days before the visit is no longer detectable at the surface; but by digging down a foot (.30 m.) or so, evidence of a recent soaking rain can be found. Another story is told by circular sweep marks in the sand under bushes whose twig tips angle or arch so that they are in contact with the ground. The graceful curves drawn in the sand are indicative of strong winds that whipped the ends of the shrubs back and forth. Where the streaks intersect, charming patterns are traced in the drifts much like the elaborate penmanship exercises of Victorian times. Smaller plants, particularly annuals, are often dehydrated, damaged, or partially buried by high wind. Tiny drifts banked around belly plants or the presence of grains blown into tufts of dense foliage hints that windstorms have scourged the area in the not-so-distant past. If lizards become active just at sunrise and thriving ephemerals show signs of recent wilting or drying, the weather is warming rapidly to high temperatures, and the nights are failing to cool to midspring norms. On the other hand, if these small reptiles deliberately bask in the open sun, and the wildflowers maintain their jauntiness, chances are that the night before has been cool, though probably not cold. Any visitor then will have a day of pleasant breeze and warmth, without the extremes so typical of this part of the world.

After a mild spring night, when the nocturnal animals have been active, the surface of a dune records much coming and going on the part of its residents and visitors. If you are fortunate enough to find one that has been tunneled by kangaroo rats (look for such a colony near creosote or other bushes where the root network provides support for the runways and prevents cave-ins), the entrances to their burrows will sprout trails leading to numerous intersections where their tracks cross each other. As these agile creatures hop about, they leave lines of double prints where their hairy hind feet land simultaneously, with elongate depressions where their tails hit the ground in rhythm with their progress. Two converging trails that have been disrupted by scattered sand and other marks of scuffle are unmistakable evidence that two rats were disputing territory or possessions, or engaging in strenuous play, all characteristic behavior traits in these attractive but often aggressive animals. Smaller dune-dwelling rodents such as grasshopper mice and little pocket mice have such diminutive feet that they barely dimple the surface of the sand.

More ominous are the doglike tracks of hunting coyotes. Each of the four claw marks is commonly quite visible if the sand is firm enough to keep the imprint. Owls, on the other hand, like most avian predators, seldom leave terrestrial evidence of their skill in attack unless a struggle ensues before the victim is borne off. Sidewinders, small horned rattlers well-adapted to travel on unstable ground, leave unmistakable traces. As the snake advances, it does so sideways with a peculiar looped motion resulting in a series of diagonal depressions, parallel to each other. This method of travel provides more traction with less drag on sandy surfaces. Long wiggling traces in the sand are characteristic of other snakes. It is rather difficult for an untrained person to distinguish between the various types of snakes by marks alone. The heavy-bodied species such as Mojave green rattlers leave broader, deeper marks, while the smaller types make shallower impressions whose undulations are closer together; this generalization is only true, however, of adults. An encounter between a constricting snake, such as a desert gopher snake, and a rodent is commonly marked by some signs of disturbance. Both predator and prey are equally determined to survive, one by eating and the other by escaping.

Most desert snakes are nocturnal, even those species whose habits are diurnal in less rigorous environments, and escape to underground retreats such as rodent dens during the daytime heat. Two exceptions, however, are the western patch-nose snake and the coachwhip, one subspecies of which is the desert's red racer. Research on reptilian eyes has uncovered a most interesting adaptation. Diurnal snakes have a yellow lens that is naturally achromatic (like modern camera lenses) for sharper vision. Nocturnal species such as the rear-fanged venomous California lyre snake have a colorless lens that is more efficient in collecting weak light. The vertical pupil typical of many nocturnal and crepuscular reptiles can be closed to a greater degree and more easily than a circular one, though the latter is found in a number of night-active snakes and lizards.

When snakes emerge from hibernation, they are lean from the long fast. On mild spring nights, one can often see a goodly aggregation of these reptiles on the pavement of the less traveled roads. Cold-blooded animals, they have interrupted their hunting to warm their bellies, as the road surface retains heat long after the sun has set. One can soon learn to identify some of the more common desert snakes. The rattlers are unmistakable with their horny tail ends. Long-nosed and shovel-nosed snakes are attractively banded, some quite spectacularly in black and red. The glossy snake has dusky spots on a light-gray background. Rosy boas have blunt tails; yellow-bellied and red racers are the color their names suggest. Desert gopher snakes generally have a paler ground color than their brush or woodland cousins but are similarly marked. Patch-nose snakes have yellow or tan stripes down their backs, often with dark edging. Very few lizards are nocturnal, but one of the most delightful, the banded gecko, is night-active, fortunately, as his velvety pink skin is covered with tiny, granular scales that are not as protective as those covering most other lizards.

As the morning progresses, it becomes noticeably warmer. The now limbered lizards are wary of the harsher sun and scud over the sandy hillocks from bush to bush. Zebra-tailed and leopard lizards are miniature dinosaurs as they charge along on their hind feet, front legs held near their bellies. Where the grains are fine and loosely compacted, the scurrying feet of the larger lizards push aside little heaps of sand like strings of diminutive crater rims. Dragging tails make streaks when lizards are moving slowly. During bursts of speed, they are held off the ground. A series of miniscule dunes with parallel troughs reveals the temporary hiding places of several sand-burrowing lizards—horned lizard and fringe-toed lizard. The last is as adjusted to its dune environment as its far-distant cousin, the sidewinder. It not only has fringes or special scales on its toes which help it "swim" through the sand, but the ear, eye, nose, and mouth openings are protected by flaps, valves, and other structural devices. The long-tailed brush lizard, though a sand-burrowing form on occasion, is one of the very few southwestern lizards that are largely arboreal. When stretched out along twigs, it closely resembles the perch to which it clings, a good example of protective disguise. Sand-burrowing and shrub- or tree-climbing are both effective ways of escaping ground surface temperatures that can be lethal for many desert dwellers.

Bird tracks multiply during the morning activity peak. One is obvious. Freshly made crosses, 2 inches (6 cm.) long, hint that a roadrunner, or paisano, is bent on breakfast. It is no surprise then to see this large bird striding along, usually away from the observer, with a limp leopard, whiptail, or other small lizard dangling from its bill. Its large feet help it negotiate the soft dune sand. Snakes are not neglected by this ungainly looking ground cuckoo. Red racers, one of the few day-active snakes, range over the sand hills long after night-hunting species have taken to seclusion during the warmer part of the day.

Other creatures now wander over the hummocks. Here is a strip of needlework stitched by the feet of a large beetle, one of the acrobat beetles perhaps. It is known by several names—tumblebug, stinkbug, and pinacate—but the reference to its head-standing ability is most apt. Small ridges, like cording on a quilt, mark the wanderings of the wingless female and larval forms of the nocturnal sand dune cockroach. They move about just under the surface of the sand, occasionally emerging to add another kind of embroidery. These insects cope with the summer heat on unshaded dunes by digging down at least 12 inches (30 cm.) where the temperatures are only 93° F. (34° C.)—compared with surface temperatures of 158° F. (70° C.)—and the relative humidity is high enough for these little creatures actually to absorb water vapor from the air. Other ways in which insects are adapted to the heat and dryness of the desert environment include waterproofed exoskeletons and the quite astonishing ability to regulate respiratory water loss. Certain desert beetles breathe through tubes that lead to a tiny moist cavity between the wings and the abdomen rather than directly to the dry outside air. By many behavioral characteristics such as dry season dormancy and retreating to burrows, rocky crevices, and even to the north or shady side of trees and shrubs (for example, cicadas) during the heat of the day, they manage to escape dehydration. Moist plant and animal food also aids in maintaining water balance.

Hot though the day might be, not all the mammals have retreated to burrow or shelter, though most take care to avoid prolonged exposure to the powerful noonday sun even on a day not overly hot. They remain in the shade when they can. A quiet observer of dune life can sometimes catch a glimpse of an antelope or a round-tailed ground squirrel out foraging or a jack rabbit digesting moisture-rich vegetation under a shrub or tree. Though able to withstand considerable overheating, it has light-colored pelage that reflects a large amount of solar radiation, and the blood vessels of its ears can be dilated or constricted depending upon the amount of heat stress. If the jack rabbit takes refuge in a cooler, for example, shady, environment, the vasodilated ears radiate body heat. When the animal is forced to remain in the hot sun, the vessels constrict, reducing heat transfer from surroundings to organism. Crested iguanas, relatively large vegetation-eating lizards, also endure surprisingly high air temperatures. They are often observed scampering over sandy hillocks in the full heat of a summer day.

The desert's harsh demands on life have forced its animals to adapt as well as its plants. Both types of living organisms need and use water. Because all living cells are largely fluid, several processes are common to the two kingdoms. Food, wastes, and other dissolved substances are transported in a liquid medium, blood in the case of the higher animals, sap in the more advanced plants. Both plants and animals respire, converting food to energy through oxidation. One of the by-products of this chemical reaction is water, a factor of extreme importance. Leaf structures of most desert perennials are considerably modified to prevent water waste. Such modifications are relatively simple. Some are permanent adaptations typical of desert plants—resinous coatings and the like. The leaf pores, where most gas exchange occurs and water vapor is lost, are smaller in size and recessed within the epidermis. In addition—and this is true for most plants, not just those in desert regions—each stomate is enclosed between two guard cells. During drought, when the plant is in danger of wilting by losing too much water through its stomata, the cells become flabby, the pore closes, and transpiration stops.

Water conservation for the higher animals involves a whole complex of anatomical features, physiological processes, and behavioral procedures. Respiration occurs externally (in contrast to internal gas exchange which involves oxidation within the individual cell) in but one set of organs, gills in tadpoles and fish, lungs and connected respiratory passages in reptiles and warm-blooded animals. Therefore, loss of water vapor from a centralized area such as a lung should be subject to easy regulation. No such adaptations, however, have evolved within the higher animals which, on the face of it, seems somewhat inefficient. There are no automatic or self-regulatory devices to decrease respiration rates within the lungs themselves. If water is to be conserved, other systems must be employed, and many have developed that help maintain water balance—some specific to a limited group of organisms and some common to a large number of desert dwellers. Regardless of degree of restriction, such adaptive machinery works, or it would have been tossed onto the biological scrapheap long ago by the ruthless hand of evolution.

Animals also lose water in ways other than through respiration. All terrestrial animals facilitate the passing of solid wastes with liquid, the amounts of which vary from species to species. With the exception of those that hibernate or experience normal diurnal fluctuations in body warmth, warm-blooded animals maintain a constant temperature when healthy. Not only must they produce and conserve heat during exposure to cold, they must have ways by which they can lower body temperatures when those of the environment at large are higher. These are of real significance in arid regions where the mechanisms for this decrease involve potentially harmful water loss.

One device is to use the natural cooling resulting from evaporation. One of the first lessons taught in high school science classes is that when water changes its state from liquid to vapor there is an accompanying loss of heat. Man has made use of this handy little physical principle ever since the first tribesman thought to hang an oozing skin bag of water in a tree to catch the breeze. He could very well have been inspired by his own body. Countless sweat glands are scattered in much of the human skin. When perspiring animals are warm, water is shunted out into the sweat glands from the blood. The glands open, water is flushed out over the skin, it evaporates, and the body is cooled; a breeze is enjoyed on a hot day because it speeds evaporation. However, the human species is unusual, for most other terrestrial vertebrates have fewer sweat glands. Evaporative cooling can only occur where there is moist skin, or tissue such as the mucus-secreting membranes of nose, mouth, throat, and the lung itself. Many desert animals open their mouths and some even pant while under heat duress, exposing as much moist surface as possible to the open air. The long, dripping tongues of overheated canine friends point up the usefulness of saliva as a moisture source for evaporative cooling. Some ground squirrels, the cactus mouse, and Merriam's kangaroo rat have been seen to actually spread saliva around on their heads and chests as a last-ditch method of keeping body temperatures below lethal levels.

Though water is very scarce over much of the desert, the animals living here must maintain a liquid level in their body cells. At the same time, its loss is unavoidable through several vital processes: respiration, voiding wastes, and keeping cool. In addition, a great drain is placed on the internal water resources of females in the production of young. Amphibians have an even harder time. They are prone to desiccation and must keep their skin surfaces moist at all times.

Needless to say, the story of the maintenance of water balance by animals in the desert is one of ultimate triumph, though the delicate equilibrium is sometimes upset by climatic or other conditions that place great stress on some or all desert populations. In general, animals rely on a number of features that enable them to avoid water deficit, not just one alone. None of the vertebrates is without some protective skin cover, and many have additional epidermal features. Reptilian scales, for instance, are quite effective in retarding water vapor loss. Feathers and fur, like the hairs of leaves, insulate the body from heat as well as cold.

The wastes of vertebrate animals are usually discharged while suspended in fluid or in a moist state. Many desert species absorb most of the liquid passing through the lower intestines, and the discharged feces are relatively dry. In birds and reptiles, the urine is concentrated to the point where its solid particles precipitate out as crystals of uric acid. They are voided with the feces with little loss of water. In some of the desert rodents, urinary wastes are almost pasty in consistency, in contrast with the liquid discharge of more water-spending species. Many amphibians have water-storing urinary bladders, internal resources upon which they can draw when moisture is scarce.

The desert tortoise apparently has moisture-retaining sacs under its upper shell in addition to the use of the urinary bladder. These extraordinary creatures plod with seemingly inexhaustible reserves of patience over the desert in search of the vegetation they need for food, burrow sites, and mates. In spite of thick, protective shells, desert tortoises are dormant in both winter and the heat of summer when adverse temperatures are common, and they spend the time in burrows, which they dig in wash banks and other suitable terrain.

By following certain patterns of behavior, organisms can regulate the need for water. The simplest ways are to decrease daytime activity and to seek cooler environments. Though low metabolic rates generally are typical of many desert animals, minimal exertion during the warmer hours reduces the amount of water used in temperature regulation and respiration. Such curtailment ranges all the way from resting under a shady bush during the summer afternoon to complete withdrawal from the hot, dry environment and cessation of most activity. The length to which each species goes depends partly on its structural water-conserving modifications and partly on what moisture sources are available.

A number of desert animals are restricted to a damp or aquatic environment, if they are to survive. They rarely, if ever, expose themselves to desiccating air and heat. Toads and frogs are among those unable to live far from moisture. Both the red-spotted and spadefoot toads retreat to damp burrows and crannies to become dormant when their pools contract following the rain's departure. During this time intake of neither food nor water is needed in what amounts to a state of suspended animation. When awake they usually confine activity to the cooler hours of evening and night. Some amphibians, including Couch's spadefoot toad, can absorb water by contact with moist soil if dehydration threatens. The diurnal California treefrog relies on the evaporative cooling of its moist skin to reduce body temperature. For these desert amphibians, rainy spells are times of busy activity, which are usually coincidental with an increased insect supply. (There is evidence that red-spotted toads are awakened from their subterranean slumber by vibrations from thunderstorms.) Breeding often takes place during the same period of optimum conditions. Omniverous to the point of cannibalism and more tolerant of heat than adults, the newly hatched young waste little time in developing into froglets and toadlets.

Though some aquatic forms such as the little pupfish are confined to permanent water, brine shrimp can exist for years as viable eggs encased in the dried mud of a playa bed. When rains and runoff create temporary lakes or puddles in these basins, almost miraculously they hatch into lively little crustaceans, swarming in the salty water. Fairy shrimp, near relatives, behave in the same way, but they cannot survive highly saline solutions.

All but a few desert species must somehow take in liquid. For many, diet alone is sufficient—succulent leaves and fruit, juicy insects, and other animal tissue. Several lizards—chuckwallas and desert iguanas—utilize fresh, moisture-rich vegetation such as flowers, leaves, and stems. Others supplement it with water when it is available. Snakes have been observed to drink from temporary rain pools; on the other hand, quite a large group of animals must drink regularly. Bighorn sheep have their waterholes which they visit on their rounds. Coyotes dig for water in washes when pools are scarce.

Most birds habitually seek water. Limited as such resources are in most deserts, one would suppose that few birds would live and be active here the year around. The resident population of birds is surprisingly large and includes a number of carnivores and carrion feeders, species which, because their kidneys work harder, need more liquid for excretion. The fresh-killed diet of many desert birds of prey provides them with sufficient water. Vultures circle in the hot updrafts. Prairie falcons, red-tailed and sparrow hawks (American kestrel) quarter the washes and slopes below. Screech and great horned owls move in on the night shift. Occasionally, the diminutive elf owl moves over from Arizona where it usually keeps to the giant saguaros serving as its home. Shrikes and roadrunners harvest the lizards that dart about under the sparse cover.

A host of insectivorous and seed-eating birds are rarely encountered away from desert haunts. In common with all species living here, they must defend themselves against desert hostility. Fortunately for birds, they are what has been called preadapted to arid environments. Like many animals of hot and dry lands, desert birds are tolerant of high body temperatures. Some species such as the white-winged dove can lose up to 40 percent of body weight by dehydration but in a matter of minutes can regain normal weight if water is available. In other words, these birds are able to sustain severe water stress if alleviated by periodic visits to oases and other sources of open water. It has already been noted that their disposal of fecal and urinary wastes is very water conservative in nature. In addition, they are insulated by feathers which they hold close to their bodies when temperatures are high. Few birds, however, spend much time in the open sun of a summer day. Though they may sing or bask on unprotected perches for short periods of time, most seek the shade of foliage, buildings, and other sheltering places while the sun is at its worst and may pant in an effort to reduce body heat. The power of flight allows them to be more mobile than most other desert animals. They can cover wide distances, ranging over arid heights and plains, looking for water, spotting oases and streams, seeking cover.

Say's phoebe is one of the more colorful of the resident flycatchers, a drab group in general. Its orange-tinted belly contrasts with a body mostly brown. Though it has a wide distribution, extending from Mexico to Alaska, it is permanently settled in the desert of the Southwest where it seemingly fares well. Another desert flycatcher is not only one of the most gayly clad of its group, but one of California's brilliantly plumaged birds. The vermillion flycatcher is unmistakable. The male is a puff of flame as he waits on a twig or pursues his food with the agile forays so typical of his family. He keeps to the Colorado Desert, but is occasionally seen in the southern Mojave. Two tiny birds are restricted to the southwestern deserts, verdin and black-tailed gnatcatcher. The former has a bright yellow face and cap. Look for it in mesquite patches where it builds a baseball-round nest that opens at the side. The other mite is almost wrenlike, with a long flexible tail it often holds straight up. Though the bird is named for this sooty appendage, the cap of the male is just as black. For these and other insectivorous birds, the body juices of their diet supply much-needed liquid.

One of the desert's most moving experiences is hearing the silvery waterfall of notes poured out by the canyon wren. Though not as exquisite as the fluting of the hermit thrush, its song is one of the most beautiful to be heard anywhere. It is a bird of dry, rocky hillsides. The other characteristic wren of the desert is the cactus wren, one of many birds making use of the natural protection afforded by this spiny vegetation. It builds its nest among the stems of cholla, a formidable type of cactus, and stutters its *chur-r-r* from the needled tips. Several other cactus dwellers are very closely related. They are all large birds with the long curving bills that place them in the thrasher group—Le Conte's, the rare Bendire's, and an occasional crissal.

White-winged, mourning, and common ground-doves and Gambel's quail are often seen as they come to tanks and pools for a drink. The California Fish and Game Department has constructed "guzzlers," primarily for the use of such avian visitors, in many desolate areas of the desert, where natural water is hard to find. The most characteristic bird of the open desert is the phainopepla. The male is jet black, and the female gray-brown. Both have sprightly crests peaked over red eyes and startlingly white wing patches. Fond of mesquite clumps, it feeds on berries of infesting mistletoe. Several sparrows compete with the rodents for the seeds of ephemerals and shrubs—black-throated and Bell's among them.

A number of nonresident birds winter over on the desert: western and mountain bluebirds, water pipits, Townsend's solitaires, and yellow-rumped warblers among others. Some of these same species are found throughout large areas of low-land California during the cool season, and the desert perhaps is peripheral to the center of the range. A few seem to prefer the desert in the summer—Costa's hummer and hooded oriole—while one, Lucy's warbler, occurs in California only in the extreme southeastern corner of the state, where it nests in the hotter part of the year. It has also been noted as a summer resident in Morongo Valley northeast of Palm Springs. The brown-crested flycatcher, a species more commonly encountered in southern Arizona, has established a small breeding population here. By far, the avian activity peak is in the spring when both residents and migrants make the most of the desert's awakening. Warblers, tanagers, lazuli buntings, orioles, and a whole host of colorful feathered creatures pause on their migratory wanderings.

With springtime sprouting seeds, rejuvenated shrubs, and restored water supplies, the smaller worlds of legs and wings stir to life. The larvae of sphinx, owlet, and measuring-worm moths work over the flourishing vegetation, crawling about on pudgy pads. Longhorn beetles find their solitary way along tree limbs, venturing down to the blossoms of the ephemerals, but seldom further. They leave the ground surfaces to the scarab and acrobat beetles. Blister beetles, some strikingly marked, often cling in clusters to perennial shrubs. A number of butterflies—swallowtails, painted ladies, monarchs, and queens—along with several kinds of bees visit the wild gardens. Cicadas begin their shrill rattle in tamarisks and cottonwoods to be continued through most of the summer. Grasshoppers and crickets move out through the cultivated fields. Life in abundance bursts forth from pupa cases, both the original species and those that have parasitized them. At dusk the ground seems to quiver as solpugids, centipedes, sand dune cockroaches, Jerusalem crickets, and scorpions take the place of velvet "ants," roving cadres of harvester and honey ants, and spiders.

Tarantula and tarantula hawk, fly and flycatcher, larva and lizard—take their places in ever-expanding food webs. Seed-eating birds, insects, and rodents begin round-the-clock assaults on the mature annuals and fruiting shrubs, while jack rabbits, gophers, ground squirrels, and wood rats compete for tender shoots and other moist vegetation. The carnivores feast on the burgeoning numbers of plant and insect feeders. The whole desert has become a picnic ground.

The migrants leave when the portions become skimpy; when the annuals have dried to straw, the seeds are picked over, and much of the insect world rests in eggs and pupa cases underground or in hidden crannies. Now the days bake in the pitiless summer sun. Waterholes constrict, and the runoff streams in the desert ranges shrivel and disappear. The year-round inhabitants adjust in many ways. One of the most common is to either cease or abate daytime activity. Some just relax under cover, jack rabbits in forms hollowed out of compact vegetation, speckled rattlesnakes in the shade of rocks. Coyotes rest deep under leafy shade hardly caring about the birds that may share shrub or tree. The lizards continuing to forage throughout the summer day minimize contact with the hot ground surface. They never linger long out in the open sun, but quickly scamper from one shade patch to another, usually holding their bellies and tails up from the scorching earth. Although some species such as the fringe-toed and horned lizards bury themselves under a protective layer of sand, many reptiles rely on a physiologically sophisticated way to regulate body temperature. A "bed" or network of tiny blood vessels lies right under the skin. If the animal is cold, it basks, heating the subsurface capillaries. The warm blood then returns to deeper tissues, and the reptile is soon warm throughout. When in danger of being overheated, the animal is able to cut off partially some of the blood flow to the subcutaneous network, slowing internal heat gain. Additionally, many lizards—

crested iguana and collared among them—may pant when uncomfortably warm. Unfortunately, this use of evaporative cooling is water-wasteful. It has been discovered recently that the abdominal cavity of many diurnal desert lizards has a black lining, presumably to shield internal organs from excessive ultraviolet radiation.

The antelope ground squirrel is one of the few mammals that continue to be day-active throughout the summer, though it may retreat into its burrow during the warmest part of the day. Though essentially a seed eater, juicy plant—such as juniper berries and cactus—and animal material contributes liquid to its diet. In addition to being one of the ground squirrels that employs salivation as a means of reducing its heat load, this attractive little rodent, in common with many other desert dwellers, is able metabolically to withstand high temperatures.

It has often been pointed out that animals living in warm climates have larger appendages than those living in colder areas. The desert kit fox is an excellent example of this general rule. Though it is smaller in size than its cousins, the gray fox of the brushlands and the forest-dwelling red fox, its ears are much larger. Presumably, this allows it more body surface from which heat can radiate. It shares with all furred desert animals the insulating advantage of pelage. Apparently there are other benefits, for instance, any air movement that stirs the hairy coat transports heat away from the animal. A covering of coarse hair prevents sand from entering the ear orifices of the kit fox, and its feet are thickly tufted with hair to form natural "snowshoes" for traveling over sand.

The most industrious hours of a number of animals are those of dawn and dusk. They are crepuscular rather than strictly diurnal or nocturnal species. Some of the latter, however, extend their foraging times into early morning and evening, such as bats and the cottontail rabbit. Two crepuscular birds are of particular interest, poorwill and nighthawk. Both are desert residents and closely related. Though much of their insect hunting is at dusk, they continue pursuit throughout the night, though not so intently. The soft *poor-will, poor-will* of the former is one of the desert's most attractive calls. While diving, the nighthawk rips apart the air, creating a little sound shiver quite audible to human ears below. Both make use of gular flutter, that is, rhythmically and rapidly moving the mucus-covered membrane of the upper throat while open-mouthed. This is a most effective way of exposing moist areas to evaporative cooling.

The desert has many strictly nocturnal animals. These include the several kangaroo rats, pocket mice, wood rats, grasshopper mice and many of their predators—snakes, kit foxes, and owls. Though some merely tuck into shaded nooks or holes, most of the rodents have underground runways in which they seek refuge when morning comes. Unless you have very tough-soled feet, don't try to walk barefoot over a sand dune, at noon, on a sunny July day in the desert. Surface soil temperatures of 180° F. (82° C.) and even higher have been recorded. Yet, as we have noted, only a few inches of vertical depth can make a tremendous difference as soil is excellent insulation. Soil temperatures can fall 100° F. (38° C.) from burrow entrance to nest level. Air temperatures drop accordingly, so what better place to wait out the broiling heat of a summer day than in your own microenvironment, a burrow where it is but 80° F. (27° C.) and the humidity is far higher than in the open air. Because of the animal's inactivity and cool surroundings, respiration and evaporation rates drop considerably, and its water balance can restabilize after the busy night. The burrow serves as hiding place for food caches, as well. Much food gathering involves the transport of seeds and other plant material to underground storage places or nests.

Several mammalian species avoid the problem of summer existence by estivating. Sometime in August, the Mojave ground squirrel disappears into underground hideaways and becomes torpid, automatically reducing its metabolic and water-spending rates. The ground squirrel's sleep is not broken after the onset of autumn. It continues in dormant state through the chill months. Though technically it is now hibernating, rather than estivating, there is no real physiological difference between the two states. Thus it is active only during spring and early summer, when conditions are at their best. Investigators working with desert mammals have discovered that a number of species, including the cactus mouse, have daily patterns of dormancy. These periods of torpor can occur at any time of the year when the food supply is limited. The California pocket mouse, in company with several other small rodents, adjusts the length of its torpor period to the amount of food available—the less food the more time is spent in dormancy.

Hibernation is not a rare phenomenon in the desert. Though this region, particularly in lower altitudes, rarely becomes very cold, high desert winter nights regularly drop below freezing. Reptiles, being cold-blooded, can little tolerate temperature extremes. Most of them and several rodents avoid this trying time by remaining underground, quiescently dormant. Until just recently, it was thought that birds did not hibernate. Several years ago, however, Dr. Edmund Jaeger, famed desert naturalist, found a torpid poorwill, much to his amazement, in a rocky crypt near the Chuckawalla Mountains. Many other such individuals have been observed since, and it appears that other bird species may reduce body temperatures to alleviate heat loss on cold nights.

The deserts of California have more animal residents than is often suspected, bound as we are by our own diurnal activity patterns. They get their water when and where they can, from crunchy grubs and cactus pads, waterholes and dripping faucets. Through various types of adjustment, they husband their intake and spend it as frugally as possible. One animal, however, is the "desert rat" supreme, the kangaroo rat, whose defense of territory is part of the nightly drama of the dunes. It is one of the few animals in the world that need no external liquid source. It never drinks, and it eats only seeds. When carbohydrates (starch- or sugar-based food) are converted to energy in the body, the by-products are water and carbon dioxide. But most animals cannot live on the small amount of fluid obtained in this way. Not so the kangaroo rat. Being strictly nocturnal, having highly efficient kidneys and many of the other water-hoarding devices and behavior characteristics mentioned in this chapter, it thrives on its seed diet. Many species of desert reptiles, birds, and mammals depend upon oxidation water, as this metabolically derived moisture is called, to supplement their intake of water from external sources.

Many of the adaptive mechanisms and behavior patterns that enable animals to cope with a desert habitat protect them also from their predators. The sparse plant cover of much of the desert provides some protection, but the refuge-seeking habits of much of its animal population foil attempts by enemies. Species ranging from harvester ants to kangaroo rats plug their entrance holes to retain humid air and keep out both heat and foraging invaders. Speed not only takes lizards and ground squirrels into coverts away from the punishing sun,

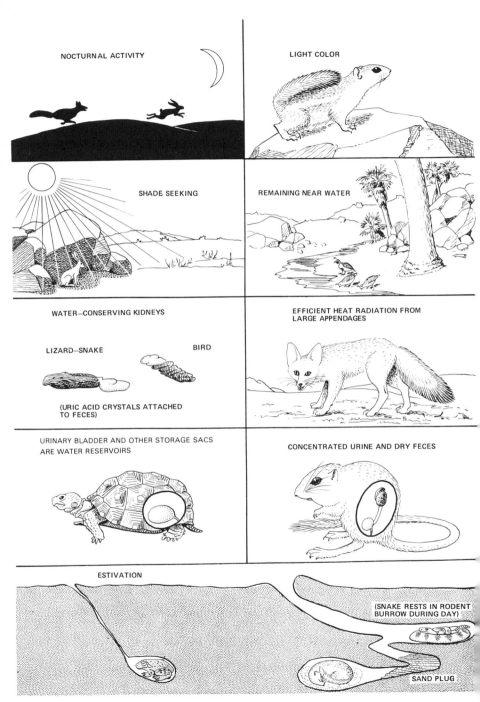

Figure 23. *Adaptations of animals to desert conditions*

but removes them from predatory interest. Most small desert animals are very light in color. This may serve to reflect both heat and light, another mechanism for the control of temperature and water balance. There is no doubt, too, that blending with one's background is a good way to escape detection. The horned lizards are capable of very subtle shifts in population color. One group may be light gray, matching the dull gravel of its territory, while a neighboring assemblage is the tan or pale rust of its sandy home.

Desert vegetation looks no different under moonlight than it does at noon. April seems little changed from October, except for its wild gardens which are by no means universal or annually dependable. The desert plains, unless disturbed by man, appear much the same as they did a hundred years ago, and will a hundred years hence. The successional patterns we note in the hills and valleys of the coastal ranges are, for the most part, missing here. No foliage canopy will shade out the scrubby shrubs. They are the best the desert can do, except for the few arboreal species in more favored sites. The living rhythms here pulse in time with its animals. Each dawn and dusk, triggered by the ebb and flow of light, one host retires and gives way to another that takes up in turn its struggle to survive in a land that is only occasionally generous. So with the seasons. Like the tide, spring rises and falls, releasing the hibernating creatures, stimulating reproduction, inviting the migrants to make use of the desert when it is most hospitable.

Joshua Tree near Olancha

19. The Small World of a Joshua Tree

Deserts have a way of turning out peculiar-looking trees, almost as if someone sat at a drawing board and deliberately thought up parodies, grotesque foolery of these familiar features of the natural world. The deserts of Africa have their dragon trees whose branches are tipped with masses of foliage that give the appearance of iris leaves, cut, tied together and glued into place. Baja California's Viscaino Desert has, among other oddities, boojum trees (*Idria columnaris*)—giant hairy asparagus stalks that twist and bend until the tip of the stem may be but 6 inches (15 cm.) from the ground. The Mojave Desert has Joshua trees which are actually more treelike in form than many of the exotic species from other desert areas. They have trunks from which spring branches and leaves of a sort. Webster's *College Standard Dictionary* defines trees as "a perennial woody plant having a single self-supporting trunk, the whole ranging from about 10 feet (3 m.) to a considerable height." *Yucca brevifolia* is closely related to the lily family, yet it has a woody trunk, lives for many years, and is often taller than 10 feet (3 m.). With its precise tufting of spiky leaves that becomes a shaggy thatch when dead, it may not look like the elm in Aunt Cora's back yard in Schenectady, but it is one of the most fascinating trees of the California deserts.

Yucca is a common genus in southern California. *Yucca whipplei*, our Lord's candle, is a tall white flame of creamy blossoms erupting from a spike-guarded base. It is thick on chaparral and coastal sage scrub hillsides of the southern counties in late spring. Spanish bayonet and Spanish dagger (Mojave yucca) are two other types of yucca extending east from desert California to Arizona, Nevada, and south down into northern Mexico. The word "yucca" is derived from a native name for cassava or manihot, a food plant of South America from which tapioca is produced. The plants actually have nothing in common, and it is one of the flukes of natural history, no doubt from the time of energetic but sometimes misguided plant explorers, that the two genera became confused. The name "Joshua" was supposedly given to *Y. brevifolia* by Mormon pioneers who might have been inspired by its aged, bearded appearance and uplifted arms.

Joshua trees are not confined to California, but occur also in Nevada, Utah, and Arizona. However, they are restricted to the higher desert, between 2,500 and 5,000 feet (750–1,500 m.). Their occurrence marks the southern boundary of the Mojave Desert on the slopes of the Little San Bernardino Mountains, where Joshua Tree National Monument is located. Though there are fine groves in the monument, by no means are they the most extensive nor are the individual trees particularly large. There are excellent stands of these tree lilies (a number of books on desert flora refer to them as such even though they actually belong to the closely related agave family) in many places in the Mojave: Cima Dome, a unique geological feature that has dense groves of the tallest Joshua trees, variety *jaegeriana*, on the desert side of the Transverse Range from Mount San Antonio (Mount Baldy) to Mount San Gorgonio, and scattered stands in the Antelope Valley. Unfortunately, ruthless bulldozing has severely depleted their ranks throughout much of their range. For the most part they are confined to gentle sandy or gravelly slopes skirting the mountains of the region. They extend roots that make use of surface water and underground moisture draining off the higher elevations.

Unlike plants of the lower deserts, Joshuas are able to withstand a fair amount of frost. In fact, they appear to need winter chilling to develop properly, as evidenced by their demise when transplanted to mild coastal areas. A favorite shot of photographers is a Joshua swansdowned with snow, and it is a real bonanza if the tree happens to be in bloom with bursts of musty-smelling, six-petaled white blossoms at the ends of its angled boughs. The blue-white of snow on the eggshell tint of its flowers is unforgettable.

The differences between the Mojave and the Sonoran deserts are those which allow Joshuas to live in the former, but not in the latter. The western and northern Mojave is higher by 2,000 to 3,000 feet (600–900 m.) on the average. Its higher elevation and more northerly latitude encourage increased rainfall, particularly on the mountain slopes so common to this broken country. Being higher it is also cooler, and the hot season is neither as long nor as severe as in the lower desert.

Like all desert plants, Joshuas have features which enable them to withstand prolonged drought, heat, and drying winds, three characteristics of the world's hot deserts. The dark green spearpoint leaves are fearsomely dagger sharp, stiff, and leathery. The tree is considered an evergreen, though each year some of the foliage shrivels and dies, much of it eventually falling off; during the spring growing period, a ring of new spikes encircles the tip of each living branch. These rings accompany the flowers which appear during the same season. Though most Joshuas have one inflorescence or two every year after maturity, heavy blooming, with clusters of white on almost every branch end, is irregular. Several years may pass between times of massive flowering.

A sequential change in foliage appearance is an outstanding feature of Joshua trees. New leaves, either on the upright poles of youth or sprouting from the branches of older trees, resemble numerous green bayonets thrust into the woody tissue, points outward. It is this stage when the seasonal leaf growth rings are most observable. Leaves more than a year old tend to lose their stiffness and droop, finally dying and becoming part of a bristling thatch that covers a good portion of the plant. After an interval some of this shaggy matting drops off the trunk and larger branches, exposing the bark beneath. Only a relatively small part of the plant has green leaves; it is uneconomical to support more food-making foliage than necessary. In common with most woody desert plants, a balance is needed between water-absorbing devices—roots—and water-spending organs—leaves. The specific name, *brevifolia,* refers to the fact that its leaves are shorter than those of most other yucca species; relatively small leaf size helps control evaporation. Its gaunt, awkward posture is intensified by the pattern of branching. Unlike ordinary trees whose boughs move gracefully from the supporting trunk, Joshuas branch into arms twisting and gesturing in upsettingly human fashion. Young trees are unbranched until they are old enough to flower when about 8 to 10 feet (2.4–3 m.) tall. Then shoots fork out at oblique angles to the parent stem just below the dead flower stalk. As the same thing happens to the young branch when it blossoms, the stiff-jointed pattern repeats itself again and again as the tree adds to its size and years. A few observers are of the opinion that branching will not occur unless injury such as insect infestation triggers the production of an offshoot. Recent work seems to indicate that differences in embryonic growing points may vary from plant to plant.

Joshua trees do not live alone though there are few other plants of the desert that compare with them in size. California junipers and pinyon accompany them on some of the higher slopes and hills. Together they form a woodland with shade and shelter reminiscent of moister areas. Desert shrubs and ephemeral herbs are joint residents with tree yuccas, occupying the spaces between the larger plants. A scrubby undercover of creosote bush, Mormon tea, brittle bush, bladder sage, cheese bush, spiny menodora, and, in places, blue sage commonly shares their gravel slopes and sandy stretches. Joshuas seldom can afford to live too close to one another, though underground lateral roots produce shoots around the bases of vigorous trees, and occasionally one will see several adults entwined together in clumsy embrace.

Camera enthusiasts would do well to visit a stand of Joshua trees in April of a wet year. When the rain gods have been kind, there is an emblazonment of yellow, white, lavender, orange, and pink displayed by desert dandelions, several kinds of evening primrose, sand verbena, thistle sage, broad gilia, nama, poppies and mallow, and other flowers typical of the western Mojave Desert. Then Scott's orioles sing from gray-green knife-blade leaves and the wind is sweet with fresh stem and petal, sun and bird chorus.

A number of organisms spend much or all of their lives in or close to a single Joshua tree, some of them so dependent on it for a variety of reasons that they would not exist except for its presence. In fact, there is such a close relationship among several species living in or with Joshua trees that it seems unbelievable considering the chance directions taken by the flow of the tides of life during evolutionary history. Here, for instance, are a moth, a lizard, and one-celled animals called protozoa. The first two are so intimately associated with Joshua trees that there would be no tree but for the moth and no lizard but for the tree.

The story of the *Tegeticula* moths and yuccas is a classic example of mutualism, the interactive or symbiotic pattern of mutual benefit to both organisms involved. Lilies, like all flowers, must be pollinated for seed production. Insects rather than wind carry out the task because of the nature of the pollen. Instead of being dust-dry like the pollen of pines and grasses, that of the lily and closely related families is sticky and needs the instinctive efforts of an insect rather than the chance attentions of a wayward wind to ensure the transportation of these vital cells to their seed-producing counterparts. *Tegeticula* moths are crepuscular, flying at dusk, when they are attracted to the white blossoms of yuccas. Collecting pollen from one flower and working it into a tiny ball, the female moth flies to others for additional material until her burden is of proper size. Now she prepares to lay her eggs which she does by inserting her ovipositor, a needlelike egg-laying organ, into the ovary, the portion of the yucca flower containing the tiny ovules, or embryonic seeds. She ensures the development of seed by depositing enough pollen grains on the stigma of the flower so that all the ovules are fertilized, and the seeds will grow. Later the newly hatched larvae of the moth feed on these seeds. Only a few are consumed, the small price the Joshua tree pays for the privilege of pollination. Somewhere and at some time in the long history of the southwestern deserts, yuccas and moths joined in a mutual task of producing more yuccas and moths, and the partnership still continues.

More creatures than moths depend on these huge "lilies." Living parts such as branch ends and shoots are homesteaded by several insects having special requirements for food and shelter. The giant yucca skipper lays eggs on the leaves of sprouts clustering around the parent trunk. After the larvae hatch, they burrow into the stems of the young shoots and feed on their pithy hearts. Finally, they reach the roots, in which case the sprouts will eventually die. Yucca boring weevil larvae prefer working over the woody material out at limb tip. As Joshuas do not have long, stabilizing taproots, they occasionally blow over in the high winds of the desert. A forest of yuccas is cluttered here and there with piles of slowly decaying trunks and boughs. These are the homes of colonies of termites, beetles, and other insects. Often the interior of an older branch or trunk is hollow as the central cortex dries and disintegrates. Though Joshuas do not have real annual rings, being more like palm stems rather than true wood, rings have been noted in cross-sections of the trunk. Unlike their more herbaceous cousins, these near-lilies have woody portions under the bark, particularly in older parts of the plant. The periodic increment of fiber between bark and the central cortex results in ring-type growth. The cortex is not woody and readily rots away.

Joshua tree trunks, whether downed or upright, are easily penetrated and become the homes of many animals such as flickers and ladder-backed woodpeckers. Other birds take over their abandoned nesting holes. Ash-throated flycatchers, house wrens, American kestrels—a long list of feathered desert dwellers makes use of these conveniently placed apartments as well as the concealing clumps of spiky foliage.

Termites prefer dead wood and, by staying deep in the tissues beneath the bark, avoid the desiccation inherent in this climate. They digest the fibrous material by means of the protozoa and bacteria in their intestines, chemically breaking it down and initiating a vital step in the return of minerals to the soil. In this way, termites perform a most useful task, one of great benefit to Joshua tree, shrub, and annual alike. The food web begun by plant, protozoa, and termite is not at an end, for a number of animals eat termites. *Xantusia,* the yucca (desert) night lizard, makes its home in the masses of overlapping dried leaf spears covering much of the deadfall. One of the smallest of the American lizards, it is a dainty thing, almost fragile in appearance with its soft, easily desiccated skin. Living in the Joshua's discarded limbs or toppled body, sheltered by its foliage, feeding on its insects, *Xantusia* is another dependent, another dweller in this complex microhabitat. This is not to say that these little lizards do not occur elsewhere. They can be found in many places in the high desert, occasionally where yuccas do not even occur. However, they are typical of Joshua forest, and one can see them by overturning a dead branch or two, uncovering their hiding places where they often avoid exposure to the most trying times of the day. The common name implies night activity or nocturnalism but diurnal and crepuscular behavior is more typical. If *Xantusia* is active during the darker hours it runs the risk of meeting a number of formidable enemies, screech owls, rattlesnakes, and leaf-nosed and night snakes. The food web widens out in patterns of interrelationships involving many inhabitants of the high-desert woodland.

Individual Joshuas offer shelter to various other species. Wood rats, often called pack or trade rats, build huge nests of desert debris at the bases of the larger yuccas and on accumulations of fallen material. These rodents are common to most of California, wherever there is green vegetation. Unlike their kangaroo rat relatives, they cannot metabolize all their water needs from a dry grain diet and must depend on juicy food for necessary liquid. Succulent cactus pads and fruits are harvested for this purpose. Wood rats show amazing agility in maneuvering themselves over the obstacle course of a cholla cactus. They also eat the new green Joshua leaves and use them for nest building. Several other features of physiology and behavior make it possible for the wood rat to live comfortably in the desert. Its nest under the shade of a tree yucca or other cover shelters it from the intense heat of the direct desert sun. It is able to eat cacti and plants toxic to most animals because of high concentration of oxalic acid.

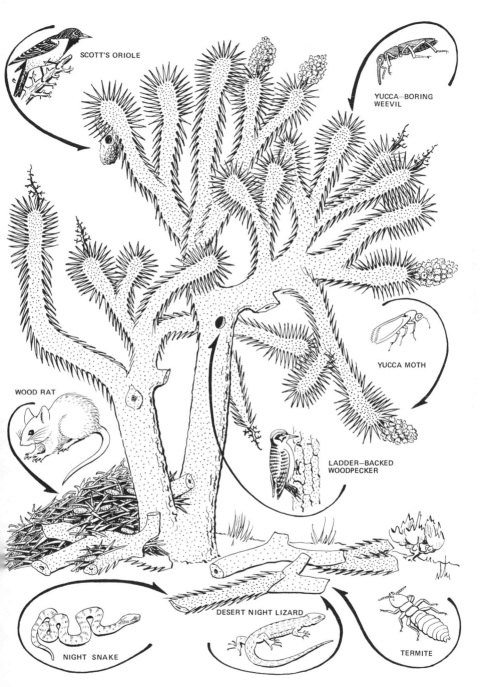

Figure 24. The small world of a Joshua tree

Both of these rodents and many more related species of the higher desert are potential meals to a red-tailed hawk perching on the outflung arm of a Joshua, keeping a close lookout for just such a dinner. Other common predators are great horned owls, whose great yellow eyes move on silent wings through the ghostly skyline of a Joshua forest at night. One bird in particular prefers to nest in the spiky foliage. Black and yellow, the Scott's oriole is a warm flash of color as it slips swiftly and gracefully under the overlapping leaves. Not only does the tree give it protection, but the nest is woven from yucca fibers, and much feeding is done on the plant itself as the birds consume both nectar and flower parts as well as the insects attracted to this source of food.

A small world it is, a world nourishing and giving shelter to insects, birds, rats, and lizards; a world that has accepted the harsh conditions of the upland heart of the desert; a world of leaves and wood and flowers, dead and living, hospitable in its way to all who seek it.

Burned Oaks in Fog, Santa Monica Mountains

20. Hollywood's Real Natives

From any freeway on a hazy day in September, coastside southern California is ugly. What undeveloped hills filter out of the smog appear all but barren, their vegetation a desiccated, stunted scrub interrupted by fire-blackened patches of brush or dead grass. The only stretches of inviting green are golf courses, parks, and cemeteries. Foothill and valley seem destined to become desert (or one huge city) in a year or so.

But be patient. Wait until Old Baldy dominates the northern sky like an enormous, unflavored snowcone, the winter-ripened berries of toyon smolder on the slopes of Griffith Park, and the sky is a rain-rinsed blue. Or wait until April when the hills above Gorman (Interstate 5 at State Highway 138) spread quilts of lavender, gold, and indigo over their rounded thighs. Or look for the latest burn in the Santa Monica Mountains. Given good rains, the depressing hillsides of strewn ash and charred snags will have turned into wild gardens whose color and lushness are unimaginable to those not acquainted with fire-following plant growth. Even summer has its surprises, from the shag carpetry of scarlet penstemon on Mount Pinos abuzz with hummingbirds to the lemon lilies hovering like a touch of sunlight by a shady spring near Idyllwild. California fuchsias spray tiny red explosions on rocky cliffs of mountainous roadsides in the wildflower-deserted months of late July and August.

The author has lived all her life in Los Angeles, and though she appreciates the dramatic beauty of the Mendocino coast and the high country along the John Muir Trail, she is delighted to introduce the reader to "her" California in this and the following chapters. There are several points of view as to what constitutes southern California. Many naturalists draw an imaginary boundary from Point Conception east to Fort Tejon and northeast to the northern end of Death Valley, excluding the Owens Valley and the White and Inyo mountains. The area so defined includes both the Mojave and the Colorado deserts, which, though already dealt with in considerable detail in three previous chapters, are considered here in terms of the interface between the arid and more humid sections of this part of California. We, however, have chosen to shift the coastal end of the borderline north to Point Sal, in this way including the Santa Inez Mountains, an important area of transition, in the region to be discussed. The first two chapters on southern California are primarily concerned with the Transverse and the Peninsular ranges and the valleys and hills lying coastwise to them. It has long been customary for botanists and other naturalists to refer to the area west of the summit of these ranges as *cismontane,* or "this side of the mountain," and *transmontane* is the region east of the divide. We shall make use of these handy terms where appropriate.

These mountains are no mere slag heaps. The two tallest peaks of the Transverse Range are Mount San Gorgonio (Old

Grayback)—11,499 feet (3,450 m.)—and Mount San Antonio (Mount Baldy)—10,064 feet (3,019 m.). Mount San Jacinto—10,804 feet (3,241 m.)—and Santa Rosa Peak—8,046 feet (2,414 m.)—dominate the Peninsular Range. Both mountainous chains are geologically young and highly dissected and are the products of compressive forces generated by a complex system of more or less related faults. Rocks ranging in age from Precambrian gneiss (1.7 billion years B.P.) to recently deposited fanglomerates—coarse accumulations in alluvial fans—were extensively faulted and folded, particularly in the Pleistocene. Uplift continues as evidenced by the 3-foot (1 m.) tall scarp created by the San Fernando earthquake in 1971.

The San Andreas Fault, the zone of contact between the North American Continental Plate and the Pacific Plate, has influenced the topography of southern California for many thousands of years. The land west of the fault is moving north at a generalized rate of more than an inch (2.5 cm.) a year, and at some time in the future Los Angeles will be where San Francisco is now, a thought not happily received by most residents of that city. The dog-leg angle of the San Andreas Fault to the southeast, just west of Mount Pinos, appears responsible for the east-west orientation of the Transverse Range, one of two such trending ranges in the contiguous forty-eight states (the other is the Uinta Range of northeastern Utah).

The Transverse Range extends east from the Santa Inez Mountains of Santa Barbara County and includes the Topatopa Mountains of Ventura County, the Santa Monica Mountains, the San Gabriel Mountains, and their northern extension, the Sierra Pelona, of Los Angeles County, and the San Bernardino and Little San Bernardino mountains of San Bernardino and Riverside counties. Some of the individual ranges such as the San Gabriel and San Bernardino mountains have cores of ancient crystalline igneous and metamorphic rocks. Consistent with its role in determining the direction of the Transverse Range, the San Andreas Fault is the northern boundary of the San Gabriel Mountains, but because of the southeast trend of the fault-mountain complex, it marks the southern edge of the San Bernardino and Little San Bernardino ranges. The Cajon Pass, an important transportation corridor for many years, is largely the fault's trace where it separates the two mountain ranges.

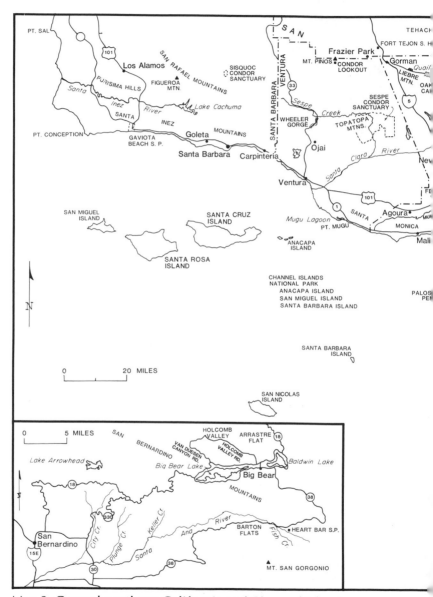

Map 3. Coastal southern California and Channel Islands

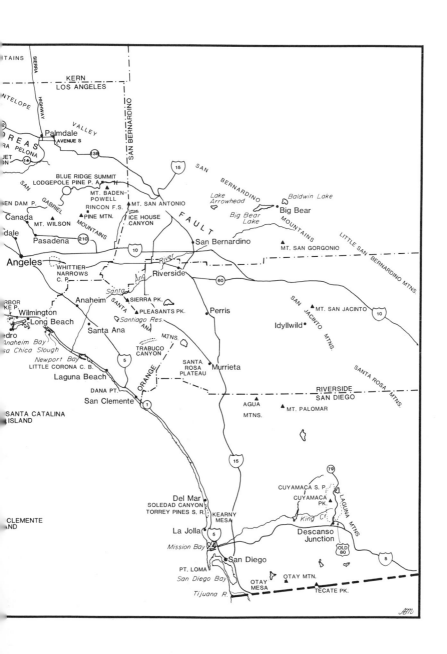

Two fault systems account primarily for the northern portion of the Peninsular Range. Massive blocks of gabbro and other plutonic rocks have been thrust up between the Elsinor and San Jacinto faults, great crustal cracks that parallel each other in a northwest-southeast trending direction. The San Jacinto, Santa Rosa, Agua Tibia, and Laguna (Cuyamaca) mountains, with their western outlier, the Santa Ana Mountains, extend south in a welter of ridges, peaks, mesas, and broad shallow valleys, cut here and there by streams into steep-walled canyons. World-famed Mount Palomar with its 200-inch (508-cm.) telescope is but one of the crestline vantage points from which one can have spectacular views of both desert and coastal southern California. The Los Angeles Basin is actually a plain tucked between the Santa Monica Mountains of the Transverse Range and the coastal foothills of the Peninsular Range. It is largely composed of sediments recently, geologically speaking, deposited by streams outflowing from neighboring mountains.

The climatic patterns of southern California, in common with the rest of the state, are determined by latitude, relief, and distance from the sea. The average annual precipitation for Los Angeles—12.4 inches (31.5 cm.)—is much less than that for San Francisco—21 inches (53 cm.)—for several reasons. Summer drought is longer in the south as the rainy season seldom begins before mid-November and usually ends in March or early April. In addition, recurrent ridges of high pressure often push the winter storm track north of Point Conception, abetted by the interference of the Transverse Range. Since 1877, annual rainfall above 20 inches (51 cm.) has been recorded for Los Angeles in only nineteen years whereas during sixty years there has been precipitation of 15 inches (38 cm.) or less.

Rain increases where relief features induce orographic cooling. Mount Wilson, 5,709 feet (1,713 m.) in elevation, has an annual average precipitation of 35 inches (89 cm.) in contrast to Pasadena, roughly 5,000 feet (1,500 m.) lower in altitude, which receives about 20 inches (51 cm.) of rainfall yearly. In general, there is a precipitation gradient from the drier coast to the moister high elevations throughout cismontane southern California.

Frost is rare along the coast, but sheltered inland valleys and uplands above 4,000 feet (1,200 m.) can expect freezing temperatures at numerous times during the winter. Rainshadow in the lee of the two major ranges of southern California has been discussed in the desert chapters of this book, but small differences in annual rainfall can often be attributed to local rainshadows produced by specific topographical features. Santa Ana, on the coast side of the Santa Ana Mountains, receives an average yearly precipitation of 13 inches (33 cm.), 3 inches (8 cm.) more than Perris to the leeward of this small range.

The southern coast, in common with the rest of maritime California, benefits from onshore ocean breezes. A typical summer day at the beach may get no warmer than 68° F. (20° C.), while inland in the San Fernando Valley, for example, the thermometer reads in the 90°s F. (30°s C.). The same cold current offshore northern and central California produces spring and summer coastal fog in the southern part of the state. On most evenings from mid-April to mid-September it pushes up against shoreline hills and penetrates the lowland basins that are open to onshore wind. The distance inland depends upon the depth of the marine layer and the strength of the ocean breeze. It "burns off" the following morning, the time varying with its thickness and closeness to the sea. The valleys cut off from the nightly influx of fog by topographical barriers also have temperatures less affected by sea breeze. They tend to have warmer summer days and, in general, wider ranges of temperature, climatic patterns that are transitional between the cooler coast and the warmer desert. In late spring and early summer a local cyclonic, the so-called Catalina eddy, often develops, which deepens the marine layer and holds the fog over both coast and inland basin alike. The succession of one cool, overcast day after another depresses both traffic to the beach and the spirits of the tourists here for the famed California sunshine.

Several weather conditions are either peculiar to or are more typical of the southern part of the state: Santa Ana winds, summer rain from tropical storms, and that worrisome nuisance, smog. Though warm dry Santa Ana wind patterns can develop any time in the year, most occur in fall. As if wiped away by the deft fingers of some extraterrestrial Houdini, the usual haze disappears, and the mountains loom like stage sets. At first it is a pleasant change from the smog-choked days of September. But as the humidity plummets and fingers touching metal door handles jump with electric shock, those living near brush-covered hills become apprehensive, and rightfully so. This is fire weather when millions of dollars worth of property can become ashes in a matter of minutes. Flowing down out of huge interior high pressure cells, the winds are heated by compression as they squeeze through canyons and passes on their way to the sea. Scrub and grassland, already dry from months of drought, are as flammable as open cans of gasoline, and the winds, once a fire starts, can whip quiet hillsides into raging holocausts within moments.

Very different weather circumstances occasionally bring unseasonable but welcome rain to the same fire-prone dry slopes. Every summer great spirals of high atmospheric pressure are generated in the Gulf of Mexico that extend tongues of warm humid air to the northwest as far as southern California. For the most part, they carry only enough moisture to build soap-sud-white thunderheads above Mount Baldy and neighboring peaks or cause flash flood warnings in the desert. Tropical hurricanes known as *chubascos* regularly develop in the same season along the west coast of Mexico. Once in a great while they leave their normal storm track and advance northward and inland, bringing an inch or so (2.5 cm.) of rain in the unlikely months of July through September.

Edaphic features, the third group of controls operating on the vegetation mosaic, apparently are no less assertive here than they are in the northern part of the state, even though serpentine soils are relatively rare. The southernmost extension of the Franciscan Formation, however, occurs in the San Rafael and Santa Inez mountains of Santa Barbara County, and serpentine outcrops are noteworthy features of Figueroa Mountain and neighboring slopes. The southernmost groves of Sargent cypress are largely confined to soils derived from this parent rock on steep hillsides north of the summit. As we shall see, several small serpentine sites are primarily responsible for stands of knobcone pine in the Santa Ana Mountains. The Purisima forest of bishop pine in western Santa Barbara County keeps to diatomaceous shale deposits while adjacent slopes of coastal sage scrub are restricted to clay soils. Recent research on a number of species of this scrub has revealed strong substrate preferences, which will be discussed later in the chapter. Direction of slope face continues to account for many specific mosaic patterns. Its influence will be noted when the various communities are described in detail.

From the foregoing summary of the physical features of southern California, it is apparent that climatic differences are largely responsible for the absence not only of a number of natural communities but many species encountered in the northern two-thirds of the state. Much of the topography is similar—coastal hills giving way to interior valleys and high mountains abutting deserts to the east—but rainfall averages are not. Aridity, in general, and prolonged warm season drought, in particular, eliminated the closed-cone pines and other more mesic species that were once so widespread in southern California at relatively low altitudes—1,500 feet (450 m.)—during the cooler, wetter climate of the Pleistocene.

Today digger pine extends no farther south than the San Rafael mountains of Santa Barbara County and the Sierra Pelona of northern Los Angeles County possibly because its seeds need colder winters for germination. On the mainland, bishop pine is now confined to western Santa Barbara County, and knobcone pine is found in only two places in southern California. Coast redwood once extended as far south as Carpenteria in Ventura County. (Recent discoveries of stream-drifted fossil redwood have extended its former range to at least Los Angeles County during the late Pleistocene.) As for community types, a case in point is mixed evergreen forest. It occurs in southern California, but it varies in both composition and character from place to place. Tanbark oak and Douglas-fir reach down as far as the hilly country north of Point Conception in Santa Barbara County. California bay and coast live oak, however, are characteristic of the community throughout much of southern California.

The mountains of Santa Barbara County have been repeatedly mentioned as having the southernmost extensions of a number of important species. The Santa Inez Mountains, in particular, are the Hadrian's Wall of California flora. This east-west trending range does not actually block the southerly expansion of plants more typical of the northern part of the state, but being a part of the storm-obstructing Transverse Range, it probably has had a role in the climatic changes that confine the more mesophytic species to the north. San Diego County is another boundary area. Such widespread trees as big-leaf maple and black oak venture no farther south; on the other hand a number of species typical of Baja California—Shaw's agave, for one—reach their northern terminus just above the border. The following list of natural communities occurring in southern California has been compiled from several sources. The choice of names as well as organization is admittedly arbitrary, the author herself having contributed some notions of nomenclature as well as format. The asterisks refer to communities whose southern and western extensions have been discussed elsewhere.

Cismontane wetlands
  Coastal salt marsh*
  Freshwater marsh
Cismontane scrub and brushlands
  Coastal strand*
  Coastal sage scrub
  Chaparral
Cismontane woodland and forest
  Southern oak woodland
  Mesic slope woodland (southern mixed evergreen forest)
  Riparian woodland
  Closed-cone conifer forest
Grassland
Lower montane pine forest
  Coulter pine forest
  Yellow pine forest
Upper montane forest
  White fir-sugar pine forest
  Subalpine forest
Mountain meadow
Alpine rockfield
Desert scrub and woodland
  Pinyon-juniper woodland*
  Joshua tree woodland*
  Sagebrush scrub*
  Creosote bush scrub*
  Shadscale scrub*
  Oasis and riparian woodland*
  Alkali sink*

Freshwater Marsh. Most of the larger bodies of freshwater here are reservoirs, and shoreline and aquatic vegetation often has difficulty in becoming established because of fluctuations of the water level. Many small marshlike habitats, however, have developed in their shallower backwaters, particularly where streams feed into the lakes. Some can be found around Lake Cuchuma in Santa Barbara County, Santiago Reservoir in Orange County, and at the eastern end of Hansen Dam in the San Fernando Valley parallel to Wentworth Street. Natural ponds are rare, but they are scattered here and there, often where water has collected in depressions created by movement along an earthquake fault. Some of these sag ponds, such as those along the Post Road between Gorman and Quail Lake, are sapphire surprises surrounded by a basketry of cattails, sedges, and tules and other bulrushes, and the limbs and branches of ancient willows. Other patches of freshwater marsh have taken hold along the edges of slow-moving rivers such as the Santa Inez in Santa Barbara County and the Santa Ana in Riverside and Orange counties. Largely because of the migratory and resident shorebird populations attracted to these habitats, a number of them have either been preserved, such as Harbor Lake (Bixby Slough) in Wilmington, or actually developed, for example, the lakes at Whittier Narrows, both sites in Los Angeles County.

Basket rush is endemic to southern California, and the Indians of the area made use of its fibrous stem in pursuit of the painstaking craft of basket making. The Chumash of the Santa Barbara region, for instance, used it as a sewing strand in making their coiled baskets. Stems of other rushes were used in bundles of three as foundation for the coils that were then bound together to form the rounded, bowllike shape. The colors used to make the decorative patterns were produced by using treated or naturally dried parts of the rush stems. Deep burnt-orange came from parts of the stem that grow below the surface. Dark tan colors appeared when the stalks were drawn by hand through beds of warm ashes. The tips dried to a lighter tan without further treatment, and the black color was produced when the stems were buried for several weeks in organic mud, abundant in freshwater marshes.

Coastal Sage Scrub. As noted in "Patterns on the Hills," this community is gradually replaced by northern coastal scrub from San Luis Obispo County northward. It has been divided into three subtypes, each with its characteristic plants, though some species such as California buckwheat and California sagebrush are common to all three. The sea bluff (maritime) succulent subtype is already familiar from the second chapter, "Sea Cliff," in which we discussed the adversities of the habitat and the types of plants it supports. Succulents such as live-forever are very abundant, and prickly pear and coast cholla cacti occur at various localities along the southern coast. One can still find specimens of velvet cactus, coast barrel cactus, snake cholla, and Shaw's century plant (agave) in coastal San Diego County (personal communication from Dr. Reid Moran, curator of botany, San Diego Museum of Natural History), but urbanization has all but obliterated them from this northern outpost of their range.

From Tijuana south, fleshy leaves of the agave often clump together in interlocking thickets that would impede the progress of the most intrepid hiker. Snarls of velvet and galloping cacti can be almost as difficult to negotiate. This spiny succulence dominates sea-facing benches and headlands in what is a maritime desert as the average annual rainfall at San Quintin, roughly 200 miles (322 km.) below the border, is only 5 inches (12.7 cm.).

The maritime sage scrub of southern California is more diverse in species, and it includes such woody shrubs as coyotebrush, lemonadeberry, and its frost-susceptible cousin, laurel sumac as well as a number of subshrubs, for example, deerweed, black and purple sage, California buckwheat, and California sagebrush. It is rather a drab collection for the most part, but in spring it is enriched by the bright green drapery of wild cucumber, the purple velvet of wild canterbury-bell, the sky-tinted whorls of chia, and other annuals. Perennials such as canyon lupine and yellow yarrow and flowering shrubs, including yerba santa, the two prominent sages, and bush monkeyflower, add lavender and gold to the coastal hills. In places the scrub is profuse enough to have three layers. The evergreen laurel sumac often commands a large share of the landscape; the subshrubs—California sagebrush and black sage—soften the terrain beneath. Grasses and other low-growing herbs fill in the cover while in season.

The drought-adapted features allowing the scrub to cope with the generally lower rainfall along the coast also enable it to survive the warmer interior below 3,000 feet (900 m.). This third subtype, inland sage scrub, is further modified where it occupies wash floors. Toyon, mountain mahogany, and holly-leaf cherry are common components, which drift in from adjacent stands of chaparral. Our Lord's candle, at times producing unusually tall flowering stems, and scalebroom are other characteristic alluvial species. Brittle bush, a spectacular mound of yellow when in bloom, has ventured over from the desert to the east on dry inland sites though it reaches the coast in San Diego County.

Investigation has revealed that most of the representative species of sage scrub have preferential sites. Bush sunflower, for example, has a tendency toward sandstone soils; California buckwheat, on the other hand, favors granitic substrates. Other factors include amount of litter, soil texture, maximum and minimum seasonal temperatures, soil chemistry, and degree of disturbance. As in all natural communities, species tend to group together in associations where they find congenial conditions. In this instance, the purple sage-laurel sumac and black sage-laurel sumac associations are more typical of south-facing slopes that have relatively deep soils and are near the coast. On the other hand, the white sage-California sagebrush-California buckwheat group keeps to the bases of interior granitic slopes. Though the scrub as a whole has been described as predominately south-facing, several associations, notably California sagebrush-coyotebrush-giant wildrye, apparently prefer steep north-facing hillsides.

The relationship between the two major brushlands of low-elevation cismontane southern California varies from noncompetitive neighborliness, to sharing many species, to dynamic successional interaction. Because of their shallow root system, the subshrubs of the coastal sage scrub are unable to utilize deep bedrock sources of moisture, and their foliage tends to be mesophytic rather than sclerophyllous. In several of the more common species such as black and white sage, this disadvantage is compensated for by having hairy, light-deflecting leaves that are either drought-deciduous or smaller in size during the warmer months. Both devices are effective in reducing the loss of transpiratory water. Evergreen brush continues some metabolic activity during the dry season. The leaf-dropping subshrubs, however, enjoy a brief but productive growing season before virtually shutting down, emulating, if you will, the drought-evading lifestyle of annual plants. As a result, sage scrub is well equipped for survival on the steep, hot, dry slopes that even the stalwart chaparral generally avoids.

Two patterns of stable relationship have evolved between the two communities. Coastal sage scrub is typical of lower, warmer elevations—from sea level to 3,000 feet (900 m.)—particularly south-facing hillsides, and chaparral dominates the more mesic sites—cooler, shadier, north-facing slopes and higher elevations that receive increased rainfall. The types of brushy cover are also kept apart by edaphic influences. Scrub occasionally occurs on fine-grained soils such as clay. The shallow-rooted subshrubs utilize moisture trapped close to the surface because of the nature of the substrate. Chaparral shrubs favor slopes where deep bedrock sources of water are available for their long roots.

These essentially consistent patterns are complicated by fire, landslides, grazing, road building, and other disturbances. As we have noted, many of the typical sage scrub plants are semiwoody. Lignified stems support fast-growing herbaceous twigs. Though most of them crown-sprout to some extent, reproduction is primarily accomplished by means of lightweight, wind-dispersed seeds. These weedlike characteristics are advantageous in exploring freshly opened territory. Following a brush fire, sage scrub seedlings infiltrate the germinating and resprouting chaparral shrubs attempting postburn growth, particularly on the sunnier slopes. During the next few years much of the seedling growth of both communities is destined for failure. The small sclerophyllous shrubs that survive are joined by the now-flourishing resprouters. Together they eventually replace the short-lived subshrub elements, primarily because of increasing shade. Some stands of black sage, however, appear to be able to reseed themselves and remain indefinitely. Most herbaceous fire-followers are annuals, and their reign is short, lasting but one growing season. A number of perennials and subshrubs continue to be strong contenders for the ever-shrinking open spaces for several years. Some of these species such as deerweed are important producers of nitrogen for the reestablishing chaparral. It appears that their leaf detritus contributes nutrients as well.

Burned north-facing slopes do not usually experience a successional stage of sage scrub domination; the resprouting sclerophylls recover too vigorously.

The ecotones between coastal sage scrub and grassland, a community generally indicative of a drier climate, are often as complex. Wild oats and other introduced grasses weave through scrubby patches as did native bunchgrasses such as wildrye before the advent of foreign species. In many places the border between the two communities is distinct. In Santa Barbara County, for instance, scrub claims exposures of Monterey shale that are unsuitable for grassland. Some naturalists support the theory that terpenes (highly volatile toxic compounds released from black and other sages) inhibit the germination of herbaceous plants. Preferential grazing may also restrict the growth of grass and favor the pungent, unpalatable sages. Other grass-inhibiting factors currently under investigation include the effects of reduced fire frequency, the depletion of soil nitrogen and moisture, and the shade cast by the taller brushy plants.

Chaparral. Chamise, manzanita, and scrub oak are already familiar to us from previous chapters. All are members of the sclerophyllous mixture that blankets our foothills, but each is typical of its own subtype of chaparral that, by and large, is restricted to specific homegrounds. Chamise chaparral, sometimes referred to as "warm" chaparral, is prevalent below 3,300 feet (990 m.) on ridgetops, south-facing hillsides and similar xeric habitats where soils are thin and organically poor. (Interestingly enough, sage scrub soils are often more fertile than those under some types of chaparral. The deciduous leaves add nitrogen and other nutrients.) Where more moisture is available in arroyos, on shady slopes, or in deeper soils, it includes ceanothus, manzanita, coffeeberry, silk tassel, and other larger-leafed shrubs. Sugarbush, lemonadeberry, and laurel sumac, sclerophyllous members of sage scrub, often associate with them. All three are closely related and are restricted to southern California and northern Baja California. They are largely responsible for the woody nature of many stands of coastal sage scrub. Our Lord's candle, another scrub species, is a frequent associate on the drier slopes where cover is sparse.

Chamise chaparral grades into "cool" chaparral, primarily manzanita, at roughly 3,500 feet (1,050 m.), an elevation at which snow and freezing temperatures can be expected during periods of colder weather. The crowded thickets of this subtype apparently require not only gentler slopes but more mesic conditions, which may be provided by denser shade, soils capable of holding more moisture, and cooler temperatures. Scrub oak chaparral also commands more favorable environments and forms thick clusters, often with larger shrubs as mountain mahogany and hollyleaf cherry, on shadier slopes and on sunny hillsides above 3,000 feet (900 m.). A shrubby variety of interior live oak and chaparral whitethorn are occasional companions, particularly at higher elevations.

Fire is an additional determining factor in the distribution of these species and their respective communities. Steeper slopes retain less ash, attracting chamise, a notable resident of impoverished soils, whereas deeper ash deposits persist on more level terrain where manzanita is more at home. Fire is less frequent in this subtype presumably because of more mesic conditions. The denser cover and greater accumulations of litter, however, produce very destructive burns, which wipe out, temporarily, the manzanitas and companion shrubs.

The role of short-lived subshrubs in fire recovery has already been discussed. Certain species of ceanothus perform the same function. Chaparral whitethorn and hoaryleaf ceanothus, for instance, are prolific fire-seeders and nitrogen fixers, as well. They drop out after a number of years, but they have paid for the hospitality of their host community, particularly chamise chaparral, by adding nutrients to the soil. It has been suggested that chamise becomes depauperate unless it is burned at regular intervals, primarily because of depleted nitrogen.

The story of fire in the brushlands of southern California is incomplete without reference to the marvelous displays following fire, especially if the postburn rains have been heavy. In the past few years, the author has seen overwhelming spreads of color in the Santa Monica Mountains along Mulholland Drive and connecting roads from Agoura west to Malibu after the fires that were, unfortunately, disastrous for many families residing in the area. Little comfort to those who lost homes and property, but unusually wet winters brought springtime wild gardens of great beauty. Hillsides rich with the fire-following fire poppy and large-flowered phacelia shared their orange and pink with thousands of lavender-tinted mariposa lilies, magenta-and-white Chinese houses, and great beds of wild Canterbury-bells, species casually present in unburned brush, in a display reminiscent of the muted splendor of an old Isfahan rug. In the years that followed, other flowers such as deerweed, nightshade, creamy-white ear drops, and the sunshine-blossomed canyon sunflower replaced this first startling assemblage.

Two special subtypes of chaparral are confined to the southern part of the state. The rare red shanks, or ribbonwood, is a much more striking plant than its close cousin, chamise, because of its size—6.5 to 20 feet (2–6 m.) in height—feathery foliage, and long strips of reddish, peeling bark. Though most of these relatively open stands are confined to elevations above 2,000 feet (600 m.) in the Peninsular Range, it also occurs disjunctly in the Santa Monica Mountains and in northern Santa Barbara and San Luis Obispo counties.

In the other subtype elements of coastal sage scrub and chaparral mingle with desert woodlands and scrubs from 2,000 to 5,000 feet (600–1,500 m.) on the desert side of southern California's dividing ranges. Many plants—scrub oak, bigberry manzanita, chamise, our Lord's candle, and the semiwoody deerweed and black sage—are common to both coastal and arid inland environments. Some species appear to be more numerous on the dry side—California juniper, flannel bush, bush poppy (a fire-follower), and Mexican manzanita. California buckwheat, an abundant cismontane species, is also one of the important shrubs of the desert chaparral and tends to group itself around the widely spaced woodier plants. A number of "pair" species—similar species restricted to one side of the range or the other—have evolved. Examples include the largely transmontane desert ceanothus and the cismontane buckbrush, scrub oak and desert scrub oak, and western mountain mahogany and desert mountain mahogany.

In general, desert chaparral tends to be less diverse, less dense, and shorter in stature than its coastal counterpart. In spite of the sparsity of cover, fire does occur occasionally. Post-fire recovery is slower than in the more mesic cismontane chaparral, primarily because of the lack of soil moisture and the absence of a successional stage of fire-following herbaceous growth. Slope-face direction plays a role in the distri-

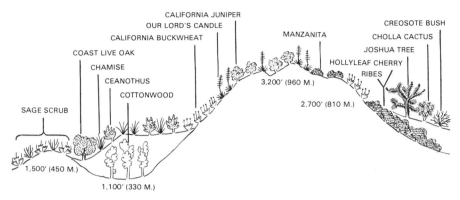

Figure 25. Idealized transect along the Antelope Valley Freeway (State Highway 14) from cismontane (left) to transmontane (right)

bution of some species. Bigberry manzanita and scrub oak, for instance, occur most frequently on north-facing hillsides. Additional influences include distance from the ocean and topographical features that modify the impact of the desert climate.

The Antelope Valley Freeway (State Highway 14) is an excellent introduction to the gradual shift from cismontane brushlands to desert vegetation. In the canyon-dissected country near Newhall, tight masses of chaparral dominate most of the higher ridges well back from the highway. On the nearer shoulders and slopes, it mingles with elements of coastal sage scrub. Where burnt off, an annual event during the fire season someplace along the freeway, grasses and other herbaceous growth temporarily dislodge the shrubs. About 12 miles (19 km.) east of the turn-off from Interstate 5, the brush almost imperceptibly thins out to a low cover of buckwheat interrupted by the sticklike stalks of our Lord's candle. At 2,000 feet (600 m.) in altitude, solitary, stunted California junipers stray in, accompanied by bladderpod, goldenbush, and little collections of cholla cactus. Just after the Pearblossom Highway takes off to the right from the freeway, one gets a glimpse of Joshua trees. After a mile or so (1.6 km.) into the desert, the first creosote bushes appear, and the big change has taken place.

Those interested in geology would do well to continue on the freeway (State Highway 14) toward Palmdale, passing the famous "cut" where highway construction has exposed the sedimentary rock strata of the Anaverde formation (Pliocene) that have been twisted and tortured by movement along the San Andreas Fault. It is a dramatic illustration of tectonic interaction between two continental plates. Downslope to the right of the cut are several sag ponds. At the intersection of Avenue S and the Sierra Highway is one of the very few places where the matrix shrubs of the two great desert scrubs actually mingle, timidly probing, as it were, each other's territory. Great Basin sagebrush and creosote bush grow side by side in the alluvium sloping down to these little basins.

Foothill Woodland. That gracious comradeship of valley oak, blue oak, and digger pine, enlivened by the bright dollops of California buckeye, is largely absent south of the thirty-fifth parallel. There are two exceptions. The San Rafael Mountains in the heart of Santa Barbara County have scattered woodlands of this nature though lacking California buckeye. The latter species, in company with the other typical trees of this woodland, does occur in northern Los Angeles County, and the author believes that this is the most accessible area in southern California for those wishing to become acquainted with this extensive and attractive native landscape. Turn east from Gorman on State Highway 138 and then follow Los Angeles County N2 as it meanders back and forth along the San Andreas Fault zone. Looking south up the northern slopes of Liebre Mountain, the viewer will notice the typical, slightly off-balance silhouette of digger pines. Blue oaks, canyon live oaks, and California buckeye are scattered along the narrow road, and a small but splendid grove of valley oaks with a surprising understory of Great Basin sagebrush is a feature of Oakdale Canyon just west of Three Points. Mottled slopes of intervening or understory chaparral are as characteristic here as they are in the Sierran foothills or the interior Coast Ranges. If you plan your visit in late April, look for thistle sage on grassy slopes to the north of the road as it winds down to Three Points and, if one is lucky, carpets of goldfields unroll between the scattered sagebrush. It is an enchanting little byway, a happy introduction to this type of rural California.

Southern Oak Woodland. This kind of community, so characteristic of the foothills of central and northern Califor-

nia, is less common in the southern part of the state. Dr. Lyman
Benson, well-known botanist at Claremont Colleges, is reputed
to have commented that southern oak woodland occurs in
patches surrounded by an almost continuous sea of brush
whereas to the north the chaparral occurs primarily as islands
surrounded by oak woodland. In the Santa Monica Mountains
it is typical of deeper soils in broad valleys and on the rolling
flanks of the northern edge of the range. It was quite prevalent
in much of southern Ventura County, and, where allowed to
remain, dominates parts of the Ojai Valley and adjacent hills.
One authority on the San Gabriel Mountains describes it as
confined there to clay benches and lower cismontane slopes.
Discontinuous spreads of southern oak woodland once extended south from the hills around Covina, where those driving on Interstate 10 and State Highway 60 (San Bernardino and
Pomona freeways) can still see fragments, to the Mexican border and below. The combination of urbanization and subtropical fruit tree culture has taken its toll, particularly in Orange
and San Diego counties, but it still can be found in wide valleys
in the San Diego backcountry as well as the lower slopes of
canyons in the Santa Ana Mountains. Some of the best examples of southern oak woodland occur on the Santa Rosa Plateau, a southeasterly extension of the range that is a series of
rolling tablelands rather than the collection of steep canyons
typical of the western face. In the San Bernardino Mountains,
north-facing slopes of the cismontane foothills and lower canyon floors support some southern oak woodland.

Valley oak remains a strong component on the inland side of
the Santa Monica Mountains and in rolling country to the
north and west of the San Fernando Valley. Apparently it is
uncommon in the rugged western part of Ventura County
though it is prominent in the interior of much of Santa Barbara
County. There is evidence that it hybridized with Engelmann
oak in the Pasadena area. A lone, oft-cited hybrid with desert
scrub oak is believed to be the large tree growing at Live Oak
Tank in Joshua Tree National Monument, of all places!

Arboreal forms of interior live oak have a limited distribution in southern California. Though the species occurs as small
trees in the Santa Ana Mountains and other ranges, large
shrubs are more typical, and they are an element of chaparral
rather than woodland.

Coast live oak is the ranking member of the genus in woodlands throughout cismontane southern California, particularly on moister slopes and in canyon bottoms where it is often joined by canyon live oak. Southern California walnut is by no means a constant companion, but groves of this handsome little tree with its parallel fingerlings of richly green foliage are scattered on north-facing slopes from Orange County to Ventura County. There is speculation that this deciduous tree may have crept in during moister times and remains in more mesic sites where its unusual way of life can be accommodated.

Engelmann, or mesa, oak is southern California's native son though it does occur in the Sierra Juarez Mountains of Baja California, roughly 40 miles (64 km.) below the border. It was once widespread from eastern Los Angeles County to San Diego County in a foothill belt approximately 50 miles (80 km.) wide and 15 to 20 miles (24–32 km.) from the sea. A few can still be seen in the Pasadena area—on the campus of the California Institute of Technology, the grounds of the Huntington Library, and on broad slopes above Claremont and other nearby towns. The oak is scattered in the Santa Ana Mountains, particularly on the mesas of the Santa Rosa Plateau west of Murrieta. Avocado groves and other land use threaten what remains of this lovely woodland, but patches of Engelmann oak and coast live oak still grace many of the gentler slopes of cismontane Orange and central San Diego counties. In spring the grassy floor is bright with blue dicks, checker bloom, owl's clover, lupine, and yellow violet. California sagebrush and sugarbush add their touch of scrub to these pleasant hillsides. Acorn woodpeckers, cockades held high, cling to the rough bark of branch and tree, and an occasional white-tailed kite forages for meadow mice and other small rodents.

A white oak, Engelmann oak is related to blue oak both in appearance and ecological status. It has bluish, semipersistent, wavy-edged leaves and, like its northern cousin, tends to form savannalike groves on drier sites in contrast to coast live oak that usually claims more mesic slopes. Engelmann oak appears to be more stress-tolerant than blue oak since it occurs in areas that have greater extremes of rainfall and experience somewhat higher temperatures.

Fire, as always, wags its dictatorial finger. In this vulnerable environment, its whims are restricted by several deterrent factors. Woodland, in general, suffers less damage since grass is the conveyor. It makes a much "cooler" blaze, and the canopy is above the source of heat. Coast live oak is commonly considered to be one of the more fire-resistant species because of its thick bark, the ability to readily root-crown- and branch-sprout, and its choice of homesite—rocky outcrops that act as fire buffers and moister slopes. Saplings, usually, are more vulnerable to fire injury because of thin bark. Recent studies, however, have disclosed that the saplings of Engelmann oak may be safeguarded by bark thicker than that of young coast live oaks, and the buds, from which later resprouting will take place, appear to be protected from burn destruction. Though both these phases of southern oak woodland tend to avoid association with chaparral, Engelmann oak evidently permits more inclusions of brush than coast live oak. Its fire resistance may also help account for its occurrence in drier, and thus more conflagration-susceptible, places.

Mesic Slope Woodland. This community is also referred to as southern mixed evergreen forest and canyon woodland. The cooler, especially the north-facing, canyonsides of cismontane southern California are host to larger or less drought-resistant shrubs and trees just as they are in Marin or Mariposa counties. There is a noticeable thickening of vegetation as coast live oak joins California bay, canyon live oak, and big-leaf maple, accompanied by a number of shrubs that thrive in deep soils and a cooler, moister environment—toyon, flowering ash, California coffeeberry, poison oak, redberry, and fuchsia-flowering gooseberry. These are the places to look for the burgundy-red trumpets of pitcher sage, the lavender skirts of fiesta flower, white fairy lanterns that appear to be bowing in their own tiny ballet, and Chinese houses, particularly in mountains near the coast.

Madroño, that colorful adjunct of mixed evergreen forest, has relinquished much of southern California. There are only four relictual populations of this tree south of Santa Barbara County—western Ventura County, on the north slope of Pine Mountain above the Rincon Forest Station in the San Gabriel Mountains, on the north face of Trabuco Canyon in the Santa Ana Mountains, and near Mount Palomar in San Diego County.

Canyon live oak belongs to many communities, but it is a dominant tree in mesic slope woodland. Not only do its ecological requirements favor moister slopes, fire kill in more exposed sites may be inevitable for several reasons. The species has thin, dry outer bark. When fire girdles the trees exposing the woody layers, eventually most of them die. Partially burned trees, however, both canopy- and stump-sprout. An herbaceous stage of recovery is succeeded by brush cover until the oaks are tall enough to discourage the latter. The coniferous members of these shady slopes will be discussed in the transitional cone-bearer section of the next chapter.

Riparian Woodland. Where soil moisture is readily available for much of the year such as in streambeds and the bottoms of canyons, the woodlands of the moister hillsides merge almost imperceptibly with lush riparian growth, intervals of welcome shade in the smoggy heat of summer. Along the edge of the south-facing and other more xeric slopes the ecotone is more abrupt, and the heavy, green canopy of Fremont cottonwood's summer foliage is lavish in contrast to the tired, drought-quiescent brush and scrub. Several willows and western sycamore are other typically riparian trees that are often joined by California bay, coast live oak, and canyon live oak. Big-leaf maple and white alder are important elements of streamside vegetation, the latter more frequently above 2,000 feet (600 m.). Arizona ash has a scattered cismontane representation. Herbaceous growth is rank, even well into summer—California mugwort, mule fat, streamside monkeyflower, and the introduced bull nettle. A special delight in exploring the riparian habitat is to come across patches of flamelike scarlet monkeyflower crowding close to the edge of the running water.

Much of southern California's riparian woodland, unfortunately, is periodically removed by torrential winter rains that tear out plant growth, or it has been permanently destroyed by flood control projects. Examples of such vegetation can still be seen along parts of the Santa Clara and Santa Ana rivers, the latter primarily because of the determination of local citizens to preserve this richly endowed wild heritage. Most flood-damaged streamside growth eventually returns if so permitted, but barren heaps of water-strewn boulders are often abundant on the washbeds and stream floors of both the San Gabriel and San Bernardino mountains. Numerous smaller streams, permanent or intermittent, have retained relatively undisturbed riparian vegetation in the Transverse and Peninsular ranges, and they are worth seeking out. The author suggests the little waterfalls and pools of Sespe Creek and Wheeler Gorge in Ventura County. Though Bouquet Canyon north of Newhall has a number of weekend as well as permanent residents, as do many of the other smaller canyons in the area, enough of the original plant life remains to provide the ambience of this delightful environment.

Grassland. Although one of the most ubiquitous biomes, natural grassy areas are rare in this part of California. Agricultural, suburban, and industrial growth threatens the remnants, a destiny shared by many other natural landscapes. The remaining patches are often overgrazed, trampled, and show other types of livestock abuse. For the most part, southern California grasslands are confined to valley floors, surrounding rolling hills and terraces, and *potreros*. They are frequently encountered in Santa Barbara and Ventura counties, less so in the southern mountains. The native species, as elsewhere in the state, were mostly perennials such as thin grass, California brome, needlegrass, purple needlegrass, and pine bluegrass. The same combination of disasters that drove the native species to near extinction in the northern parts of the state overcame them in southern California. Soft chess and wild oats are the most common species present today.

The role of grassland in the cismontane mosaic is multifaceted. Annual forbs and grasses form postdisturbance successional stages in recovering brush and scrub. Grass is the typical ground cover in oak woodland, and each natural community of southern California has its representative grasses adapted to particular environmental demands. Many of the swards that push aside neighboring chaparral and sage scrub reflect the nature of the substrate. On the Santa Rosa Plateau, grassy areas intrude where shale beds underlie the ground surface. Many of the hillside *potreros* of Santa Barbara County have fine-grained soils of low permeability derived from marine claystones and shales. As in the Central Valley, low rolling hills and terraces support grassland on clay loams. Some of them are deep, and others have drainage blocked by shallow claypans.

Vernal marshes and pools are rare, but they occur sporadically from Kearny and Otay mesas in San Diego County to the gentle terrain near Los Alamos north of the Santa Inez River in western Santa Barbara County. A number of seasonally wet habitats on the Santa Rosa Plateau have been investigated recently. Some of them are designated as vernal marshes rather than pools, largely because of the abundance of several spike-rushes, members of the sedge family, whose underground rhizomes are able to survive severe desiccation even though most species of this group require consistently damp soil. Both occur in shallow depressions on the basalt-capped mesas of the plateau and have the characteristic successional sequence of plants as the pools dry out. April's blue and white froth of *Downingia* and popcorn flower gives way to the rare endemic grass, *Orcuttia californica*, and the tiny tubes of *Navarretia*, among other dry-bed flowering species. San Diego mesa mint is another endemic of the pool habitat, in this case extremely limited in geographical range.

These vulnerable hills, prone as they are to fire, flood, and human encroachment, are ubiquitous. Anyone spending any time at all in southern California soon becomes aware of their dominance of the landscape, even through the smog. Los Angeles is the only major city in the world cut in two by a mountain range. One drives over hills, around them, and through passes between them that are now mainly conduits for freeways. Some are almost entirely converted to stepside housing. Others are practically untouched wilderness such as in northern Ventura County, which has only two paved connecting roads north of the Ojai Valley. But there they are, created by forces that from time to time remind us that man is a guest on a very unstable planet.

Black Oaks in San Bernardino Mountains

21. Upward

Although this chapter is primarily concerned with plants of higher elevations, a number of important species and several small communities described here actually are encountered on the coast or in chaparral and mesic slope and riparian woodlands at altitudes ranging from 1,000 to 4,000 feet (300–1,200 m.). The decision to include no conifers in Chapter 20 is admittedly arbitrary, but it was made in view of the length of the chapter and the fact that many of the cone-bearing trees shortly to be discussed ascend to the lower montane forest and become very much a part of it.

The following chapter discusses the Channel Islands, whose ecological and biogeographical importance is becoming better understood because of the research that has been and currently is being done by the University of California at Santa Barbara, the Santa Barbara Museum of Natural History, the botanic garden of the same city, and many other institutions. The California condor is being reserved for this chapter particularly since some of the best places for viewing these rare creatures are on or near Mount Pinos, an area we shall discuss in our exploration of mountaintop southern California. This brings up another point. Some readers may have noticed the near absence of references to the animals of this part of the state. No need to worry; we shall discuss them but in a rather different context than heretofore.

Lowland and Transitional Conifers. This encompassing term includes the closed-cone conifer forest, the Coulter pine forest, and several cone-bearing trees of limited distribution. Two of the closed-cone pines, bishop and Monterey, are no longer found in mainland southern California south of Santa Barbara County and San Luis Obispo County, respectively, though both occur in Baja California (see pp. 94–102). There is much evidence that they were strongly represented in various coastal forests from the Miocene to the late Pleistocene. Knobcone pine with its affinity for serpentine and other inhospitable substrates could be expected to continue in quantity far to the south of its present range. In fact, it is known to occur naturally in only three areas south of San Luis Obispo County. One is in City Creek, Plunge, and Keller Creek canyons on the cismontane side of the San Bernardino Mountains. Another is in the Santa Ana Mountains around Pleasants Peak, and the third grove is south of Ensenada in Baja California. This species, however, has been planted in various places in the San Gabriel Mountains for erosion control and landscape aesthetics, a practice now no longer followed.

The two disjunct sites in southern California are quite different edaphically. The San Bernardino Mountains stand occupies southern faces of the range at elevations from 2,000 to 4,500 feet (600–1,350 m.) on shallow rocky soils derived from granite whose inability to hold water intensifies the effects of summer drought. The Santa Ana group grows on what has been described as hydrothermally altered serpentinite, a rock type rare south of Santa Barbara County. Its chemically hostile nature is not only augmented but is perpetuated by steep, continually eroding terrain. The stunted, sparse shrubby undergrowth consists of a dozen or so species in contrast to the dense, diversified chaparral surrounding the serpentinite bedrock. Chamise and Eastwood manzanita provide roughly 50 percent of the plant cover.

As elsewhere in California, knobcone pine tolerates both the lack of essential nutrients and the ultrabasic nature of serpentine, features that discourage competitive scrub and tree species, but, at the same time, it benefits from the soil's capacity to retain moisture. Not only does serpentine often weather into soils of high water content, but, in this case, the end result is a fine-textured clay, which becomes saturated in the wetter months. Both stands of this pine are on seaward faces of their respective ranges and profit from this topographical advantage. The Santa Ana population as well as the inland City Creek groves receive orographically induced higher amounts of rainfall, and the former group encounters winter "tule-type" fogs as well as the coastal marine stratus of late spring and summer. The pines are excellent collectors of condensed air moisture. Fog drip amounting to an average of 2.26 inches (5.7 cm.) per month for May and June has been recorded in a study conducted by Dr. R. J. Vogl of California State University, Los Angeles. There seems little doubt that the knobcone pines of the Santa Ana Mountains make use of this additional source of moisture.

Coulter pine is another drought-tolerant endemic of the California Floristic Province, but its distribution is southern and coastal rather than northern and Sierran. It extends from the Mount Diablo area south to the mountains of northern Baja California and, like knobcone pine, is an arboreal companion of upland mixed chaparral—1,000 to 7,000 feet (300–2,100 m.). It is transitional between the sprawling spreads of brush and the coniferous forests of higher elevations. A medium-sized tree with thick clusters of long, dark green needles, it has heavy, massive cones whose scales look as though they had been carved by a skillful whittler and glued to a central solid core. Numerous groves occur in the Peninsular Range and the Santa Ana, San Bernardino, and San Gabriel mountains where they share drier inclines and ridges with chamise, ceanothus, shrubby canyon live oak, and other sclerophyllous species. At higher elevations this pine may join black oak, but the broadleaf tree often monopolizes the deeper, moister soils of north-facing hillsides. Like knobcone pine, Coulter pine has special adaptations for reproduction in the highly fire-prone chaparral environment. The cones are not indefinitely closed, but they retain seed until winter when the worst of the fire season is over. Then they open, and seedling establishment is possible during the following spring. Like so many California trees, Coulter pine germinates best in open mineral soils, and early growth is characterized by deep root penetration and rapid photosynthesis. Even with these safeguards against the elimination of the stands by fire, repeated burning apparently favors the entrance of chaparral, particularly manzanita, which is frequently a strong element in the ecotone between brush and Coulter pine forests. Recurrent fire tends to restrict the pine to steeper, less fertile slopes and other unsuitable manzanita habitats (see Figure 26). Seed-sprouting, short-lived species of ceanothus drop flammable deposits of leaves and other dead material. This quickly accumulates, and, as fire follows fire, the pines are gradually pushed up to higher elevations, unable to compete with these transitory but aggressive shrubs.

Big-cone Douglas-fir is often referred to as big-cone spruce, but its close taxonomic relationship to Douglas-fir (same genus) and the similarity of environmental requirements justify the use of the perhaps less well-known name. It is endemic to southern California and extends along the Transverse and Pe-

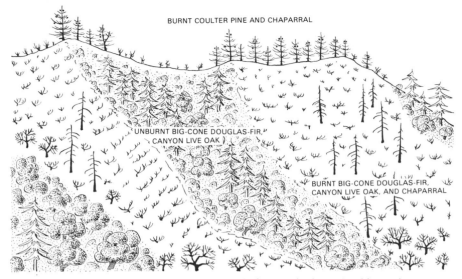

BURNT COULTER PINE AND CHAPARRAL

UNBURNT BIG-CONE DOUGLAS-FIR,
CANYON LIVE OAK

BURNT BIG-CONE DOUGLAS-FIR,
CANYON LIVE OAK, AND CHAPARRAL

Figure 26. Typical burn pattern on a north slope in the Santa Ana Mountains

ninsular ranges from central Santa Barbara County—just 21 miles (34 km.) from the southernmost grove of Douglas-fir—to central San Diego County, ranging from 900 to 8,000 feet (270–2,400 m.) in elevation. Its silhouette is unmistakable. A raggedy collection of tapering, spokelike branches radiates from the trunk. The more densely foliaged trees have feathery twigs that droop in a manner resembling Douglas-fir. It appears to have a wider range of ecological tolerance than its close relative, stepping down with coniferous dignity into shaggy chaparral as well as joining the montane forest of higher elevations. Though some stands occupy dry rocky outcrops, the greater majority of these trees at the lower part of their range tend either to remain in islandlike groves in sheltered canyons or on north-facing inclines that have escaped the invasion of fire-induced chaparral. In the Santa Ana Mountains, however, big-cone Douglas-firs are almost as numerous on the south faces of the range where increased precipitation and fog counteract the more intense solar radiation. It also appears to prefer the gentler gradients, and, as one study reveals, the fastest-growing and denser stands are on less steep terrain.

Depending on these and other factors, its companions vary from the extremely summer drought-adapted California sagebrush and buckwheat of the more xeric sites to canyon live oak and California bay of shady, deep-soiled slopes and draws. It associates with two of the southernmost colonies of madroño in upper Trabuco Canyon in the Santa Ana Mountains, emphasizing its mesic preferences. Above 5,000 feet (1,500 m.) it expands with canyon live oak in a more or less open forest over large areas of steep canyon walls and other precipitous tracts. The oak is very susceptible to fire destruction because of its thin bark, but certain features of these forests make them less vulnerable to fire damage than neighboring chaparral which consists mainly of patches of short, multistemmed forms of canyon live oak, mountain mahogany, and deerbrush. The tree-sized canyon live oaks apparently protect their coniferous associates from high heat damage, and the rugged topography helps contain the spread of fire. If big-cone Douglas-fir is not too severely damaged or is old enough to have developed thick bark, it, unlike its relative, can resprout from the trunk and larger branches.

It is thought by some investigators that reproduction benefits from the litter-free soil and opened canopy following fire, but seedlings have been observed beginning life in duff-covered soils and, more importantly, in the deep shade of the understory. A number of researchers make the point that shade may be necessary for the regeneration of big-cone Douglas-fir. Its absence, after a burn, could be a factor in the slow return of this conifer to some fire-devastated areas. Most agree, however, that growth is slowed under shade, and the saplings respond well to increased sunlight when they finally grow up through the oak canopy.

Though both coniferous trees are found in the same general area, big-cone Douglas-fir is seldom in actual contact with Coulter pine. The latter species shares exposed ridges and hillsides with its highly combustible chaparral confederates whereas big-cone Douglas-fir and canyon live oak forests tend to perch on steep-sided, north-facing inclines or in narrow, shaded gullies that escape the full wrath of a fire storm. This preference is a nice example of ecological sorting out, a kind of gentleman's agreement—I remain where my territory and choice of broadleaf companions suit my needs; the rest I leave to you.

Two cypresses are endemic to southern California and adjacent Baja California. Both consort with chaparral and have very restricted distributions. The only known population of Cuyamaca cypress in the United States—a grove of this cypress has been reported recently from the Sierra Juarez Mountains in northern Baja California—occurs on upper King Creek from 3,000 to 4,000 feet (900–1,200 m.) on the southwest side of Cuyamaca Peak straddling the border between the Cuyamaca State Park and the Cleveland National Forest in San Diego County. Like Piute cypress, another rare species limited to the Greenhorn Mountains of Kern and southern Tulare counties, it is closely related to Arizona cypress, and some authorities claim the two species should be subspecies of the latter. It is a handsome tree with rich red bark and foliage that has a slightly bluish tinge though new growth is somewhat greener. Coulter pines are scattered through the stand whose upper edge blends into the conifers of the lower montane forest.

Tecate cypress (considered by some to be a subspecies of Guadalupe cypress, native to islands offshore Baja California) has a slightly wider distribution. One population is on the northwest slope of Sierra Peak between 1,400 and 2,600 feet (420–780 m.) in the Santa Ana Mountains, and several larger stands and isolated groups are scattered around Otay Mountain and Tecate Peak at roughly 1,000 to 4,500 feet (300–1,350 m.) in southern San Diego County and similar terrain south of the border for 150 miles (241 km.). The most accessible grove and well worth a visit is just south of old U.S. Highway 80 on a hill above the now abandoned Guatay campground. Take Interstate 8 to State Highway 79 and look for the grove to the right of the old highway about 3 miles (5 km.) east of Descanso Junction.

Both cypresses have the closed-cone habit of their relatives to the north, a feature that has enabled these species to cope with the repeated ravages of fire. Burning also provides the duff-free soil and plentiful sunlight favorable for reproduction. Too frequent fires, however, have been blamed for the attrition of Cuyamaca cypress and the dwarfing of several groups of Tecate cypress. Intense competition from the better drought-adapted chaparral has also pushed these populations into relictual status. They are remnants of more extensive tracts that flourished in preglacial times. Tecate cypress typically occupies acidic, infertile slopes that apparently discourage competing chaparral. Cuyamaca cypress is confined to a gabbro-derived substrate with high water-retaining capacity. The isolation of Tecate cypress as a community is exemplified by the presence of a number of endemics, for example, Otay manzanita and Otay ceanothus.

Of the two remaining California conifers restricted to the southern part of the state, one is a pinyon, or nut pine. Unlike the closely related one-, two-, and three-needled pinyons, it generally has four needles in each bundle. Parry, or four-leaved, pinyon extends south 220 miles (354 km.) from Riverside County into Baja California at elevations ranging from 3,500 to 6,000 feet (1,050–1,800 m.). On the desert-facing slopes of the Santa Rosa Mountains it does not appear to be part of a pinyon-juniper woodland since it most often occurs where chaparral nudges into the lower edge of the montane coniferous forest. It is also found on the eastern slope of the Laguna Mountains of San Diego County where it is scattered about with a few one-leaved pinyons. Apparently it forms more extensive woodlands in Baja California.

The final conifer endemic to the southern part of the California Floristic Province to be discussed in this section of the chapter is perhaps the least understood ecologically, primarily because of the lack of published literature, but it is widely known for its picturesque dominance of the coastal bluffs on both sides of Soledad Canyon north of Del Mar in San Diego County. Most of the Torrey pine groves on the south side of the small river valley are in a state reserve. They are justly famed for their rarity and scenic embellishment. Restricted now to the two small relict sites—the ravine-broken bluffs referred to above and Santa Rosa Island—the species is also the only true low-elevation pine in mainland southern California south of Santa Barbara County. It usually has five needles in a bundle like a number of California pines (whitebark and limber), and because of its chunky, 5-inch (13 cm.) long cones, it has been placed with Coulter and digger pines in a "big-cone" subgroup.

Torrey pine has often been cited as a primary example of a California relict species, even though no fossil cones have ever been found that would have extended its ancient range. At any rate, these tiny populations cling to their fog-wrapped maritime habitats, which approximate the more humid conditions of the mid-Tertiary when, presumably, the pines were more widespread. Both mainland and island stands are found on sandy soil, an edaphic feature which may have paleontological significance. Evidently Torrey pines are resistant to salt spray, but those more exposed to harrying onshore breeze are typically deliquescent and wind-pruned into the attractive shapes we associate with the Japanese art of bonsai. The sheltered pines, particularly those growing back from the sea on north-facing slopes, are taller and straighter.

Fire has influenced the evolution of this species, but it has not exerted as strong a selective pressure as it has on bishop or knobcone pines probably because it has not been as frequent in these coastal groves. In consequence, Torrey pine cones are only somewhat serotinous. They can open at maturity, when three years old, or persist as long as fifteen years. Seedling establishment, however, is precarious. Much of the seed crop is consumed by California ground squirrels and other rodents, and 90 percent of the seedlings that attempt establishment fail to survive through the first year. Some die from summer drought, others from fungal infestation if there is too much soil moisture. Fire has other positive roles, nevertheless; it removes competing species, reduces rodent populations, and increases soil nutrients. The San Diego groves have an undercover that varies from sparse to dense of mixed coastal sage scrub and chaparral that includes the more common brushland species—California sagebrush, toyon, scrub oak, laurel sumac, and bush sunflower. More noteworthy species are barranca-brush, endemic to San Diego County and adjacent Baja California; mission manzanita; bushrue—one of the three wild members of the citrus family in California—the less rare but the only native mainland species of rock rose; and surprisingly enough, Mojave yucca. Its presence along with a number of cacti is indicative of the low yearly rainfall averages on the San Diego coast.

Lower Montane Pine Forest. Those more familiar with the Sierra Nevada's Great Green Wall and its rich assortment of canopy and understory trees and shrubs could at first be put off by the smaller number of species and the open, relatively dry character of the forests of the southern mountains. Remember that this reflects the transitional position of Mediterranean climates. As representative species of the Pacific Northwest rainforest extend into the Klamath Mountains of the northern border, so do a few stalwart conifers such as white fir, incense cedar, and Jeffrey, sugar, Coulter, knobcone, and lodgepole pines straggle down into the mountains of northern Baja California, no farther south, however, than latitude thirty degrees.

Yellow and Jeffrey pines are the most abundant conifers of this forest in the Transverse and Peninsular ranges. The former is more characteristic of cismontane slopes, meeting Coulter pine, black oak, and assorted chaparral shrubs in a broad ecotone that varies in elevation from 4,500 to 6,500 feet (1,350–1,950 m.). Jeffrey pine, more tolerant of aridity and temperature extremes, is typical of higher, more exposed sites and, almost exclusively, the transmontane slopes of the San Bernardino Mountains and the Peninsular Range. The two species are closely related and habitually hybridize when they are in contact.

Along much of the Angeles Crest (State Highway 2) and Rim-of-the-World (State Highway 18) highways, the pines seem to hold each other at arm's length. The open stance of these generally drought-resistant conifers and the paucity of undergrowth, particularly the absence of large-leaved mesophytic shrubs, give these forests the same impression of borderline survival as the islands of pine forest in the Mono Basin east of the Sierra.

A number of factors are responsible for the comparative lack of ground cover. Much of this rugged country has been carved into steep hillsides that are rapidly eroding even in the dry season when downslope creep is common. Such unstable substrates are poor footing for the establishment of shrubby growth. Probably one limiting factor is the long dry season, interrupted only by sporadic, short-lived showers that are local and very unpredictable.

There are more mesic intervals such as on north- and east-facing sides of canyons where yellow pine is joined by big-cone Douglas-fir, incense cedar, and canyon live oak, and at higher elevations, white fir and sugar pine. The montane chaparral of these altitudes includes Eastwood and pinkbract manzanitas, bracken, deerbrush, and coffeeberry. Where Jeffrey pine is transmontane its coniferous companions may be one-leaved pinyon and mountain juniper. At higher elevations or on moister slopes its shrubby associates are those that also consort with yellow pine even if this is the drier side of the range—bush chinquapin, snowbush, greenleaf manzanita, and Parish snowberry. Great Basin sagebrush and rabbitbrush are common understory transmontane plants, reminding the visitor that the desert is not far below. Black oaks are often abundant, particularly where competing conifers have been removed by fire. Canyon live oak continues up into the forest on the south and west faces of the ranges, losing ground at about 8,000 feet (2,400 m.).

An unusual substrate has led to the development of a dozen or so relatively treeless "islands" of low-growing, sparse vegetation called pavement plains. They are scattered about on the northeast—desert side—flanks of the San Bernardino Mountains at elevations ranging from 6,000 to 7,500 feet (1,800–2,250 m.). The surrounding forest of Jeffrey pine, pinyon, mountain juniper, and mountain mahogany halts abruptly and surrenders to little tufts of Sandberg's bluegrass, basal rosettes of Parish rock cress, tiny cushions of Bear Valley buckwheat, and Bear Valley sandwort, four of the thirty-three species found on the plains. The last two plants are endemic to this substrate, testifying to the age and stability of these flat or gently sloping patches of open terrain. Confined to valleys north and south of the Big Bear-Baldwin lakes basin, they are located on remnants of an ancient, possibly Pleistocene, lake bed. The soils contain much clay, poorly drained in the wet season and dried out in summer. The resultant expansion and contraction of the substrate is partially responsible for the lack of tree seedling establishment. Other factors include frost-heave and the absence of soil litter and shade, which, particularly in the warmer months, allows the soil to heat to potentially lethal temperatures. Some pinyon and other tree seedling encroachment occurs around the edge of the plain under the shade of mature trees, but for the most part, the annuals and stunted perennials capable of coping with the harsh conditions dominate the inhospitable habitat.

Some of these fascinating bald patches can be viewed easily as from State Highway 18 around the north end of Baldwin Lake. Others can be seen on Van Duesen Canyon Road (F.R. 3N09) and Holcomb Valley Road (F.R. 3N16). Arrastre Flat on F.R. 3N04 is a particularly fine area with large expanses of the low-growing dwarf sagebrush whose small size is all the more noticeable because of the much taller Great Basin sagebrush in the nearby forest.

The word *pavement* refers to the closely packed reddish pieces of rock (Saragossa quartzite) that litter the ground. Pavements occur where a thin cover of vegetation grows on subsoils containing many rock fragments of varying sizes. The cobbles are thrust upward by alternating periods of freezing and thawing, moisture and drought. The finer soil particles are removed by the unimpeded action of water and wind, leaving the coarser, heavier fragments to settle into place on the surface.

Upper Montane Forest. The white firs and sugar pines that found comfortable outposts such as shady canyonsides and other more mesic sites in the yellow pine zone form their own community at elevations from 5,500 to 8,500 feet (1,650–2,550 m.), particularly on steep, north- and east-facing gradients. In both the San Gabriel and San Bernardino mountains it allows typically open Jeffrey pine stands to dominate the drier slopes and flats as high as 9,500 feet (2,850 m.), but it claims the moister areas for its own richer collection of trees and shrubs. Incense cedar is a frequent associate up to roughly 8,200 feet (2,460 m.). As in the eastern Sierra, mountain juniper occupies exposed ridges and high rocky slopes from 7,700 to 9,500 feet (2,310–2,850 m.) in the San Gabriel Mountains. It is especially abundant on the dry hillsides surrounding Big Bear Lake from 6,700 feet (2,010 m.) and higher. The older trees often twist as though wrenched into shape by colossal hands that in the process capriciously pulled away a limb or two and rearranged the foliage in haphazard tufts and clumps. On this desert side of the range its companions are Jeffrey pine, one-leaved pinyon, and tree-size mountain mahogany, species we have already encountered surrounding the pavement plains.

Subalpine Forest. The mountain juniper, Jeffrey pine, and white fir discussed above ascend high enough to join, here as in the Sierra, lodgepole pine, the dominant subalpine tree. From as low as 6,500 feet (1,950 m.) on shady, north-facing inclines to 8,500 feet (2,550 m.), it forms large tracts of forest that extend either to the crest of the mountain or to timberline, depending on the peak's elevation. Shrubs at these altitudes include bush chinquapin, greenleaf and Parry manzanita, snow bush, and squaw currant. Like all trees of great elevation, it huddles in stunted, twisted patches of *krummholz* where it is exposed to the cold harsh winds of winter. The only other truly timberline tree in southern California is limber pine, which finds precarious footholds in crevices between boulders or dry, rocky promontories and other timberline sites from Mount Pinos, through the San Gabriel, San Bernardino, and San Jacinto mountains to the Santa Rosa Mountains of Riverside County. It becomes *krummholz* on Mount San Gorgonio, the tallest peak in southern California.

The high elevation trees of this part of the state have some interesting statistics. The largest of all known mountain junipers is in Ice House Canyon on the cismontane side of Mount Baldy. The trunk of the tree is 47.6 feet (14.3 m.) in circumference, and it is estimated to be a venerable 3,000 years old. A lodgepole pine, reputed to be the largest known individual of its species, reaches a height of 110 feet (33 m.). It is located south of Big Bear Lake on a trail one quarter of a mile (394 m.) from the end of F.R. 2N10. Limber pines have reached the girth of over 25 feet (7.5 m.) on Mount San Gorgonio, and ages of over 1,700 years have been noted for limber pines on Mount Baden-Powell. These are enviable records for trees either at or close to the southern edge of their distribution. Reminiscent of the oldsters of the White Mountains, large portions of many of these trees are dead except for a few tufts of needles kept alive by strips of living tissue.

Only two aspen groves—the location of both groves is indicated on the U.S. Forest Service map of the San Bernardino National Forest—remain in the southern mountains. One is on Fish Creek just south of Heart Bar State Park, and the other is a tiny patch in a gully below F.R. 2N04, southeast of Big Bear Lake and just north of State Highway 38. The author was lucky indeed that the owner of the four-wheel-drive camper she was in happened to pause at just the right place on a barely negotiable forest track. The grove was visible several hundred feet (100 m.) below, the twinkling green leaves and white bark unmistakable through binoculars. These isolated bits are all the more remarkable in light of the fact that sizable patches of aspen occur far to the south in the San Pedro Martir Mountains of Baja California.

Mountain Meadow. Only San Gorgonio was glaciated during the Pleistocene and not very much at that. The other mountainous areas of southern California escaped the fingers of ice that scrubbed into peaks and ridges or carved *U*-shaped canyons in other ranges of the West, depriving them of the legacy of lakes and meadows that enriches the high country elsewhere. A few basins and stream valley floors—for example, Barton Flats on the upper Santa Ana River—in the San Bernardino and San Jacinto mountains support the lush green growth of summer-moist habitat. So-called snow melt gullies are more typical of the San Gabriel Mountains on north-facing slopes in white fir-sugar pine-lodgepole pine forests. In such moist places, often called *cienegas,* one can see summertime landscapes whose colors range from the pink of shooting star to the green-and-white of corn lilies and the blue of flag iris and the lavender of lupine. These bright openings, especially if surrounded by thick forest with a dense understory, most closely resemble the rich assortment of Sierran vegetation. Even tiny seepage streaks along trail and highway or the banks of small streams have flourishing displays of scarlet monkeyflower and red-and-yellow columbine. In damp draws and gullies riparian vegetation includes several willows and black cottonwood up to an altitude of 7,500 feet (2,250 m.), but big-leaf maple and white alder rarely extend above 6,500 feet (1,950 m.).

Alpine Rock Fields. Semibarren patches have developed on the tops of Mount Baldy and Mount San Gorgonio. Such characteristic cushion and basal rosette plants as Kennedy buckwheat and pumice hulsea and the shrubbier mountain heather (farthest south location) and littleleaf cream bush hug the rocky surface between the scattered prostrate conifers that have managed to reach the summit. Interlocking patches of lichens cover the scattered boulders.

Those wishing to see with a minimum of inconvenience the representative conifers of southern California's forests would do well to take three trips. There is some overlap, but all three are enjoyable, easily reached by freeway, and take no more than one day each. For the City Creek-Baldwin Lake trip, leave Interstate 10 at State Highway 30 and drive north to its junction with State Highway 330. Continue east on that road until it meets State Highway 18, which will take you to State Highway 38 at the west end of Big Bear Lake. Drive on the north side to Baldwin Lake and return on State Highway 38, the long but scenically attractive route through Barton Flats, or continue down into the desert on State Highway 18, where Joshua trees reach uncharacteristic altitudes, or complete the Rim-of-the-

World extension to Lake Arrowhead on the same highway. From here there are a number of roads which eventually have access to the Interstate 15 system.

The author suggests the City Creek (State Highway 330)-State Highway 18-State Highway 38 route because three of the important lower elevation conifers are immediate to the road, easily recognizable, and are nicely snuggled into their most typical habitats. Because a fire swept through the area some years ago, chubby young knobcone pines are now beginning to overtop the returning chaparral. A number of picturesque old fellows are perched on rocky promontories, their branches gesturing as if to invite the photographer to pose them against the blue of the mountain sky. Mingling with them at about 4,000 feet (1,200 m.) are the taller, longer-needled Coulter pines, which continue another 2,000 to 3,000 feet (600–900 m.) higher on the dry slopes that both species find comfortable. In gullies and other shady places big-cone Douglas-fir thrusts up its spindlelike trunks through thickets of canyon live oak. At about 5,000 feet (1,500 m.) black oak and yellow pine become noticeable, but white fir, incense cedar, and sugar pine wait until about 6,500 feet (1,950 m.) where they begin to replace Coulter pine. The forest continues, varying more open hillsides with shadier patches, until a pronounced shift begins on the north shore of Big Bear Lake. The desert influence becomes apparent as Jeffrey pine now meets mountain juniper and some higher outliers of pinyon on the dry margin of the montane coniferous forest. If you wish to see the pavement plains described earlier, look for them via the forest roads leading to and through Holcomb Valley north of the lake or continue to the north shore of Baldwin Lake. To find lodgepole pine in this vicinity, one reference suggests a stand at the southwest corner of Big Bear Lake not far from the dam.

If you missed this pine on the preceding trip, we urge driving the Angeles Crest Highway (State Highway 2), accessible from Interstate 210 in La Cañada, north of Glendale. It is a long, winding but well worthwhile drive with picnicking and camping breaks in forests that, by and large, are open and often free of brushy undergrowth, particularly on the drier slopes. One of these recreation spots, appropriately named Lodgepole Pine Picnic Area, has a short trail leading out to a small stand of these higher elevation pines. If you drive on and park in the lot provided at Blue Ridge Summit, look west at

Mount Baden-Powell. Even the naked eye can pick out the limber pines scattered on its upper slopes.

For a closer look at this timberline tree, a third trip is recommended. Going north on Interstate 5, pass Gorman and take the turnoff to Frazier Park. Continue west following, incidentally, the San Andreas Fault (watch for sag ponds along the way) to the well-marked turnoff to Mount Pinos Recreation Area. The pinyons which have accompanied you for several miles (kilometers) give way to Jeffrey pine at about 6,000 feet (1,800 m.). Black oak and canyon live oak are in evidence along with white fir. Incense cedar and sugar pine are noticeably absent, and though the forest is dense in places, it is poor in species representation. The three places worth a pause are at or near the summit. The paved road ends at a magnificent meadow, one of the best in southern California. In early summer it is splendid with lupine, blue flag iris, and corn lilies. A short trail around the meadow leads to a picnic and camp site, which by late July has a vivid display of scarlet penstemon. This is hummer heaven, and the bird watchers will have their binoculars out faster than one can say *Stellula calliope*.

Any car with sufficient clearance and good shock absorbers can negotiate the dirt road—1.7 miles (2.7 km.)—leading to the summit. One enjoyable experience is guaranteed—the feel of timberline, the bright, windy world of the high country. Here is a delightful grove of old, gnarled limber pine with a few storm-harassed Jeffrey pines and white firs. In the rocky meadow around and under the trees, mats of spreading phlox and little plants such as dwarf lousewort and Pursh's sheeppod contribute a distinctly alpine character to this most accessible of all the high peaks of southern California.

The other experience is not guaranteed, but if it occurs, it is unforgettable. This is an official California condor lookout, one of the few places where one can hope, but only that, to get a glimpse of one of the world's rarest birds.

Though there appears to be some confusion in the public mind about what kind of a bird it is, the California condor belongs to the American vulture family. It includes seven carrion-feeding species—Andean condor, California condor, king vulture, yellow-headed vulture, greater yellow-headed vulture, turkey vulture, and black vulture. The population of our famous bird has dwindled to between twenty and thirty in number, steadily losing ground because of shooting, death from eating poisoned animals, human disturbance while attempting to breed and during other sensitive times, loss of major feeding areas, and a naturally slow reproductive rate. Even under optimum conditions, each pair only produces one chick every two years. Like many of California's rare and endemic species, the condor is a relict whose range once extended from British Columbia to Baja California and across the continent to Texas and Florida. Its present hunting grounds are confined to the southern Sierra and the Tehachapi Mountains west to the Mount Pinos-Frazier Mountain complex and the mountainous country in northern Ventura County and eastern Santa Barbara County. Two reserves have been established in the Los Padres National Forest—the Sespe Condor Sanctuary and the smaller Sisquoc Condor Sanctuary. They contain most of the known nesting sites, which are usually in rocky crevices and small caves.

Condors have the largest wingspread (9 feet—2.7 m.) of any North American land birds, and they use their huge wings magnificently. Taking advantage of the numerous updrafts in their rugged homegrounds, once airborne, they soar with effortless grace over the conifers and brush of mountain crests and canyons. California condors are unmistakable once they are close enough for the observer to note a few details. The head is bare and usually reddish in color, and it is much larger than that of the more common turkey vulture. Seen from beneath, other distinctive features of the mature bird are a large patch of white on the undersurface of the wing and slotted primary wing feathers.

Because this unique creature is so close to extinction, several projects to ensure its preservation have been proposed. One advocates capturing subadults to begin a supervised breeding program. Organizations opposed to this plan because of the well-known sensitivity of this species to human interference suggest upgrading the environment to provide sufficient food and protection. And there are those who feel that all such efforts will, in the long run, be in vain and the condors should be allowed a dignified exit from a now too-hostile world.

Channel Islands

22. Outward

Most of the material in the preceding two chapters has been confined to the plants of southern California, admittedly because they are the most obvious indicators of changes in climate, soils, and the other factors that determine the structure of natural communities. Each of the biotic units of the southern part of the state also has typical animal members. Many of them are the same species as those occurring in central and northern California. Wrentits and rufous-sided towhees slip in and out of the chaparral of both the Santa Monica Mountains and the foothills of Eldorado County. The lodgepole chipmunk is just as agile a stump-jumper in the San Bernardino Mountains as it is in the Tuolumne Meadows. There are, however, some pronounced changes in the distribution of California's terrestrial vertebrates from north to south, coast to desert. Many of these patterns are even more complex because of one of California's most famed biotic features, its wealth of endemic species. Before we cope with the evolutionary challenges of the Channel Islands, it might be well to take a brief look at some of these configurations of dispersal.

Like all living organisms, our vertebrate species live in environments to which they have adapted. Some consist of small populations that are restricted to just one area, for example, the endemic Mount Lyell shrew and limestone salamander of the central Sierra Nevada. Others have broad tolerance ranges that allow them to occupy a number of habitats at various altitudes over large geographical areas of North America—coyote and mule deer. Many species such as the dipper, a bird that lives near and feeds in fast-flowing streams, are widespread but are confined to a particular habitat within their range.

A large group of organisms takes advantage of California's peculiar geographical position, sharing as it does neighboring biotic regions—Pacific Northwest, Great Basin, and Southwestern desert. Like our flora, our fauna is enriched by species typical of these regions whose corners and edges spill over the political borders of California. The amphibians, about which we shall have more to say later, give us three examples. The northwestern salamander lives on the humid coast from southeastern Alaska to its southernmost extension in Sonoma County; the range of the Great Basin spadefoot toad includes the sagebrush scrub and pinyon-juniper woodland just west of the Nevada border; the red-spotted toad of the Southwest and southern plains is locally confined to the Mojave and Colorado deserts. Many species are more widely distributed but are restricted to certain latitudinal ranges. A number of inhabitants typical of the central and northern portions of the state are absent from the southern section, and the reverse is true as well. The Sierra's pika, Douglas squirrel, and Belding ground squirrel do not occur in the southern mountains, and a large group of amphibians, including twelve endemic species, are limited to the northern half of California. On the other hand, many species of mammals and reptiles, adjusted to dry environments, keep to the southern half.

The majority of both the plants and animals of California are shared with other areas of the West, but the presence of species typical of such contrasting environments as the north humid forest and the Southwestern desert is only partly responsible for the biotic diversity that is such a hallmark of California's natural heritage. The other contributor is endemism—the pro-liferation of unique species and subspecies that inevitably make detailed distribution maps of our fauna look like jigsaw puzzles. We have met such developmental patterns before, particularly in regard to our native pines and oaks.

The parent form evolved into a group of related organisms, each with its own distinguishing features and limited to a char-acteristic range. As these genetically different types bubbled up out of the gene pool, they spread into that part of the sur-rounding environment for which they were suited. If isolated by physical or biological factors from other related popula-tions, they continued to maintain these differential traits, be-coming at last new taxonomic units. A case in point is the slen-der salamander, or the genus *Batrachoseps*. This amphibian is often called the "worm salamander" because of its slimness and grooves in its skin that give it a segmented appearance. Like most amphibians, it requires moist surroundings like damp places in underground passages dug by other creatures or beneath pieces of wood or rocks.

Salamanders are largely restricted to north temperate re-gions. Those present in both the New and Old World tropics appear to favor higher, cooler altitudes. Slender salamanders belong to the lungless salamander family, which is believed to have originated in the eastern part of North America. Five gen-era of lungless salamanders occur in California. Two of them—*Plethodon* and *Aneides*—are common east of the Mississippi River and are thought to have migrated to the West millions of years ago. The parent form that produced *Batrachoseps* and *En-satina* reached western North America during the early Ter-tiary when woodland and forest covered much of the area. At present these two genera are confined to California, northern Baja California, and Oregon. A fifth genus, *Hydromates*, has five species, three in California and the other two in Europe, a most astonishing example of disjunction!

Using new techniques of genetic research, several investiga-tions have led to the construction of a possible "scenario" for the speciation of slender salamanders. Presumably, the various types of this genus began radiating from the interior of southern California when it was warmer and wetter than at present, and neotropical vegetation was abundant. Subsequent geomorphic changes and the drying out of the climate tended to isolate populations and stimulate specific differentiation. By 10 million years ago (early Pliocene) the ancestor of the Oregon and Inyo slender salamanders was east of the hills that preceded the Sierra Nevada. The line leading to the Kern and Tehachapi species was established around the southern end of the protorange, and the forebears of the Pacific and California slender salamanders had already evolved along with the ancestral form of *B. nitriventris*, a newly recognized species that ranges from Orange County to southern Monterey County. It is believed to have occupied the woodlands and savanna present at that time in what is now the Mojave Desert. It also extended along a portion of the coast of that epoch. The forerunner of the California slender salamander had moved to a mixed evergreen forest north of the then submerged Sacramento Valley, and the form that gave rise to the Pacific slender salamander and its subspecies extended coastwise from central California down to Baja California. (A new classification, based on this research, reduces the relictual and garden slender salamanders to subspecies of the Pacific slender salamander.)

Tectonic activity along the San Andreas and other faults continued to rearrange thoroughly the geography of coastal California. The offshore archipelago, part of the ancestral base of the Coast Ranges, began to coalesce, forming large islands and peninsulas that isolated segments of the biota present at the time. These geomorphic changes and increasing aridity, by restricting populations, encouraged speciation. At the end of the Pliocene selective pressure from these environmental modifications produced most of the known species and subspecies of slender salamanders that have evolved from the five basic genetic strains. The Ice Age, coincidental with mountain uplift and other physiographic fluctuations such as the closing of seaways and the establishment of land connections, on the one hand, assisted isolation, and, on the other, expansion and recontact of the various populations. The spread of the garden subspecies through the Transverse Range at this time probably gave rise to yet another species, the desert slender salamander, now a relict restricted to a palm oasis in Riverside County.

The slender salamanders contribute seven of the forty-six species of amphibians now listed as occurring in California. (Please bear in mind that the numbers used in this discussion of California vertebrates are approximate in that no authority seems to agree with all his colleagues on just how many species of particular animals occur in California, let alone what they are and how they should be named.) Twenty-one types of salamanders, toads, and frogs are found in southern California, but only seven are restricted to this part of the state. These statistics have interesting implications. More than half of the amphibians of California do not occur this far south. Like the slender salamanders—only two are presently found in southern California—they are not equipped to cope with the increasing aridity, unreliability of precipitation, and the relative absence of suitable habitat. Some such as the red-bellied newt are endemic to the humid northwest region of the state. Others are species characteristic of Puget Sound and coastal British Columbia and extend south as far as the north coastal counties. The fact that of the fifteen species endemic to California twelve are limited to the northern half of the state is additionally indicative of the northern concentration of amphibious forms.

Of the seven that are confined to the southern half of California, six are desert species. One is the endemic desert slender salamander; the other five are common throughout much of the arid West. Several such as Woodhouse's toad and the Colorado River toad tend to depend on the moisture resources of that great desert river, including bottomlands and irrigation canals. Others, such as the red-spotted toad, are less restricted and are found in many places in the desert where open water is available for breeding—rainpools or where permanent water in streams, irrigation ditches, oases, and the like is present.

The general pattern of concentrations of certain species and attrition as distance widens from the center of distribution is repeated many times among the vertebrates of western North America but with numerous variations. The preponderance of amphibians in the northern and central parts of the state is more than counterbalanced by the greater number of reptiles in the south, augmented as it is by the strictly desert types. Though reptiles occur throughout much of the world, they have proliferated in its warmer regions, and many have adapted in physiology, morphology, and behavior to dry climates as well. About eighty-four species of reptiles live in or make an occasional appearance in the state or its off-shore waters, such as green turtles that have been found near warmwater discharge outlets. Some seventy occur in southern California, and of these, thirty-four are restricted here and to neighboring desert states. They occupy the full range of available habitats with perhaps the exception of timberline and above. Some range widely throughout much of the state as part of a broader distribution in the West, for example, western fence lizard. Others are very restricted such as the small-scaled lizard that barely nudges into the Peninsular Range from Baja California. A few are lowland forms—the San Joaquin blunt-nosed leopard lizard (officially declared endangered as are many of our endemics)—and many like the handsome red, yellow, and black mountain kingsnake, which extends from Oregon to Baja California, prefer higher elevations. This species is an excellent example of reptilian genetic diversity. It has differentiated into five subspecies, each occupying its own stretch of upland. The Coachella Valley fringe-toed lizard is one of few reptilian full species endemic to California, though several species have very limited occurrences outside of the state. The reptiles, as do the amphibians, exhibit distribution gradients from cool and damp to warm and dry environments, though in the opposite direction. It is probable that many of our desert forms became established in southern California only after the retreat of the Pleistocene glaciers when the climate became warmer and drier.

The mobility of birds tends to free them from narrow geographic restrictions. As a result only a few are endemic to the California Biotic Province—wrentit, California thrasher, yellow-billed magpie, and Nuttall's woodpecker. Much of our avifauna is seasonal and spends only a part of the year in the state. Some species only pass through. They breed in the north and spend the winter south of the Mexican border. Others also nest in more northern latitudes, but they overwinter in California. A third group arrives to nest here in the summer but migrates south in the fall. These are the regulars, species which one would expect to see each year. The accidentals, the rare types so coveted by life-list-keeping birdwatchers, seem to increase in number each year and to expand their ranges. It has become almost commonplace to see what used to be considered unusual birds such as the black-and-white warbler, particularly in the migratory seasons. Some of the more casual visitors are more common along the coast in spring and tend to appear in the interior in the fall. Though many vagrants seem to turn up more frequently in particular locations such as the Tijuana

River bottom and Point Loma in San Diego County, perhaps because these are favorite haunts for sharp-eyed birders, they can appear anywhere—the Farallon Islands, Scotty's Castle in Death Valley, Pacific Grove in the Monterey area, and even one's own backyard. (The author claims a broad-billed hummingbird in her garden on Mount Washington in Los Angeles.)

Resident birds account for only 31 percent of California's avifauna. Only a few species such as the common raven range widely through the state, making use of many natural communities from sea level to timberline. Some are statewide but have strong habitat preferences, for example, meadowlarks and red-winged blackbirds. The former frequent open areas of natural grassland or cultivated fields; the latter rely on marshy places for nesting but commonly feed in surrounding croplands or natural environments. A number of these species are sedentary and rarely move from their homegrounds—the acorn woodpecker of oak woodlands and the brown towhee of brush and scrub. A third group breeds in the mountains of the state but migrates downward and at times south for the cooler season. It includes red-breasted nuthatches and ruby-crowned kinglets. A number of resident birds such as Lewis' woodpecker breed in northern California and on occasion overwinter in the south. Still others such as the ruddy duck move from the interior to spend the cool season on coastal lagoons or cismontane freshwater ponds and lakes. Several species are true desert residents and are rarely seen away from their special environment—ladder-backed woodpecker and Gambel's quail. Counterpart species, in this case, Nuttall's woodpecker and California quail, take their places in the western part of the state and are, by and large, cismontane. They are examples of oft-noted patterns of species replacement in adjacent but differing environments. A few residents are confined to specific localities within the state. The "gray-crowned" rosy finch is an alpine species widely distributed through Alaska, the Rocky Mountains, the Cascades, and the Sierrra. Whether the "gray-crowned" rosy finch ever lived in the mountains of southern California is debatable, but at present they do not. Like many Arctic-alpine plants and animals, it is possible they never did reach the southern ranges, even during the Ice Age. They gray jay and ruffed grouse are also confined to the northernmost part of the state.

A number of resident species have been differentiated into

recognizable taxonomic units. At least fourteen subspecies of song sparrow have been described for California. Some are desert and valley; others are coastal and mountain, and migratory patterns further complicate matters. Nevertheless, they provide other examples of the vertebrate mosaic with which we are becoming so familiar.

Southern California again appears to be the winner in the numbers contest. The avifauna is enriched by a dozen or so southwestern and tropical species such as the Gila woodpecker, zone-tailed hawk, and great-tailed grackle that regularly visit or may even breed in the Colorado Desert. The Salton Sea and the lower Colorado River regularly attract postbreeding blue-footed boobies, roseate spoonbills, and other tropical species.

The supremacy of southern California in terms of both reptiles and birds reverses for mammals. Of the 157 species of native mainland nonmarine mammals, ninety-six occur both in southern California and elsewhere in the northern two-thirds of the state. Twenty-two are restricted to southern California, but sixty-four are not found here. The state as a whole is rich in mammalian endemics, additional examples of genetic diversification.

There are five genera in the New World rodent family, Heteromyidae. These are pocket mice, kangaroo rats, kangaroo mice, and two genera of spiny pocket mice, which are confined mostly to Middle America and northern South America. Contrary to what their common names imply, the entire group is more closely related to ground squirrels and pocket gophers than to mice and rats. The two species of kangaroo mice are restricted to the Great Basin, but pocket mice and kangaroo rats are widespread throughout much of the drier West and are worth a little further exploration.

Both are burrow dwellers and have fur-lined external cheek pouches in which they carry seed, their principal source of food, but the kangaroo rats are larger, hop about on elongated hind legs, and rely on moisture metabolically derived from their granivorous diet, though several species appear to supplement this with juicy leaves during the breeding season. Pocket mice also rely upon metabolized water, but they are smaller and quadripedal in motion. Many smaller heteromyids hibernate or enter interrupted torpor during the cool season, particularly when food is scarce.

The family evolved during the mid-Tertiary, the pocket mice in the early Miocene and the kangaroo rats later. At present, species of both extend to southwestern Canada and down into Mexico. Of the twenty-six species of pocket mice, more than one half—fourteen—occur in the Californias, and nine are endemic to this region. Ten species occur in Arizona, but only one is restricted to that state and neighboring Sonora. Kangaroo rats have a similar pattern of distribution. Twenty-two species have been described for the arid and semi-arid West. Eighteen occur in either Baja California or California or both, of which twelve are restricted to these states.

The evolutionary expansion of the family appears to have begun in the grasslands, scrubs, and dry woodlands which in the mid-Tertiary dominated much of what is now the drier West and northern Mexico. Fossil remains of Miocene pocket mice have been recorded in such widely separated areas as Nebraska and California. As precipitation decreased east of the rising major mountain chains, the heteromyids adapted to ever increasing environmental stress. Speciation continued. Some forms have wide ranges, covering much of the dry western interior. Others are endemics, kept in pockets isolated from the gene flow. Where many species coexist, a number of strategies allow them to avoid excessive competition for limited resources. The seed-eating pocket mice and kangaroo rats compete with other granivores—birds, insects, and other rodents. Aggressive reaction to potential competitors is one behavioral response. Also important are preferences in food and substrate. Vegetation type and density, differences in the manner of food-getting, and success in avoiding predators are significant factors.

Competition between heteromyids appears intense, particularly where several species occur in the same habitat. Though there is overlap, well-developed niche structures allow efficient use of resources. Because of their agile bipedality, the larger kangaroo rats forage for widely scattered clumps of seeds that collect in more open terrain, while the smaller pocket mice scurry about hunting for seeds in denser vegetation. This division of territory is illustrated by a study of four pocket mice in Arizona. Silky pocket mice preferred low, fairly dense grass, and hispid mice utilized dense, high grass. Bailey and desert species were "bush mice," needing brush cover.

Eventually the heteromyids encountered the great diversity of habitats now present in both Californias as well as the geographical barriers of intervening mountain ranges, large valley troughs, and the sea that now cuts off most of Baja California and the western edge of California from terrestrial contact. Populations were isolated because of changes in landform and climate, and selective pressure completed the process of evolutionary development.

At last we are ready to begin our journey to those offshore jewels, the Channel Islands. Rounding the breakwater that protects the harbor from the open ocean, we can begin to look for the various marine mammals that enrich California's fauna. The cetaceans most often encountered are those graceful charmers, the common and the bottle-nosed dolphins. Two larger members of the family, killer whale and false killer whale, also live in the eastern Pacific waters but are less frequently seen. Seven other dolphins make appearances, but as many of them are most numerous in tropical waters, they are rare. Several other species visit alongshore—Dall's and harbor porpoises and, on occasion, the pilot whale, or "blackfish."

The gray whale is the cetacean everyone interested in California's wildlife wants to see. Of the twelve species of whale that enter our coastal waters, only a few can be viewed with any regularity—minke, hump-backed, and the Pacific gray. This last species has become of great interest to the public largely because of its migratory predictability in terms of numbers, time, and route, and publicity arising from its close escape from extinction. As a result, several sportsfishing enterprises in San Pedro and other nearby harbors schedule "whale-watch" cruises during the months of gray whale migration. They usually have trained naturalists on board to help identify marine mammals and discuss their habits and behavior. (Be prepared—the water is often rough, and seasickness can ruin any pleasure in viewing these splendid creatures.) It is an exhilarating experience! The anticipation and excitement of boarding is contagious. Everyone hopes for a close look at one if not several gray whales. The more knowledgeable cannot help but wish to see the animal breaching, that is, jumping out of the water to turn over and fall back with a great splash. More commonplace sights are spouts as atomized sea water is blown skyward when the giant creature explosively exhales air from its lungs through a blowhole on top of its head in preparation for breathing in fresh air. This accomplished, it dives or engages in a series of dives, often with a wonderful display of its tail flukes as it plunges for descent. Once down, it idles or swims until it needs to replenish its supply of oxygen. Then up, "there she blows!" and the little cruise vessels, usually several out at a time, turn as quickly as possible to catch up with the great beasts.

The migratory routes of the gray whale were well known during the last century when whalers twice pursued it to the point of near demise. Not a toothed species, it spends the summer in the Bering Sea feeding on amphipods and other bottom-dwelling crustaceans, which it strains through plates of whalebone, or baleen. The whales are fat and ready for their long trek south in early fall, and by November the first few are seen off the California coast. Finally, they arrive at their destination, the quiet waters of Scammons Lagoon and other lagoons in Baja California. Mating having taken place in the previous winter season (the gestation period is roughly eleven months long), the calves are born in these protected stretches of warm, calm water behind barrier sand bars. In a month or two they are ready to depart for northern seas, the newborn calves swimming alongside their mothers. It has been warmly debated as to whether or not they feed in the lagoons or en route to their summer and winter destinations. Aerial surveillance has disclosed that some food is taken from the floor of the lagoons, but over 90 percent of their food intake occurs during the months spent in their Arctic feeding grounds.

One of the author's most delightful memories is awakening at dawn on a tuna clipper anchored in Scammons Lagoon. Literally hundreds of whales were either "spy-hopping," balancing on their tails while slowly lifting their bodies straight out of the shallow water, or blowing silvery plumes against the light of the just-rising sun. Access to some of these lagoons is controlled at present, but the persevering can join tours that sail, drive, or fly down for memorable times observing these huge but gentle creatures.

Whichever Channel island you choose to visit, somehow it is unexpected. You know it is out there, you should be rising land soon, but suddenly there it is, ephemeral in the morning mist. Its subtle solidity seems to be a piece of California torn from some rugged coastline and dropped with a splash into the encircling sea foam. Here and there steep-sided canyons empty out to pockets of narrow sandy or rock-strewn beaches, separated by huge cliffs where only a few sea birds and stunted shrubs find a foothold.

Four of the eight—Anacapa, Santa Cruz, Santa Rosa, and San Miguel—are neatly aligned west of Point Mugu and are referred to as the northern Channel Islands. The other four— Santa Catalina, Santa Barbara, San Nicolas, and San Clemente—are the corners of a rectangle south of Santa Monica Bay. Three of the islands comprise the Channel Islands National Park—Anacapa, Santa Barbara, and San Miguel. Ninety percent of Santa Cruz Island is owned by the Santa Cruz Island Company. The current arrangement is that at a future date this portion will become the property of The Nature Conservancy. Access at present is confined to a limited area along the north shore. Visits can be made through special arrangement with The Nature Conservancy. Santa Catalina was for many years the private domain of the Wrigley family, but in 1975 the family gave 86 percent of the island to a nonprofit foundation, the Santa Catalina Island Conservancy (no relationship to the national organization), which presently has jurisdiction. Santa Rosa Island remains in private hands, and San Nicolas and San Clemente are under the control of the U.S. Navy.

Another collection of islands is scattered off the coast of northern Baja California from Los Coronados Islands off Tijuana to Cedros Island off Viscaino Bay. Many of them have plants and animals that are closely related to or are the same as species on the Channel Islands, and apparently most, with the exception of the volcanic Guadalupe Island, share the same geologic history. Collectively, they are all known as the California Islands.

For a time it was thought that these dramatic bits of California were merely westward extensions of the Transverse and Peninsular ranges. They are now believed to have a somewhat different origin and are part of what is called the California Borderland. During the mid-Tertiary the coastal slope and offshore shelf were broken into a series of basins and ridges because of a change in the interaction between the Pacific Plate and the North American Continental Plate. One began to slide past the other instead of converging, creating tectonic stress. Volcanic activity accompanied this crustal movement.

In following epochs local uplift fluctuated with subsidence, alternately emptying and flooding basins, raising and lowering ridges. The Palos Verdes Peninsula, the headlands upon which the Del Mar groves of Torrey pines are located, and possibly the Santa Monica Mountains were part of an archipelago as were offshore rises that are now inundated. The Ventura and Los Angeles basins were periodically underwater from the Pliocene to comparatively recent times. The islands were even larger thousands of years ago, but the postglacial rise in sea level drowned their edges and separated the four northern islands, which for a time were part of one large mass. Wave-cut terraces have been considered indicative of fluctuations in sea level during the Pleistocene when it rose and fell in accordance with the growth and shrinkage of the great ice masses, but because of differences in elevation and other inconsistencies, it is now thought that the uncoordinated rise and subsidence of individual crustal blocks could also help account for these distinctive features.

It appears the islands are not merely eroded chunks of mainland ranges projecting into the ocean. Rather, these intransigent morsels of rock are evidence of a long and complex history of crustal movement in what amounts to a mini-basin-and-range province that includes features of the present shoreline as well as the California Islands. In other words, what we see today are the tips of only a few of the many knolls, banks, and ridges that, with the interlying basins, comprise the continental borderland. Whether or not there was a Pleistocene land bridge connecting the northern Channel Islands to the mainland has long been a subject of controversy and conjecture. This will be covered later when we discuss some of the problems arising from the distribution of certain extant and fossil species.

Now that we have some background for understanding why the islands are there, we can raise other questions. What organisms live there, and where did they come from? For starters: three handsome trees that occur nowhere else in the world, a hundred or so other endemic plants, impressive groves of tree-size chaparral shrubs, and more species of pinnipeds (seals and their relatives) than anywhere else on the Pacific Coast of North America, south of Alaska. Why this richness of unusual species on these small humps of land? Our old friend, isolation, along with geographical location and its partner, climate, are primarily responsible. The islands share the same climatic regime as the mainland—cool, wet winters and warm, dry summers, but it is modified by the surrounding sea. Average annual temperature fluctuations are small, frost is quite rare, and fog reduces the effect of summer heat and drought. Prevailing winds, chilled by contact with the sea surface, also lower air temperatures, particularly on the smaller outer islands and the exposed sides of the larger ones. There is some difference in precipitation from north to south. It varies from a yearly average of 20 inches (52 cm.) on Santa Cruz to 10.5 inches (27 cm.) on San Clemente.

It is widely accepted that this maritime climate accounts for the presence of such relictual species as bishop pine on Santa Rosa and Santa Cruz and the endemic ironwood on Santa Catalina, Santa Rosa, Santa Cruz, and San Clemente. Both trees were abundant in woodlands that dominated much of southern California during the gentle climate of the mid-Tertiary (Miocene). As the great drying trend continued, it restricted both species to the only places in California with an acceptably equable climate, the coast and the offshore archipelago. The pine was able to maintain small populations on the mainland, but island ironwood is now strictly insular. There are two subspecies. The Santa Rosa, Santa Cruz, and San Clemente populations have markedly incised leaves, which appear to resemble fossils of this species found in the mainland interior. The other subspecies is restricted to Santa Catalina, and its unpatterned leaf margins are like those of fossil remains discovered in coastal California.

The Channel Islands are different in size, position, amounts of precipitation, soil type, and topography. As a result, the natural communities they support vary as well. Taking them as a group, about ten community types occur somewhere among them—tide pool, beach and dune, coastal salt marsh, coastal sage scrub, maritime cactus (succulent) scrub, chaparral, grassland, riparian woodland, oak woodland, and closed-cone pine forest. Regardless of the large number of endemics, the communities themselves are much poorer than they are on the mainland. The Santa Monica Mountains have 312 genera of terrestrial plants; Santa Cruz and Santa Catalina are each listed as having 237, the largest number among the eight islands.

The insular seaweeds, however, are as rich and diverse as those of the mainland southern coast and for the same reason. As mentioned in Chapter 1, the eastward trend of the continental edge from Point Conception south modifies the effect of the cold California Current, which continues equatorward west of that great curve of shoreline often referred to as the Southern California Bight. The offshore system of islands and submerged banks, probably augmented by certain conditions of wind speed and direction, produces eddies or changes in the flow pattern of the California Current. Some are small and short-lived, but one is more persistent. This is the Southern California Eddy, formed as part of the California Current swings eastward offshore Ensenada and flows north up into the Southern California Bight.

It is most developed in summer and fall, and, as this countercurrent is relatively weak, it stagnates alongshore to become much warmer than the parent current. The eddy continues northwest until it meets the cooler, south-moving main stream at Point Conception. This mingling creates local counterclockwise swirls that bring cooler water to the northern sides of Santa Rosa and Santa Cruz.

The sea life of the Southern California Bight is affected in several ways. Nutrient enrichment is provided by the movement of upwelling and eddying water, greatly increasing the supply of plankton, and the temperature gradient between the two currents alters the composition of both mainland and insular marine organisms. The most striking result of the meeting of cool and warm water off the southwest corner of Santa Barbara County is the richness of both algae and invertebrates. It is a transition zone which the northern species enter to be stopped from southern expansion by encountering the warmth of the Southern California Eddy, and many southern species are prevented from northward invasion because of the colder California Current. The interisland distribution of these organisms appears to be based upon these thermal gradients. The outer islands—San Miguel and San Nicolas—are surrounded by cooler water, and their intertidal life has more northern species than southern. Santa Catalina and San Clemente, on the other hand, are exposed to warmer water, and their percentage of southern species is correspondingly higher. The remaining islands have intermediate population trends, indicative of the mixing of water temperatures in their vicinity. Because of differences in substrate type and stability, length of exposure to desiccation, range of water temperature, nutrient availability, and degree of human disturbance and pollution, insular tidal life is in general richer and more prolific than on the mainland. Today some of the thickest beds of the southern sea palms occur offshore Santa Catalina. Cursory glimpses into the depleted tide pools around the Palos Verdes Peninsula and, by contrast, into those of Anacapa, for example, confirm this, but one wonders how long the pristine abundance of island tidal organisms can withstand the intensified pressure of more and more visitor use. It is hoped that the relative isolation of the Channel Islands will continue to protect these vulnerable resources.

Most of them have active dunes, particularly on sites exposed to the prevailing northwesterly winds. Much of San Miguel is covered by dunes that have advanced clear across the island from the windward side. These areas support characteristic strand and dune species such as sand verbena, beach silverweed, sea rocket, sea fig, and ice plant, an aggressive invader that by increasing the salt content of the soil discourages native plants. Two species, bush lupine and a form of beach primrose, introduce northern elements into typically southern assemblages.

A few patches of coastal salt marsh occur on the larger islands. Pickleweed, *Frankenia, Jaumea,* sea blite, several saltbushes, and salt grass have been recorded on Santa Catalina. Small mud flats are also located on Santa Rosa and San Nicolas.

Once up on the bluffs and headlands we begin to encounter some of the endemics for which the islands are noted—Saint Catherine's lace, a large, spectacular buckwheat of Santa Catalina, San Clemente, and Santa Barbara, island tarweed, and silver-lace, a shrubby perennial of the daisy family restricted to the Channel Islands. Joining them are many plants typical of southern mainland coastal bluffs—giant coreopsis—and some species restricted to northern sea cliffs—seaside daisy and golden yarrow, again reflecting the influence of cooler sea surface temperatures off some of the islands.

About one hundred species are presently considered to be indigenous only to the California Islands. The list was longer at one time, but mainland representatives are being continually discovered, much to the consternation of many amateur and professional naturalists for whom these islands have their own special appeal. They help compensate for a poverty of species and give certain communities a unique character. The flora as a whole is considered to be relictual, but it appears that a few genera have developed species that are restricted to the islands. This is not surprising as it has long been recognized that islands are natural laboratories of evolution. Surrounded by water, they are among the most isolated of all geographical features. We know from previous discussions of speciation that populations of organisms segregated from each other tend to differentiate. Thus, the Channel Islands, even though they are close to the continental shoreline, should not only have produced some endemic species, but each island should have evolved a number of its own unique organisms. As it happens, they have, and one example is live-forever, a group of succulent plants widely distributed on sea bluffs and xeric sites from Oregon to Baja California. Of the nine types found in the Channel Islands, seven are endemic species or subspecies. Two are restricted to Santa Rosa, one to Santa Catalina, one to Santa Barbara, and one to Santa Cruz. Of the remaining two types, one is confined to Santa Cruz and Santa Rosa. Only one, Greene live-forever, has a wider distribution and occurs on four islands—Santa Cruz, Santa Rosa, San Miguel, and Santa Catalina.

Other evolutionary variations have been noted for the Channel Islands. Among the most conspicuous are certain color trends, toward the pink in both endemic and nonendemic flowers, and gray in leaf tones. It has been speculated that the latter has a selective advantage, particularly when associated with hairiness, for resistance to herbivorous pressure and salt spray damage. Large size is another outstanding attribute of many insular species, either for the entire plant or its separate parts such as leaves. There has been some debate as to whether this is an example of genetic insular gigantism, which has been documented for other islands, or it is the result of environmental factors such as the recent absence of repeated fires or the feeding habits of large herbivorous mammals which forces plants to grow above the browse line. Comparisons of island

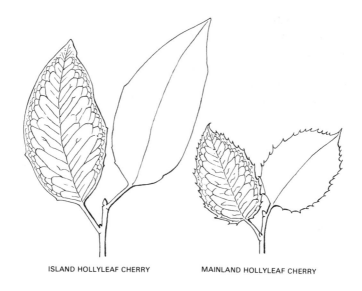

ISLAND HOLLYLEAF CHERRY   MAINLAND HOLLYLEAF CHERRY

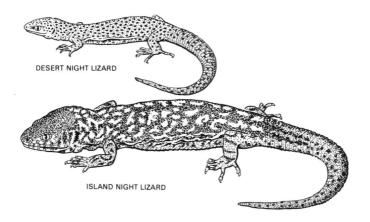

DESERT NIGHT LIZARD

ISLAND NIGHT LIZARD

Figure 27. Variation in related island and mainland forms

and mainland populations of several chaparral shrubs indicate
that not only are the leaves of the island representatives larger
than those of mainland sites, but the total leaf area is greater as
well. If we remember that small leaf size is one of the adaptations to xeric habitats, we could conclude that the moist

maritime climate in conjunction with other advantageous environmental factors such as water-retaining soils permits the extravagance of larger-sized and more abundant foliage.

On the other hand, the numerous windy exposures have induced what appears to be genetic dwarfism in many species that are taller on the mainland. California buckwheat and chamise are two examples of this phenomenon. Several additional evolutionary trends have been described—woodiness in genera that are commonly herbaceous, unusually long-blooming periods, a high degree of hybridization, aggressive spread on the part of some species, and, on the contrary, resistance of others to dispersal.

Above and mingling with the plants of the sea bluffs are the typical members of the coastal sage scrub, particularly on rocky, south-facing slopes—California sagebrush, black and white sages, bush sunflower, coyotebrush, and lemonadeberry. San Clemente and Santa Catalina, in keeping with their southern locations, have substantial populations of velvet cactus, a constituent of maritime cactus scrub. Coast cholla has a much broader distribution—from Santa Rosa to San Clemente. The two coastal prickly pears and their hybrids are probably the most prominent plants in brushy Santa Catalina perhaps because browsing pressure by feral animals has eliminated many of the more palatable competing plants.

Chaparral is restricted to the larger islands. It ranges from woodlandlike open groves of tree-size toyon, summer holly, and other shrub species that are arboreal in the island environment to wind-pruned mats on exposed coastlines. It appears to be most extensive in canyons and on north-facing slopes, and the composition varies from island to island. Scrub oak is abundant throughout the larger islands, but manzanita is more restricted. According to P. A. Munz's *A Flora of Southern California* (University of California Press, 1974), all island manzanitas are endemics. Santa Cruz has its own species as well as a subspecies, Santa Rosa claims one for itself, as does Santa Catalina. A fourth species is shared by Santa Cruz and Santa Rosa, though each of these two islands has its own subspecies. Most of them have the ability to become small trees that, because of their reddish bark, strikingly resemble their close relative, madroño. The two types of ceanothus are also insular endemics, but they seldom form extensive stands. One species attains small-tree size. Interestingly enough, chamise, which often dominates mainland chaparral, is very limited in distribution and is found in only a few places. Primarily because of animal overuse, steep cliffs have remained refuges for a number of rare or endemic species, including island alumroot, island redberry, Greene liveforever, Lyon phacelia, and Nevin gilia.

One would have supposed that sheep and other grazing animals introduced long ago would have severely disrupted the grasslands of the islands, but extensive areas remain although the native species have been largely replaced by foreign annuals. Such prairies favor deep soils as they do over much of California and brighten springtime with many colorful charmers—mariposa lilies, blue dicks, California poppy, owl's clover, and shooting star.

Several woodlands and one forest comprise the remaining communities of the larger islands. Small areas of riparian woodland follow the few streambeds that have either small permanent or intermittent flows of water. For the most part they consist of black and Fremont cottonwood and several willows. Santa Cruz boasts a few stands of big-leaf maple on its north side, and elderberry is often part of streamside thickets on Santa Catalina along with viny tangles of poison oak, clematis, and wild grape. Small seeps and moist grottoes support ferns in protected gullies.

The larger woodlands have few species, but some of them are of great interest. Coast live oak occupies its characteristic habitats in canyon or valley bottoms on Santa Cruz (and presumably on Santa Rosa), but its place is taken by the island cherry on Santa Catalina where the oak does not occur. A number of unique trees such as ironwood, island oak, the winter-deciduous MacDonald oak, supposedly a hybrid between scrub oak and valley oak (a tree no longer present in the islands), and the arboreal shrubs mentioned above form groves on steep, north-facing slopes where conditions are more mesic. Santa Cruz has two small stands of madroño, another northern affiliate whose presence is justified by the higher precipitation on this island, but golden cup oak is more ubiquitous. Island tree mallow has a strange history. Though widely planted in southern California as an ornamental, its wild populations have been reduced to several isolated remnants. One is on Bird Rock just south of the Santa Catalina isthmus. A healthy green patch of this attractive pink-flowered tree grows in startling contrast to the pure-white ring of guano surrounding it. Only here, it seems, could it escape the dangerous attention of nibbling goats.

Two conifers occur on the northern larger islands, Torrey pine on Santa Rosa and the much-debated island pine on both Santa Cruz and Santa Rosa. Though some authorities list this as a separate species, many botanists now feel that it belongs to the bishop pine complex. Thicker needles, more symmetrical cones, smoother scales, and smaller prickles supposedly distinguish island from bishop pine, but there appears to be enough variation in the latter to accommodate these differences. The groves are high enough in elevation to be in contact with the lower edge of the marine layer. The resulting fog drip no doubt contributes to their continued existence.

The author recently walked through a grove of dead pines uphill from Pelican Bay on Santa Cruz. The huge gray ghosts were crowded with hundreds of closed and open cones, but the absence of offspring was both striking and thought-provoking. A fire struck the area sometime around 1930, and saplings should be replacing the burn-damaged parent trees. The lack of regeneration is primarily because of what has proved to be the most persistent foe of this unique assemblage of plants—introduced animals. Almost as soon as the seedlings are established, grazing sheep destroy them, and the grove is unable to reproduce itself.

Ranching and farming have had a long history on most of the islands. As far back as 1852, cattle, and probably sheep and pigs, had been released on Santa Cruz, and Santa Rosa had as many as 10,000 sheep around the same period. The list of nonnative mammals includes black rats, domestic cats, rabbits, goats, horses, and such exotic species as wild turkeys, mule deer, and bison. (Attempts are presently being made to reintroduce breeding colonies of bald eagles on Santa Catalina where they were once quite common.) Each island has its own combination of foreign populations. Some do little damage to the native plants and animals, but rats and cats threaten sea bird colonies, and sheep, pigs, rabbits, and, in particular, goats because of their indiscriminate appetites and tree-climbing ability, account for much wholesale destruction of vegetation.

Not only is the endemic and other plant life endangered, but the removal of plant cover and hoof impaction has resulted in severe gullying and erosion. Drought and fire have always played havoc with California's vegetation, even on the Channel Islands, but man and his imported creatures have had a tremendous impact on these outposts rich with unique species.

Of the three islands in the Channel Islands National Park, only Santa Barbara still has a significant population of a foreign herbivore, the New Zealand rabbit, but attempts to control it are under review. Present owners are aware of the problems caused by sheep (Santa Cruz) and goats (Santa Catalina) on their respective islands. Much of the land on Santa Cruz has been fenced off from sheep trespass since 1958. This should allow a wonderful collection of plants to maintain itself. The multiplication of prickly pear on Santa Catalina is probably the result of the suppression of tastier species, but it has proved helpful in another way. Clumps of them serve as refuges for other plants which are thus protected by the sharp needles of their companion.

Only a small number of native animals persist on the Channel Islands. Three salamanders, one treefrog, five lizards, seven snakes, eleven nesting sea birds, fifty-six breeding land birds, fourteen nonmarine mammals (seven of which are bats), and six pinnipeds have been recorded here in recent times. Island populations are determined by and subject to certain biogeographical controls. The farther they are from the mainland, the fewer the number of immigrants that manage to colonize the new territories. This generalization is modified, however, by the type of organism involved. It is much easier for animals capable of flight to populate islands than reptiles or mammals which must depend upon rafting, swimming, or "stowing away," to reach distant shores. Size is also important. The smaller the island, the fewer available habitats and the greater chance of elimination during times of adversity. Isolation, however, encourages evolutionary expansion, or speciation. So island organisms come, go, and develop in accordance with these regulatory factors and mechanisms.

Leaving aside the whole question of ancient and recent land bridges and other means of arrival for the time being, we shall investigate why some groups of island organisms are so small, considering the closeness of the neighboring continent (five island lizards compared with thirty-two mainland species), and then discuss the astonishing success of some of the few that developed endemic forms.

As noted before, southern California is rich in the number of reptiles that are primarily residents of the desert and dry slopes of the Peninsular Range. These are not and perhaps never were near enough to the coast to be a source of immigrants. Species adapted to warm, dry environments that were present on what is now the cismontane mainland prior to the Ice Age were pushed south by the change in climate and became unavailable for colonization. Similarly adapted species already on the islands during the same epoch were removed by the adversity of the Pleistocene environment. Only four lizards were able to become established and persist in spite of cooler, wetter times— southern alligator, western skink, side-blotched, and western fence. All four have widespread distributions but require relatively mesic as opposed to desert habitats.

The other lizard is an island endemic, the island night lizard. Some authorities give it additional taxonomic status by placing it in a genus of its own, *Klauberina,* rather than retaining it in *Xantusia,* the genus of the other night lizards. Regardless, it is larger and more strongly marked than its mainland cousins (see Figure 27), and its diet includes plant material, a big departure in feeding habits. It is found on three southern islands—San Nicolas, Santa Barbara, and San Clemente. As the former two were underwater during the Pleistocene, the conjecture is that the island night lizard arrived first on San Clemente in the late Tertiary, survived the glacial period, and then pioneered on the two smaller islands. Meanwhile, the original mainland population disappeared, leading one to the assumption that life is easier, for them at least, on the islands. A more equable climate and the lack of both predators and competing species are additional factors in the success of their invasion.

Endemism is a trend in insular avifauna, as well. Out of the thirty-two species of breeding land birds on Santa Cruz, ten have subspecies confined to the islands. Evidently a number of species first moved into the northern islands, dispersed south, and rapid evolutionary development followed, particularly in the last 20,000 years. Variability appeared in such anatomical characteristics as body size, bill size, and wing and tail length. Some differences developed because of selection for changes in diet, others as adaptations that would tend to prevent accidental wing-lift out to sea.

The Santa Cruz Island scrub jay has often been mentioned as an example of a high degree of avifaunal endemism. It is a well-defined subspecies of the mainland scrub jay despite the fact that the wings of this particular bird are too weak to permit an overwater flight of 18 miles (29 km.). It either flew when the Santa Barbara Channel was narrower, possibly assisted by storm winds, or it arrived by some other means, floating debris, etc. It has not pioneered to neighboring islands, further reducing the possibility that it came over on its own power. Once it arrived on Santa Cruz, its divergence indicates that it has had a long history of genetic isolation.

The mammalian counterpart of reptilian and avifaunal endemism is the island gray fox. It has species status, but of even more interest, each of the six islands it inhabits has its own subspecies. Now classified as a rare species, it has managed to hold its own even though major changes have taken place in its homegrounds. One of its main sources of food, presumably, is deer mice, a species of even more diversity. Each of the eight islands has its subspecific representative of deer mouse, the only insular small mammal to have undergone such morphological divergence. Gene flow could first have come from the then-connected northern islands south to the other islands or from Santa Catalina which was also closer to the mainland when the channel was narrower.

The six marine mammals that breed on the shores of the islands obviously swam there, but they, too, have a complicated story though somewhat different from those of the other vertebrates we have discussed. Harbor seals are common throughout much of the area and breed regularly along the coast and all eight Channel Islands. Though the California sea lion is also abundant in the Southern California Bight, 90 percent breed on San Nicolas and San Miguel. The other four pinnipeds have undergone dramatic changes in their populations in the last twenty or thirty years. The northern elephant seal nearly became extinct late in the last century, but it has made a remarkable recovery and now breeds on several islands offshore Baja California and on San Nicolas and San Miguel (recently on Año Nuevo, as well). The Steller sea lion appears to be caught in a reverse trend. Its numbers are steadily declining in the Channel region, and today it is found only on San Miguel and nearby islets. Populations are decreasing also on the

Farallones and Año Nuevo. The Guadalupe fur seal also suffered a drastic decrease in territory, but the species is beginning to expand its range southward. Occasional individuals turn up from time to time on San Miguel. The northern fur seal has recently established small breeding colonies here as well. From the above it appears that this little chunk of drifting sand is home or rest stop for more species of pinnipeds than anywhere else along our coast.

We have left the big question for the last. Was any of this dispersal between the mainland and the islands or interisland accomplished by means of a land bridge? For many years it was assumed that a Pleistocene land connection had to exist because of the fossil mammoth remains found on several of the islands. Current thinking tends to disagree with this hypothesis. The channel between the northern islands and the mainland coast is too deep to have completely emptied during the low sea level intervals of the Ice Age. It is thought that it narrowed to 3.25 miles (6 km.), a distance which it is now known can be swum by African elephants. Additional arguments against the land bridge emphasize the absence of pocket gophers, ground squirrels, and many other ubiquitous species that would have utilized the islands' many unoccupied ecological niches.

Other possibilities of transport are not lacking. Those of us who have experienced the torrential downpours that plague southern California every so often—the so-called one-hundred-year meteorological episodes—can well imagine rain-swollen rivers, normally no larger than small streams, sweeping huge loads of storm-uprooted debris out to sea. This must have happened frequently in the pluvial periods of the Pleistocene, and animals, most probably, had many chances to cross safely the narrow channels of that time on such impromptu rafts.

Indian use of the islands has also shared a long history. Bones of a number of animals, including skunks, have been found in insular middens, suggesting the dietary preferences of the Indians did not prevent them from exploiting any convenient sources of protein. Some species may have been deliberately carried in the Indians' seaworthy canoes, but some may have been inadvertently transported as stowaways.

As for the plants, seeds, though incapable of voluntary movement, can be dispersed across intervening bodies of water in many ways—by wind, in the digestive tracts or on the bodies of mobile animals, and by floating or adherence to other floating objects. It is possible that mid-Tertiary land connections did exist, but not necessarily so.

It is difficult if one is not an experienced boat owner to reach islands other than Santa Catalina. Publicly advertised tours to Santa Cruz and the islands under the auspices of the National Park Service are regularly scheduled by various organizations such as the American Cetacean Society. For the casual traveler, however, Santa Catalina is the most accessible via ship and air transport, and it is prepared to handle large numbers of day and weekend visitors.

For this reason we suggest that readers wishing to become acquainted with the unique life of the islands take a trip to Santa Catalina. Though one cannot drive freely over the island, guided bus tours are available, hikers are welcome in many places, and the environs of Avalon are fun to explore. One strongly advised suggestion is to take the tram to the botanic garden. Many of the famed endemics are grown here, and, as there is no other easy introduction to this unique flora, we urge a visit. Be sure and look for the brilliantly orange garibaldis flashing around the rocks below the docking area.

The islands are difficult to leave. The spuming wake curves back to coves and headlands now darkening under the sunset sky. Gulls call across the wind-quickened foam, heightening the sense of loss, of leaving behind a very special place. One must remember that it will be there for future visits. After all, these islands have been around for a long, long time.

Sequoia Trunks, Sequoia National Park

23. Epilogue: Return to an Island

The singer of the Songs of Solomon was not only a consummate lover, but an articulate observer of his natural environment. In one of the Bible's most lyrical passages, he speaks of spring, the special spring of a dry land blessed with a wet winter:

Rise up, my love, and come away.
For lo, the winter is past, the rain is over and gone.
The flowers appear upon the earth, and the time of
the singing of birds is come, and the voice of the
turtledove is heard in our land.

Such a plea would have particular meaning to someone who, as a child, perhaps, herded the family's sheep over the hot and barren slopes of summer. In spite of all the references to a "land of milk and honey," stony wilderness and drought were common enough in ancient Palestine to serve as threatened destinies for backsliders and idol worshippers. But a warm, thyme-scented hillside, sung to by larks and carpeted with anemones and crocuses is wonderfully appealing. Who could resist such a tempting rendezvous?

Many early visitors to California were as enchanted. Charles F. Saunders, whose *With the Flowers and Trees in California* (McBride, Nast, 1914) is a delightful if slightly self-conscious introduction to natural California, quotes from the diaries of Father Crespi: "Both sides of our way were lined with rose bushes of Castile, from which I broke one bunch with six roses opened and about twelve in bud." David Douglas, Scottish gardener whose name appears in much California botanical nomenclature, wrote enthusiastically in 1832 of "the beautiful wild gooseberry not surpassed in beauty by the finest fuchsia," and, "a humble but lovely plant, the harbinger of spring," which we know by the rather sentimental name of baby-blue-eyes.

Though many of the flower fields of the valleys and foothills have been inundated by the Human Wave, they remain symbolic of the Golden State. Few postcard stands lack pictures of poppy fields or of a sea cliff, startlingly magenta from the

massed flowers of mesembryanthemum, a South African genus that has donated a number of colorful species now so common to coastal bluffs that they are usually thought to be native.
Impressive floral displays are characteristic of all subtropical
wet-winter, dry-summer climatic systems. The plains of southwestern Australia are bright with Sturt pea, everlasting, clumps
of kangaroo paw, and multicolored shrubs. Some of the most
glorious displays are concentrated in the Cape region of South
Africa. For mile after mile the brilliant whorls of mesembryanthemum and related succulents; flame and sun-tinted gerberas
and gazanias; ixias, gladioli, and other Cape bulbs are spread
in a unending carpet. Scattered through the scrub of central
Chile are open patches of wood sorrel, yellow gum plant, and
the blue trumpets of nolana.

Lavish wildflowers, of course, are not confined to Mediter-
ranian and climatically sister lands. Alpine and Arctic tundra,
mountain meadows, prairies, and heaths offer bright collections of blossoms when at their best. But none of these communities comes close to the arid or summer-dry subtropics in
terms of numbers of species. Nine-tenths or 14,400 of the
16,000 South African flowering plants are confined to the Cape
coastal strip.

Though species count alone is sufficiently impressive to un-
derscore the uniqueness of Mediterranean climate-type floral
kingdoms and those of their desert edges, a large number of
endemics is another outstanding feature. Santa Lucia fir, a
conifer restricted to the coastal mountains of central California, has its Mediterranean counterpart, *Abies hebrodensis,* native to the northern coast of Sicily. The Cape's silverleaf and
western Australia's honey-myrtles are endemic types that, as
attractive ornamentals, have traveled far from their original
and limited homegrounds.

Known as "bush" in South Africa and *macchia* or *maquis* in
the Mediterranean lands, drought-resistant chaparral-type
scrub is an additional shared characteristic of the summer-dry
subtropics. Photographs of brush-covered hills from all five regions are so similar in appearance that only experts can readily
distinguish between them. The firm hand of physical environment nowhere exercises more control than here in the olive
tree latitudes. Bear this in mind when you next visit a botanical
garden featuring specimens from many areas of the world.

Any shrub with small, thick, light-colored, evergreen leaves is likely to be from these climatic regions.

One can become so fascinated by differences between California and the rest of the United States that one forgets that the state is part of a larger whole. It is attached to a land mass, and its ecological, physiographic, and climatological isolation can be overemphasized. Political boundaries are seldom coincidental with ecotones. Extending far south of the misted inlets of the Alaska panhandle, a slender ribbon of spruce and cedar follows the California coast until it finally unravels in the increasing summer drought. A mantle of Utah juniper, sagebrush, and pinyon pine, triumvirate species of the intermountain West, folds a ragged edge over the highlands of eastern California. Palo verde, trees of the Southwest arboreal desert, winds along wash floors as far west as San Diego County; and Mexican palo verde is reported to have become naturalized in parts of the Mojave Desert, far from its center of distribution in Sonora, Mexico. Moreover, a number of far-ranging species such as yellow and limber pine, Great Basin sagebrush, and Douglas-fir serve to knit California firmly into the vegetation complex of the West. Mariposa lilies may be called sego lilies in Utah, but they are basically the same flower. Poppies are as richly yellow in the Arizona desert as they are in California.

Nevertheless, the California Floristic Province is truly an "island called California," a singular piece of country with extremes unknown in more temperate or less diverse regions. Frozen peaks reach up over scorched valleys. Lichen-shrouded sea-mist forest is but an hour's drive from a mineral-encrusted dry lake. Prairie and the world's tallest forest are only a few feet apart. Not many landscapes are as dull and unattractive as the littered, weed-patch fields of the southern San Joaquin Valley. On the other hand, the cypress-crowned coves of Point Lobos and carved ivory of the Sierran scarp west of Independence are among the world's most magnificent scenes.

Isolated by sea, mountain range, and desert, this area has developed in its own way and at its own pace; evolutionary history here has woven numerous distinctive patterns of interaction between life form and the land. Like the fire pines and cypresses, many such patterns are tag ends, remnants of much larger biological designs. Others, like chaparral and coniferous forest, run repeatedly through the warp and woof of natural California.

Such are the patterns of survival through a rainless summer, on a serpentine slope, in a Sierran canyon; patterns that have similarities but no exact duplicates elsewhere in the world; patterns that are incredibly intricate, multiple, and unfortunately irreplaceable if obliterated by man's heedlessness, apathy, or greed.

Selected Bibliography

General Ecology

Benton, A. H., and Werner, W. E., Jr. *Field Biology and Ecology*. McGraw-Hill, 1974.

Buchsbaum, R., and Buchsbaum, M. *Basic Ecology*. Boxwood Press, 1957.

Dice, L. R. *Natural Communities*. University of Michigan Press, 1952.

Farb, P., and the editors of *Life*. *Ecology*. Time, Inc., 1963.

Foin, T. C., Jr. *Ecological Systems and the Environment*. Houghton Mifflin, 1976.

Hanson, H. C. *Dictionary of Ecology*. Philosophical Library, 1962.

Knight, C. B. *Basic Concepts of Ecology*. Macmillan, 1965.

Kormondy, E. J. *Concepts of Ecology*. Prentice-Hall, 1969.

Lewis, W. H. *Ecology Field Glossary*. Greenwood Press, 1977.

Martin, A. C., Zim, H. S., and Nelson, A. L. *American Wildlife and Plants*. McGraw-Hill, 1951.

Odum, E. P. *Ecology*. Holt, Rinehart, and Winston, 1963.

Odum, E. P., and Odum, H. T. *Fundamentals of Ecology*. Saunders, 1959.

Richardson, J. L. *Dimensions of Ecology*. Williams and Wilkins, 1977.

Shelford, V. E. *The Ecology of North America*. University of Illinois Press, 1963.

Whitaker, R. H. *Communities and Ecosystems*. Macmillan, 1970.

Plant Ecology

Billings, W. D. *Plants and the Ecosystem*. Wadsworth, 1964.

Dansereau, P. *Biogeography*. Ronald, 1957.

Daubenmire, R. F. *Plants and Environment*. John Wiley, 1947.

Gleason, H. A., and Cronquist, A. *The Natural Geography of Plants*. Columbia University Press, 1964.

Humphrey, R. R. *Range Ecology*. Ronald, 1964.

Oosting, H. J. *The Study of Plant Communities*. W. H. Freeman, 1958.

Reimold, R. J., and Queen, W. H. *Ecology of Halophytes.* Academic Press, 1974.

Spurr, S. *Forest Ecology.* Ronald, 1964.

Weaver, J. E., and Clements, F. E. *Plant Ecology.* McGraw-Hill, 1938.

Animal Ecology

Kendeigh, S. C. *Animal Ecology.* Prentice-Hall, 1961.
———. *Ecology with Special Reference to Animals and Man.* Prentice-Hall, 1974.

Ricciuti, E. R. *Wildlife of the Mountains.* Henry N. Abrams, Inc. (Chanticleer Press), 1979.

Sutton, A., and Sutton, M. *Wildlife of the Forests.* Henry N. Abrams, Inc. (Chanticleer Press), 1979.

Wagner, F. H. *Wildlife of the Deserts.* Henry N. Abrams, Inc. (Chanticleer Press), 1980.

Soils

Buckman, H. O., and Brady, N. C. *The Nature and Properties of Soils.* Macmillan, 1974.

Farb, P. *Living Earth.* Harper & Row, 1959.

Foth, H. D. *Fundamentals of Soil Science.* John Wiley, 1978.

Kellogg, C. E. *The Soils That Support Us.* Macmillan, 1961.

Marine Environment

Abbott, I. A., and Hollenberg, G. J. *Marine Algae of California.* Stanford University Press, 1976.

Amos, W. H. *The Life of the Seashore.* McGraw-Hill, 1966.

Ballard, R. D., et al. *The Ocean Realm.* National Geographic Society, 1978.

Baxter, J. L. *Inshore Fishes of California.* California Department of Fish and Game, 1960.

Carefoot, T. *Pacific Seashores: A Guide to Intertidal Ecology.*

University of Washington Press, 1977.

Chapman, V. J. *Salt Marshes and Salt Deserts of the World.* Von J. Cramer, 1974.

Conradson, D. R. *Exploring Our Baylands.* Palo Alto Chamber of Commerce, 1966.

Dawson, E. Y. *Seashore Plants of Northern California.* University of California Press, 1966.
———. *Seashore Plants of Southern California.* University of California Press, 1966.

Fitch, J. E., and Lavenberg, R. J.

Marine Food and Game Fishes of California. University of California Press, 1971.

―――. *Tidepool and Nearshore Fishes of California.* University of California Press, 1975.

Hedgpeth, J. W. *Introduction to Seashore Life of the San Francisco Bay Region and the Coast of Northern California.* University of California Press, 1964.

Hinton, S. *Seashore Life of Southern California.* University of California Press, 1969.

Ingmanson, D. E., and Wallace, W. J. *Oceanology: An Introduction.* Wadsworth, 1973.

Jensen, A. C. *Wildlife of the Oceans.* Henry N. Abrams, Inc. (Chanticleer Press), 1979.

Light, S. F., et al. *Intertidal Invertebrates of the Central California Coast.* University of California Press, 1975.

McConnaughey, B. H. *Introduction to Marine Biology.* C. V. Mosby, 1978.

Moore, H. B. *Marine Ecology.* John Wiley, 1958.

Munz, P. A. *Shore Wildflowers of California, Oregon, and Washington.* University of California Press, 1964.

North, W. *Underwater California.* University of California Press, 1976.

Orr, R. T. *Marine Mammals of California.* University of California Press, 1972.

Reid, G. K. *Ecology of Inland Waters and Estuaries.* Reinhold, 1961.

Reish, D. J. *Marine Life of Southern California.* Published by the author, 1972.

Ricketts, E. F., Calvin, J., and Hedgpeth, J. W. *Between Pacific Tides.* Stanford University Press, 1968.

Sumich, J. L. *Biology of Marine Life.* W. C. Brown, 1976.

Sverdrup, H. U., Johnson, M. W., and Fleming, R. H. *The Oceans.* Prentice-Hall, 1942.

Tierney, R. J., et al. *Exploring Tidepool Life.* Berkeley-Tidepool Associates, 1966.

Weihaupt, J. G. *Exploration of the Oceans.* Macmillan, 1979.

Freshwater Environment

Amos, W. H. *The Life of the Pond.* McGraw-Hill, 1967.

―――. *Wildlife of the Rivers.* Henry N. Abrams, Inc. (Chanticleer Press), 1981.

Macan, T. T. *Freshwater Ecology.* Longman, 1963.

Mason, H. L. *A Flora of the*

Marshes of California. University of California Press, 1957.

Needham, J. G., and Needham, P. R. *A Guide to the Study of Freshwater Biology.* Holden-Day, 1962.

Niering, W. A. *The Life of the*

Marsh. McGraw-Hill, 1966.
Pennack, R. W. *Fresh-Water Invertebrates of the United States.* Ronald, 1953.
Usinger, R. L. *Aquatic Insects of California.* University of California Press, 1956.
———. *The Life of Rivers and Streams.* McGraw-Hill, 1967.
Whitton, B. A. *River Ecology.* University of California Press, 1975.

Birds

Bent, A. C. "Life Histories of the Birds of North America." Smithsonian Institution United States National Museum, Bulletins 107,113, 121, 126, 130, 135, 142, 162, 167, 170, 176, 191, 195, 196, 197, 203, 211 (Dover editions published 1961-1968).
Cogswell, H. L. *Water Birds of California.* University of California Press, 1977.
Dawson, W. L. *The Birds of California,* Vols. 1-4. South Moulton Co., 1923.
Garrett, K., and Dunn, J. *Birds of Southern California.* Los Angeles Audubon Society, 1981.
Grinnell, J., and Miller, A. H. *The Distribution of the Birds of California.* Pacific Coast Avifauna, No. 27. Cooper Ornithological Club, 1944.
Grinnell, J., and Wythe, M. W. *Directory of the Bird Life of the San Francisco Bay Region.* Pacific Coast Avifauna, No. 18. Cooper Ornithological Club, 1927.
Hoffman, R. *Birds of the Pacific States.* Houghton Mifflin, 1927.
Peterson, R. T. *A Field Guide to Western Birds.* Houghton Mifflin, 1969.
Robbins, C. S., Bruun, B., and Zim, H. S. *Birds of North America.* Golden Press, 1966.
Small, A. *The Birds of California.* Collier, 1975.
Udvardy, M. D. F. *The Audubon Society Field Guide to North American Birds* (western region). A. A. Knopf, 1977.
Welty, J. C. *The Life of Birds.* Saunders, 1962.

Reptiles and Amphibians

Behler, J. L. *The Audubon Society Field Guide to North American Reptiles and Amphibians.* A. A. Knopf, 1979.
Klauber, L. M. *Rattlesnakes* (abridged edition). University of California Press, 1982.
Stebbins, R. C. *Amphibians and*

Reptiles of Western North America. McGraw-Hill, 1954.
———. *Reptiles and Amphibians of the San Francisco Bay Region.* University of California Press, 1959.

———. *Field Guide to Western Reptiles and Amphibians.* Houghton Mifflin, 1966.
———. *California Amphibians and Reptiles.* University of California Press, 1972.

Mammals

Berry, W. D., and Berry, E. *Mammals of the San Francisco Bay Region.* University of California Press, 1959.

Booth, E. S. *Mammals of Southern California.* University of California Press, 1968.

Grater, R. *Discovering Sierra Mammals.* Yosemite Natural History Association and Sequoia Natural History

Association, 1978.

Hall, E. R. *Mammals of North America.* John Wiley, 1981.

Ingles, L. G. *Mammals of the Pacific States.* Stanford University Press, 1965.

Whitaker, J. O. *The Audubon Society Field Guide to North American Mammals.* A. A. Knopf, 1980.

Insects

Borrer, D. J., and White, R. E. *Field Guide to the Insects of America North of Mexico.* Houghton Mifflin, 1970.

Brown, L. R., and Eads, C. O. *A Technical Study of Insects Affecting the Oak Tree in Southern California.* California Agricultural Experiment Station, Bulletin 810, n.d.

Essig, E. O. *Insects and Mites of*

Western North America. Macmillan, 1926.

Powell, J. A., and Hogue, C. L. *California Insects.* University of California Press, 1979.

Smith, A. C. *Western Butterflies.* Lane, 1961.

Tilden, J. W. *Butterflies of the San Francisco Bay Region.* University of California Press, 1965.

California Flora

Arno, S. *Discovering Sierra Trees.* Yosemite Natural History Association and Sequoia Natural History Association, 1973.

Axelrod, D. I. *History of the*

Coniferous Forests, California and Nevada. University of California Press, 1976.

Barbour, M. G., and Major, J. *Terrestrial Vegetation of California.* John Wiley, 1977.

Bowerman, M. L. *The Flowering Plants and Ferns of Mount Diablo, California.* Gillick Press, 1944.

Brockman, C. F. *Trees of North America.* Golden Press, 1968.

Burcham, L. T. *California Range Lands.* California Department of Natural Resources, Division of Forestry, 1957.

Collins, B. J. *Key to Coastal and Chaparral Flowering Plants of Southern California.* California State University Foundation, n.d.

————. *Key to Trees and Wildflowers of the Mountains of Southern California.* California State University Foundation, n.d.

Crampton, B. *Grasses in California.* University of California Press, 1974.

Critchfield, W. B., and Little, E. L. *Geographic Distribution of the Pines of the World.* Forest Service, United States Department of Agriculture, Miscellaneous Publication 991, 1966.

Ecology, Management, and Utilization of California Oaks. Pacific Southwest Forest and Range Experiment Station (General Technical Report PSW–44), 1980.

Ferlatte, W. J. *A Flora of the Trinity Alps of Northern California.* University of California Press, 1974.

Ferris, R. S. *Native Shrubs of the San Francisco Bay Region.* University of California Press, 1968.

Fowells, H. A. *Sylvics of Forest Trees of the United States.* Agriculture Handbook 271, Forest Service, United States Department of Agriculture, 1965.

Griffin, J. R., and Critchfield, W. B. *The Distribution of Forest Trees in California.* United States Department of Agriculture, Forest Service Research Paper PSW–82, 1976.

Grillos, S. J. *Ferns and Fern Allies of California.* University of California Press, 1966.

Harvey, H. T., Shellhammer, H. S., and Stecker, R. E. *Giant Sequoia Ecology.* United States Department of the Interior, National Park Service, 1980.

Hoover, R. F. *The Vascular Plants of San Luis Obispo County, California.* University of California Press, 1970.

Howell, J. T. *Marin Flora.* University of California Press, 1970.

Jain, S. *Vernal Pools: Their Ecology and Conservation.* Institute of Ecology, University of California, Davis, Publication No. 9, n.d.

Lanner, R. M. *The Pinon Pine.* University of Nevada Press, 1981.

Latting, J., ed. *Plant Communities of Southern California.* California Native Plant Society, Special Publication No. 2, 1976.

Lloyd, R. M., and Mitchell, R. S. *A Flora of the White Mountains, California and Nevada.* University of California Press, 1973.

Mabry, T. J., Hunziker, J. H., and Difeo, D. R., Jr. *Creosote Bush.* John Wiley, 1977.

McMinn, H. E. *An Illustrated Manual of California Shrubs.* University of California Press, 1964.

Metcalf, W. *Native Trees of the San Francisco Bay Region.* University of California Press, 1960.

Mirov, N. T. *The Genus Pinus.* Ronald, 1967.

Munz, P. A. *California Spring Wildflowers.* University of California Press, 1961.

————. *California Mountain Wildflowers.* University of California Press, 1963.

————. *A Flora of Southern California.* University of California Press, 1974.

Munz, P. A., and Keck, D. D. *A California Flora.* University of California Press, 1973.

Niehaus, T. F. *Sierra Wildflowers.* University of California Press, 1974.

Niehaus, T. F., and Ripper, C. L. *Field Guide to Pacific States Wildflowers.* Houghton Mifflin, 1976.

Ornduff, R. *California Plant Life.* University of California Press, 1974.

Orr, R. T., and Orr, D. B. *Mushrooms and Other Common Fungi of the San Francisco Bay Region.* University of California Press, 1968.

Peattie, D. C. *A Natural History of Western Trees.* Houghton Mifflin, 1953.

Peterson, P. V. *Native Trees of Southern California.* University of California Press, 1966.

————. *Native Trees of the Sierra Nevada.* University of California Press, 1975.

Raven, P. H. *Native Shrubs of Southern California.* University of California Press, 1966.

Raven, P. H., and Axelrod, D. I. *Origins and Relationships of the California Flora.* University of California Press, 1978.

Raven, P.H., and Thompson, H. J. *Flora of the Santa Monica Mountains, California.* University of California, Los Angeles, 1966 (revised 1977).

Sampson, A. W., Chase, A., and Hedrick, D. W. *California Grasslands and Range Forage Grasses.* College of Agriculture Bulletin 724. University of California, 1951.

Sampson, A. W., and Jesperson, B. S. *California Range Brushlands and Browse Plants.* Division of Agricultural Sciences, Manual 33, University of California, 1963.

Sands, A. *Riparian Forests in California.* Institute of Ecology, University of California, Davis, Special Publication No. 15, n.d.

Sharsmith, H. K. "The Flora of the Mount Hamilton Range of California." *American Midland Naturalist.* Vol. 34, no. 2 (September 1945).

————. *Spring Wildflowers of the San Francisco Bay Region.* University of California Press, 1965.

Simpson, B. B. *Mesquite.* John Wiley, 1977.

Smith, C. F. *A Flora of the Santa*

Barbara Region. Santa Barbara Museum of Natural History, 1976.

Spellenberg, R. *The Audubon Society Field Guide of North American Wildflowers* (western region). A. A. Knopf, 1979.

Sudworth, G. B. *Forest Trees of the Pacific Slope.* United States Department of Agriculture, Forest Service, 1908 (Dover reprint published 1968).

Thomas, J. H. *Flora of the Santa Cruz Mountains of California.* Stanford University Press, 1961.

Thomas, J. H., and Parnell, D. R. *Native Shrubs of the Sierra Nevada.* University of California Press, 1974.

Twisselmann, E. *A Flora of Kern County.* University of San Francisco, 1967.

Geology

Bascom, W. *Waves and Currents.* Doubleday, 1964.

Bowen, O. E. *Rocks and Minerals of the San Francisco Bay Region.* University of California Press, 1966.

Dott, R. H., Jr., and Batten, R. L. *Evolution of the Earth.* McGraw-Hill, 1981.

Fenniman, N. M. *Physiography of the Western United States.* McGraw-Hill, 1931.

Geologic Guidebook: Along Highway 49—Sierran Gold Belt. Bulletin 141. California Department of Natural Resources, Division of Mines, 1948.

Geologic Guidebook of the San Francisco Bay Counties. Bulletin 154. California Department of Natural Resources, Division of Mines, 1951.

Hill, M. *Geology of the Sierra Nevada.* University of California Press, 1975.

Howard, A. D. *Evolution of the Landscape of the San Francisco Bay Region.* University of California Press, 1962.

———. *Geologic History of Middle California.* University of California Press, 1979.

Hunt, C. B. *Physiography of the United States.* W. H. Freeman, 1967.

Iacopi, R. *Earthquake Country.* Lane, 1964.

Norris, R. M., and Webb, R. W. *Geology of California.* John Wiley, 1976.

Strahler, A. N. *Physical Geography.* John Wiley, 1969.

Climate and Weather

Bailey, H. P. *Climate of Southern California.* University of California Press, 1966.

Felton, E. L. *California's Many Climates.* Pacific Books, 1965.

Gilliam, H. *Weather of San Francisco Bay Region.* University of California Press, 1966.

Desert Environment

Benson, L., and Darrow, R. A. *Trees and Shrubs of the Southwest Deserts.* University of Arizona Press, 1981.

Brown, G. W., Jr. *Desert Biology.* Academic Press, Volume I, 1968, Volume II, 1974.

Costello, D. *The Desert World.* Thomas Y. Crowell, 1972.

Cowles, R. B., and Bakker, E. S. *Desert Journal.* University of California Press, 1977.

Dawson, E. Y. *Cacti of California.* University of California Press, 1966.

Jaeger, E. *The California Deserts.* Stanford University Press, 1933.

——. *Desert Wildflowers.* Stanford University Press, 1967.

——. *Our Desert Neighbors.* Stanford University Press, 1950.

Kearney, T. H., and Peebles, R. H. *Arizona Flora.* University of California Press, 1960.

Larson, P. *The Deserts of the Southwest.* Sierra Club Books, 1977.

Munz, P. A. *California Desert Wildflowers.* University of California Press, 1962.

Schmidt-Nielsen, K. *Desert Animals: Physiological Problems of Heat and Water.* Oxford University Press, 1964.

Soltz, D. L., and Naiman, R. J. *The Natural History of Native Fishes in the Death Valley System.* Natural History Museum of Los Angeles County, 1978.

Sutton, A., and Sutton, M. *The Life of the Desert.* McGraw-Hill, 1966.

Regional Guides

Barbour, M., et al. *Coastal Ecology: Bodega Head.* University of California Press, 1973.

Hunt, C. B. *Death Valley: Geology, Ecology, and Archaeology.* University of California Press, 1975.

Jaeger, E., and Smith, A. C. *Introduction to the Natural History of Southern California.* University of California Press, 1966.

Miller, A. H., and Stebbins, R. C. *The Lives of Desert Animals in Joshua Tree National Monument.* University of California Press, 1964.

Muir, J. *The Yosemite.* Century Co., 1912.

Philbrick, R. N. *Proceedings of the Symposium on the Biology of the California Islands.* Santa Barbara Botanic Gardens, 1967.

Power, D. M. *The California Islands.* Santa Barbara Museum of Natural History, 1980.

Smith, A. C. *Introduction to the Natural History of the San Francisco Bay Region.* University of California Press, 1963.

Smith, G. Schumacher, ed. *Deepest Valley: Guide to Owens Valley and Its Mountain Lakes, Roadsides, and Trails.* Revised edition, Sierra Club Books, 1978.

Storer, T. I., and Usinger, R.

Sierra Nevada Natural History. University of California Press, 1963.

Whitney, S. *The Sierra Nevada.* Sierra Club Books, 1979.

Winkler, D. W. *An Ecological Study of Mono Lake, California.* Institute of Ecology, University of California, Davis, Publication No. 12, 1977.

List of Animals

Abalone, black, *Haliotis
cracherodii*
Abalone, red, *Haliotis rufescens*
Alder-fly, *Sialis* spp.
Amphioxus (California lancelet),
Branchiostoma californiense
Amphipod, Amphipoda
Ant, California harvester,
Pogonomyrmex californicus
Ant, carpenter, *Camponotus* spp.
Ant, honey, *Myrmecocystus* spp.
Ant, velvet, Mutillidae
Antelope, pronghorn,
Antilocapra americana
Aphid, Aphididae
Auklet, Cassin's, *Ptychoramphus
aleuticus*
Aurelia, Aurelia aurita
Avocet, American, *Recurvirostra
americana*

Backswimmer, Notonectidae
Badger, *Taxidea taxus*
Banana slug, *Ariolimax
columbianus*
Barnacle, acorn, *Balanus glandula*
Barnacle, leaf (gooseneck),
Pollicipes polymerus
Barnacle, southern acorn,
Chthamalus fissus
Barracuda, *Sphyraena argentea*
Bass, *Micropterus* spp.
Bat, Chiroptera
Batrochoseps nigriventris (see also
Salamander: Slender)
Beach hopper, *Orchestia
traskiana, Orchestoidea
californiana*

Bear, black, *Ursus americanus*
Bear, grizzly, *Ursus arctos* (*U.
californicus* has been used to
designate the California
grizzly bear)
Beaver, golden, *Castor canadensis*
ssp. *subauratus*
Beaver, mountain, *Aplodontia
rufa*
Bee, carpenter, *Xylocopa* spp.
Beetle:
Acrobat (pinecate, stinkbug,
tumblebug), *Eleodes* spp.
Bark, Scolytidae
Blister, Melodae
Cone, *Conophthorus ponderosae*
Diving (predaceous water),
Dytiscidae
Flat-headed borer, Buprestidae
Longhorn (big tree cone scale
borer), *Phymatodes nitidus*
Longhorn, Cerambycidae
Pine engraver, *Ips* spp.
Riffle, Elmidae
Scarab, Scarabaeidae
Bittern, American, *Botaurus
lentiginosus*
Blackbird, red-winged, *Agelaius
phoeniceus*
Blackbird, yellow-headed,
Xanthocephalus xanthocephalus
Blenny, common rock,
Hypsoblennius gilberti
Blenny family, Blenniidae
Bluebird, mountain, *Sialia
currucoides*
Bluebird, western, *Sialia mexicana*
Bluegill, *Lepomis macrochirus*

Bobcat, *Lynx rufus*
Booby, blue-footed, *Sula nebouxii*
Borer, western sycamore,
   Ramosia resplendens
Bryozoa, Bryozoa
Bubble shell (see Snail)
Buffalo, American (bison), *Bison
   bison*
Bug, boxelder, *Leptocoris
   rubrolineatus*
Bullfrog, *Rana catesbeiana*
Bullhead, *Ictalurus* spp.
Bunting, lazuli, *Passerina amoena*
Bushtit, *Psaltriparus minimus*
Butterfly:
   California sister, *Limenitis
      bredowii*
   Hairstreak, California, *Strymon
      californica*
   Hairstreak, canyon oak,
      Habrodais grunus
   Monarch, *Danaus plexippus*
   Painted lady, *Vanessa cardui*
   Queen, *Danaus gilippus*
   Silver blue, *Glaucopsyche
      lygdamus*
   Swallowtail, *Papilio* spp.
   Tailed copper, *Lycaena arota*

Caddisfly, Trichoptera
Carp, *Cyprinus carpio*
Centipede, *Scolopendra* spp.
Chat, yellow-breasted, *Icteria
   virens*
Chickadee, chestnut-backed,
   Parus rufescens
Chickadee, mountain, *Parus
   gambeli*
Chickaree (Douglas squirrel),
   Tamiasciurus douglasii
Chipmunk:
   Alpine, *Eutamias (Tamias)
      alpinus*
   Least, *Eutamias (Tamias)
      minimus*

Lodgepole, *Eutamias (Tamias)
   speciosus*
Merriam, *Eutamias (Tamias)
   merriami*
Sonoma, *Eutamias (Tamias)
   sonomae*
Yellow-cheeked, *Eutamias
   (Tamias) ochrogenys*
Chiton (sea cradle), Amphineura
Chub, Mojave, *Gila bicolor
   mohavensis*
Cicada, Cicadidae
Cichlid, Zill's, *Tilapia zillii*
Clam:
   Bean, *Donax gouldi*
   Bent-nosed, *Macoma nasuta*
   Boring, Pholadidae,
      Teredinidae
   Gaper, *Tresus nuttalli*
   Manila, *Corbicula manilensis*
   Pismo, *Tivela stultorum*
   Razor, *Siliqua patula*
   Sand, *Macoma secta*
Cockle, basket, *Clinocardium
   nuttalli*
Cockroach, sand dune, *Arenivaga*
   spp., *Eremoblatta* spp.
Condor, Andean, *Vultus gryphus*
Condor, California, *Gymnogyps
   californianus*
Coot, *Fulica americana*
Copepod, Copepoda
Coral, solitary (northern),
   Balanophyllia elegans
Coral, solitary (southern),
   Astrangia lajollaensis
Cormorant, Brandt's,
   Phalacrocorax penicillatus
Cormorant, double-crested
   (Farallon), *Phalacrocorax
   auritus*
Cormorant, pelagic,
   Phalacrocorax pelagicus
Cowry, chestnut brown, *Cypraea
   (Zonaria) spadicea*

Coyote, *Canis latrans*
Crab:
  Fiddler, *Uca crenulata*
  Hermit, *Pagurus* spp.
  Hermit, hairy, *Pagurus hirsutiusculus*
  Kelp, *Pugettia producta*
  Market, *Cancer magister*
  Masking, *Loxorhynchus crispatus, Scyra acutifrons*
  Mud-flat, *Hemigrapsus oregonensis*
  Pea, *Fabia subquadrata*
  Pea, fat innkeeper, *Pinnixa* spp., *Scleroplax granulata*
  Porcelain sand, *Lepidopa myops*
  Rock, *Cancer* spp.
  Sand (mole), *Emerita analoga*
  Shore, *Hemigrapsus nudus*
  Shore, lined (striped), *Pachygrapsus crassipes*
Crayfish, *Astacus* spp.
Creeper, brown, *Certhia familiaris*
Cricket, Gryllidae
Cricket, Jerusalem, *Stenopelmatus fuscus*
Crossbill, red, *Loxia curvirostra*
Crow, common, *Corvus brachyrhynchos*
Crustacean, Crustacea
Cuckoo, yellow-billed, *Coccyzus americanus*
Curlew, long-billed, *Numenius americanus*
Cutworm (see Moth: Cutworm)

Dace, speckled, *Rhinichythys osculus*
Damselfly, Zygoptera
Daphnia, *Daphnia* spp.
Deer, black-tailed, *Odocoileus hemionus columbianus*
Deer, mule, *Odocoileus hemionus*
Dipper (water ouzel), *Cinclus mexicanus*

Dobson-fly, Corydalidae
Dolphin, bottle-nosed, *Tursiops gilli*
Dolphin, common, *Delphinus delphis*
Dove, mourning, *Zenaida macroura*
Dove, white-winged, *Zenaida asiatica*
Dowitcher, short-billed, *Limnodromus griseus*
Dragonfly, Anisoptera
Duck:
  Canvasback, *Aythya valisineria*
  Gadwall, *Anas strepera*
  Goldeneye, common, *Bucephala clangula*
  Mallard, *Anas platyrhynchos*
  Merganser, common, *Mergus merganser*
  Pintail, *Anas acuta*
  Redhead, *Aythya americana*
  Ruddy, *Oxyura jamaicensis*
  Scaup, greater, *Aythya marila*
  Scaup, lesser, *Aythya affinis*
  Shoveler, northern, *Anas clypeata*
  Teal, blue-winged, *Anas discors*
  Teal, cinnamon, *Anas cyanoptera*
  Teal, green-winged, *Anas crecca (A. carolinensis)*
  Widgeon, American, *Anas americana*
Dunlin, *Calidris alpina*

Eagle, bald, *Haliaeetus leucocephalus*
Earthworm, *Lumbricus* spp., Oligochaeta
Egret, great, *Casmerodius albus*
Elk, Rocky Mountain, *Cervus elaphus (C. canadensis) nelsoni*
Elk, Roosevelt (Olympic), *Cervus elaphus (C. canadensis) roosevelti*

Elk, tule, *Cervus elaphus (C. canadensis) nannodes*
Empidonax, *Empidonax* spp.

Falcon, prairie, *Falco mexicanus*
Fat innkeeper (see Tube worm)
Filbertworm, *Melissopus latiferreanus*
Finch:
  Cassin's, *Carpodacus cassinii*
  Darwin's, *Geospiza* spp.
  House (see Linnet)
  Purple, *Carpodacus purpureus*
  Rosy, "brown," *Leucosticte arctoa australis*
  Rosy, "gray-crowned," *Leucosticte arctoa dawsoni*
Flat bug, *Aradus* spp.
Flea, sand (beach), *Orchestia* spp., *Orchestoidea* spp.
Flicker, "red-shafted," *Colaptes auratus (C. cafer)*
Fly, bot, rodent, *Cuterebra* spp.
Fly, brine, *Ephydra riparia*
Flycatcher:
  Ash-throated, *Myiarchus cinerascens*
  Brown-crested (Wied's crested), *Myiarchus tyrannulus*
  Dusky, *Empidonax oberholseri*
  Gray, *Empidonax wrightii*
  Olive-sided, *Contopus (Nuttallornis) borealis*
  Vermillion, *Pyrocephalis rubinus*
  Western, *Empidonax difficilis*
  Willow (Traill's), *Empidonax traillii*
Fox, gray, *Urocyon cinereoargenteus*
Fox, island gray, *Urocyon cinereoargenteus littoralis*
Fox, kit, *Vulpes macrotis*
Fox, red, *Vulpes fulva*

Gallinule, common, *Gallinula chloropus*
Gannet, *Morus bassanus*
Garibaldi, *Hypsypops rubicundus*
Gastropod, Gastropoda
Girdler, oak twig, *Agrilus angelicus*
Gnatcatcher, black-tailed, *Polioptila melanura*
Gnatcatcher, blue-gray, *Polioptila caerulea*
Godwit, marbled, *Limosa fedoa*
Goldfinch, *Carduelis (Spinus)* spp.
Goose, Canada, *Branta canadensis*
Goose, snow, *Anser (Chen) caerulescens*
Goose, white-fronted, *Anser albifrons*
Gopher, pocket, *Thomomys* spp.
Gorgonian coral, Gorgonacea (two southern California genera: *Lophogorgia, Eugorgia*)
Grackle, great-tailed, *Quiscalus (Cassidix) mexicanus*
Grasshopper, Acrididae
Grebe, eared, *Podiceps nigricollis*
Grebe, western, *Aechmophorus occidentalis*
Gribble, *Limnoria* spp.
Grosbeak, black-headed, *Pheucticus melanocephalus*
Grosbeak, blue, *Guiraca caerulea*
Grosbeak, evening, *Coccothraustes vespertinus (Hesperiphona vespertina)*
Grosbeak, pine, *Pinicola enucleator*
Ground-dove, common, *Columbina passerina*
Grouse:
  Blue (Sierra, sooty), *Dendragapus obscurus*
  Ruffed, *Bonasa umbellus*

Sage, *Centrocercus urophasianus*
Sharp-tailed, *Tympanuchus*
 (Pedioecetes) phasianellus
Spruce, *Canachites canadensis*
Grunion, *Leuresthes tenuis*
Guillemot, pigeon, *Cepphus*
 columba
Gull, California, *Larus californicus*
Gull, glaucous-winged, *Larus*
 glaucescens
Gull, herring, *Larus argentatus*
Gull, western, *Larus occidentalis*

Hare, snowshoe, *Lepus*
 americanus
Hawk:
 Cooper's, *Accipiter cooperii*
 Marsh (northern harrier),
  Circus cyaneus
 Red-shouldered, *Buteo lineatus*
 Red-tailed, *Buteo jamaicensis*
 Sparrow (see Kestrel)
 Swainson's, *Buteo swainsoni*
 Zone-tailed, *Buteo albonotatus*
Heron, black-crowned night,
 Nycticorax nycticorax
Heron, great blue, *Ardea herodias*
Heron, green, *Butorides striatus*
 (B. virescens)
Hummingbird, Allen's,
 Selasphorus sasin
Hummingbird, broad-billed,
 Cynanthus latirostris
Hummingbird, Costa's, *Calypte*
 costae
Hummingbird, rufous,
 Selasphorus rufus
Hydroid, Hydrozoa

Ibis, white-faced, *Plegadis chihi*
Isopod, Isopoda

Jay:
 Crested (Steller's), *Cyanocitta*
  stelleri
 Gray, *Perisoreus canadensis*
 Pinyon, *Gymnorhinus*
  cyanocephalus
 Scrub, *Aphelocoma coerulescens*
 Scrub, Santa Cruz Island,
  Aphelocoma coerulescens
  insularis
Jellyfish, Scyphozoa
Junco, dark-eyed, *Junco hyemalis*

Kestrel, American, *Falco*
 sparverius
Killdeer, *Charadrius vociferus*
Killifish, *Empetrichthys* spp.
Kingbird, western, *Tyrannus*
 verticalis
Kingfisher, belted, *Ceryle*
 (Megaceryle) alcyon
Kinglet, golden-crowned,
 Regulus satrapa
Kinglet, ruby-crowned, *Regulus*
 calendula
Kite, white-tailed, *Elanus*
 leucurus
Knot, red, *Calidris canutus*

Lagomorph, Lagomorpha
Lamprey, *Entosphenus tridentatus*
Lark, horned, *Eremophila alpestris*
Limpet, file, *Acmaea limatula*
Limpet, giant keyhole,
 Megathura crenulata
Limpet, shield, *Acmaea pelta*
Linnet (house finch), *Carpodacus*
 mexicanus
Littorines (periwinkle), *Littorina*
 spp.
Lizard:
 Alligator, northern,
  Gerrhonotus coeruleus

Alligator, southern,
Gerrhonotus multicarinatus
Brush, long-tailed, *Urosaurus
graciosus*
Chuckwalla, *Sauromalus obesus*
Collared, *Crotaphytus collaris
(Crotaphytus insularis)*
Fringe-toed, *Uma* spp.
Fringe-toed, Coachella Valley,
Uma inornata
Gecko, banded, *Coleonyx
variegatus*
Horned, *Phrynosoma* spp.
Iguana, crested (desert),
Dipsosaurus dorsalis
Leopard, *Crotaphytus
(Gambelia) wislizenii*
Leopard, blunt-nosed San
Joaquin, *Crotaphytus
(Gambelia) silus*
Night, island, *Klauberina
(Xantusia) riversiana*
Night, yucca (desert), *Xantusia
vigilis*
Sagebrush, *Sceloporus graciosus*
Side-blotched, *Uta stansburiana*
Skink, *Eumeces* spp.
Skink, western, *Eumeces
skiltonianus*
Small-scaled, *Urosaurus
microscutatus*
Spiny, desert, *Sceloporus
magister*
Spiny, granite, *Sceloporus orcutti*
Western fence, *Sceloporus
occidentalis*
Whiptail, western,
Cnemidophorus tigris
Zebra-tailed, *Callisaurus
draconoides*
Lobster, California spiny,
Panulirus interruptus
Loon, *Gavia* spp.
Louse, rock, *Ligia occidentalis*
Louse, sea (kelp), *Idothea* spp.

Magpie, black-billed, *Pica pica*
Magpie, yellow-billed, *Pica
nuttalli*
Marmot, yellow-bellied, *Marmota
flaviventris*
Marten, pine, *Martes americana*
Mayfly, Ephemeroptera
Meadowlark, western, *Sturnella
neglecta*
Midge, net-winged,
Blephariceridae
Millipede, Diplopoda
Minnow, Cyprinidae
Mockingbird, *Mimus polyglottos*
Mole, *Scapanus* spp.
Mollusc, Mollusca
Molly, sailfin, *Molliensia latipinna*
Mosquito, Culicidae
Mosquitofish, *Gambusia affinis*
Moss animal, Bryozoa
Moth:
  Cutworm, Noctuidae
  Measuring-worm,
    Geometridae
  Needleminer, Gelechiidae
  Oak, *Phryganidia californica*
  Owlet, Noctuidae
  Pinecone, *Eucosma bobana*
  Sphynx, Sphingidae
  Tent caterpillar, *Malacosoma*
    spp.
  Yucca, *Tegeticula* spp.
Mountain lion, *Felix concolor*
Mouse:
  Brush, *Peromyscus boylii*
  Cactus, *Peromyscus eremicus*
  California, *Peromyscus
    californicus*
  Deer (white-footed), *Peromyscus*
    spp.
  Grasshopper, *Onychomys* spp.
  Harvest, *Reithrodontomys
    megalotis*
  Harvest, salt marsh,
    Reithrodontomys raviventris

Jumping, *Zapus* spp.
Kangaroo, dark, *Microdipodops megacephalus*
Meadow (vole), *Arborimus* spp., *Clethrionomys* spp., *Lagurus* spp., *Microtis* spp., *Phenacomys* spp.
Pinyon, *Peromyscus truei*
Pocket, Bailey's, *Perognathus baileyi*
Pocket, California, *Perognathus californicus*
Pocket, desert, *Perognathus penicillatus*
Pocket, Great Basin, *Perognathus parvus*
Pocket, hispid, *Perognathus hispidus*
Pocket, little, *Perognathus longimembris*
Pocket, San Joaquin, *Perognathus inornatus*
Pocket, silky, *Perognathus flavus*
Red tree vole, *Arborimus longicaudus*
Rock, *Peromyscus difficilis*
Sagebrush vole, *Lagurus curtatus*
White-footed, *Peromyscus* spp.
Murex, *Maxwellia gemma*, *Pteropurpura festivus*
Murre, California (common), *Uria aalge*
Murrelet, Xantus', *Endomychura hypoleuca*
Mussel, bay, *Mytilus edulis*
Mussel, California, *Mytilus californianus*
Mysid, opossum, Mysidacea

Needleminer (see Moth: Needleminer)
Newt, California (water dog), *Taricha torosa*

Newt, red-bellied, *Taricha rivularis*
Nighthawk, *Chordeiles* spp.
Nudibranch (sea slug), Nudibranchia
Nutcracker, Clark's, *Nucifraga columbiana*
Nuthatch, pygmy, *Sitta pygmaea*
Nuthatch, red-breasted, *Sitta canadensis*
Nuthatch, white-breasted, *Sitta carolinensis*

Octopus, *Octopus* spp.
Olivella, purple, *Olivella biplicata*
Opaleye, *Girella nigricans*
Oriole, hooded, *Icterus cucullatus*
Oriole, northern, "Bullock's," *Icterus galbula*
Oriole, Scott's, *Icterus parisorum*
Ostracod, Ostracoda
Owl:
　Burrowing, *Athene (Speotyto) cunicularia*
　Elf, *Micrathene whitneyi*
　Great horned, *Bubo virginianus*
　Long-eared, *Asio otus*
　Pygmy, *Glaucidium gnoma*
　Screech, common, *Otus asio*
　Spotted, *Strix occidentalis*
Oyster, Ostreidae
Oyster borer, Japanese, *Ocenebra japonica*
Oystercatcher, black, *Haematopus bachmani*
Oyster drill, *Urosalpinx cinereus*

Pecten, Pectinidae
Pelican, brown, *Pelecanus occidentalis*
Perch, Percidae
Periwinkle (see Littorines)
Phainopepla, *Phainopepla nitens*

Phalarope, northern, *Phalaropus (Lobipes) lobatus*
Phalarope, Wilson's, *Phalaropus (Steganopus) tricolor*
Phoebe, Say's, *Sayornis saya*
Piddock, Pholadidae
Pigeon, band-tailed, *Columba fasciata*
Pika (cony), *Ochotona princeps*
Pinniped, Pinnipedia
Plover, black-bellied, *Pluvialis squatarola*
Plover, snowy, *Charadrius alexandrinus*
Poorwill, common, *Phalaenoptilus nuttallii*
Porcupine, *Erethizon dorsatum*
Porpoise, Dall's, *Phocoenoides dalli*
Porpoise, harbor, *Phocoena phocoena*
Puffin, tufted, *Lunda cirrhata*
Pupfish:
　Desert, *Cyprinodon macularis*
　Devil's Hole, *Cyprinodon diabolis*
　Owens, *Cyprinodon radiosus*
　Salt Creek, *Cyprinodon salinus*
　Saratoga Springs, *Cyprinodon nevadensis nevadensis*

Quail, California, *Callipepla (Lophortyx) californica*
Quail, Gamble's, *Callipepla (Lophortyx) gambelii*
Quail, mountain, *Oreortyx pictus*

Rabbit, brush, *Sylvilagus bachmani*
Rabbit, cottontail, desert, *Sylvilagus audubonii*
Rabbit, jack, *Lepus californicus*
Rabbit, pygmy, *Brachylagus idahoensis*
Raccoon, *Procyon lotor*
Rail, black, *Laterallus jamaicensis*

Rail, clapper, *Rallus longirostris*
Rail, Virginia, *Rallus limicola*
Rat, kangaroo, Great Basin (chisel-toothed), *Dipodomys microps*
Rat, kangaroo, Heermann's, *Dipodomys heermanni*
Rat, kangaroo, Merriam's, *Dipodomys merriami*
Rat, kangaroo, San Joaquin, *Dipodomys nitratoides*
Rat, wood, desert, *Neotoma lepida*
Rat, wood, dusky-footed, *Neotoma fuscipes*
Raven, common, *Corvus corax*
Ray, Elasmobranchii
Ringtail, *Bassariscus astutus*
Roadrunner, *Geococcyx californianus*
Robin, American, *Turdus migratorius*
Rotifer, Rotifera

Salamander:
　Ensatina, *Ensatina eschscholtzi*
　Giant, *Dicamptodon ensatus*
　Limestone, *Hydromantes brunus*
　Northwestern, *Ambystoma gracile*
　Santa Cruz long-toed, *Ambystoma macrodactylum croceum*
Slender:
　California, *Batrachoseps attenuatus*
　Desert, *Batrachoseps aridus*
　Garden, *Batrachoseps pacificus major*
　Inyo, *Batrachoseps campi*
　Kern, *Batrachoseps simatus*
　Oregon, *Batrachoseps wrighti*
　Pacific, *Batrachoseps pacificus*
　Relictual, *Batrachoseps pacificus relictus (B. relictus)*

Tehachapi, *Batrachoseps stebbinsi*
Tiger, *Ambystoma tigrinum (A. californiense)*
Salmon, *Oncorhynchus* spp.
Sand dollar, *Dendraster excentricus*
Sanderling, *Calidris alba*
Sandfly, Ceratopogonidae
Sandpiper family, Scolopacidae
Sandpiper, western, *Calidris mauri*
Sapsucker, Williamson's, *Sphyrapicus thyroideus*
Sapsucker, yellow-bellied, *Sphyrapicus varius*
Scale, oak pit, *Asterolecanium* spp.
Scallop, Pectinidae
Scorpion, Scorpionida
Sculpin, tide pool, *Clinocottus analis, Oligocottus maculosus*
Sea anemone, aggregated, *Anthopleura elegantissima*
Sea anemone, burrowing, *Anthopleura artemisia, Cerianthus aesturi*
Sea anemone, solitary green, *Anthopleura xanthogrammica*
Sea cucumber, *Holothuroidea*
Sea fan, Gorgonacea
Sea lion, California, *Zalophus californianus*
Sea lion, Steller (northern), *Eumetopias jubata*
Sea otter, *Enhydra lutris*
Sea pansy, *Renilla kollikeri*
Sea pen, *Acanthoptilum gracile, Stylatula elongata*
Sea spider, Pycnogonidae
Sea squirt, Ascidiacea
Sea star:
    Brittle (serpent), Ophiuroidea
    Sand star, southern, *Astropecten armatus*

Starfish, blue, *Piaster giganteus*
Starfish, common (ochre), *Piaster ochraceous*
Starfish, red, *Henricia leviuscula*
Sunflower, star, *Pycnopodia helianthoides*
Sea urchin, giant red, *Strongylocentrotus franciscanus*
Sea urchin, purple, *Strongylocentrotus purpuratus*
Sea whip, Gorgonacea
Seal, elephant, northern, *Mirounga augustirostris*
Seal, fur, Guadalupe, *Arctocephalus townsendi*
Seal, fur, northern, *Callorhinus ursinus*
Seal, harbor, *Phoca vitulina*
Shark, Elasmobranchii
Sheep, bighorn (mountain), *Ovis canadensis*
Shell, slipper (see Snail: Slipper shell)
Shipworm (see Clam: Boring)
Shrew, Mount Lyell, *Sorex lyelli*
Shrew, Trowbridge, *Sorex trowbridgii*
Shrike, loggerhead, *Lanius ludovicianus*
Shrimp:
    Brine (desert), *Artemia salina*
    Broken back, *Spirontocaris* spp.
    Clam, *Cyzicus mexicanus*
    Fairy, Phyllopoda
    Ghost, *Callianassa californiensis*
    Gray, *Crago* spp.
    Mud, *Upogebia pugettensis*
    Pistol (snapping), *Crangon* spp.
    Skeleton, *Caprella* spp.
    Transparent, *Spirontocaris paludicola, S. picta*
Silverfish, Lepismatidae
Skate, Elasmobranchii
Skipper, giant yucca, *Megathymus yuccae*

Skunk, spotted, *Spilogale gracilis*
(*S. putorius*)
Skunk, striped, *Mephitis mephitis*
Snail:
  Barrel, Acteonidae
  Basket, Nassariidae
  Basket, channeled, *Nassarius fossatus*
  Bubble, Atyidae, Bullidae
  Bubble shell, cloudy, *Bulla gouldiana*
  Horn, Cerithiidae
  Horn, California, *Cerithidea californica*
  Moon, Naticidae
  Moon, northern, *Polinices lewisi*
  Moon, southern, *Polinices reclusianus*
  Rock, Muricidae
  Slipper shell, *Crepidula* spp.
  Top, Trochidae
  Tube, *Aletes squamigerus*
  Turban, *Tegula* spp.
  Turban, black, *Tegula funebralis*
  Tusk, Scaphopoda
  Tusk, polished, *Dentalium semipolitum*
  Wavy top, *Astraea undosa*
Snake:
  Boa, rosy, *Lichanura trivirgata*
  Boa, rubber, *Charina bottae*
  Coachwhip, *Masticophis flagellum*
  Coral, *Micrurus fulvius*
  Garter, *Thamnophis* spp.
  Glossy, *Arizona elegans*
  Gopher, *Pituophis melanoleucus*
  Gopher, Great Basin, *Pituophis melanoleucus deserticola*
  King, *Lampropeltis getulus*
  King, mountain, *Lampropeltis zonata*
  Leaf-nosed, *Phyllorhynchus decurtatus*
  Long-nosed, *Rhinocheilus lecontei*

  Lyre, California, *Trimorphodon vandenburghi* (*Trimorphodon biscutatus vandenburghi*)
  Night, *Hypsiglena torquata*
  Patch-nosed, western, *Salvadora hexalepis*
  Racer, red, *Masticophus flagellum piceus*
  Racer (yellow-bellied), *Coluber constrictor*
  Rattlesnake, Mojave green, *Crotalus scutulatus*
  Rattlesnake, Pacific, northern, *Crotalus viridis oreganus*
  Rattlesnake, Pacific, southern, *Crotalus viridis helleri*
  Rattlesnake, speckled, *Crotalus mitchelli*
  Rattlesnake, western, *Crotalus viridis*
  Sharp-tailed, *Contia tenuis*
  Shovel-nosed, *Chionactis occipitalis*
  Sidewinder, *Crotalus cerastes*
Snipe, common (Wilson's), *Gallinago gallinago*
Solpugid, Solpugida
Sow bug, *Porcellio* spp.
Sparrow:
  Black-chinned, *Spizella atrogularis*
  Black-throated, *Amphispiza bilineata*
  Brewer's, *Spizella breweri*
  Chipping, *Spizella passerina*
  Fox, *Passerella iliaca*
  Lincoln's, *Passerella lincolnii*
  Rufous-crowned, *Aimophila ruficeps*
  Sage (Bell's), *Amphispiza belli*
  Savanna, *Ammodramus sandwichensis*
  Song, *Passerella melodia*
  Vesper, *Pooecetes gramineus*
  White-crowned, *Zonotrichia leucophrys*

Spider, Araneida
Sponge, Porifera
Spoonbill, roseate, *Ajaia ajaja*
Springtail, Collembola
Squawfish, *Ptychocheilus grandis*
Squirrel, flying, *Glaucomys sabrinus*
Squirrel, gray, *Sciurus griseus*
Squirrel:
Ground, antelope, *Ammospermophilus leucurus*
Ground, Belding, *Spermophilus beldingi*
Ground, California, *Spermophilus beecheyi*
Ground, golden-mantled, *Spermophilus lateralis*
Ground, Mojave, *Spermophilus mohavensis*
Ground, round-tailed, *Spermophilus tereticaudus*
Stilt, black-necked, *Himantopus mexicanus*
Stone-fly, Plecoptera
Storm-petrel, ashy, *Oceanodroma homochroa*
Sucker, Catostomidae
Sucker, Owens, *Catostomus fumeiventris*
Surfbird, *Aphriza virgata*
Swan, whistling, *Cygnus columbianus*
Sweet potato cucumber, *Molpadia arenicola*
Swift, black, *Cypseloides niger*
Swift, Vaux, *Chaetura vauxi*

Tanager, summer, *Piranga rubra*
Tanager, western, *Piranga ludoviciana*
Tarantula, *Aphonopelma* spp.
Tarantula hawk, *Pepsis* spp.
Tattler, wandering, *Heteroscelus incanus*
Termite, Isoptera

Tern, *Sterna* spp.
Tern, least, *Sterna albifrons*
Thrasher, Bendire's, *Toxostoma bendirei*
Thrasher, California, *Toxostoma redivivum*
Thrasher, crissal, *Toxostoma dorsale*
Thrasher, Le Conte's, *Toxostoma lecontei*
Thrasher, sage, *Oreoscoptes montanus*
Thrush, hermit, *Catharus guttatus (Hylocichla guttata)*
Thrush, Swainson's (russet-backed), *Catharus ustulatus (Hylocichla ustulata)*
Thrush, varied, *Zoothera naevia (Ixoreus naevius)*
Titmouse, plain, *Parus inornatus*
Toad:
Colorado River, *Bufo alvarius*
Red-spotted, *Bufo punctatus*
Spadefoot, Couch's, *Scaphiopus couchi*
Spadefoot, Great Basin, *Scaphiopus intermontanus*
Spadefoot, western, *Scaphiopus hammondi*
Western, *Bufo boreas*
Woodhouse's, *Bufo woodhousei*
Toebiter, *Abedus indentatus*
Tortoise, desert, *Gopherus agassizi*
Towhee, brown, *Pipilo fuscus*
Towhee, green-tailed, *Pipilo chlorurus (Chlorura chlorura)*
Towhee, rufous-sided, *Pipilo erythrophthalmus*
Townsend's solitaire, *Myadestes townsendi*
Treefrog, California, *Hyla cadaverina*
Treefrog, Pacific, *Hyla regilla*
Trout, *Salmo* spp., *Salvelinus* spp.
Trout, cutthroat, *Salmo clarkii*
Trout, golden, *Salmo aguabonita*

Trout, steelhead, *Salmo gairdnerii gairdnerii*
Tube worm, a number of families in Polychaeta including Maldanidae, Pectinariidae, Sabellariidae, Serpulidae
Tube worm, fat innkeeper, *Urechis caupo*
Tunicates, Urochordata *(Tunicata)*
Turkey, wild (common), *Meleagris gallopavo*
Turnstone, black, *Arenaria melanocephala*
Turtle, green, *Chelonia mydas*
Turtle, western pond, *Clemmys marmorata*

Unicorn shell, *Acanthina spirata*

Velella (by-the-wind-sailor), *Velella velella*
Verdin, *Auriparus flaviceps*
Vireo:
Bell's, *Vireo bellii*
Hutton's, *Vireo huttoni*
Solitary, *Vireo solitarius*
Warbling, *Vireo gilvus*
Vole (see Mouse)
Vulture:
Black, *Coragyps atratus*
King, *Sarcoramphus papa*
Turkey, *Cathartes aura*
Yellow-headed, *Cathartes burrovianus*
Yellow-headed, greater, *Cathartes melambrotus*

Warbler:
Black-and-white, *Mniotilta varia*
Black-throated gray, *Dendroica nigrescens*
Hermit, *Dendroica occidentalis*

Lucy's, *Vermivora luciae*
MacGillivray's, *Oporornis tolmiei*
Nashville, *Vermivora ruficapilla*
Orange-crowned, *Vermivora celata*
Wilson's, *Wilsonia pusilla*
Yellow, *Dendroica petechia*
Yellow-rumped, *Dendroica coronata*
Yellowthroat, *Geothlypis trichas*
Wasp, braconid, Braconidae
Wasp, chalcid, chalcidoidea
Wasp, cynipid (gall), Cynipidae
Water boatman, Corixidae
Water bug, creeping, Naucoridae
Water bug, giant, Belostomatidae
Water dog (see Newt, California)
Water pennies, Psephenidae
Water strider, Geridae
Weasel, *Mustela frenata*
Weevil, California acorn, *Curculio uniformis*
Weevil, yucca-boring, *Scyphophorus yuccae*
Whale:
False killer, *Pseudorca crassidens*
Hump-backed, *Megaptera novaeangliae*
Killer, *Orcinus orca*
Minke, *Balaenoptera acutorostrata*
Pacific gray, *Eschrichtius robustus (E. gibbosus)*
Pilot, *Globicephala scammonii*
Whimbrel, *Numenius phaeopus*
Whitefly, crown, *Aleuroplatus coronatus*
Wildebeest, *Connochaetes taurinus*
Willet, *Catoptrophorus semipalmatus*
Wolverine, *Gulo gulo*

Woodpecker:
Acorn, *Melanerpes formicivorus*
Downy, *Picoides (Dendrocopos) pubescens*
Gila, *Melanerpes uropygialis*
Hairy, *Picoides (Dendrocopos) villosus*
Ladder-backed, *Picoides (Dendrocopos) scalaris*
Lewis', *Melanerpes (Asyndesmus) lewis*
Nuttall's, *Picoides (Dendrocopos) nuttallii*
Pileated, *Dryocopus pileatus*
Three-toed, *Picoides arcticus*
White-headed, *Picoides (Dendrocopus) albolarvatus*
Wood-pewee, western, *Contopus sordidulus*

Worm, bristle (polychaete), Polychaeta
Worm, sand-castle, *Phragmatopoma californica*
Wren:
Bewick's, *Thryomanes bewickii*
Cactus, *Campylorhynchus brunneicapillus*
Canyon, *Catherpes mexicanus*
House, *Troglodytes aedon*
Marsh, *Cistothorus (Telmatodytes) palustris*
Winter, *Troglodytes troglodytes*
Wrentit, *Chamaea fasciata*

Yellowlegs, greater, *Tringa melanoleuca (Totanus melanoleucus)*

Zebra, *Equus burchelli*

List of Plants

Abies hebrodensis
Acacia, *Acacis* spp.
Agave, *Agave* spp.
Agave, Shaw's, *Agave shawii*
Alder, mountain, *Alnus tenuifolia*
Alder, red, *Alnus rubra*
Alder, white, *Alnus rhombifolia*
Alkaligrass, *Puccinellia* spp.
Alkali sacaton, *Sporobolus airoides*
Allscale (common saltbush),
    Atriplex polycarpa
Aloe, *Aloe* spp.
Alpine flames, *Haplopappus
    apargioides*
Alpine gold, *Hulsea algida*
Alumroot, *Heuchera* spp.
Alumroot, island, *Heuchera
    maxima*
Apache plume, *Fallugia paradoxa*
Arnica, serpentine, *Arnica cernua*
Arrow-grass, *Triglochin* spp.
Arrowhead, *Sagittaria* spp.
Arrowweed, *Pluchea sericea*
Ash, Arizona, *Fraxinus velutina*
Ash, flowering, *Fraxinus dipetala*
Ash, Oregon, *Fraxinus latifolia*
Ash, single-leaf, *Fraxinus
    anomala*
Aspen, quaking, *Populus
    tremuloides*
Aster, *Aster* spp.
Aster, alpine, *Aster peirsonii*
Aster, Mojave, *Aster mohavensis*
Avocado, *Persea* spp.
Azalea, western, *Rhododendron
    occidentale*

Baby-blue-eyes, *Nemophila
    menziesii*
Baldcypress, *Taxodium distichum*
Barberry, *Berberis* spp.
Barley, mouse, *Hordeum
    leporinum*
Barranca-brush, *Ceanothus
    verrucosus*
Basswood, *Tilia* spp.
Bay, California, *Umbellularia
    californica*
Beach silverweed (beach bur),
    Franseria chamissonis
Bearberry, *Arctotstaphylos
    Uva-ursi*
Beech, *Fagus* spp.
Bee plant, *Cleome* spp.
Bentgrass, *Agrostis* spp.
Big tree (giant sequoia),
    Sequoiadendron giganteum
Birch, paper, *Betula papyrifera*
Birch, water, *Betula occidentalis*
Bird's beak, *Cordylanthus
    maritimus*
Bird's-foot trefoil, *Lotus* spp.
Bitterbrush, antelope, *Purshia
    tridentata*
Bitterbrush, desert, *Purshia
    glandulosa*
Bitterroot, pygmy, *Lewisia
    pygmaea* (*L. sierrae* is also a
    dwarf subalpine-alpine
    species)
Blackberry, *Rubus vitifolius*
Blackbrush, *Coleogyne
    ramosissima*

Bladderpod, *Isomeris arborea*
Bladderwort, *Utricularia* spp.
Blazing star, *Mentzelia* spp.
Bleeding heart, *Dicentra formosa*
Blueberry, mountain, *Vaccinium occidentale*
Blue dicks, *Brodiaea pulchella*
Blue-eyed grass, *Sisyrinchium bellum*
Bluegrass, maritime, *Poa douglasii*
Bluegrass, pine, *Poa scabrella*
Bluegrass, Sandberg, *Poa sandbergii*
Bluejoint grass, *Calamagrostis canadensis*
Boojum tree, *Idria columnaris*
Boxelder, *Acer negundo*
Boxthorn (desert thorn), *Lycium* spp.
Bracken, *Pteridium aquilinum*
Brass buttons, *Cotula coronopifolia*
Brittle bush, *Encelia farinosa*
Brodiaea, harvest, *Brodiaea elegans*
Brome, *Bromus* spp.
Brome, California, *Bromus carinatus*
Brome, red, *Bromus rubens*
Buck brush, *Ceanothus cuneatus*
Buckeye, California, *Aesculus californica*
Buckwheat:
   Bear Valley, *Eriogonum kennedyi* ssp. *austromontanum*
   California, *Eriogonum fasciculatum*
   Cushion, *Eriogonum caespitosum*
   Dune (desert), *Eriogonum deserticola*
   Great Basin, *Eriogonum microthecum*
   Ione, *Eriogonum apricum*
   Kennedy, *Eriogonum kennedyi*
   Lobb's, *Eriogonum lobbii*
   (North coast) *Eriogonum latifolium*
   Ocher-flowered, *Eriogonum ochrocephalum*
Bud-sage, *Artemisia spinescens*
Buffaloberry, *Shepherdia argentea*
Bulrush, *Scirpus* spp.
Burning bush, western, *Euonymus occidentalis*
Bur-sage, *Ambrosia dumosa* (*Franseria dumosa*)
Bushrue, *Cneoridium dumosum*
Buttercup, aquatic, *Ranunculus aquatilis*
Buttercup, desert, *Ranunculus cymbalaria*
Buttonbush, *Cephalanthus occidentalis*

Cactus:
Barrel, *Ferocactus acanthodes*
Barrel, coast, *Ferocactus viridescens*
Cholla, *Opuntia* spp.
Cholla, coast, *Opuntia prolifera*
Cholla, dwarf, *Opuntia pulchella*
Cholla, snake, *Opuntia parryi* (*O. serpentina*)
Fishhook, *Mammillaria* spp., *Phellosperma tetrancistra*
Galloping, *Pitaya agria*
Prickly pear, *Opuntia* spp.
Prickly pear, coastal, *Opuntia littoralis*, *O. oricola*
Prickly pear, Mojave, *Opuntia mojavensis*
Saguaro, *Carnegiea gigantea* (*Cereus giganteus*)
Velvet, *Bergerocactus emoryi*
Calico plant, *Langloisia matthewsii*
Camas, *Camassia leichtlinii*
Campion, moss, *Silene acaulis*

Canterbury-bell, wild, *Phacelia minor*
Carpet clover, *Trifolium monanthum*
Cassava, *Manihot esculenta*
Cassiope, *Cassiope mertensiana*
Catclaw, *Acacia greggii*
Cattail, *Typha* spp.
Ceanothus:
Blue blossom, *Ceanothus thyrsiflorus*
Blue blossom, prostrate, *Ceanothus thyrsiflorus* var. *repens*
Chaparral whitethorn, *Ceanothus leucodermis*
Coville's, *Ceanothus pinetorum*
Desert, *Ceanothus greggii*
Hoaryleaf, *Ceanothus crassifolius*
Jepson (muskbrush), *Ceanothus jepsonii*
Otay, *Ceanothus otayensis*
Cedar, Alaska, *Chamaecyparis nootkatensis*
Cedar, incense, *Calocedrus decurrens*
Cedar, Port Orford, *Chamaecyparis lawsoniana*
Cedar, pygmy, *Peucephyllum schottii*
Cedar, western red (canoe), *Thuja plicata*
Century plant, *Agave* spp.
Cercocarpus (see Mountain mahogany)
Chamise, *Adenostoma fasciculatum*
Chara, *Chara* spp.
Cheatgrass, *Bromus tectorum*
Checker bloom, *Sidalcea malvaeflora*
Cheese bush, *Hymenoclea salsola*
Cherry, bitter, *Prunus emarginata*
Cherry, hollyleaf, *Prunus ilicifolia*

Cherry, island, *Prunus lyonii* (*P. ilicifolia* ssp. *lyonii*)
Chess, soft, *Bromus mollis*
Chia, *Salvia columbariae*
Chiming bells, *Mertensia ciliata*
Chinch weed, *Pectis papposa*
Chinese houses, *Collinsia heterophylla*
Chinquapin, bush, *Chrysolepis sempervirens* (*Castanopsis sempervirens*)
Chinquapin (giant), *Chrysolepis chrysophylla* (*Castanopsis chrysophylla*)
Chokecherry, *Prunus virginiana*
Chuparosa (beloperone), *Beloperone californica*
Cinquefoil, Brewer's, *Potentilla breweri*
Cinquefoil, Mount Rainier, *Potentilla flabellifolia*
Cinquefoil, shrubby, *Potentilla fruticosa*
Clarkia, *Clarkia* spp.
Clematis (virgin's bower), *Clematis* spp.
Cliff rose, *Cowania mexicana*
Clintonia, red, *Clintonia andrewsiana*
Club moss, *Lycopodium* spp.
Coffeeberry, *Rhamnus californica*
Coldenia, Palmer, *Coldenia palmeri*
Columbine, alpine, *Aquilegia pubescens*
Columbine, blue, *Aquilegia coerulea*
Columbine, red, *Aquilegia formosa*
Cone flower, *Rudbeckia californica*
Cordgrass, *Spartina foliosa*
Cordia, *Cordia* spp.
Coreopsis, desert, *Coreopsis bigelovii, C. calliopsidea*
Coreopsis, giant, *Coreopsis*

gigantea
Coreopsis, maritime, *Coreopsis maritima*
Cotton thorn, *Tetradymia spinosa*
Cottonwood, black, *Populus trichocarpa*
Cottonwood, Fremont, *Populus fremontii*
Cow clover, *Trifolium wormskjoldii*
Cow parsnip, *Heracleum lanatum*
Coyotebrush, *Baccharis pilularis* ssp. *consanguinea*
Cranesbill, *Geranium richardsonii*
Cream bush, littleleaf, *Holodiscus microphyllus*
Cream bush (ocean spray), *Holodiscus discolor*
Cream cup, *Platystemon californicus*
Creosote bush, *Larrea tridentata*
Croton, *Croton californicus*
Croton, Wiggins (desert), *Croton wigginsii*
Crucifixion thorn, *Holacantha emoryi*, *Koeberlinia spinosa*
Cryptomeria japonica
Cucumber, wild, *Marah fabaceus*
Currant, *Ribes* spp.
Currant, alpine prickly, *Ribes montigenum*
Currant, golden, *Ribes aureum*
Currant, mountain pink, *Ribes nevadense*
Currant, red-flowering, *Ribes sanguineum* var. *glutinosum*
Currant, squaw, *Ribes cereum*
Cushion-cress (see Draba: Lemmon's)
Cycad, *Cycas* spp.
Cypress:
Abrams, *Cupressus abramsiana*
Arizona, *Cupressus arizonica*
Arizona, smooth, *Cupressus glabra*
Cuyamaca, *Cupressus stephensonii*

Gowen, *Cupressus goveniana*
Guadalupe, *Cupressus guadalupensis*
Macnab, *Cupressus macnabiana*
Modoc, *Cupressus bakeri*
Monterey, *Cupressus macrocarpa*
Piute, *Cupressus nevadensis*
Pygmy (Mendocino), *Cupressus pygmaea*
Sargent, *Cupressus sargentii*
Tecate, *Cupressus forbesii*

Daisy, Clokey's, *Erigeron clokeyi*
Daisy, dwarf alpine, *Erigeron pygmaeus*
Daisy, seaside, *Erigeron glaucus*
Dalea, Mojave, *Dalea arborescens*
Dalea, Nevada, *Dalea polyadenia*
Dandelion, *Taraxacum officinale*
Deerbrush, *Ceanothus integerrimus*
Deergrass, *Muhlenbergia rigens*
Deerweed, *Lotus scoparius*
Desert almond, *Prunus fasciculata*
Desert apricot, *Prunus fremontii*
Desert bells, *Phacelia campanularia*
Desert blite, *Suaeda fruticosa*
Desert dandelion, *Malacothrix glabrata*
Desert holly, *Atriplex hymenelytra*
Desert marigold, *Baileya* spp.
Desert peach, *Prunus andersonii*
Desert star, *Monoptilon bellioides*
Desert-sunflower, *Geraea canescens*
Desert sweet, *Chamaebatiaria millefolium*
Desert trumpet, *Eriogonum inflatum*
Desert willow, *Chilopsis linearis*
Dock, *Rumex* spp.
Dock, curly-leafed, *Rumex crispus*
Dodder, *Cuscuta* spp.
Dogwood, creek, *Cornus stolonifera*

Dogwood, Pacific (mountain),
   Cornus nuttallii
Douglas-fir, *Psuedotsuga menziesii*
Douglas-fir, big-cone,
   Psuedotsuga macrocarpa
Downingia spp.
Draba:
   Comb, *Draba oligosperma*
   Dense-leaved, *Draba densifolia*
   Lemmon's, *Draba lemmonii*
   Snow, *Draba lonchocarpa* (*D.
   nivalis* var. *elongata*)
   White Arctic, *Draba fladnizensis*
Dragon tree, *Dracaena draco*
Duckweed, *Lemna* spp.
Dunegrass, Eureka, *Swallenea
   alexandrae*

Eardrops, white, *Dicentra
   ochroleuca*
Eel-grass, *Zostera marina*
Elderberry, *Sambucus* spp.
Elderberry, red, *Sambucus
   microbotrys*
Elephant's head, *Pedicularis
   attolens*, *P. groenlandica*
Elephant tree, *Bursera microphylla*
Elm, *Ulmus* spp.
Eriophylum spp.
Eschscholzia californica (see also
   Poppy: California)
Eucalyptus spp.
Everlasting, alpine, *Antennaria
   alpina*
Everlasting, pearly, *Anaphalis
   margaritacea*
Everlasting, rosy, *Antennaria
   rosea*

Fairy bells, *Disporum hookeri*
Fairy duster, *Calliandra eriophylla*
Fairy lantern, *Calochortus albus*
Farallon weed, *Lasthenia minor*
Farewell-to-spring, *Clarkia* spp.

Fern:
   Chain, *Woodwardia fimbriata*
   Duckweed, *Azolla filiculoides*
   Five-finger, *Adiantum pedatum*
   var. *aleuticum*
   Lady, *Athyrium filix-femina* var.
   californicum
   Maidenhair, *Adiantum* spp.
   Sword, *Polystichum munitum*
   Wood, *Dryopteris* spp.
Fescue, European, *Festuca
   dertonensis*
Fescue, foxtail, *Festuca megalura*
Fescue, sixweeks, *Festuca
   octoflora*
Fiddleneck, *Amsinckia* spp.
Fiesta flower, *Pholistoma* spp.
Fig, *Ficus* spp.
Filaree, *Erodium* spp.
Fir:
   Grand (lowland), *Abies grandis*
   Noble, *Abies procera*
   Red, *Abies magnifica*
   Saint Lucia, *Abies bracteata*
   Silver, *Abies amabilis*
   Subalpine, *Abies lasiocarpa*
   White, *Abies concolor*
Fivespot, *Malvastrum
   rotundifolium*
Flannel bush, *Fremontodendron
   californicum*
Flax, western, *Linum perenne*
Forget-me-not, *Myosotis* spp.
Four-o'clock, *Mirabilis bigelovii*
Frankenia, *Frankenia grandifolia*
   (*F. palmeri*, San Diego County
   and south)
Fringe cup, Alaska, *Tellima
   grandiflora*
Fuchsia, California, *Zauschneria
   californica*

Gaillardia, *Gaillardia* spp.
Galleta, big, *Hilaria rigida*

Garrya (silk tassel), *Garrya* spp.
Gazania, *Gazania*, spp.
Gentian, blue, *Gentiana* spp.
Gentian, green, *Frasera speciosa*
Gerbera, *Gerbera* spp.
Ghost flower, *Mohavea* spp.
Gilia:
  Bird's eye, *Gilia tricolor*
  Broad, *Gilia latiflora* (also called bird's eye)
  Golden, *Linanthus aureus*
  Granite, *Leptodactylon pungens*
  Nevin's, *Gilia nevenii*
  Scarlet, *Ipomopsis aggregata*
Ginger, wild, *Asarum caudatum*
Gingko, *Gingko biloba*
Gladiolus spp.
Goatgrass, *Aegilops* spp.
Goatnut (jojoba), *Simmondsia chinensis*
Gold carpet, *Gilmania luteola*
Goldenbush, *Haplopappus* spp.
Goldenrod, *Solidago* spp.
Goldenrod (north coastal), *Solidago spathulata*
Goldenstar, *Bloomeria crocea*
Goldfields, *Lasthenia chrysostoma*
Gooseberry, alpine, *Ribes lasianthum*
Gooseberry, fuchsia-flowering, *Ribes speciosum*
Goosefoot family, Chenopodiaceae
Grape, wild, *Vitis californica*
Grass, American dune, *Elymus mollis*
Grass, beach, *Ammophila arenaria*
Grass nut (Ithuriel's spear), *Brodiaea laxa*
Grass, surf, *Phyllospadix* spp.
Grass, thin, *Agrostis diegoensis*
Gray thorn, *Condalia lycioides*
Greasewood, big, *Sarcobatus vermiculatus*
Greasewood, little, *Sarcobatus*

baileyi
Groundsel, *Senecio* spp.
Gum plant, *Grindelia* spp.

Hackberry, netleaf, *Celtis reticulata*
Hairgrass, *Aira* spp., *Deschampsia* spp.
Hairgrass, silver, *Aira caryophyllea*
Hairgrass, tufted, *Deschampsia caespitosa*
Harebell, *Campanula rotundifolia*
Hazelnut, *Corylus cornuta* var. *californica*
Heart's ease, *Viola ocellata*
Heather, mock, *Haplopappus ericoides*
Heather, red mountain, *Phyllodoce breweri*
Hemlock, mountain, *Tsuga mertensiana*
Hemlock, western, *Tsuga heterophylla*
Hibiscus, California, *Hibiscus californicus*
Hickory, *Carya* spp.
Hollyhock, wild, *Sidalcea reptans*
Honey-myrtle, *Callistemon* spp.
Honeysuckle, *Lonicera* spp.
Hopsage, spiny, *Grayia spinosa*
Horehound, *Marrabium vulgare*
Horsebrush, *Tetradymia* spp.
Horsetail, *Equisteum* spp.
Hottentot fig, *Carpobrotus (Mesembryanthemum) edulis*
Huckleberry, *Vaccinium* spp.
Hulsea, alpine (see Alpine gold)
Hulsea, pumice, *Hulsea vestita*

Ice plant, *Gasoul (Mesembryanthemum) crystallinum*
Indigo bush, *Dalea fremontii*

Inkweed, *Suaeda torreyana* var.
    ramosissima
Iodine bush, *Allenrolfea*
    occidentalis
Iris, blue flag, *Iris missouriensis*
Iris, Douglas, *Iris douglasiana*
Iris, Sierra, *Iris hartwegii, I.*
    macrosiphon
Ironwood, desert, *Olneya tesota*
Ironwood, island, *Lyonothamnus*
    floribundus
Ivesia, clubmoss, *Ivesia*
    lycopodioides
Ivesia, dwarf (pygmy), *Ivesia*
    pygmaea
Ivesia, Shockley's, *Ivesia shockleyi*
Ixia, *Ixia* spp.

Jaumea, *Jaumea carnosa*
Jewel flower, mountain,
    Streptanthus tortuosus
Johnny tuck, *Orthocarpus*
    erianthus
Joshua tree, *Yucca brevifolia*
July gold, *Dedeckera eurekensis*
Juniper:
    Alligator, *Juniperus deppeana*
    Ashe, *Juniperus ashei*
    California, *Juniperus californica*
    Common, *Juniperus communis*
    Creeping, *Juniperus horizontalis*
    Drooping, *Juniperus flaccida*
    Mountain, *Juniperus occidentalis*
    ssp. *australis*
    One-seed, *Juniperus*
    monosperma
    Red-berry, *Juniperus pinchotii*
    Rocky Mountain, *Juniperus*
    scopulorum
    Utah, *Juniperus osteosperma*
    Western, *Juniperus occidentalis*
    ssp. *occidentalis*

Kangaroo paw, *Anigozanthos*
    manglesii
Knotweed, dwarf, *Polygonum*
    minimum
Kobresia, *Kobresia myosuroides*

Labrador tea, *Ledum glandulosum*
Larch, alpine, *Larix lyallii*
Larch, western, *Larix occidentalis*
Lasthenia, *Lasthenia glabrata*
Laurel, American (alpine),
    Kalmia polifolia
Laurel sumac, *Malosma laurina*
Lavender, *Lavandula*
Lemonadeberry, *Rhus integrifolia*
Lenscale, *Atriplex lentiformis*
Lichen, pendant, *Usnea,*
    Ramalina
Lichen, reindeer, *Cladina pacifica*
Lichen, staghorn, *Letharia*
    vulpina
Lily:
    Alp, *Lloydia serotina*
    Corn, *Veratrum californicum*
    Desert "Easter," *Hesperocallis*
    undulata
    Globe (see Fairy lantern)
    Lemon, *Lilium parryi*
    Mariposa, *Calochortus* spp.
    Mariposa, Kennedy,
    Calochortus kennedyi
    Sierra, *Lilium kelleyanum*
    Star, *Zigadenus fremontii*
    Water (wocas), *Nuphar*
    polysepalum
Liquidambar (sweet gum),
    Liquidambar
Live-forever, *Dudleya* spp.
Live-forever, Greene, *Dudleya*
    greenei
Locoweed, *Astragalus* spp.
Locoweed, alpine spring,
    Astragalus kentrophyta

Locust, *Robinia* spp.
Lotus (see Bird's-foot trefoil)
Lousewort, dwarf, *Pedicularis semibarbata*
Lupine:
  Annual blue, *Lupinus nanus*
  Brewer's, *Lupinus breweri*
  Bush (dune), *Lupinus chamissonis*
  Canyon, *Lupinus latifolius* var. *latifolius*
  Harlequin, *Lupinus stiversii*
  Silvery, *Lupinus argenteus*
  Tree, *Lupinus arboreus*
  Varied, *Lupinus variicolor*

Madroño, *Arbutus menziesii*
Magnolia, *Magnolia* spp.
Mallow, apricot, *Sphaeralcea ambigua*
Mallow, island, *Lavatera assurgentiflora*
Manzanita:
  Bigberry, *Arctostaphylos glauca*
  Eastwood, *Arctostaphylos glandulosa*
  Greenleaf, *Arctostaphylos patula*
  Ione, *Arctostaphylos myrtifolia*
  Mexican, *Arctostaphylos pungens*
  Mission, *Xylococcus bicolor*
  Otay, *Arctostaphylos otayensis*
  Parry, *Arctostaphylos manzanita*
  Pinemat, *Arctostaphylos nevadensis*
  Pinkbract, *Arctostaphylos pringlei*
  White-leaf, *Arctostaphylos viscida*
Manzanita, Channel Islands:
  Arctostaphylos catalinae (Santa Catalina Island)

Arctostaphylos confertiflora (Santa Rosa Island)
Arctostaphylos insularis (Santa Cruz Island)
Arctostaphylos tomentosa (Santa Cruz Island, Santa Rosa Island)
Arctostaphylos tomentosa ssp. *subcordata* (Santa Cruz Island)
Maple, big-leaf, *Acer macrophyllum*
Maple, vine, *Acer circinatum*
Marsh pennywort, *Hydrocotyle verticillata*
Meadowfoam, *Limnanthes* spp.
Meadow rue, alpine, *Thalictrum alpinum*
Melicgrass, *Melica* spp.
Menodora, smooth, *Menodora scabra*
Menodora, spiny, *Menodora spinescens*
Mesquite, honey, *Prosopis juliflora*
Mesquite, screwbean, *Prosopis pubescens*
Miner's lettuce, *Montia perfoliata*
Mint, San Diego mesa, *Pogogyne abramsii*
Mistletoe, desert, *Phoradendron californicum*
Mistletoe, oak and other broadleaf trees, *Phoradendron villosum*
Miterwort, *Mitella breweri*
Mock orange, *Philadelphus lewisii*
Molly, green, *Kochia americana*
Molly, rusty, *Kochia californica*
Monkeyflower:
  Bigelow, *Mimulus bigelovii*
  Brewer's, *Mimulus breweri*
  Bush, *Mimulus aurantiacus, M. longiflorus*
  Mojave, *Mimulus mohavensis*
  Scarlet, *Mimulus cardinalis*

Yellow (streamside,
seep-spring), *Mimulus
guttatus*
Monkshood, *Aconitum
columbianum*
Mormon tea, *Ephedra* spp.
Morning glory, beach, *Convolulus
soldanella*
Moss, sphagnum, *Sphagnum*
spp.
Mountain mahogany, birch-leaf,
Cercocarpus betuloides
Mountain mahogany, curl-leaf
(desert), *Cercocarpus ledifolius*
Mountain misery, *Chamaebatia
foliolosa*
Mugwort, *Artemisia douglasiana*
Mule fat, *Baccharis viminea*
Mustang clover (yellow-throated
gilia), *Linanthus montanus*
Mustard, *Brassica* spp.

Nama, *Nama demissum*
Navarretia, *Navarretia* spp.
Needlegrass, desert, *Stipa
speciosa*
Needlegrass, purple, *Stipa pulchra*
Needlegrass, western, *Stipa
occidentalis*
Neostapfia, Neostapfia colusana
Nettle, *Urtica gracilis*
Nightshade, *Solanum* spp.
Ninebark, *Physocarpus capitatus*
Nitgrass, *Gastridium ventricosum*
Nolina, *Nolina* spp.
Nutmeg, California, *Torreya
californica*

Oak:
Black, *Quercus kelloggii*
Blue, *Quercus douglasii*
Canyon, *Quercus chrysolepis*
Deer, *Quercus sadleriana*

Desert scrub, *Quercus turbinella*
Eastern white, *Quercus alba*
Engelmann, *Quercus
engelmannii*
Garry, *Quercus garryana*
Holly-leaf (Palmer), *Quercus
palmeri (dunnii)*
Huckleberry, *Quercus
vaccinifolia*
Island, *Quercus tomentella*
Leather, *Quercus durata*
Live, coast, *Quercus agrifolia*
Live, interior, *Quercus wislizenii*
MacDonald, *Quercus
macdonaldii*
Scrub, *Quercus dumosa*
Valley, *Quercus lobata*
Oat, slender, *Avena barbata*
Oat, wild, *Avena fatua*
Oatgrass, *Danthonia*, spp.
Ocean spray (see Cream bush)
Ocotillo, *Fouquieria splendens*
Onion, wild, *Allium* spp.
Orchid, coralroot, *Corallorhiza
maculata*
Orchid, rein, *Habenaria dilatata*
var. *leucostachys*
Orchid, stream, *Epipactis gigantea*
Orcuttia, Orcuttia spp.
Orcuttia, California, *Orcuttia
californica*
Oregon grape, *Berberis aquifolium,
B. nervosa*
Our Lord's candle, *Yucca whipplei*
Owl's clover, *Orthocarpus
purpurascens*
Oxalis, *Oxalis* spp.

Paintbrush, dwarf alpine,
Castilleja nana
Paintbrush, desert, *Castilleja
chromosa*
Paintbrush, Lemmon, *Castilleja
lemmonii*

Paintbrush, shortlobe, *Castilleja brevilobata*
Palm, blue, *Erythea armata*
Palm, native fan, *Washingtonia filifera*
Palo verde, *Cercidium floridum*
Palo verde, littleleaf, *Cercidium microphyllum*
Palo verde, Mexican, *Parkinsonia aculeata*
Pea, beach, *Lathyrus littoralis*
Pea, chaparral, *Pickeringia montana*
Pea, Sturt, *Clianthus formosus*
Pea, sweet, *Lathyrus* spp.
Pearlwort, Arctic, *Sagina saginoides*
Pebble pincushion, *Chaenactis carphoclinia*
Pecan, *Carya* spp.
Pennyroyal, *Monardella* spp.
Penstemon, creeping, *Penstemon davidsonii*
Penstemon, scarlet, *Penstemon bridgesii, P. labrosus* (common on Mount Pinos)
Persimmon, *Diospyros* spp.
Phacelia, large-flowered, *Phacelia grandiflora*
Phacelia, Lyon, *Phacelia lyonii*
Phlox, carpet, *Phlox caespitosa*
Phlox, Coville's (alpine), *Phlox covillei*
Phlox, spiny, *Phlox stansburyi*
Phlox, spreading, *Phlox diffusa*
Pickleweed, *Salicornia* spp.
Pickleweed, Bigelow's, *Salicornia bigelovii*
Pine:
    Aleppo, *Pinus halepensis*
    Apache, *Pinus engelmannii*
    Beach, *Pinus contorta* ssp. *contorta*
    Bishop, *Pinus muricata*
    Bristlecone, *Pinus aristata*
    Chihuahua, *Pinus leiophylla*
    Coulter, *Pinus coulteri*
    Digger, *Pinus sabiniana*
    Foxtail, *Pinus balfouriana*
    Island, *Pinus remorata*
    Japanese, *Pinus densiflora*
    Jeffrey, *Pinus jeffreyi*
    Knobcone, *Pinus attenuata*
    Limber, *Pinus flexilis*
    Lodgepole, *Pinus contorta* spp. *murrayana*
    Monterey, *Pinus radiata*
    Norfolk Island, *Araucaria excelsa*
    Pinyon, four-leaved, *Pinus quadrifolia*
    Pinyon, Mexican, *Pinus cembroides*
    Pinyon, one-leafed, *Pinus monophylla*
    Pinyon, two-leaved, *Pinus edulis*
    Southwestern white, *Pinus strobiformis*
    Stone, *Pinus pinea*
    Sugar, *Pinus lambertiana*
    Torrey, *Pinus torreyana*
    Washoe, *Pinus washoensis*
    Western white (silver), *Pinus monticola*
    Whitebark, *Pinus albicaulis*
    Yellow, *Pinus ponderosa*
Pinedrops, *Pterospora andromedea*
Pink, California, *Silene californica*
Pipevine, *Aristolochia californica*
Pitcher plant, California, *Darlingtonia californica*
Podistera, Sierra, *Podistera nevadensis*
Poison oak, *Toxicodendron diversilobum*
Polemonium, showy, *Polemonium pulcherrimum*
Pond weed, *Potamogeton* spp.
Popcorn flower, *Plagiobothrys* spp.

Poplar, Lombardy, *Populus nigra*
Poppy:
California, *Eschscholzia*
californica and related species
Fire (flame), *Papaver californicum*
Prickly, *Argemone munita*
Tree (bush), *Dendromecon rigida*
Wind, *Stylomecon heterophylla*
Potentilla, *Potentilla* spp.
Pride-of-California, *Lathyrus*
splendens
Primrose, evening, beach (sun
cup), *Camissonia cheiranthifolia*
Primrose, evening, birdcage
(noonflower), *Oenothera*
deltoides
Primrose, evening, yellow cups,
Camissonia brevipes
Primrose, fairy, *Primula*
augustifolia
Primrose, Sierra, *Primula*
suffrutescens
Prince's plume, *Stanleya pinnata*
Pussy paws, *Calyptridium*
umbellatum

Rabbitbrush, *Chrysothamnus*
nauseosus
Radish, wild, *Raphanus sativus*
Ratany, *Krameria parvifolia*
Rattlesnake weed, *Euphorbia*
albomarginata
Redberry, *Rhamnus crocea*
Redberry, island, *Rhamnus crocea*
var. *pirifolia*
Redbud, *Cercis occidentalis*
Red shanks (ribbonwood),
Adenostoma sparsifolium
Redwood, coast, *Sequoia*
sempervirens
Redwood, dawn, *Metasequoia*
glyptostroboides
Reed, *Phragmites communis*

Reedgrass, *Calamagrostis* spp.
Reedgrass, Pacific, *Calamagrostis*
nutkaensis
Ricegrass, *Oryzopsis* spp.
Ricegrass, Indian, *Oryzopsis*
hymenoides
Ripgut, *Bromus rigidus*
Rock cress, *Arabis* spp.
Rock cress, Parish, *Arabis parishii*
Rock fringe, *Epilobium*
obcordatum
Rock rose, *Helianthemum*
scoparium
Rose-bay (coast rhododendron),
Rhododendron macrophyllum
Roseroot, *Sedum rosea* ssp.
integrifolium
Rose, wild, *Rosa californica*
Rush, *Juncus* spp.
Rush, basket, *Juncus textilis*
Rush, Mexican, *Juncus mexicanus*
Rust, white pine blister,
Cronartium ribicola

Sage:
Black, *Salvia mellifera*
Bladder, *Salazaria mexicana*
Blue, *Salvia dorrii*
Mojave, *Salvia mohavensis*
Pitcher (hummingbird), *Salvia*
spathacea
Purple, *Salvia leucophylla*
Thistle, *Salvia carduacea*
White, *Salvia apiana*
Sagebrush:
Alpine, *Artemisia rothrockii*
Black, *Artemisia arbuscula*
California, *Artemisia californica*
Dwarf, *Artemisia nova*
Flat, *Artemisia bigelovii*
Great Basin (big), *Artemisia*
tridentata
Low, *Artemisia arbuscula*

Mountain big, *Artemisia
tridentata* ssp. *vaseyana*
Silver (hoary), *Artemisia cana*
Sagewort, beach, *Artemisia
pycnocephala*
Saint Catherine's lace, *Eriogonum
giganteum*
Salal, *Gaultheria shallon*
Saltbush, *Atriplex* spp.
Saltbush, four-winged, *Atriplex
canescens*
Saltbush, Parry, *Atriplex parryi*
Salt grass, *Distichlis spicata*
Salt grass, interior, *Distichlis
stricta*
Saltwort, *Batis maritima*
Sand food, *Ammobroma sonorae*
Sand verbena, common desert,
Abronia villosa
Sand verbena, pink-flowering
coastal, *Abronia maritima*
Sand verbena, yellow-flowering
coastal, *Abronia latifolia*
Sandwort, alpine, *Arenaria
obtusiloba*
Sandwort, Bear Valley, *Arenaria
ursina*
Sandwort, Nuttall's, *Arenaria
nuttallii*
Saxifrage, goldenbloom,
Saxifraga serpyllifolia
Scalebroom, *Lepidospartum
squamatum*
Scarlet bugler, *Penstemon
centranthifolius*
Scarlet pimpernel, *Anagallis
arvensis*
Sea blite, *Suaeda californica*
Sea fig, *Carpobrotus aequilaterus
(Mesembryanthemum chilense)*
Sea lavender, *Limonium
californica*
Sea rocket, *Cakile maritima*,
native species, *Cakile edentula*
ssp. *californicum*

Seascale, *Atriplex leucophylla*
Seaweed:
Agarweed, *Gelidium* spp.
Alga, coralline, Corallinacaea
Braided hair, *Plocamium
coccineum* var. *pacificum*
Delicate sycophant, *Microcladia*
spp.
Gigartina, *Gigartina* spp.
Green rope, *Spongomorpha
coalita*
Kelp, bladder, *Macrocystis
pyrifera*
Kelp, bull, *Nereocystis leutkeana*
Kelp, elk, *Pelagophycus porra*
Kelp, feather boa, *Egregia
menziesii, E. laevigata*
Lissom red sea fire, *Farlowia*
spp.
Mermaid's hair, *Gracilaria* spp.
Nailbrush, *Endocladia muricata*
Oar weed (blade), *Laminaria*
spp.
Ocean pincushion, *Cladophora*
spp.
Red fan, *Hymenena* spp.,
Cryptopleura spp.
Red laver, *Porphyra* spp.
Red point, *Prionitis* spp.
Red sea feather, *Erythrophyllum
delesserioides*
Rockweed, *Fucus* spp., *Pelvetia
fastigiata, Hesperophycus
harveyanus*
Ruffled sword, *Dictyoneurum
californicum*
Sea grapes, *Botryocladia
psuedodichotoma*
Sea lettuce, *Ulva* spp.
Sea palm, northern, *Postelsia
palmaeformis*
Sea palm, southern, *Eisenia
arborea*
Sea sacks, *Halosaccion
glandiforme*

Seersucker, *Costaria costata*
Tassel wing, *Pterochondria woodii*
Turkish towel, *Gigartina* spp.
Sedge, *Carex* spp.
Seep willow, *Baccharis glutinosa*
Sequoia, giant (see Big tree)
Service berry, *Amelanchier
alnifolia*
Shadscale, *Atriplex confertifolia*
Sheeppod, Pursh's, *Astragalus
purshii*
Shooting star, alpine,
Dodecatheon alpinum
Shooting Star, Jeffrey's,
Dodecatheon jeffreyi
Sierra pride, *Penstemon newberryi*
Silk tassel (see Garrya)
Silver-lace, *Eriophyllum nevinii*
Silverleaf, cape, *Leucadendron
argenteum*
Silver mat, *Raillardella argentea*
Sky pilot, Sierra, *Polemonium
eximium*
Smartweed, *Polygonum coccineum*
Smoke tree, *Dalea spinosa*
Snakeweed, *Gutierrezia* spp.
Snakewood, California,
Colubrina californica
Sneezeweed, *Helenium* spp.
Snowberry, *Symphoricarpos* spp.
Snowberry, desert,
Symphoricarpos longiflorus
Snowberry, mountain,
Symphoricarpos vaccinioides
Snowberry, Parish,
Symphoricarpos parishii
Snow bush, *Ceanothus cordulatus*
Snow plant, *Sarcodes sanguinea*
Solomon's seal, *Smilacina* spp.
Sorrel, alpine, *Oxyria digyna*
Sorrel, redwood, *Oxalis oregana*
Spanish bayonet (banana yucca),
Yucca baccata
Spanish dagger (Mojave yucca),
Yucca schidigera

Spanish needles, *Palafoxia linearis*
Spice bush, *Calycanthus
occidentalis*
Spikenard, *Aralia californica*
Spike rush, *Eleocharis* spp.
Spiraea, *Spiraea* spp.
Spiraea, rock, *Petrophytum
casespitosum*
Spruce:
Blue, *Picea pungens*
Engelmann, *Picea engelmannii*
Sitka, *Picea sitchensis*
Weeping, *Picea breweriana*
White, *Picea glauca*
Squaw bush, *Rhus trilobata*
Squaw cabbage (desert candle),
Caulanthus inflatus
Squaw mat, *Ceanothus prostratus*
Squirreltail, *Sitanion hystrix*
Stinkweed, *Cleomella obtusifolia*
Stonecrop, *Sedum* spp.
Strawberry, beach, *Fragaria
chiloensis*
Sugarbush, *Rhus ovata*
Sugar scoop, *Tiarella unifoliata*
Sulfur flower, *Eriogonum
umbellatum*
Summer holly, *Comarostaphylis
diversifolia*
Summerpoppy, *Kallstroemia
grandiflora*
Sunflower, *Helianthus* spp.
Sunflower, bush, *Encelia
californica*
Sunflower, canyon, *Venegasia
carpesioides*
Sunflower, white-leafed,
Helianthus niveus ssp.
tephrodes
Swamp whitehead,
Sphenosciadium capitellatum
Sweetbush, *Bebbia juncea*
Sweet gum (see Liquidambar)
Sycamore, western, *Platanus
racemosa*

Tamarix, *Tamarix gallica*
Tanoak (tanbark oak), *Lithocarpus densiflora*
Tar weed, *Hemizonia* spp., *Layia* spp., *Madia* spp.
Tar weed, island, *Hemizonia clementina*
Thimbleberry, *Rubus parviflorus*
Thrift, *Armeria maritima* var. *californica*
Ticklegrass, *Agrostis scabra*
Tidytips, *Layia platyglossa*
Tobaccobrush, *Ceanothus velutinus*
Toyon, *Heteromeles arbutifolia*
Trillium, *Trillium ovatum*
Trisetum, nodding, *Trisetum cernuum*
Tule, *Scirpus acutus*
Tumbleweed (Russian thistle), *Salsola iberica*
Turpentine broom, *Thamnosma montana*
Twinberry, *Lonicera involucrata*

Umbel family, Umbelliferae

Vetch, *Vicia* spp.
Violet, *Viola* spp.
Violet, Sierra white, *Viola macloskeyi*

Wallflower, *Erysimum* spp.
Walnut, northern California

black, *Juglans hindsii*
Walnut, southern California black, *Juglans californica*
Water starwort, *Callitriche* spp.
Waterweed, yellow, *Ludwigia peploides*
Wax myrtle, *Myrica californica*
Wheatgrass, *Agropyron* spp.
Whispering bells, *Emmenanthe penduliflora*
Wildrye, basin, *Elymus cinereus*
Wildrye, blue, *Elymus glaucus*
Wildrye, giant, *Elymus condensatus*
Willow, alpine (Arctic), *Salix anglorum (S. arctica)*
Willow, short-fruited, *Salix brachycarpa*
Willow herb (fireweed), *Epilobium* spp.
Wingscale, *Atriplex canescens*
Winter fat, *Eurotia lanata*
Wintergreen, *Pyrola* spp.
Woodland star, *Lithophragma* spp.
Wormwood, *Artemisia* spp.

Yarrow, alpine, *Achillea lanulosa* var. *alpicola*
Yarrow, golden, *Eriophyllum confertiflorum*
Yerba santa, *Eriodictyon* spp.
Yew, western, *Taxus brevifolia*
Yucca, Mojave (see Spanish dagger)

Index

Page numbers in italics refer to illustrations.

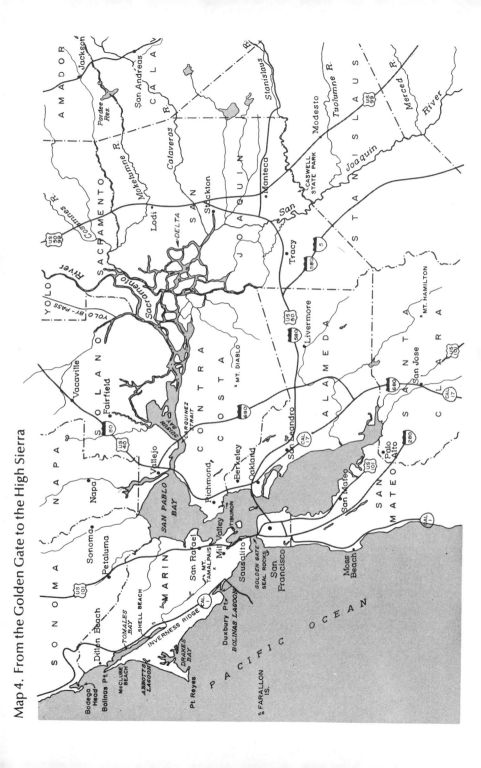

Map 4. From the Golden Gate to the High Sierra

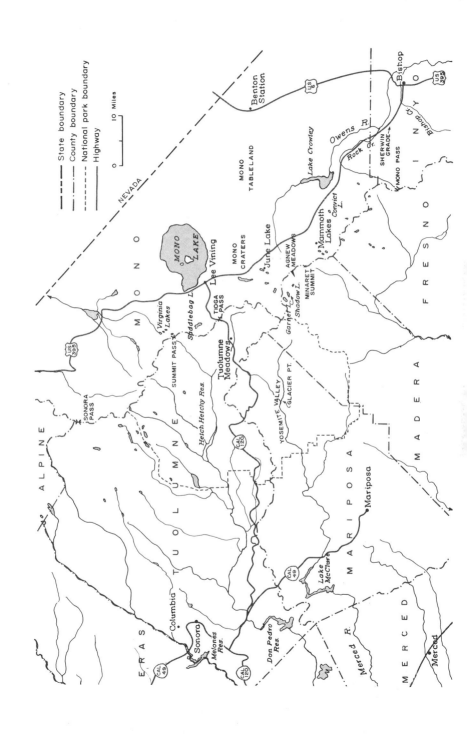

State boundary
County boundary
National park boundary
Highway

0   10 Miles

NEVADA

Benton Station

US 6

Owens R.

Bishop
Bishop Cr.
US 395

SHERWIN GRADE
MONO PASS

Lake Crowley
Rock Cr.

MONO TABLELAND

MONO

Mammoth Lakes
Convict L.

MONO CRATERS

June Lake
AGNEW MEADOWS
MINARET SUMMIT

Shadow L.
Garnet L.

Lee Vining
Tioga Pass
Spddiebag L.

MONO LAKE

Virginia Lakes
SUMMIT PASS

US 395

Tuolumne Meadows

Hetch Hetchy Res.

SONORA PASS

FRESNO

GLACIER PT.
YOSEMITE VALLEY

CAL 120

ALPINE

TUOLUMNE

MADERA

Mariposa

CAL 49

Lake McClure

Columbia
Sonora
Melones Res.

CAL 49

CAL 120

Don Pedro Res.

MARIPOSA

Merced R.

MERCED

Merced

...ERAS